Ancient Christian Texts

Latin Commentaries on Revelation

Commentary on the Apocalypse
Victorinus of Petovium

*Explanation of the Revelation
by the Most Learned Man,
Apringius, Bishop of Pax (Julia)*
Apringius of Beja

Exposition on the Apocalypse
Caesarius of Arles

*The Exposition of the Apocalypse
by Bede the Presbyter*
Bede the Venerable

EDITED AND TRANSLATED WITH AN
INTRODUCTION AND NOTES BY

William C. Weinrich

SERIES EDITORS

Thomas C. Oden and Gerald L. Bray

IVP Academic
An imprint of InterVarsity Press
Downers Grove, Illinois

InterVarsity Press
P.O. Box 1400, Downers Grove, IL 60515-1426
World Wide Web: www.ivpress.com
E-mail: email@ivpress.com

InterVarsity Press® is the book-publishing division of InterVarsity Christian Fellowship/USA®, a movement of students and faculty active on campus at hundreds of universities, colleges and schools of nursing in the United States of America, and a member movement of the International Fellowship of Evangelical Students. For information about local and regional activities, write Public Relations Dept., InterVarsity Christian Fellowship/USA, 6400 Schroeder Rd., P.O. Box 7895, Madison, WI 53707-7895, or visit the IVCF website at <www.intervarsity.org>.

The LS Graeca® II font used to print this work is available from Linguist's Software, Inc., P.O. Box 580, Edmonds, WA 98020-0580 USA tel (425) 775-1130.

Design: Cindy Kiple
Images: Saints Peter and Paul by Carlo Crivelli at Accademia, Venice/Art Resource, NY
    Monogrammatic cross: Early Christian monogrammatic cross from Monastero, at Kunsthistorisches Museum, Vienna, Austria. Erich Lessing/Art Resource, NY

ISBN 978-0-8308-2909-5

Printed in the United States of America ∞

Library of Congress Cataloging-in-Publication Data
Latin commentaries on Revelation / Victorinus of Petovium . . . [et al.]
; translated and edited by William C. Weinrich.
    p. cm.—(Ancient Christian texts)
  Includes bibliographical references and index.
  ISBN 978-0-8308-2909-5 (hardcover: alk. paper)
  1. Bible. N.T. Revelation—Commentaries. I. Victorinus, Saint,
Bishop of Poetovio, d. 304? II. Weinrich, William C.
  BS2825.53.L39 2011
  228'.07—dc23

              2011023282

P	26	25	24	23	22	21	20	19	18	17	16	15	14	13	12	11	10	9	8	7	6	5	4	3	2	1
Y	34	33	32	31	30	29	28	27	26	25	24	23	22	21	20	19	18	17	16	15	14	13	12	11		

CONTENTS

CAESARIUS OF ARLES
Exposition on the Apocalypse

BEDE THE VENERABLE
The Exposition on the Apocalypse by Bede the Presbyter

GENERAL INTRODUCTION

Ancient Christian Texts (hereafter ACT) presents the full text of ancient Christian commentaries on Scripture that have remained so unnoticed that they have not yet been translated into English.

The patristic period (A.D. 95–750) is the time of the fathers of the church, when the exegesis of Scripture texts was in its primitive formation. This period spans from Clement of Rome to John of Damascus, embracing seven centuries of biblical interpretation, from the end of the New Testament to the mid-eighth century, including the Venerable Bede.

This series extends but does not reduplicate texts of the Ancient Christian Commentary on Scripture (ACCS). It presents full-length translations of texts that appear only as brief extracts in the ACCS. The ACCS began years ago authorizing full-length translations of key patristic texts on Scripture in order to provide fresh sources of valuable commentary that previously were not available in English. It is from these translations that the ACT series has emerged.

A multiyear project such as this requires a well-defined objective. The task is straightforward: *to introduce full-length translations of key texts of early Christian teaching, homilies and commentaries on a particular book of Scripture.* These are seminal documents that have decisively shaped the entire subsequent history of biblical exegesis, but in our time have been largely ignored.

To carry out this mission each volume of the Ancient Christian Texts series has four aspirations:

1. To show the approach of one of the early Christian writers in dealing with the problems of understanding, reading and conveying the meaning of a particular book of Scripture.

2. To make more fully available the whole argument of the ancient Christian interpreter of Scripture to all who wish to think with the early church about a particular canonical text.

3. To broaden the base of the biblical studies, Christian teaching and preaching to include classical Christian exegesis.

4. To stimulate Christian historical, biblical, theological and pastoral scholarship toward deeper inquiry into early classic practitioners of scriptural interpretation.

For Whom Is This Series Designed?

We have selected and translated these texts primarily for general and nonprofessional use by an audience of persons who study the Bible regularly.

In varied cultural settings around the world, contemporary readers are asking how they might grasp the meaning of sacred texts under the instruction of the great minds of the ancient church. They often study books of the Bible verse by verse, book by book, in groups and workshops, sometimes with a modern commentary in hand. But many who study the Bible intensively hunger to have available as well the thoughts of a reliable classic Christian commentator on this same text. This series will give the modern commentators a classical text for comparison and amplification. Readers will judge for themselves as to how valuable or complementary are their insights and guidance.

The classic texts we are translating were originally written for anyone (lay or clergy, believers or seekers) who wished to reflect and meditate with the great minds of the early church. They sought to illuminate the plain sense, theological wisdom, and moral and spiritual meaning of an individual book of Scripture. They were not written for an academic audience, but for a community of faith shaped by the sacred text.

Yet in serving this general audience, the editors remain determined not to neglect the rigorous requirements and needs of academic readers who until recently have had few full translations available to them in the history of exegesis. So this series is designed also to serve public libraries, universities, academic classes, homiletic preparation and historical interests worldwide in Christian scholarship and interpretation.

Hence our expected audience is not limited to the highly technical and specialized scholarly field of patristic studies, with its strong bent toward detailed word studies and explorations of cultural contexts. Though all of our editors and translators are patristic and linguistic scholars, they also are scholars who search for the meanings and implications of the texts. The audience is not primarily the university scholar concentrating on the study of the history of the transmission of the text or those with highly focused interests in textual morphology or historical-critical issues. If we succeed in serving our wider readers practically and well, we hope to serve as well college and seminary courses in Bible, church history, historical theology, hermeneutics and homiletics. These texts have not until now been available to these classes.

Readiness for Classic Spiritual Formation

Today global Christians are being steadily drawn toward these biblical and patristic sources for daily meditation and spiritual formation. They are on the outlook for primary classic sources of spiritual formation and biblical interpretation, presented in accessible form and grounded in reliable scholarship.

These crucial texts have had an extended epoch of sustained influence on Scripture interpretation, but virtually no influence in the modern period. They also deserve a hearing among modern readers and scholars. There is a growing awareness of the speculative excesses and spiritual and homiletic limitations of much post-Enlightenment criticism. Meanwhile the motifs, methods and approaches of ancient exegetes have remained unfamiliar not only to historians but to otherwise highly literate biblical scholars, trained exhaustively in the methods of historical and scientific criticism.

It is ironic that our times, which claim to be so fully furnished with historical insight and research methods, have neglected these texts more than scholars in previous centuries who could read them in their original languages.

This series provides indisputable evidence of the modern neglect of classic Christian exegesis: it remains a fact that extensive and once authoritative classic commentaries on Scripture still remain untranslated into any modern language. Even in China such a high level of neglect has not befallen classic Buddhist, Taoist and Confucian commentaries.

Ecumenical Scholarship

This series, like its two companion series, the ACCS and Ancient Christian Doctrine (ACD), are expressions of unceasing ecumenical efforts that have enjoyed the wide cooperation of distinguished scholars of many differing academic communities. Under this classic textual umbrella, it has brought together in common spirit Christians who have long distanced themselves from each other by competing church memories. But all of these traditions have an equal right to appeal to the early history of Christian exegesis. All of these traditions can, without a sacrifice of principle or intellect, come together to study texts common to them all. This is its ecumenical significance.

This series of translations is respectful of a distinctively theological reading of Scripture that cannot be reduced to historical, philosophical, scientific, or sociological insights or methods alone. It takes seriously the venerable tradition of ecumenical reflection concerning the premises of revelation, providence, apostolicity, canon and consensuality. A high respect is here granted, despite modern assumptions, to uniquely Christian theological forms of reasoning, such as classical consensual christological and triune reasoning, as distinguishing premises of classic Christian textual interpretation. These cannot be acquired by empirical methods alone. This approach does not pit theology against critical theory; instead, it incorporates critical historical methods and brings them into coordinate accountability within its larger purpose of listening to Scripture.

The internationally diverse character of our editors and translators corresponds with the global range of our audience, which bridges many major communions of Christianity. We have sought to bring together a distinguished international network of Protestant, Catholic and Orthodox scholars, editors and translators of the highest quality and reputation to accomplish this design.

But why just now at this historical moment is this need for patristic wisdom felt particularly by so many readers of Scripture? Part of the reason is that these readers have been longer deprived of significant contact with many of these vital sources of classic Christian exegesis.

The Ancient Commentary Tradition

This series focuses on texts that comment on Scripture and teach its meaning. We define a commentary in its plain-sense definition as a series of illustrative or explanatory notes on any work of enduring significance. The word *commentary* is an Anglicized form of the Latin *commentarius* (or "annotation" or "memoranda" on a subject, text or series of events). In its theological meaning it is a work that explains, analyzes or expounds a biblical book or portion of Scripture. Tertullian, Origen, John Chrysostom, Jerome, Augustine and Clement of Alexandria all revealed their familiarity with both the secular and religious commentators available to them as they unpacked the meanings of the sacred text at hand.

The commentary in ancient times typically began with a general introduction covering such questions as authorship, date, purpose and audience. It commented as needed on grammatical or lexical problems in the text and provided explanations of difficulties in the text. It typically moved verse by verse through a Scripture text, seeking to make its meaning clear and its import understood.

The general western literary genre of commentary has been definitively shaped by the history of early Christian commentaries on Scripture. It is from Origen, Hilary, the *Opus imperfectum in Matthaeum*, John Chrysostom and Cyril of Alexandria that we learn what a commentary is—far more so than in the case of classic medical, philosophical or poetic commentaries. It leaves too much unsaid simply to assume that the Christian biblical commentary took a previously extant literary genre and reshaped it for Christian texts. Rather it is more accurate to say that *the Western literary genre of the commentary (and especially the biblical commentary) has patristic commentaries as its decisive pattern and prototype.*

It is only in the last two centuries, since the development of modern historicist methods of criticism, that modern writers have sought more strictly to delimit the definition of a commentary so as to include only certain limited interests focusing largely on historical-critical method, philological and grammatical observations, literary analysis, and socio-political or economic circumstances impinging on the text. While respecting all these approaches, the ACT editors do not hesitate to use the classic word *commentary* to define more broadly the genre of this series. These are commentaries in their classic sense.

The ACT editors freely take the assumption that the Christian canon is to be respected as the church's sacred text. The reading and preaching of Scripture are vital to religious life. The central hope of this endeavor is that it might contribute in some small way to the revitalization of religious faith and community through a renewed discovery of the earliest readings of the church's Scriptures.

An Appeal to Allow the Text to Speak for Itself

This prompts two appeals:

1. For those who begin by assuming as normative for a commentary only the norms considered typical for modern expressions of what a commentary is, we ask: Please allow the ancient commentators to define *commentarius* according to their own lights. Those who assume the preemptive authority and truthfulness of modern critical methods alone will always tend to view the classic Christian exegetes as dated, quaint, premodern, hence inadequate, and in some instances comic or even mean-spirited, prejudiced, unjust and oppressive. So in the interest of hermeneutical fairness, it is recommended that the modern reader not impose upon ancient Christian exegetes modern assumptions about valid readings of Scripture. The ancient Christian writers constantly challenge these unspoken, hidden and indeed often camouflaged assumptions that have become commonplace in our time.

We leave it to others to discuss the merits of ancient versus modern methods of exegesis. But even this cannot be done honestly without a serious examination of the texts of ancient exegesis. Ancient commentaries may be disqualified as commentaries by modern standards. But they remain commentaries by the standards of those who anteceded and formed the basis of the modern commentary.

The attempt to read a Scripture text while ruling out all theological and moral assumptions—as well as ecclesial, sacramental and dogmatic assumptions that have prevailed generally in the community of faith out of which it emerged—is a very thin enterprise indeed. Those who tendentiously may read a single page of patristic exegesis, gasp and toss it away because it does not conform adequately to the canons of modern exegesis and historicist commentary are surely not exhibiting a valid model for critical inquiry today.

2. In ancient Christian exegesis, chains of biblical references were often very important in thinking about the text in relation to the whole testimony of sacred Scripture, by the analogy of faith, comparing text with text, on the premise that *scripturam ex scriptura explicandam esse*. When ancient exegesis weaves many Scripture texts together, it does not limit its focus to a single text as much modern exegesis prefers, but constantly relates them to other texts, by analogy, intensively using typological reasoning, as did the rabbinic tradition.

Since the principle prevails in ancient Christian exegesis that each text is illumined by other texts and by the whole narrative of the history of revelation, we find in patristic comments on a given text many other subtexts interwoven in order to illumine that text. In these ways the models of exegesis often do not correspond with modern commentary assumptions, which tend to resist or rule out chains of scriptural reference. We implore the reader not to force the assumptions of twentieth-century hermeneutics upon the ancient Christian writers, who themselves knew nothing of what we now call hermeneutics.

The Complementarity of Research Methods in this Series

The Ancient Christian Texts series will employ several interrelated methods of research, which the editors and translators seek to bring together in a working integration. Principal among these methods are the following:

1. The editors, translators and annotators will bring to bear the best resources of *textual criticism* in preparation for their volumes. This series is not intended to produce a new critical edition of the original-language text. The best urtext in the original language will be used. Significant variants in the earliest manuscript sources of the text may be commented upon as needed in the annotations. But it will be assumed that the editors and translators will be familiar with the textual ambiguities of a particular text and be able to state their conclusions about significant differences among scholars. Since we are working with ancient texts that have, in some cases, problematic or ambiguous passages, we are obliged to employ all methods of historical, philological and textual inquiry appropriate to the study of ancient texts. To that end, we will appeal to the most reliable text-critical scholarship of both biblical and patristic studies. We will assume that our editors and translators have reviewed the international literature of textual critics regarding their text so as to provide the reader with a translation of the most authoritative and reliable form of the ancient text. We will leave it to the volume editors and translators, under the supervision of the general editors, to make these assessments. This will include the challenge of considering which variants within the biblical text itself might impinge upon the patristic text, and which forms or stemma of the biblical text the patristic writer was employing. The annotator will supply explanatory footnotes where these textual challenges may raise potential confusions for the reader.

2. Our editors and translators will seek to understand the *historical context* (including socioeconomic, political and psychological aspects as needed) of the text. These understandings are often vital to right discernment of the writer's intention. Yet we do not see our primary mission as that of discussing in detail these contexts. They are to be factored into the translation and commented on as needed in the annotations, but are not to become the primary focus of this series. Our central interest is less in the social location of the text or the philological history of particular words than in authorial intent and accurate translation. Assuming a proper social-historical contextualization of the text, the main focus of this series will be upon a dispassionate and fair translation and analysis of the text itself.

3. The main task is to set forth the meaning of the biblical text itself as understood by the patristic writer. The intention of our volume editors and translators is to help the reader see clearly into the meanings which patristic commentators have discovered in the biblical text. *Exegesis* in its classic sense implies an effort to explain, interpret and comment upon a text, its meaning, its sources and its connections with other texts. It implies

a close reading of the text, utilizing whatever linguistic, historical, literary or theological resources are available to explain the text. It is contrasted with *eisegesis*, which implies that interpreters have imposed their own personal opinions or assumptions upon the text. The patristic writers actively practiced intratextual exegesis, which seeks to define and identify the exact wording of the text, its grammatical structure and the interconnectedness of its parts. They also practiced extratextual exegesis, seeking to discern the geographical, historical or cultural context in which the text was written. Our editors and annotators will also be attentive as needed to the ways in which the ancient Christian writer described his own interpreting process or hermeneutic assumptions.

4. The underlying philosophy of translation that we employ in this series is, like the Ancient Christian Commentary on Scripture, termed *dynamic equivalency*. We wish to avoid the pitfalls of either too loose a paraphrase or too rigid a literal translation. We seek language that is literary but not purely literal. Whenever possible we have opted for the metaphors and terms that are normally in use in everyday English-speaking culture. Our purpose is to allow the ancient Christian writers to speak for themselves to ordinary readers in the present generation. We want to make it easier for the Bible reader to gain ready access to the deepest reflection of the ancient Christian community of faith on a particular book of Scripture. We seek a thought-for-thought translation rather than a formal equivalence or word-for-word style. This requires the words to be first translated accurately and then rendered in understandable idiom. We seek to present the same thoughts, feelings, connotations and effects of the original text in everyday English language. We have used vocabulary and language structures commonly used by the average person. We do not leave the quality of translation only to the primary translator, but pass it through several levels of editorial review before confirming it.

The Function of the ACT Introductions, Annotations and Translations

In writing the introduction for a particular volume of the ACT series, the translator or volume editor will discuss, where possible, the opinion of the writer regarding authorship of the text, the importance of the biblical book for other patristic interpreters, the availability or paucity of patristic comment, any salient points of debate between the Fathers, and any special challenges involved in translating and editing the particular volume. The introduction affords the opportunity to frame the entire commentary in a manner that will help the general reader understand the nature and significance of patristic comment on the biblical text under consideration and to help readers find their critical bearings so as to read and use the commentary in an informed way.

The footnotes will assist the reader with obscurities and potential confusions. In the annotations the volume editors have identified Scripture allusions and historical references embedded within the texts. Their purpose is to help the reader move easily from passage to passage without losing a sense of the whole.

The ACT general editors seek to be circumspect and meticulous in commissioning volume editors and translators. We strive for a high level of consistency and literary quality throughout the course of this series. We have sought out as volume editors and translators those patristic and biblical scholars who are thoroughly familiar with their original language sources, who are informed historically, and who are sympathetic to the needs of ordinary nonprofessional readers who may not have professional language skills.

Thomas C. Oden and Gerald L. Bray, Series Editors

ABBREVIATIONS

Series

ACW	Ancient Christian Writers
ANF	Ante-Nicene Fathers
CCL	Corpus *Christianorum*, Series Latina
CS	Cistercian Studies
CSEL	Corpus *Scriptorum Ecclesiastinorum Latinorum*
FC	Fathers of the Church
GCS	Die *grichische christliche Schriftsteller* der *ersten [drei] Jahrhunderte*
JEH	*Journal of Ecclesiastical History*
NPNF[2]	*Nicene and Post-Nicene Fathers, Series 2*
PG	*Patrologia Graeca*
PL	*Patrologia* Latina
SC	Sources *Chrétiennes*
TEG	Traditio *exegetica graeca*
TS	Texts and Studies

Bible Versions

LXX	Septuagint

Technical

c.	circa (about)
d.	died
MS/MSS	manuscript/s

TRANSLATOR'S INTRODUCTION

This volume presents English translations of four early Latin commentaries on the Revelation of Saint John, that of Victorinus of Petovium, Apringius of Beja, Caesarius of Arles and Bede the Venerable. Each of these commentaries has a special significance and a special place in the Western tradition of the interpretation of the Revelation. From the beginning, texts of the Revelation went west rather than east. This perhaps explains why the authority of the Revelation was never doubted in the West and from early on was consistently used and interpreted. In Africa Tertullian (c. 220) and Cyprian (d. 258) made significant use of the Revelation, as did the *Shepherd* of Hermas (c. 140) in Rome. Evidence exists, however, that not merely incidental use but more extended commentary on the Revelation existed by the third and perhaps already in the second century. According to Jerome, Justin Martyr and Irenaeus "interpreted" (*interpretatur*) the Revelation,[1] although this may mean that they commented on various passages rather than the whole book. Eusebius mentions that Melito of Sardis wrote a work entitled *On the Devil and the Apocalypse of John*.[2] Perhaps this was something like a commentary, but the work is lost and we do not know. We may be more certain with Hippolytus of Rome (c. 230). Jerome writes that Hippolytus wrote "various commentaries on the Scriptures" and mentions among them *On the Apocalypse*.[3] This may refer to the *Apology for the Apocalypse and Gospel of John*, a defense of the common authorship of the Revelation and the Gospel against some who denied it.[4]

Despite this attestation of early interpretation of the Revelation in the west, the earliest commentary on the whole of the Revelation that we possess is that of Victorinus, bishop of Petovium, who wrote in the latter half of the third century and is usually thought to have been martyred in the persecution of Diocletian (c. 304). With Victorinus the western interpretative tradition of the Revelation begins, and with Apringius, Caesarius and Bede that tradition continues and acquires its fundamental consensus.[5]

---

[1]Jerome *On Illustrious Men* 9.6 (*NPNF*[2] 3:364; FC 100:20). The two English translations have "wrote commentaries" which perhaps over-interprets the Latin.

[2]Eusebius *Ecclesiastical History* 4.26.2 (*NPNF*[2] 1:203). It is possible that this title indicates two separate works (so Jerome and Rufinus), but the Greek MSS of Eusebius suggest only one: τὰ περὶ τοῦ διαβόλου καὶ τῆς ἀποκαλύψεως Ἰωάννου (PG 20:392).

[3]Jerome *On Illustrious Men* 61.2 (*NPNF*[2] 3:375; FC 100:87). The Latin here is *scripsit nonnullos in Scripturas commentarios*.

[4]The fragments of this commentary in French translation are in Pierre Prigent, "Hippolyte, commentateur de l'Apocalypse," *Theologische Zeitschrift* 28 (1972): 391-412; and in Pierre Prigent and R. Stehly, "Les fragments du De Apocalypsi d'Hippolyte," *Theologische Zeitschrift* 29 (1973): 313-33.

[5]For general discussion concerning the early history of Latin interpretation of the Revelation, see E. Ann Matter, "The Apoca-

Victorinus of Petovium

Life and Work of Victorinus

Although the work of Victorinus was well known into the early middle ages, information about his person and life are known only through a brief report in Jerome's *De viris illustribus*:

> Victorinus, bishop of Poetovio, did not know Latin as well as he did Greek; as a result, his works, which are excellent in content, seem inferior in composition. His works are: *Commentaries On Genesis, On Exodus, On Leviticus, On Isaiah, On Ezekiel, On Habakkuk, On Ecclesiastes, On the Canticle of Canticles, On the Apocalypse of John, Against the Heresies* and numerous others. At the end he received the crown of martyrdom.[6]

In the third century the city of Petovium was an important commercial, military and governmental center.[7] Raised to the status of a colony under Trajan, Petovium was the headquarters of the Roman province of Upper Pannonia. During the reign of Hadrian the city became a major port and was the base of the great Danubian fleet (*Classis Flavia Pannonica*). The province became especially important under Gallienus (260–268) and was the base for the two Danubian legions of the *V Macedonica* and the *XIII Gemina*. Petovium was furthermore the commercial crossroads between the east and west and especially for the amber traffic between Aquileia and the Baltic regions. In view of such a cosmopolitan center, not surprisingly the imperial cults of Isis, Cybele and Mithras were well represented.

All evidence of Christianity in Petovium can be dated only after the time of Victorinus. Nonetheless, given its importance and cosmopolitan character and that in Victorinus the city had a Christian bishop, a Christian community most probably predated Victorinus by some few decades. After a brief review of the evidence, Dulaey concludes: "Whatever the origins of the church at Poetovio might be, it was already solidly established at the time of Victorinus, since it had a bishop. The opinion of those who would locate its origin under the Severians is probable."[8]

What do we know of Victorinus? Not much, and from the entry of Jerome one might

---

lypse in Early Medieval Exegesis," in *The Apocalypse in the Middle Ages*, edited by Richard K. Emmerson and Bernard McGinn (Ithaca, N.Y.: Cornell University Press, 1992), pp. 38-50; Roger Gryson, "Les commentaires patristiques latins de l'Apocalypse," *Revue théologique de Louvain* 28 (1997): 305-37, 484-502.

[6]Jerome *On Illustrious Men* 74.1-3 (NPNF[2] 3:377; FC 100:105-6). For discussion of Victorinus see Martine Dulaey, *Victorin de Poetovio premier exégète latin*, 2 vols. (Collection des Études Augustiniennes 139, 140; Paris: Institut d'Études Augustiniennes, 1993); M. Dulaey, *Victorin de Poetovio. Sur L'Apocalypse et autres écrits* (SC 423; Paris: Les Éditions du Cerf, 1997), pp. 15-41; Kenneth B. Steinhauser, *The Apocalypse Commentary of Tyconius: A History of Its Reception and Influence* (European University Studies; Series XXIII, Theology 301; Bern: Peter Lang 1987), pp. 29-44; F. F. Bruce, "The Earliest Latin Commentary on the Apocalypse," *The Evangelical Quarterly* 10 (1938): 352-66.

[7]Petovium is the modern city of Ptuj in Slovenia (former Yugoslavia) on the river Drava. The Latin name of the city was Poetovio. Sometimes the name of the city is given in its German form, Pettau.

[8]Dulaey, *Victorin de Poetovio*, 1:15 (my translation). The dynasty of the Severians would date the origins of the church at Poetovio to the early third century, from Septimius (193–211) to Alexander (222–235).

wonder whether he knew much apart from the reading of Victorinus's works. All evidence suggests that Victorinus was active during the latter half of the third century. The only heretics mentioned in his extant works are the Gnostics, although Optatus of Mileve mentions that he also refuted Sabellius. This, together with the fact that Victorinus makes no mention of Manichaeanism or Arianism, suggests the theological context of the third century. Moreover, Dulaey notes that within the various lists of ancient authors that are chronologically ordered Victorinus is to be located firmly within the third century. For example, in his *On Illustrious Men* Jerome places him between Anatolius, bishop of Laodicea (d. 283), and Pamphilus, the friend of Eusebius (d. 309). Ambrosiaster places Victorinus after Tertullian and before Cyprian (d. 258). "One might think, therefore, that [Victorinus] was younger than Cyprian, but wrote a part of his works at a time when Cyprian was writing his own."[9] In Jerome's judgment Victorinus "did not know Latin as well as he did Greek."[10] This has led some to the conclusion that Victorinus was Greek. However, the name Victorinus is Latin, and Eusebius of Caesarea seems not to know him, despite his considerable literary output. Most probably Victorinus was from Pannonia itself whose cosmopolitan character suffices to explain his facility in Greek rather than in good rhetorical Latin.[11] On one occasion Jerome speaks of him as "our Victorinus" which very likely refers to their common region of origin.[12] The date of the martyrdom of Victorinus is given by Jerome in the broadest of terms, "at the end." Usually this is taken to refer to the persecution of Diocletian, and the martyrdom is dated c. 304. Dulaey, however, thinks that an earlier persecution, perhaps one under Numerian (283–284), is possible.[13]

As the listing of Jerome makes clear, the work of Victorinus was primarily exegetical. He mentions eight commentaries on the Old Testament books and one on a New Testament book, namely, the commentary on the Revelation. In addition, Jerome mentions "numerous others" (*multa alia*). Among these must be *De fabrica mundi*, the only other work of Victorinus that is known to us,[14] and a commentary on Matthew that is mentioned by Jerome.[15] In addition, Victorinus was an imitator of Origen and edited some of Origen's commentaries "not in exact versions but in independent paraphrases."[16] The

---

[9]See Dulaey, *Victorin de Poetovio*, 1:11-12 (my translation). For Ambrosiaster, see *in Rom* 5.14 (CSEL 81:177). Other lists place Victorinus between Tertullian and Lactantius, between Minucius Felix and Lactantius, and between Cyprian and Lactantius.

[10]An opinion which he also expressed elsewhere. *Letter* 58.10: "What he understood, he could not express well"; *Letter* 70.5: "Although he lacked erudition, he was not lacking in the desire for erudition."

[11]Concerning the Latin of Victorinus, Bruce writes, "While his meaning is usually quite plain, his grammatical constructions are the reverse. In many places they conform to no known rule of Latin syntax, classical or post-classical. He makes frequent use of the infinitive in independent clauses, the subject being sometimes in the nominative, sometimes in the accusative. He inverts the normal usages of *in* with the accusative and *in* with the ablative" ("Earliest Latin Commentary," pp. 353-54).

[12]Jerome *Letter* 36.16 (CSEL 54:283).

[13]Dulaey, SC 423:16. In the *Roman Martrology* the feast day of Victorinus is November 2. However, this may not be the date of the martyrdom but the date of the translation of the relics to Poetovio c. 472 (SC 423:16).

[14]For introduction and text, see Dulaey, SC 423:23-28, 138-49. This work is not mentioned by any ancient writer.

[15]Jerome *Commentary on Matthew*, pref. (CCL 77:5).

[16]Jerome *Letter* 61.2; 84.7 (NPNF[2] 6:132, 179).

Against Heresies listed by Jerome is not extant, unless, as some scholars have speculated, it was Victorinus's Latin translation of an early listing of heresies that was added as an appendix to Tertullian's *On Prescription Against the Heresies*.[17] The rest of Victorinus's considerable output is lost to us, probably because his chiliasm, evident in his commentary on the Revelation, made him theologically suspect. Victorinus is listed among the "apocrypha" in the so-called *Decretum Gelasianum* (c. 490).

Nonetheless, it is clear that early on Victorinus enjoyed a respected status. Indeed, on one occasion Jerome lists Victorinus among "the pillars of the church" (*columnae ecclesiae*).[18] According to Dulaey, Victorinus is mentioned at least forty-one times by ancient writers.[19] His reputation seems to have been high in Rome. Ambrosiaster mentions him, along with Tertullian and Cyprian, as a witness to early Latin versions of the Bible, and Helvidius adduces Victorinus, apparently on the basis of his Matthew commentary, as a witness for the view that Mary had natural children after Jesus.[20] In Africa Victorinus is mentioned positively by Optatus of Milevis as a defender of orthodox doctrine.[21] In the seventh century, works of Victorinus are still to be found in the library of Isidore of Seville.[22]

Victorinus's Commentary on Revelation: The Text

The legacy of Victorinus, however, continued only through his commentary on the Revelation. It is the earliest commentary on the Revelation that we have, written perhaps as early as the reign of Gallienus (c. 258–260).[23] However, the commentary of Victorinus continued into the middle ages only with significant modification. In 398 a certain Anatolius sent a copy of Victorinus's commentary to Jerome and requested an assessment of it. Jerome returned the commentary with a covering letter in which he said that he had made necessary corrections, especially removing the offending chiliastic interpretations and substituting them with comments from other writers who had more acceptable understandings:

> Various misfortunes befall those who attempt to cross the expanse of the sea. If the force of the winds should be quite vehement, the journey is fraught with fear. If the breeze makes waves upon a more calm and tranquil sea, then one fears the possibility of ambush.

---

[17]Tertullian, *Prescription Against the Heresies* 46–53. This catalogue of thirty-two heresies has been thought to be a translation of the *Syntagma* of Hippolytus (R. A. Lipsius, 1865) or perhaps an anti-Origenistic work written in Greek at the time of Bishop Zephyrinus of Rome (199–217) and translated into Latin by Victorinus (so Eduard Schwartz).

[18]Jerome *Apology against Rufinus* 1.2 (SC 303:10).

[19]Dulaey, *Victorin de Poetovio*, 1:16. This includes the twenty-two occasions in which Jerome refers to Victorinus.

[20]Ambrosiaster *in Rom* 5.14 (CSEL 81/1:176); the view of Helvidius is given by Jerome *Against Helvidius* 19 (NPNF[2] 6:343). According to Jerome, Helvidius also adduced Tertullian for his views. Jerome claims that Helvidius misunderstood Victorinus, but his words do not betray confidence.

[21]Optatus *Against Parmenian* 1.9 (CSEL 26:11). Victorinus is mentioned along with Zephyrinus and Tertullian as defenders of the church (*adsertores ecclesiae catholicae*) against Marcion, Praxeas, Sabellius and Valentinus.

[22]For discussion of the use of Victorinus by ancient writers, see Dulaey, *Victorin de Poetovio*, 1:15-16.

[23]So Dulaey, *Victorin de Poetovio*, 1:24; SC 423:15.

Such is the case, it seems to me, concerning this volume that you have sent to me and that contains the Explanation of the Revelation (*in apocalypsin explanatio*) by Victorinus.

It is dangerous to judge the works of an illustrious man, and moreover one exposes oneself to the barkings of detractors. For earlier Papias, bishop of Hierapolis, and Nepos, bishop in regions of Egypt, affirmed the thousand year kingdom even as Victorinus did. However, since you have urged me to this task by letter, I do not wish to delay. Yet, lest I disappoint you in this request, I have diligently consulted the books of the authorities (*maiorum*). I have added the opinions found in their commentaries concerning the millennial kingdom to the work of Victorinus, removing from his work those portions that he interpreted literally.

From the beginning of the book unto the sign of the cross I have corrected what was faulty because of lack of skill. From there unto the end of the volume you will notice what has been added. It is for you to exercise discernment and to confirm what is pleasing. If, however, my dearest Anatolius, he who is Life shall become our teacher (*comes*) and the Lord will give me sound judgment, we will use our abilities to the fullest extent in this book.[24]

This edition of Jerome gradually replaced the original of Victorinus until by the sixth or seventh century the original was no longer known.[25] Steinhauser notes six ways in which Jerome emended the text of Victorinus: (1) Jerome improved the imperfect Latin of Victorinus; (2) Jerome used a later translation of the Scriptures; (3) Occasionally Jerome changed the wording of Victorinus's exposition; (4) Jerome omitted what he thought false or unhelpful, especially the chiliastic passages at the end; (5) Jerome added some comments of his own[26] and some sections taken from Tyconius; (6) Jerome transposed some sections of the original.[27] The first edition of Jerome itself underwent two further more minor recensions. But the original of Victorinus remained unknown until 1916 when Johannes Hausleiter discovered the original in *Codex Ottobonian latinus 3288A* (fifteenth century).[28]

---

[24]For the Latin text of this statement of Jerome, see Hausleiter (CSEL 49:14-15); Dulaey (SC 423:124). The sign of the cross has been variously located. G. Morin located it at Rev 13:18 and thought that it was the monogram of Christ that the antichrist wished to ascribe to himself ("Hieronymus de monogrammate: Un nouvel inédit hiéronymien sur le chiffre de la bête dans l'Apocalypse," *Revue Benedictine* 20 [1903]: 225-36). Perhaps more likely, Hausleiter locates the sign at Rev 20:6 and refers it to the significant emendations that Jerome makes to Victorinus's chiliastic interpretations (CSEL 49:145).

[25]Steinhauser claims that Caesarius of Arles still knew and used the original of Victorinus: "The extensive agreement between Caesarius and Victorinus would indicate that Caesarius had access to the original commentary of Victorinus but not to Jerome-Victorinus. Beatus, on the other hand, had access to Jerome-Victorinus but not to Victorinus" (*Apocalypse Commentary of Tyconius*, p. 39).

[26]A good example of this and of Jerome's reinterpretation of Victorinus's chiliasm is Jerome's interpretation of the thousand years. He adds that the thousand years are not earthly: "The number ten signifies the Decalogue, and the number one hundred reveals the crown of virginity. For whoever preserves inviolate the intention of virginity and faithfully fulfills the precepts of the Decalogue and is watchful of impure habits and impure thoughts within the chamber of the heart lest they overcome him, that one is truly a priest of Christ and fully completing the millennial number is believed to reign with Christ and with him the devil is truly bound" (CSEL 49:145-47).

[27]Steinhauser, *Apocalypse Commentary of Tyconius*, pp. 31-32; also Bruce, "Earliest Latin Commentary," p. 355.

[28]Published in *Commentarii in Apocalypsin Editio Victorini* (CSEL 49; Leipzig: G. Freytag, 1916). The original exists also in two secondary manuscripts, *Ottobonian 3288B*, a sixteenth century copy of the former, and *Vatican 3546*, a sixteenth century copy of one or the other of the former two. See Dulaey, SC 423:28-29; Dulaey, *Victorin de Poetovio*, 1:19-21; Gryson, "Commentaires

The present translation is on the basis of the text of Hausleiter, although the text of Dulaey was at every point also consulted.[29]

Victorinus's Commentary on Revelation: Theology and Method

As one might expect from a commentary written in the middle of the third century, the commentary of Victorinus on the Revelation retains evidence of early and primitive expectations of early Christian eschatology which are largely unaffected by a later dogmatic consensus. We have already noted that any mention of Arius or Manichaeanism is absent from the work, the only heresy mentioned being that of Gnosticism. In addition, Victorinus identifies the antichrist with the emperor Nero whom he counts as the eighth king who when he comes will go to perdition.[30] Furthermore, Victorinus, perhaps following Irenaeus,[31] interprets the four living creatures in a manner differently from that given in the Jerome recension. For Victorinus Matthew is represented by the man, Luke by the calf, Mark by the eagle and John by the lion. The Jerome recension gives the later consensus: Matthew is represented by the man, Luke by the calf, Mark by the lion and John by the eagle.[32] And, of course, the chiliastic portions of Victorinus testify to a primitive eschatology which, as the letter of Jerome to Anatolius says, corresponds to that of Papias of Hierapolis, Nepos and, we might add, Irenaeus.

According to Cassiodorus, Victorinus "interpreted certain difficult passages [of the Revelation] in concise form."[33] Indeed, as a whole the commentary is not easy to characterize. It makes no attempt to interpret all portions of the Revelation, and some interpretation, as Cassiodorus notes, is quite brief. While a millenialist perspective is certainly evident, much of the commentary evinces a mild allegorical method, perhaps reflecting the influence of Origen. For example, the letters to the seven churches are interpreted to address and to represent seven classes of saints in the church. Influence by earlier writers is only implicit. Victorinus quotes no previous authorities, although Irenaeus and Hippolytus are in the background, and he makes mention of only one nonbiblical text, that of the unknown epitome of Theodore.[34]

At the same time, his use of the Scriptures is frequent and broadly based.[35] One may well surmise that the broad use of the Scriptures is due not merely to his familiarity with the Scriptures but to his deep conviction that the Scriptures comprise a singular and

---

patristiques latins," pp. 305-11.

[29]Dulaey, *Victorin de Poetovio.*

[30]Victorinus *On the Apocalypse* 13/17:2 (SC 423:106). Victorinus was apparently the first to make this identification.

[31]See Irenaeus *Against the Heresies* 3.11.8 (ANF 1:428).

[32]Victorinus *On the Apocalypse* 4.4 (SC 423:66-68; CSEL 49:50-55).

[33]Cassiodorus *Institutes on Divine and Secular Learning* 1.9.2 (PL 70:1122): *difficillima quaedam loca breviter tractavit.*

[34]Victorinus *On the Apocalypse* 4.5 (SC 423:70); see Dulaey, *Victorin de Poetovio,* 1:271-72.

[35]Bruce lists the following: Genesis, Exodus, Numbers, Job, Psalms, Proverbs, Ecclesiastes, Isaiah, Jeremiah, Ezekiel, Daniel, Joel, Micah, Zechariah, Malachi, the four Gospels (especially Matthew), Acts, Romans, 1 and 2 Corinthians, 1 and 2 Thessalonians, 2 Timothy, Hebrews, 1 Peter, Jude ("Earliest Latin Commentary," p. 356).

united revelation. Indeed, the unity of Scripture is fundamental to the hermeneutical method of Victorinus and reveals itself in his interpretations. The unity of the Scriptures consists in the fact that the one who speaks in both the Old Testament and the New Testament is one and the same, the Word of God. However, this is not merely a formal claim. The unity of the Scriptures is itself revealed and comprehended only with the coming of the Word in the flesh, with his passion and with his resurrection.[36] This is especially clear from Victorinus's comments on Rev 5:1-5 where the Lion of Judah alone is said to be capable of opening the sealed book. This was foretold when Moses came down from Sinai with veiled face, indicating to the people that "the words of preaching were veiled until the time of Christ's coming."[37] The unveiling of the Law of Moses (*revelatio*) is also an unsealing (*resignatio*) of the seven seals, that is, it is to open the Scriptures (*apertio*; *adapertio*). According to Dulaey, "The exegetical terminology of Victorinus takes up the vocabulary of Jewish literature where 'to open the book' signifies to open the meaning of the book, to make comment on the book."[38]

That Christ opens his word of the Old Testament through his word of the New Testament is given emphasis at the very beginning of the commentary.[39] Victorinus gives four arguments. First, in the initial vision of the prophet, a sharp two-edged sword is seen coming from the mouth of Christ (Rev 1:16). Since a sword both arms a soldier and kills the enemy, the sword shows that Christ both gave knowledge of the law and now gives the blessings of the Gospel. Second, a scribe of the kingdom is like a householder who brings forth things both new and old (see Mt 13:51-52). That which is old is the law and the prophets, and that which is new is the good tidings of the Gospel. Third, Victorinus refers to Jesus' command to Peter to cast his hook into the sea and bring up the first fish. In its mouth would be a shekel coin, that is, two denarii (see Mt 17:27), the two denarii referring to the two testaments. Finally, Victorinus quotes from Psalm 62:11 (61:12 LXX): "Once God has spoken, twice I have heard this." This means, comments Victorinus, that "the Lord once decreed from the beginning what was going to be unto the end."[40] Although the view that the Old and New Testaments were one because the voice behind both was one had become a traditional *theologoumenon* by the time of Victorinus, his is the first use of this Psalm to argue for the unity of the Scriptures. Dulaey writes: "Perhaps he borrowed from sources of Jewish origin, for the rabbis sometimes used this verse to explain that one and the same word of God could have several meanings."[41]

Victorinus's conviction concerning the unity of the Scriptures is reinforced by his ex-

---

[36]See Dulaey, *Victorin de Poetovio*, pp. 94-96.

[37]Victorinus *On the Apocalypse* 5.2 (SC 423:76). See Ex 34:29-33; 2 Cor 3:13-16. The Latin word for veiled is *velata*; the word for the lifting of the veil is *revelatio*.

[38]Dulaey, *Victorin de Poetovio*, p. 95.

[39]Victorinus *On the Apocalypse* 1.4 (SC 423:50).

[40]Ibid.

[41]Dulaey, *Victorin de Poetovio*, 1:90.

egetical method in interpreting the Revelation. Victorinus seems to have been the first to have interpreted the Revelation not as a continuous and successive sequence of visions but as repetitive, the trumpets and the bowls portraying the same events under different images. What governs the structure of the Revelation is not the succession of temporal moments but divine purpose: "We ought not pay too much attention to the order of what is said. For the sevenfold Holy Spirit, when he has passed in revue [the events] to the last time, to the very end, returns again to the same times and supplements what he had said incompletely. Nor ought we inquire too much into the order of the Revelation. Rather, we ought inquire after the meaning."[42] This divine purpose, as we have seen, was from the beginning centered on the coming Word incarnate whose death and resurrection open the meaning of all Scripture. Therefore Victorinus can write concerning the vision of the open door in heaven (Rev 4:10), "And now he recalls that which had been foretold in the law by means of similitudes, and through this Scripture he joins together all the previous prophets and opens the Scriptures."[43] It is an important statement of Victorinus's understanding of the Revelation. The Revelation is the synthesis of all Scripture and the key to its understanding. "It is the perfect revelation of the sense of the Scripture concerning Christ himself. The Revelation extends to all faithful that incredible privilege that the disciple of Emmaus enjoyed when Jesus 'beginning from Moses and all the prophets explained to them in all the Scriptures that which was concerning him' (Lk 24:27)."[44]

Apringius of Beja

Life and Work of Apringius

The person of Apringius is even less known to us than is that of Victorinus. Virtually all we know of Apringius comes from the title of his commentary on the Revelation: "Explanation of the Revelation by the most learned man, Apringius, Bishop of the church at Pax Iulia." The name Apringius is very rare and except for our author is unknown in the history of Spain.[45] We are told that he was the bishop of the church at Pax Iulia (*Pacensis ecclesiae*). Indeed, in the episcopal lists of this church Apringius is mentioned. The city of

---

[42]Victorinus, *On the Apocalypse* 8.2 (SC 423:88).

[43]Ibid., 4.1 (SC 423:64): *et nunc exinde recolit quae per legem in similitudinibus praenuntiata errant, et per hanc scripturam coniungit omnes priores prophetas et adaperit scripturas.*

[44]Dulaey, *Victorin de Poetovio*, 1:103. As Dulaey notes, the *adaperit scripturas* of Victorinus corresponds to the διήνοιγεν τὰς γραφάς of Lk 24:32. Dulaey notes the relationship between Irenaeus and Victorinus concerning the notion of recapitulation: as Christ recapitulates in his person the new humanity and carries it to its consummation, so the Revelation recapitulates all prophecy and perfects it. It is clear, then, that the chiliasm that Victorinus sees especially in the final chapters of Revelation corresponds to the final earthly kingdom of Christ in Irenaeus (*Against the Heresies* 5.30-36). What Irenaeus develops as a full biblical theology of recapitulation, Victorinus develops as the exegetical key for understanding the Revelation.

[45]Marius Férotin, *Apringius de Béja: son commentaire de l'Apocalypse, Écrit sous Theudis, Roi des Wisigoths (531–548)* (Bibliothéque Patrologique; Paris: Alphonse Picard, 1900), p. vi n. 4. Férotin identifies only two other persons of this name. One was a fourth-century bishop of Chalcis (Syria) who attended the Council of Ephesus (431); the other comes from the letters of Augustine who wrote to a proconsul of Africa with this name.

Pax Iulia, so named by Julius Caesar in 48 B.C., was located in the south-western region of the Roman province of Lusitania, in what today is south Portugal. Its modern name is Beja, and modern discussion is wont to use this name when referring to Apringius.[46]

The title furthermore says that Apringius was a "most learned man" (eruditissimi viri). This is echoed in virtually the only other information we have about Apringius. In his On Illustrious Men Isidore of Seville (d. 636) gives the following summary notice:

> Apringius, bishop of the church at Pax Iulia (Pacensis Hispaniarum), a man skillful and fluent in speaking (disertus lingua) and learned in knowledge (scientia eruditus), expounded the Apocalypse of the apostle John with a clear and simple meaning (subtili sensu) and a clear and plain manner of speaking (illustri sermone), and this he did perhaps better than the older ecclesiastical men had expounded it. He wrote also other works that, however, have not come to the knowledge of our own reading. He flourished during the time of Theudis, king of the Goths.[47]

Férotin notes that Isidore does not list the other works of Apringius and that he probably never knew them.[48] Gryson is skeptical: "One can hardly give credence to information so hazy and uncertain."[49]

Indeed, this "hazy and uncertain" information corresponds to the general and rapid loss of any information concerning Apringius and his commentary. Isidore informs us that Apringius was active during the reign of the Visigothic king Theudis (531–548). Yet, by the end of the sixth century information about the commentary was already in very short supply. St. Braulio of Saragossa (c. 590–651) wrote to a friend of his in Toledo, one Aemilianus, indicating that he could not locate a copy of Apringius's commentary and asking that Aemilianus search for a copy there in the Visigothic capital. Braulio mentions that he knew that a copy was in the library of a certain Count Laurentius. Braulio wished to transcribe the commentary and then return it to Aemilianus. In his return letter, Aemilianus sadly responds that "as God is his witness" his most diligent searches did not uncover a copy of Apringius's commentary on the Revelation. Unhappily, the library of Laurentius was being dispersed so it also proved unhelpful.[50] Yet, a century after this the commentary of Apringius was certainly known by Beatus of Liébana (d. c. 800) who

---

[46]The Latin Pacensis is an adjective meaning "of or belonging to Pax Iulia." The city was conquered by the Umayyad army in 713.

[47]Isidore of Seville On Illustrious Men 30 (PL 83:1098-99). The plural Hispaniarum is perhaps due to the fact that the Romans often distinguished between Nearer Spain (citerior Hispania) and Further Spain (ulterior Hispania).

[48]Férotin, Apringius de Béja, p. vii n. 1. Férotin notes that Johannes Trithemus (c. 1500) mentions a commentary on the Song of Songs as yet existing (de scriptorium ecclesiasticorum 211), but he is cautious about accepting this.

[49]Roger Gryson, Apringi Pacensis Episcopi Tractatus in Apocalypsin Fragmenta quae Supersunt (CCL 107; Turnhout: Brepols Publishers, 2003), p. 13.

[50]See Férotin, Apringius de Béja, pp. vii-viii. For the correspondence, see Braulio of Saragossa Letter 25 (PL 80:673-74); the response of Aemilianus is counted as Letter 26 of Braulio (PL 80:674-75). Who Aemilianus was is uncertain. Braulio refers to him as presbyter et abbas. The language of Braulio would suggest that he was abbot of one of the principal monasteries in Toledo, perhaps that of SS. Cosma and Damian (Férotin, p. viii n. 1).

quotes about ninety-five percent of Apringius's commentary in his own huge commentary. However, that is the only use of Apringius by any later Latin commentator. Only rarely is the name of Apringius mentioned in medieval catalogues.[51]

Apringius's Tractate on the Revelation: Text

As we have noted, copies of the commentary of Apringius on the Revelation became rare quite soon after his death. The only copy of the commentary that exists is located in the university library of Copenhagen. According to a seventeenth century note on the last page, this manuscript was copied in Barcelona in 1042. The Copenhagen text, therefore, may represent a text as early as the eighty or ninth century.[52] The manuscript at Copenhagen came to the attention of Marius Férotin in 1892 who subsequently published it in 1900.[53] Férotin made no attempt to give a critical text but was content to provide a transcription of the Copenhagen manuscript. During the twentieth century a Latin edition was published by P. A. C. Vega, and a Latin edition with Spanish translation was published by Alberto del Campo Hernandez.[54] However, a much superior critical text is that of Roger Gryson, and the present translation is based on his text.[55]

Not all of Apringius's commentary on the Revelation comes from the pen of Apringius. The commentary of Apringius on the Revelation combines comments both of Apringius himself and of whole sections taken from the tradition of Victorinus-Jerome. The first five and the last five chapters of Revelation receive explanation by Apringius himself (Rev 1:1–5:7; 18:6–22:20), while the long middle section is taken wholly from a later recension of Jerome's first editing of Victorinus.[56] How did Apringius's commentary come to possess this mixed character? Did Apringius himself insert the commentary of Victorinus-Jerome into the middle portion of his own commentary, or was Victorinus-Jerome

---

[51]Férotin (*Apringius de Béja*, pp. xi-xii) mentions an 882 inventory of the library of the cathedral of Oviedo which mentions a volume combining the work of Apringius and Junilius Africanus (c. 550). The commentary of Apringius (*liber Apringii*) also appears in the library of Bishop Gennadius of Astorga which he bequeathed to the monks of San Pedro de Montes (919). In addition, c. 1600 the archives of the cathedral of Braga (Portugal) contained the commentary of Apringius, but it is lost. Finally, at the beginning of the seventeenth century a benefactor of the cathedral of Sevilla, Luis de Sanllorente, possessed a copy. He intended to publish it but died before the project could be carried out (1621). See also Gryson (CCL 107:13-15).

[52]See the discussion of Férotin, *Apringius de Béja*, pp. xii-xvii. Dulaey explicitly refers to the Copenhagen manuscript as belonging to the eighth-ninth century (*Victorin de Poetovio*, 1:361). However, Gryson believes the 1042 date too early. The manuscript cannot be "before the 12th century" (CCL 107:14).

[53]Marius Férotin, *Apringius de Béja: son commentaire de l'Apocalypse, Écrit sous Theudis, Roi des Wisigoths (531–548)* (Bibliothèque Patrologique; Paris: Alphonse Picard, 1900). This book has recently been reprinted by Kessinger Legacy Reprints, Kessinger Publishing.

[54]P. A. C. Vega, *Apringii Pacensis Episcopi Tractatus in Apocalysin* (Scriptores Ecclesiastici Hispano-Latini Veteris et Medii Aevi, fasc. 10-11; Madrid: Typis Augustinianis Monasterii Escurialensis, 1940); Alberto del Campo Hernandez, *Comentario al Apocalipsis de Apringio de Beja: Introduccion, Texto Latino y Traduccion* (Institucion San Jeronimo 25; Estella: Editorial Verbo Divino, 1991).

[55]Roger Gryson, *Variorum Auctorum Commentaria Minora in Apocalypsin Johannis* (CCL 107; Turnholt: Brepols Publishers, 2003), pp. 11-97. See also the discussion of Apringius's text by Gryson, "Commentaires patristiques latins," pp. 322-27.

[56]For discussion see Gryson (CCL 107:17-21); Dulaey, *Victorin de Poetovio*, 1:360-62. The later recension in view was given the *signum* Φ by Hausleiter. Gryson summarizes: "La source majeure, si pas unique, d'Apringius est le commentaire de Victorin, qui lui parvient à travers la recension Φ de l'édition hiéronymienne" ("Commentaires patristiques latins," p. 324).

inserted for some other reason? Opinion on this question is divided. Dulaey claims that both in the middle section and in sections from Apringius himself the text of Victorinus-Jerome used is that of the later recension Φ.[57] Dulaey concludes: "One has the impression that it is the same manuscript that is used throughout the commentary, and it is therefore probable that it was Apringius himself who inserted a section of the commentary of Victorinus into his own."[58] Gryson, on the other hand, is of the opinion that a later copyist is responsible. From at least the eighth century copies of Apringius became increasingly rare and increasingly fragmented. Some portions became lost. In view of this, a copyist, who noted that Apringius had used Victorinus-Jerome, similarly made use of this text to fill in the large middle section that had already disappeared.[59] Certainty in this question is clearly unattainable. However, Dulaey's comment is worthy of mention: "To those who object that it is strange that Apringius would in this way reproduce whole sections from the commentary of Victorinus, one can respond that the same thing was done by Beatus."[60]

Apringius's Tractate on the Revelation: Theology and Method

Férotin gives a brief summary of the importance of Apringius's commentary on the Revelation:

> Apringius wrote during the first half of the sixth century, before the time of Saint Leander and Saint Isidore, at a time when, following upon the great barbarian invasions, Christian literature was especially meager within all of the [Iberian] peninsula. To some extent, therefore, his work serves to fill in that regrettable lacuna. One must add that the catholic bishop of Béja lived under the dominion of the Arian Visigoths, and this circumstance sufficiently explains, it seems to us, the choice of sacred text that he took as a text of his commentary.[61]

As we are informed by Isidore, Apringius was active during the reign of Theudis, king of the Visigoths (531–548). At the time, the Visigoths in Spain represented the *homoion* understanding of the Arian heresy, that is, they affirmed that the Son and the Holy Spirit were "similar" to the Father but not themselves divine according to nature. The

---

[57]Other than the middle section which is taken wholly from Victorinus-Jerome, Gryson (CCL 107:24) identifies nine places where Apringius gives another explanation, often introduced by *aliter*, taken from the Φ edition of Victorinus-Jerome (Rev 1:13, 14, 15, 16; 2:17, 28; 4:3; 5:1, 3). Apart from these nine passages, claims Gryson, no other influence from Victorinus-Jerome is discernible in sections from Apringius himself.

[58]Dulaey, *Victorin de Poetovio*, 1:361. Del Campo Hernandez also believes Apringius is responsible for inserting Victorinus into his own work (*Comentario*, 32-39). Joop van Banning also credits Apringius himself for the insertion, but his theory is perhaps too speculative to warrant assent ("Bemerkungen zur Apringius von Beja-Forschung," *Zeitschrift für antikes Christentum* 3 [1999]: 113-19, here 114-16).

[59]Gryson (CCL 107:18-20); Gryson, "Commentaires patristiques latins," pp. 325-27.

[60]Dulaey, *Victorin de Poetovio*, 1:361 (my translation).

[61]Férotin, *Apringius de Béja*, p. xxii (my translation). For the theological character of Apringius's commentary, see Gryson (CCL 107:23-25); van Banning, "Bemerkungen," pp. 116-19.

Nicene orthodox party, represented by Apringius, was perhaps in the minority. Theudis was, however, not a persecutor, and this perhaps explains why there is no explicit polemical emphasis against the Arians in Apringius's commentary.[62] Yet, Apringius repeatedly emphasizes the orthodox doctrine of the Trinity, namely, that the Son and the Spirit, together with the Father, are equal in deity and one God. At the very beginning, in his short preface, Apringius asserts that our Lord Jesus Christ is "the author of the law" and that weak humanity cannot explain it unless guided by "the mystery of the two-fold sacrament" of the two natures of Christ. Moreover, the Holy Spirit, who dwelt in Jesus, is called on to "open the door of our inner mind" so that "God (i.e., the Spirit) teaching us," Apringius might draw out the true meanings.[63] Hence, according to the understanding of Apringius, his commentary is not an abstract work of the scholar, but the writing down of divine speech through which that revealed to the seer John might now also illuminate the church. Indeed, the Revelation is the divine speech of the risen Christ, an important point to which we shall return below. Through his resurrection Christ revealed to the world the mystery of the Trinity that had remained hidden from the ages.[64] As the divine speech of the risen Christ, therefore, the Revelation is a Trinitarian text and Apringius's commentary a Trinitarian tractate.

Perhaps the most interesting and sustained passage in which Apringius affirms the deity of both the Son and the Spirit occurs at Revelation 1:8. There Christ calls himself the A and the Ω, the Alpha and the Omega. Appealing to the interpretation of certain "authorities of ours" (*maiores nostri*), Apringius notes that the numerical value of A and Ω is 801 (800 + 1), the same numerical value as περιστερά, the Greek word for "dove," the form of the Holy Spirit at the baptism of Jesus. This numerical equality was, apparently, first noted by the Marcosian Gnostics in order to claim that the dove at the baptism of Jesus was in fact none other than the Christ figure.[65] Later Gregory of Elvira and Didymus the Blind used this numerical identity to argue for the divinity of the Holy Spirit.[66] In his commentary on the Revelation, Primasius of Hadrumetum also uses this argument for the deity of the Spirit: "And so by the agreement of this number this revelation from heaven makes known that the Holy Spirit is consubstantial and co-eternal with the Father and the Son."[67] The particular argument of Apringius, however, is unique to himself. The Greek word περιστερά "moves toward A," that is, toward its final letter which has the numerical value of one. The previous letters of the word have

---

[62]Férotin (*Apringius de Béja*, p. xxiii) notes that, although Theudis was a heretic in doctrine, Isidore of Seville gives him high praise: "Although he was a heretic, he nevertheless gave peace to the church. In this regard he allowed the catholic bishops to assemble together in the city of Toledo, and they established freely and as they willed whatever was necessary for the discipline of the church" (Isidore, *Historia de regibus Gothorum* [PL 83:1068-69]).

[63]Apringius *Tractatus* pref (CCL 107:33); see also Apringius's comments in *Tractatus* 4.1 (CCL 107:59)

[64]Apringius *Tractatus* 5.7 (CCL 107:68).

[65]See Irenaeus *Against the Heresies*, 1.14.6 (ANF 1:338); Ps-Tertullian *Against All Heresies* 5.1-2 (CCL 2:1407-8).

[66]Gregory of Elvira *Song of Songs* 3.10-11; Didymus the Blind *On the Trinity* 2.14 (PG 39:696).

[67]Primasius *Commentary on the Apocalypse* 22.13 (CCL 92:306-7).

the numerical value of 800, which is also that of Ω. Apringius, therefore, draws the conclusion that the deity of the Holy Spirit is in the unity of the Trinity.

The commentary of Apringius is significant because it preserves early and independent interpretation apart from the later consensus. He does not know of the commentary of Tyconius or of later writers, such as Primasius and Caesarius, who were dependent on Tyconius. In fact, Apringius cites no previous ecclesiastical writer by name, although, as we have seen, he can refer to earlier authorities. In another instance, in commenting on Revelation 4:7, he again refers to certain "authorities of ours" (*maiores nostri*) when he identifies the figure of the lion with the Gospel of Mark.[68] By the time of Apringius this identification had become largely traditional, and it is probable that Apringius takes this identification from his edition of Victorinus-Jerome. More interesting is Apringius's appeal to certain "ecclesiastical historians" (*relatores ecclesiastici*) who place John's exile to Patmos during the reign of Claudius (41–54). John's exile is interpreted as an imperial response to the famine foretold by Agabus (Acts 11:28), and therefore the apostle's exile would be c. 45. Who these *relatores* are is not clear. The only other patristic writer who adopts this view is Epiphanius of Salamis (d. 403),[69] although the Muratorian Canon (c. 200) also dates John's writing to seven churches to be earlier than the letters of Paul to seven churches.

As we have noted, the Revelation was especially important in the western tradition. In the Iberian peninsula during the time of Apringius this was especially the case. Readings from the Revelation were especially prominent in the Visigothic/Mozarabic liturgy of the Spanish church during the period between Easter and Pentecost. This liturgical fact may be the primary reason why Apringius undertook his commentary on this biblical book. Indeed, as we know from the Fourth Council of Toledo (633), reading from the Revelation during this period of the church's liturgical calendar was commanded.[70] In view of this, it has been suggested that the commentary of Apringius may have originated as a series of homilies for this liturgical season.[71] However, the commentary does not read like a homily, and why Apringius would use a text of Victorinus-Jerome for his large middle section would remain a mystery. Yet, clearly

---

[68]Apringius *Tractatus* 4.7 (CCL 107:62-63).

[69]Epiphanius of Salamis *Against the Heresies* 51.12.2 (GCS 31/2:263-64; PG 41:909); 51.33.9 (GCS 31/2:308; PG 41:949). Van Banning positively receives this early dating. He notes that Epiphanius is an independent witness and, as a bishop on Cyprus, could have known of a local tradition of this dating ("Bemerkungen," pp. 118-19).

[70]After affirming that by the authority of many councils the Revelation has been recognized as a writing of the evangelist John and should be received among the divine books (*inter divinos libros*) in the church and that there were many who do not receive its authority and neglect to read (*praedicare contemnunt*) it in the church, Canon 17 from the Fourth Council of Toledo reads as follows: "If therefore anyone does not accept it or does not read (*praedicaverit*) it in the church at the time of the mass from Pascha until Pentecost, he shall receive the sentence of excommunication" (Mansi, *Sacrorum Conciliorum* 10:624). For the readings from the Revelation used from the Pascha to Pentecost, see PL 85:487-614. Since we know that passages from the Revelation were read, we have translated the Latin *praedicere* as "to read." It is possible that the verb refers as well to preaching on the text of the Revelation.

[71]Berthold Altaner, book review of P.A.C. Vega's edition, *Theologische Revue* 4 (1942): 119-20.

the Mozarabic liturgy guided some portions of Apringius's commentary. This is most evidently the case in Apringius's interpretation of the seven seals.[72] Apringius understands these seven seals to correspond to seven events in the life of Jesus Christ: (1) incarnation; (2) birth; (3) passion; (4) death; (5) resurrection; (6) glory; (7) kingdom.[73] These correspond closely to a practice of the Mozarabic rite. Upon recital of the Nicene Creed the priest took the largest host which is consecrated and broke it into two pieces. From one piece he further broke the host into five pieces and from the other part into four, arranging them on the paten in the form of a cross. The effect is that found in figure 1:[74]

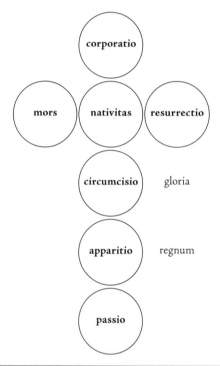

Figure 1. Events of the Life of Christ and the Seven Seals

The fact that *gloria* and *regnum*, listed among the seven seals by Apringius, lie alongside the cross is explained by the fact that they represent the status and mission of the resurrected Christ and so his activity through the sacraments of the church.[75]

[72]Apringius *Tractatus* 5.1 (CCL 107:66).

[73]Among the Greek commentaries, that of Oecumenius also interprets the seven seals to be events in the life of Jesus. For a helpful study with translations of the seven seals in medieval commentaries, see Francis X. Gumerlock, *The Seven Seals of the Apocalypse: Medieval Texts in Translation* (TEAMS Commentary Series; Kalamazoo, Mich.: Medieval Institute Publications, Western Michigan University, 2009).

[74]See PL 85:118, 557. For discussion, see E. Ann Matter, "The Pseudo-Alcuinian 'De septem sigillis'. An Early Latin Apocalypse Exegesis," *Traditio* 36 (1980): 118-22.

[75]Matter, "Pseudo-Alcuinian 'De septem sigillis'," pp. 121-22. Matter notes that the earliest example of the seven seals representing events in the life of Christ comes from Hilary of Poitiers's *Tractatus super Psalmos* (CSEL 22:7). For Hilary this interpretation

Commentary on the Revelation, so it seems, assisted to teach the faithful concerning the mystery of the Faith in which they participated when partaking of the Supper of the Risen Christ. To understand the mystery of the Trinitarian life, latent in the Old Testament but acquired by the incarnation of the divine Son and granted by the divine Holy Spirit, was not merely a matter of intellect. It involved an opening of the spiritual mind of the faithful who in the reception of the Eucharist entered through the open door. As bishop Apringius wished to teach his faithful what it was they were to see.

Caesarius of Arles

Life and Work of Caesarius

The sack of Rome by the Goths in 410 and again by the Vandals in 455 was perhaps the most spectacular indication that the Roman Empire in the west was in collapse. Yet the fall of the empire in the west had been underway for decades beforehand. Unlike in the east where the unity of empire under a centralized government was largely preserved in the Byzantine rule of Constantinople, in the west centralized rule disappeared into an agrarian society that was largely local and in which state control was weak. What centralized control existed was exercised primarily by the Germanic kings of the Visigoths, Ostrogoths, Burgundians and Franks. However, the deeply rooted remnants of popular paganism continued in this area of former Roman glory. Ensuring the continuation of Christian progress and evangelization of these western regions was the task and responsibility of local bishops and their clergy. It was to be through their efforts, along with the spiritual influence of the monasteries, that Christian faith and piety was to confront this paganism and, as it were, demystify the world so that human life might be lived according to the will of God, the Creator.

In this process no one was more steadfast in execution and of greater importance than Caesarius of Arles. The sole focus and intent of his pastoral care and work was to reorient the minds and hearts of people from their pagan habits to the practice of Christian virtue. As Peter Brown notes, this was a huge challenge that entailed the creation of a new mentality: "He had to dethrone the ancient image of the world. In his preaching, the *mundus*, the physical universe, was drained of its autonomy. It had no life of its own apart from that given to it by the will of God."[76]

There is considerable information about Caesarius of Arles in the sources. Primary bi-

---

served as an anti-Arian argument. Since Apringius was writing during the time of the Arian Theudis, perhaps this aspect of the Mozarabic rite served the same purpose. This interpretation of the seven seals appears also in Ildefonsus of Toledo (seventh century; PL 96:120) and in Beatus of Liebana (eighth century) who, however, is following the commentary of Apringius.

[76]Peter Brown, *The Rise of Western Christendom: Triumph and Diversity, A.D. 200–1000* (Oxford: Blackwell, 1996; 2nd edition 2003), p. 152. Brown's description and analysis of the move from the world of Rome to that of the early Middle Ages is excellent.

ographical information about him, however, comes from the *Vita Caesarii* written shortly after his death by Cyprian of Toulon along with other associates of Caesarius.[77] Caesarius was born in 470 into a Christian Roman-Burgundian family in the region around Chalon-sur-Saone.[78] Against the desires of his parents he was admitted to the clergy at age seventeen and two years later determined to live as a monk in the famous monastery at Lérins. Here Caesarius became familiar with a broad array of Christian authors, although Augustine served him as principal authority.[79] Failing health due to monastic rigor, and perhaps opposition among the monks at Lérins due to his restricting of the distribution of supplies, occasioned his move to the city of Arles which was the seat of Visigoth rule.[80] In Arles Caesarius was welcomed by Aeonius, bishop of Arles and a relative of Caesarius, who ordained him deacon and priest and in 499 made Caesarius abbot of the monastery in Arles. Before his death Bishop Aeonius had designated Caesarius as his successor, and when Aeonius died in 502, Caesarius was ordained bishop of Arles, a position he held until his own death in 542.

As bishop of the most important church in south Gaul, Caesarius was instrumental in promoting the interests of the Roman church in Gaul, furthered the monastic life in his regions, and promoted the ideals of asceticism, faithful pastoral care and popular preaching as suitable and right for priests and bishops. In 512/513 Caesarius was accused of treason and was brought to Ravenna to defend himself before the Ostrogothic king, Theodoric. Absolved of any wrongdoing and, indeed, receiving honor and praise, Caesarius used the occasion to visit Rome. While there Caesarius became the first bishop outside Italy to receive the *pallium*, a symbol that Caesarius was given responsibility to represent the Bishop of Rome's interests in Gaul. At the same time Pope Symmachus decided in favor of Arles over the church of Vienne, making Caesarius the metropolitan bishop of southern Gaul. In this capacity Caesarius was well-positioned to advance his ideals. In

---

[77]A translation of the *Life of Caesarius* with notes and introduction may be found in William C. Klingshirn, *Caesarius of Arles: Life, Testament, Letters* (Texts for Historians 19; Liverpool: Liverpool University Press, 1994). Cyprian was bishop of Toulon (c. 517–545) and was disciple and life-long supporter of Caesarius. Cyprian was assisted in the writing of the *Vita* by Firminus, bishop of Uzès (c. 534–552) and Viventius, bishop of an unknown see (c. 541–548). These were responsible for Book One of the *Vita*. Book Two was largely written by Messianus, a priest, and Stephanus, a deacon, both of whom were clerics of the diocese of Arles and apparently lived in the episcopal household.

[78]For full biographical information see A. Malnory, *Saint Césaire, évêque d'Arles 503–543* (Bibliothèque de l'école des hautes etudes 103; Paris: Librairie Émile Bouillon, 1894; repr. Paris: Honoré Champion; Genève: Slatkine Reprints, 1978); William E. Klingshirn, *Caesarius of Arles: The Making of a Christian Community in Late Antique Gaul* (Cambridge: Cambridge University Press, 1994). Helpful also is W. M. Daly, "Caesarius of Arles, a Precursor of Medieval Christendom," *Traditio* 26 (1970): 1-28.

[79]Among the authors read by Caesarius while at Lérins Steinhauser mentions Hilary of Arles, Vincent of Lérins, Faustus of Riez, Irenaeus, Origen, Ambrose, John Chrysostom and Ephraem the Syrian (*Apocalypse Commentary of Tyconius*, p. 45).

[80]At Lérins Caesarius held the important post of *cellerarius*. In this office Caesarius would be responsible for the storage and distribution of the monastery's food, wine, clothing and other materials for daily living. In 476/477 the Visigothic king, Euric, consolidated his rule in southern Gaul, and Arles permanently left the regions of the Roman Empire. In 508 Arles came under Ostrogoth rule, when the armies of Theodoric saved the city from a siege by Frankish and Burgundian forces. However, when in 536 the Ostrogoths required their forces to defend their Italian lands against the Byzantines under Justinian, Arles and all of the Provence came under the hegemony of the Franks.

Arles he established a women's monastery in parallel to that over which he had been abbot, and placed his sister, Caesaria, as abbess over it. For these monastic houses Caesarius wrote two monastic rules, one for the monks and one for the nuns. Moreover, to enforce greater discipline and conformity among the clergy, to make certain liturgical changes and to decide doctrinal questions, Caesarius presided over no fewer than six synods: Agde (506), Arles (524), Carpentras (527), Orange (529), Vaison (529) and Marseilles (533).[81] Historically the most important of these councils was that of Orange (529). Caesarius along with fourteen bishops and eight high-ranking laymen (*viri illustres*) met to decide questions arising from ongoing dispute over certain doctrines of Augustine on sin, grace and free will. The council affirmed Augustine's insistence that fallen humanity was under the curse of natural/original sin and possessed no capacity to make even the first step toward faith and good works and that, therefore, no human merit preceded the gift of grace (prevenient grace). Yet the council ameliorated Augustine's predestinarian views, asserting that after the grace of baptism anyone could and should, with the aid and cooperation of Christ, perform what is pleasing to God and sufficient to the soul's salvation. Predestination to evil was explicitly condemned. The central importance that the Council of Orange gave to the sacramental administrations of the church throughout the life of a person was a significant factor in the formation of the medieval church. The council of Vaison (529) made several significant changes to the Gallic liturgy. The council determined that the three-fold *Sanctus* should be recited at every mass, that the *Kyrie Eleison* be recited at matins, vespers and mass, and, importantly, that the words *sicut erat in principio* ("as he was in the beginning") be added to the *Gloria Patri*, as a liturgical affirmation of the deity of Christ against the surrounding Arians. Moreover, the name of the bishop of Rome was to be mentioned in liturgical prayers.

However, Caesarius was above all a bishop who understood himself essentially as a pastor of the people and who understood his pastoral activities in terms of the reformist agenda of Julianus Pomerius. When Caesarius first arrived in Arles, he attended the school of Pomerius and became deeply influenced by him. Pomerius himself was a devoted follower of Augustine and believed that bishops and clergy should live more like monks than aristocracy. As Roman imperial rule waned and the political authority of the Germanic kingdoms increased, the traditional outlets for the exercise of aristocratic privilege and patronage diminished. Increasingly aristocratic youth turned to the church to find opportunity for public office-holding and influence, and increasingly bishops of towns and cities were aristocratic in attitude and behavior. The reformist ideal of Pomerius directly confronted this development. Taking his cue from Augustine

---

[81]For the council at Agde, see Klingshirn, *Caesarius of Arles*, pp. 97-104; for the councils of 524, 527, 529, see Klingshirn, *Caesarius of Arles*, pp. 137-45. A helpful summary of the canons of these councils is given by Mary Magdeleine Mueller in her Introduction to the sermons of Caesarius (FC 31:xii-xv). At other councils held during the episcopate of Caesarius, Caesarius himself was not present, usually due to ill health: Auvergne (533), Orleans (533, 538, 541).

that in this age the times were mixed, Pomerius collapsed the distinction between the active life and the contemplative life. The contemplative life was not the life apart from the world, but life to be lived in the future life of bliss with God. At the same time, the contemplative life could be to some extent lived already through an ascetic manner of life that exercised both active and contemplative virtues. Thus, Pomerius advised clergy to study the Scriptures, to be free of worldly entanglements and to do works of charity such as freeing captives and feeding the poor.[82] But especially important was Pomerius's views concerning preaching. Clergy, including bishops, were to speak simply so that all could understand: "A teacher of the Church should not parade an elaborate style, lest he seem not to want to edify the Church of God but to reveal what great learning he possesses."[83] Klingshirn explains the reformist implication of this idea:

> It was the social meaning of rhetoric in late Roman Gaul that gave this [simple] standard of preaching its novelty and importance. The spoken word not only communicated information, but also defined social rank. The ability to compose and deliver complex and elegant speeches required many years of education and great expense to perfect. Because this skill was generally available only to members of the aristocracy, it served as a mark of aristocratic birth and carried with it a series of powerful associations. The refined speech of an aristocrat was calculated to reinforce feelings of solidarity with his peers, evoke a sense of deference in his inferiors, and demonstrate to everyone his knowledge and capacity for leadership. Thus, bishops who addressed their congregations in the highly ornate style of a Sidonius Apollinaris or an Avitus of Vienne did so not to confuse their congregations, but to establish their credentials as aristocrats, to reinforce their authority as leaders, and to demonstrate their status as spiritual experts."[84]

The style and content of Caesarius's many sermons and the thrust of his episcopal labors belie at every point the influence of Pomerius's reformist ideals.[85] The vast majority of Caesarius's works remaining to us are sermons.[86] He was perhaps the greatest popular preacher of the early middle ages. His sermons, many of them copied and edited from others, especially Augustine, reveal a bishop fully engaged in the articulation of Christian faith and virtue in the hope of ridding his people, high and low, from the superstitions of their residual paganism. Caesarius urged the people to pray daily, to read the Scriptures, to attend church regularly and to engage in the common charity of alms giving. Con-

---

[82]Most important is Julianus Pomerius *The Contemplative Life* (ACW 4).

[83]Julianus Pomerius *The Contemplative Life* 1.23 (ACW 4:49).

[84]Klingshirn, *Caesarius of Arles*, p. 81.

[85]The simplicity of Caesarius's sermons is reflected in this statement of Pomerius: "Such should be the simplicity and straightforwardness of the bishop's language: though this may mean less good Latin, it should be restrained and dignified so that it prevents no one, however ignorant, from understanding it but sinks with a certain charm into the heart of all who hear it" (*The Contemplative Life* 1.23 [ACW 4:49]).

[86]See especially the translations in Sister Mary Magdeleine Mueller, *Saint Caesarius of Arles: Sermons*, Volume 1 (1–80), Volume 2 (81–186), Volume 3 (187–238) in FC 31, 47, 66 (Washington, D.C.: The Catholic University of America Press, 1956, 1964, 1973).

trary to Roman practice, in which bishops alone had the right to preach (*verbum faciendi potestas*), Caesarius expanded the circle of those who had the right to preach to include priests, and if the priest was not able to do so, sermons from the Fathers were to be read by a deacon. Indeed, Caesarius intended his own sermons to be disseminated and read to the people throughout his diocese. That his sermons survive in such numbers is due to the fact that Caesarius assembled written copies of his sermons into collections which he gave to other bishops and priests and demanded that these collections be disseminated further afield. As the *Vita* expresses it, the sermons of Caesarius were carried throughout "the Frankish lands, Gaul, Italy, Spain, and other provinces."[87]

In sum, the life of Caesarius was a speech that echoed his words. He embodied as best anyone could the view of Pomerius that "not in the glitter of his words, but in the virtue of his deeds let [the bishop] place all his confidence in preaching."[88]

Caesarius's Exposition on the Revelation: Text

"With Caesarius of Arles we enter into the era of the epigones, that is, into the era of those writers whose work relies on their illustrious forebears rather than upon their own original effort. A great number of his sermons especially are a rereading of previous pieces. His commentary on the Apocalypse is no exception."[89] Indeed, the sermons and commentary of Caesarius reveal the literary form of his historical importance as a transitional figure between the patristic and early medieval periods.

Traditionally the nineteen homilies of Caesarius were attributed in most manuscripts to Augustine, and on the basis of such manuscripts the Maurists published the homilies within their edition of Augustine's works.[90] Therefore, the homilies are sometimes referred to as the pseudo-Augustinian homilies, since their ascription to Augustine himself is clearly incorrect. On the basis of one twelfth-century manuscript in Cambridge, Otto Bardenhewer attributed the homilies to Gennadius of Marseilles (end of fifth century).[91] This manuscript begins with the words, "Here begins the Tractatus of the Presbyter Gennadius of Marseilles On the Thousand Years and On the Apocalypse of the Blessed John." These words correspond to Gennadius's *De viris illustribus* 99 in which Gennadius writes of himself: "I, Gennadius, Presbyter of Marseilles have written . . . the tractates On the Thousand Years and On the Apocalypse of the Blessed John."[92]

---

[87]*Vita Caesarii* 1.55; see Klingshirn, *Caesarius of Arles*, p. 9.

[88]Pomerius *The Contemplative Life* 1.23 (ACW 4:49).

[89]Gryson, "Commentaires patristiques latins," p. 317 (my translation). For discussion of the text of Caesarius see especially Germain Morin, "Le commentaire homilétique de S. Césaire sur L'Apocalypse," *Revue Bénédictine* 45 (1933): 43-61; Steinhauser, *Apocalypse Commentary of Tyconius*, pp. 47-67; Gryson, "Commentaires patristiques latins," pp. 317-22. Still important for the western tradition of commentary on the Revelation is H. J. Vogels, *Untersuchungen zur Geschichte der lateinischen Apokalypse-übersetzung*. Düsseldorf: L. Schwann, 1920.

[90]In Migne, *Patrologie Latine*, 35:2417-52.

[91]Otto Bardenhewer, *Geschichte der altkirchlichen Literatur* (Freiburg im Breisgau: Herder & Co., 1924), 4:597-98.

[92]Cambridge, St. John's College H.6 (twelfth century): *Incipit tractatus Gennadii Presbiteri Massilie de mille annis et de Apocalypsi beati Johannis.* Gennadius of Marseilles, *De viris Illustribus* 99: *Ego Gennadius Massiliae presbyter scripsi . . . tractatus de mille*

However, the *incipit* of the manuscript of homilies was merely borrowed by a scribe from the words of Gennadius, the scribe apparently believing that in the homilies he had before him the (lost) treatises of Gennadius on the millennium and Apocalypse.[93] Although in the eighteenth century the French abbot J.-B. Morel (d. 1772) identified Caesarius of Arles as the true author of the "pseudo-Augustinian" homilies, his work remained unknown, and modern scholarly certitude of Caesarius as the author is the product of the researches of Germain Morin.[94]

The homilies of Caesarius, however, are not easily described. Morin begins his important article with this interesting claim: "One of the most strange productions of Christian literature in the high middle age is, without contradiction, the *Expositio in Apocalypsim* that is relegated by the Maurists to the end of the Appendix of volume three of their edition of Saint Augustine."[95] First of all, it is by no means evident that the comments of Caesarius are homilies. Nowhere within the work itself are the various sections called homilies, and the whole is given the title *Expositio de Apocalypsi sancti Iohannis* which suggests nothing other than an attempt at explanation. Furthermore, the various sections are introduced by the words "Here begins the continuation of the exposition of the Apocalypse" (*incipit sequentia de expositione Apocalypsi*) or simply "once more a continuation" (*item sequentia*). In addition, the style of the comments is rarely that of homily. While many of the sections are addressed to "dearest brothers" (*fratres carissimi*), others possess no such *exordium* (4, 5, 6, 8, 17) or possess no homiletic, doxological ending (2, 3, 10, 11, 12, 14, 15, 16).[96] In addition to the absence of homiletic content and style is what Morin calls the "unheard of disorder" of the text.[97] Comment on the text of the Revelation does not really begin until Revelation 1:13, the first verses passed by in complete silence. However, writes Morin, "it is above all the lack of sequence in the citations of the Apocalypse that surprises and baffles the reader."[98] To give but one example, in the second homily the author moves from Revelation 2:16 to 1:16, from there to 2:28 and 3:18. A little later he moves from Revelation 4:6 back to 1:18 and to various verses from chapter two of the Revelation. Given such disorder in the arrangement along with the recapitulations, Morin suggests that what we presently have are notes taken by Caesarius

---

annis de Apocalypsi beati Iohannis (PL 58:1120; NPNF² 3:402). The *On Illustrious Men* of Gennadius was a continuation of the work by the same name by Jerome. Its choice of "famous" men and comments about them reveals the generally semi-Pelagianism of Gennadius. The authenticity of Gennadius's self-description of his writings may perhaps be doubted, since it does appear in all manuscripts. Gennadius's self-description is §99 in the NPNF² listing and §100 in the PL listing.

[93]See Morin, "Commentaire homilétique,"pp. 49-50; Gryson, "Commentaires patristiques latins," p. 318.

[94]Morin, "Commentaire homilétique," pp. 43-61. For discussion of the work of Morel, see Morin, pp. 50-51.

[95]Morin, "Commentaire homilétique," p. 43 (my translation).

[96]Morin, "Commentaire homilétique," p. 44. Steinhauser, *Apocalypse Commentary of Tyconius*, p. 51: "Often traces of a genuine homiletic style may be found especially either at the beginning or the end of some sections. However, for the most part the work is simply an Apocalypse commentary, which has been artificially divided into homilies."

[97]Morin, "Commentaire homilétique," p. 45: *désordre inouï*.

[98]Ibid., pp. 44-46, quote p. 45 (my translation).

from various sources in preparation for a series of homilies on the Revelation.[99] If this is correct, the address to "dearest brothers" (*fraters carissimi*) might well suggest that these homilies were intended either for the fellow monks of Caesarius at his monastery in Arles or for some occasion when he would address his fellow clergy. However, Ferreiro reminds us of the importance Caesarius attached to the reading of his sermons also by the laity: "Caesarius did not believe that *lectio* should be restricted to the clergy. The laity were expected to read the divine lessons for themselves, and if they were illiterate these lessons should be read to them."[100]

Although Caesarius quotes no one explicitly, the principal sources behind the homilies are the (lost) commentary of Tyconius and the original edition of Victorinus which sometimes he uses verbatim.[101] According to Steinhauser, the fact that Caesarius often comments on verses twice can only be explained by assuming that he made use of "two different manuscripts of the same source in making the compilation." "Without a doubt Caesarius had two copies of Tyconius's commentary."[102] This is, however, not wholly evident, for it is possible that Caesarius himself is the origin of these repetitions.

The date of the homilies is also difficult to determine. Caesarius makes no certain and specific allusions to historical events. However, in Homily 10 Caesarius comments on Revelation 13 and writes that "just as formerly it was the pagans who devastated the church, so now it is the heretics."[103] And he identifies these heretics as the Arians, which must refer to the Visigoths or to the Ostrogoths, both of whom at one time exercised hegemony over Arles. This would suggest that the homilies were compiled before 537 when the Frankish Merovingian king, Childebert I, became effective ruler of Arles. The Franks were not Arian but supporters of the Nicene affirmation of the deity of Christ. Steinhauser, however, believes that a more precise dating is possible. He notes that in Homily 13 Caesarius alludes to the destruction of Jerusalem under Vespasian and Titus[104] which Steinhauser claims is "a veiled allusion to the siege of Arles" in the years 508–510 by a combined army of Franks and Burgundians. The city was saved by the intervention of the Arian Ostrogoths who assumed governance of the city from the Visigoths but whose rule was significantly more harsh than had been that of the Visigoths. In his *Sermon* 127, preached in 510, Caesarius makes a similar allusion to the siege and fall of Jerusalem. Steinhauser concludes: "The pseudo-Augustinian homilies should be dated after 510,

---

[99]Ibid., pp. 51-53.

[100]Alberto Ferreiro, "'*Frequenter Legere*' The Propagation of Literacy, Education, and Divine Wisdom in Caesarius of Arles," *JEH* 43 (1992): 7. Thus, the address *fraters carissimi* may have broader application.

[101]See Morin, "Commentaire homilétique," pp. 46-48; Steinhauser, *Apocalypse Commentary of Tyconius*, pp. 52-68; Gryson, "Commentaires patristiques latins," pp. 319-20. Gryson notes that Caesarius possessed "a superior manuscript [of Victorinus] than the sole late witness which we possess, but he did not know the edition of Jerome" (Gryson, p. 319, my translation).

[102]Steinhauser, *Apocalypse Commentary of Tyconius*, pp. 52-53. "The actual basis of the entire pseudo-Augustinian homilies is Tyconian recension A, which has been edited and partially revised by Caesarius" (p. 53).

[103]*Homily* 10 (PL 35:2435).

[104]*Homily* 13 (PL 35:2441).

namely after the unsuccessful siege of Arles. Ostrogoth rule after this date coincides very well with the references to the Arians who were then in power, especially since the Ostrogoths were stricter than the Visigoths."[105]

Although the Maurist edition in *Patrologie Latine* (PL 35:2417-52) may be more accessible, the critical edition of Caesarius's *Expositio* was published by Germain Morin in *Sancti Caesarii Episcopi Arelatensis Opera Omnia nunc Primum in Unum Collecta*, volume 2: *Opera Varia* (Maretioli: 1942), pp. 209-77. The translation of Caesarius in this volume is based on this critical edition of Morin. However, for reference in the notes I have cited the Maurist edition in *Patrologie Latine*. For his critical edition Morin used primarily four manuscripts. The most important of these is Chartres, Bibliothèque municipale, I.C.3 (end of eighth century) which is designated by C. This is the only manuscript that provides the authentic beginning of the *Expositio*. The others are London, British Museum, Egerton 874 (ninth century), designated as A; Oxford, Bodleian Library, Hatton 30 (tenth century), designated as H and perhaps from the monastery at Glastonbury where St. Dunstan had it copied; München, Staatsbibliotek, MS lat. 14469 (ninth century), designated as R.[106]

Caesarius's Exposition on the Revelation: Theology and Method
The *Expositio de Apocalypsi* of Caesarius is divided into nineteen sections.[107] While there is a rough correspondence between these divisions and the chapters of the Revelation, evidently no real correspondence exists and the divisions appear to have no structural or thematic significance. As we have noted, the homilies on the Revelation are not a sequential commentary but at times demonstrate considerable disorder, and the sections possess also considerable repetition and recapitulation. This gives support for the view of Morin that the homilies are in fact something like preliminary notes in preparation for the writing of homilies that were perhaps never written and never preached. Concerning this matter one other feature of the homilies should be noted. Most of the homilies begin with some remark that suggests that the reading of the Revelation has just occurred. Phrases such as "as the Revelation was being read" (Homilies 2, 5, 7, 14), "we have just heard" (Homilies 3, 10, 17, 19), "in the reading just recited" (Homilies 9, 11, 12, 15, 18) are used. Moreover, in the authentic introduction preserved in Manuscript C the author

---

[105]Steinhauser, *Apocalypse Commentary of Tyconius*, pp. 49-51, quote p. 50. One cannot, however, be certain: "We may set the outer limit for the composition of the pseudo-Augustinian homilies at the year 537. However, an earlier date is more probable. Thus I propose that the collection was composed between the years 510 and 537, most likely, however, in the decade after the siege of Arles when those events would still have been fresh in mind and Ostrogoth rule would have been an evident and unpleasant reality" (p. 51). For the reference to the siege of Jerusalem in *Sermon* 127.2, see FC 47:222. See also G. Langgärtner, "Der Apokalypse-Kommentar des Caesarius von Arles," *Theologie und Glaube* 57 (1967): 210-25. For the siege of Arles and its aftermath see also William E. Klingshirn, *Caesarius of Arles: The Making of a Christian Community in Late Antique Gaul* (Cambridge: Cambridge University Press, 1994), pp. 106-17.

[106]For a full listing of manuscripts, see Morin, "Commentaire homilétique," pp. 54-56.

[107]Most manuscripts join together homilies 16 and 17, resulting in eighteen homilies. Manuscript C gives the correct divisions.

seems directly to be addressing an audience: "whatever you shall hear in the recitation of the reading." It is possible that such remarks might be included in the making of notes for homilies in preparation. However, given Caesarius's habit and intention for his sermons, it is not necessarily the case that he himself would preach or read these homilies. Central to the reform efforts of Caesarius was his insistence that his sermons serve as models of teaching. It may well be, then, that the one who would read such sermons were not only clergy but also literate laity. And the audience to whom these sermons were read crossed all boundaries. In his article on *lectio* in Caesarius, Ferreiro writes: "The individuals to whom the homilies were addressed came from various levels of society, that is, not all of them were exclusively from the upper echelons. When Caesarius preached to the clergy he addressed both literate and near-illiterate bishops, abbots, parish priests, and monks. The laity to whom he preached was just as diverse in social standing: literate and illiterate estate owners, merchants, hired labourers, entire families."[108] Whether, then, the *Expositio* of Caesarius was regarded as more or less complete or merely in a preliminary stage of preparation, Caesarius may have had multiple occasions and multiple audiences in mind. It is wholly probable that he intended his words to be broadly disseminated and used for the instruction and exhortation of all classes of the people of God. At the end of the day, however, we remain unsure of the status and purpose of the text entitled *Expositio de Apocalypsi* by Caesarius of Arles.

The structure and organization of the *Expositio*, therefore, are unhelpful in revealing to us the theological convictions that are articulated. It is rather the Tyconian basis of the *Expositio* that determines the theological character of Caesarius's comments. The perspective and driving concept of Caesarius is evident at the very beginning in the authentic *exordium* solely preserved in Manuscript C. Here Caesarius compares "some of the ancient fathers" with "those who have more diligently commented" on the Revelation.[109] He names no representative of either group. However, it is clear that in these two groups Caesarius has in mind the two most important sources behind his commentary: Victorinus of Petovium and Tyconius. The ancient fathers believed that the Revelation in its totality or in its greatest part reveals "the day of judgment or the coming of the antichrist." This evidently refers to the eschatological interpretation that Victorinus represents. On the other hand, the more diligent commentators understand that the content of the Revelation has to do with what "had begun immediately after the passion of our Lord and Savior and therefore was to be fulfilled to the day of judgment." In other words, the visions of the Revelation reveal the spiritual truth of the life of the church that is lived and experienced between the time of Jesus and the last day. It was precisely Tyconius who was

---

[108]Ferreiro, "'Frequenter legere'," p. 7.
[109]Unfortunately the authentic beginning of the *Expositio*, given alone by MS C, is not printed in the Maurist edition. Their edition was based on other MSS, such as A and R (see PL 35:2417). The *exordium* given in MS C may be found in Morin, *Sancti Caesarii Opera Omnia*, 2:210.

most responsible for the revolution of interpretation from the one to the other of these positions. The *Expositio* of Caesarius is a thoroughly ecclesiological interpretation of the Revelation. Therefore, at the start Caesarius makes explicit what the hearers of the reading of the Revelation are to understand: "Whether it is of the Son of man or of stars or of angels or of lampstands, or of the four living creatures or of the eagle flying in midheaven, understand that these and everything else are reality in Christ and in the church." Similarly, the "one catholic church" is to be recognized in the seven churches in Asia, since the one Spirit of a sevenfold grace speaks to each.

Indeed, at every point Caesarius makes good on this fundamental hermeneutical perspective. A few examples will suffice. While Victorinus interprets the 144,000 of Revelation 7 to show "the number of those from the Jews who will believe" at the coming of Elijah at the end of time and those without number to be the multitude of the believing Gentiles, Caesarius interprets both groups to be "the selfsame people," the number 144,000 signifying "the fullness of the church." For this interpretation Caesarius makes use of one of his favorite strategies: the numbers seven, ten, twelve and their multiples symbolize completeness. Therefore, in the figure of the twelve tribes "the whole church both from the Jews and from the Gentiles" is shown.[110] Another interpretative strategy of Caesarius is to identify "heaven" with the church. This allows him to interpret the vision in Revelation of the woman, dragon and war in heaven in a thoroughly ecclesiological manner. For Victorinus all of these things will occur at the coming of the antichrist and during the final persecutions that his appearance will inspire. Thus the water from the dragon's mouth is persecution, and the earth's swallowing up the water is the church's deliverance from these persecutions. In the interpretation of Caesarius, on the other hand, all of this is a figure of the daily, continuous spiritual warfare that occurs between the faithful of the church and the devil and his body: "The great red dragon is the devil, who seeks to devour anyone who is born [that is, baptized] of the church."[111] The tail of the dragon symbolizes the heretics who convince some to join in their error and thus fall from heaven, that is, from the church to the earth, that is, to persons who are only wise in earthly things. In keeping with this interpretation, Michael and his angels who fight in heaven with the dragon are regarded as Christ and his saints. That they have cast the devil out of heaven is interpreted to mean that "those who believe have fully expelled the devil and no longer receive his compatriots."[112] The devil and his body of demons and heretics are cast out of the faithful hearts of the believers and are simply cast out of the church so that her faith and creed will remain heavenly.

Finally, we might call attention to one feature of Caesarius's comments that demonstrate that he was in possession of quite early and ancient ideas. The reading of Revela-

---

[110]*Homily* 6 (PL 35:2428).
[111]*Homily* 9 (PL 35:2434).
[112]*Homily* 9 (PL 35:2434).

tion 13:18 that Caesarius possessed had the number of the beast as 616. Caesarius gives no indication that he was aware of the more common 666. Already in the second century Irenaeus had noted that some manuscripts read 616, although he attributed that reading to the error of copyists.[113] Did Caesarius have at his disposal a manuscript tradition of which Irenaeus was already aware?[114] According to Caesarius this number is the number not of the antichrist himself, but the number of Christ, the Son of man. Therefore, the number is reckoned as that of Christ, whose name "the beast takes for himself among the heretics."[115] Hence, even this passage is given an ecclesiological referent: "[The number] is understood to be a sign of Christ and shows a likeness of him that the church *in reality* holds in reverence."[116]

To be sure, the interpretation of the Revelation as a vision of the spiritual warfare of the church against the powers of the devil comes to Caesarius through the commentary of Tyconius, and was probably reinforced by Caesarius's loyalty to Augustine. However, if we remember that Caesarius was primarily a preaching bishop and that he was fully engaged in the Christianizing of the populace of Gaul, we can appreciate the fact that the ability to read and interpret the Revelation in that manner made the Revelation relevant to his task, a powerful tool in his preaching and an incentive to those under his pastoral care.

The Venerable Bede

Life and Work of the Venerable Bede

Although often regarded as the greatest of all Anglo-Saxon scholars, the life of Bede was wholly uneventful, and the information we possess of his life is strangely meager in comparison to the fame he acquired as a master writer of church history and expositor of the Bible. The principal source of the few known facts of his life is the last chapter of what became his most famous book, *An Ecclesiastical History of the English People*. Here Bede gives a summary of significant moments in his life at the monastery at Jarrow and gives a listing of his many writings and translations:

> I was born on the lands of this monastery, and on reaching seven years of age, I was entrusted by my family first to the most reverend Abbot Benedict and later to Abbot Ceolfrid for my education. I have spent all the remainder of my life in this monastery and devoted myself entirely to the study of the Scriptures. And while I have observed the regular disciple and sung the choir offices daily in church, my chief delight has always been in study, teaching, and writing.

---

[113]Irenaeus *Against Heresies* 5.30.1 (ANF 1:558-59).

[114]The see of Arles was in considerable competition with that of Vienne, and Caesarius was in jurisdictional dispute with Bishop Avitus of Vienne. In the time of Irenaeus the Christian community of Vienne was closely associated with Lyons.

[115]*Homily* 11 (PL 35:2437).

[116]*Homily* 11 (PL 35:2437). Italics added: *in veritate*. The heretics only falsely hold the name of Christian; those of the true church "in truth" hold the name of Christ.

I was ordained deacon in my nineteenth year, and priest in my thirtieth, receiving both these orders at the hands of the most reverend Bishop John at the direction of Abbot Ceolfrid. From the time of my receiving the priesthood until my fifty-ninth year, I have worked, both for my own benefit and that of my brethren, to compile short extracts from the works of the venerable Fathers on Holy Scripture and to comment on their meaning and interpretation.[117]

Hereupon Bede lists his writings, his commentaries on Biblical books being listed first, perhaps because he regarded these as the most important. Among his books on the Scriptures he names also *On the Apocalypse of Saint John*: Three Books.

It is doubtful whether Bede ever left the environs of his monastery. In that sense his world was quite small. Yet, in another sense he lived and worked in an arena that was quite dynamic and even transcontinental. Although the great kingdom of Northumbria had begun its decline when Bede was born in 673, the religious environment in which Bede lived and worked was undergoing rapid change. Christianity had come to Northumbria in 627 with the conversion of Edwin. Soon afterward Celtic practice and discipline was introduced into the kingdom by Oswald (d. 642), who invited St. Aidan from Iona to teach the people. Under the leadership of Aidan the great Celtic monastery at Lindesfarne became a center of Celtic monastic piety and manuscript production. However, the future lay not with Lindesfarne and Celtic Christianity but with Canterbury and Rome. Northumbrian monks and scholars, such as Wilfred and Benedict Biscop, had traveled to Rome and become convinced of that church's role in the establishing of a universal Christian kingdom. Eventually their advocacy of Rome's primacy was vindicated at the Council of Whitby (664) when King Oswy determined that the religious loyalties of the kingdom would be with Rome and no longer with the Celtic church. Thus, despite his geographical isolation Bede would become both beneficiary and benefactor of a strong relation between English Christianity and the Church of Rome.

It is convenient to discuss the life of Bede in connection with three persons of great importance to him. The first of these is Benedict Biscop (628–690). Born into a noble Northumbrian family, Benedict would make no less than five journeys to Rome. After spending two years at Lérins where he took monastic vows, he made his third trip to Rome where he was commissioned by Pope Vitalian (657–672) to return to England with Theodore of Tarsus who would be consecrated Archbishop of Canterbury. In 674 King Ecgfrith of Northumbria, son of Oswy, gave Benedict land on which to build a monastery. This was the monastery of Monkwearmouth on whose lands Bede had been born. As Bede reports, when he was seven he was committed to Benedict and so he entered into a

---

[117]Perhaps the most accessible translation of Bede's history is *Bede: Ecclesiastical History of the English People with Bede's Letter to Egbert and Cuthbert's Letter On the Death of Bede*, The History translated by Leo Sherley-Price, revised by R. E. Latham; translation of the minor works, new Introduction and Notes by D. H. Farmer (New York: Penguin Books, 1955; revised editions, 1968, 1990). Quotation is from *History* 5.24 (*Bede*, 329).

monastic community that would be enriched and embellished by the great energies and continental contacts of its abbot. Under Benedict the monastery at Wearmouth would be built in Romanesque style with stonemasons and glaziers brought in from France. Bede describes Benedict as "untiring in his efforts" to provide for his monastery: "The ornaments and images he could not find in France he sought out in Rome." In 679 Benedict made his fourth trip to Rome where he met Pope Agatho (678–681). Bede describes the benefit to Wearmouth of the gifts and privileges that Benedict brought with him on his return. He returned with "a great mass of books of every sort"; second he returned with an "abundant supply of relics of the blessed apostles and Christian martyrs." Third, Benedict "introduced in his monastery the order of chanting and singing the psalms and conducting the liturgy according to the practice in force at Rome."[118] Benedict also brought back a letter from Pope Agatho giving Wearmouth autonomy and independence from all external interference. Finally, writes Bede, Benedict returned from Rome with "many holy pictures of the saints to adorn the church at St. Peter (Wearmouth). These pictures included one of the Mother of God, one each of the holy apostles, pictures of various Gospel stories and "scenes from St. John's vision of the apocalypse." Thus, says Bede, all who entered the church, even the illiterate, were able to contemplate the face of Christ and his saints, and "as they saw the decisive moment of the Last Judgment before their very eyes be brought to examine their conscience with all due severity."[119] We do not know with certainty, but we may well imagine that the scenes of the Apocalypse brought back by Benedict Biscop and placed in the church of St. Peter and Wearmouth were in the mind of Bede as he wrote his comments on the vision of St. John.

Gratified with the success of Wearmouth, in 682 King Ecgfrith gave further lands to Benedict for a second monastery. The result was the monastery at Jarrow. Benedict placed Ceolfirth as abbot of the new monastery, and it was to Jarrow that Ceolfrith took with him twenty monks including the young Bede. Bede's relation with Ceolfrith would be long and deep, and Bede would honor Ceolfrith as though his father: "Ceofrith was a man of acute mind, conscientious in everything he did, energetic, of mature judgement, fervent and zealous for his faith." Under Ceolfrith's tutelage Bede would be ordained deacon in 692 and priest in 703. Most importantly Ceolfrith shared with Biscop the intent to enrich the cultural and intellectual life of his monastery. Of this Bede reports the following: "[Ceolfrith] enlarged the stock of church plate, altar vessels and every kind of vestment. He doubled the number of books in the libraries of both monasteries with an ardour

---

[118]Bede informs us that to assist in this training Pope Agatho sent along with Benedict "the chief cantor of St. Peter's and abbot of the monastery of St. Martin" whose name was John. He became choirmaster at Wearmouth and "taught the monks at first hand how things were done in the churches in Rome."

[119]For this information about Benedict Biscop and his significance for developing the literary, architectural and cultural excellence of his monastery, see Bede *Lives of the Abbots of Wearmouth and Jarrow* 6. An accessible English translation of this interesting work can be found in *The Age of Bede* (New York: Penguin Books, 1965; revised 1983, reprinted 2004). Quotations above from pp. 192-93.

equal to that which Benedict had shown in founding them. He added three copies of the new translation of the Bible to the one copy of the old translation which he had brought back from Rome. One of these he took with him as a present when he went back to Rome in his old age, and the other two he bequeathed to his monasteries."[120]

Bede's mention of "three copies of the new translation of the Bible" deserves some comment. On his fifth and final trip to Rome, 678–679, Benedict Biscop took Ceolfrith with him. They returned to England with many books, but the most important seems to have been the *Codex grandior* ("larger book"), a sixth century pandect of the Bible written by or for Cassiodorus at his monastery, Vivarium, in Italy. This codex is almost certainly the "one copy of the old translation" that Bede mentions in his description of Ceolfrith.[121] Ceolfrith ordered the production of three large pandects, two of these were to remain in the libraries of the monasteries of Wearmouth and Jarrow. These have unfortunately disappeared, perhaps destroyed by Viking raids of the eighth and ninth centuries. The third pandect was intended as a gift to the papacy. In 716 Ceolfrith announced that he would leave the twin monasteries and accompany this huge Bible to Rome where he wanted to present it to Pope Gregory II. On the way, however, Ceolfrith died in Burgundy. It is possible that the monks who were with him did present the codex to the Pope, although no official report of such a gift exists. What is known is that c. 900 the codex was presented to the monastery of San Salvatore at Monte Amiata in the central Apennines. When San Salvatore was dissolved in 1786 the codex, known as Codex Amiatinus, was deposited in the Biblioteca Laurenziana at Florence, where it still exists (MS Amiatino 1).[122] Amiatinus is the oldest surviving Latin Bible in a single volume anywhere in the world. Along with the two lost pandects it is a translation of Jerome's Vulgate (hence, Bede's words, "the new translation of the Bible"). It is quite possible that Bede participated in the production of this remarkable Anglo-Saxon text of Scripture.[123]

The successor of Ceolfrith was Hwaetbehrt. Little is known of him, but he must have been a close associate and friend of Bede. Of him Bede writes: "He had been taught in

---

[120]For this information concerning Ceolfrith see Bede *Lives of the Abbots of Wearmouth and Jarrow* 15, in: *The Age of Bede*, pp. 202-3.

[121]A pandect is a single codex containing the whole of the Old and New Testaments. The *Codex grandior* was of the Old Latin version, hence in Bede's words "the old translation."

[122]For a long time the Anglo-Saxon origin of Amiatinus was unknown. The mention of Ceolfrith in the dedicatory introduction had been erased and over it the name of Petrus Langobardorum (Peter of the Lombards) was written. Apparently this Peter was an abbot of Italy who gave the huge codex as a gift to the monastery of San Salvatore. Later investigation revealed the secondary nature of this dedication, revealing as well the name of Ceolfrith and the true provenance of this famous codex.

[123]For the story of Codex Amiatinus, see Paul Meyvaert, "Bede, Cassiodorus, and the Codex Amiatinus," *Speculum* 71 (1996): 827-83. In the first quire of Amiatinus there is the famous "Ezra miniature," an illumination of the prophet dressed as a high priest sitting in front of a cabinet holding nine books. This depiction is thought to be a copy of an untitled portrait that was in the *Codex grandior*, perhaps depicting Cassiodorus himself. An illuminator of Amiatinus, however, made the image to be that of Ezra. Over the miniature is the couplet *codicis sacris hostili clade perustis, Esdra Deo feruens hoc reparavit opus* ("When the sacred books were burned by hostile attack, Ezra, out of zeal for God, repaired this work"). According to Kendall, "Bede was almost certainly the author of these verses" (*On Genesis, Bede*, translated with an introduction and notes by Calvin B. Kendall [Liverpool: Liverpool University Press, 2008], p. 49).

that same monastery from his earliest childhood to observe the discipline of the rule and had also applied himself there to solid study of the arts of writing, chanting, reading and teaching." Bede tells us that Hwaetbehrt had also traveled to Rome during the pontificate of Pope Sergius (687–701) and had remained there a long while "learning, copying down and bringing back with him all that he thought necessary for his studies."[124] Hwaetbehrt would outlive Bede who died in 735.

The lives and activities of the three abbots under whom Bede lived, wrote and dedicated his life reveal the remarkable flowering of Anglo-Saxon scholarship and erudition of which Bede himself was the most stellar representative. In addition to his many commentaries on the books of Scripture, Bede is best known for his *Ecclesiastical History of the English People*, dedicated to King Ceolwulf of Northumbria and completed in 731. It remains the most important source of information for the early history of Christianity in England.

Bede's Exposition on the Revelation: Text

The commentary of the Venerable Bede on the Revelation is prefaced by a letter addressed to "brother, Eusebius."[125] This Eusebius was Hwaetbehrt who in 716 would become abbot of Wearmouth and Jarrow and was nicknamed Eusebius because of his piety. That Bede addresses him as brother indicates that Hwaetbehrt was not yet abbot and so sets the *terminus ad quem* for the date of the Revelation commentary at 716. That is perhaps all we can say with certainty about the date. In his own listing of his writings in the *Ecclesiastical History* no indication of date or sequence is given. Nonetheless, Bonner claims that the Revelation commentary is "probably the earliest of his commentaries on Scripture, and seems to have been written between 703 and 709."[126] Gryson similarly claims that the Revelation commentary is "one of the first, if not the very first of the exegetical works of Bede." He dates the commentary "probably before 710."[127] This would explain, says Gryson, the developed hermeneutical reflections that constitute the bulk of the prefatory letter to Eusebius. In this letter Bede describes the seven rules of Tyconius and their meanings and applications. At the conclusion Bede remarks that "these rules are applicable not only in the Apocalypse, that is, in the revelation of Saint John the apostle, but also in all of the canonical Scripture and especially in the prophetic books."[128] It may well be, therefore, that the methodological discussion of Bede in the letter to Eusebius that prefaces his commentary on the Revelation suggests that this commentary was one of the first commentaries that he penned. If so, then his comments on the Revelation,

---

[124]See Bede *Lives of the Abbots of Wearmouth and Jarrow* 18, in: *The Age of Bede*, p. 206.

[125]For discussion of the text of Bede, see Gryson, "Commentaires patristiques," pp. 484-89; Steinhauser, *Apocalypse Commentary of Tyconius*, pp. 116-31.

[126]Gerald Bonner, *Saint Bede in the Tradition of Western Apocalyptic Commentary*. Jarrow Lecture 1966 (Newcastle upon Tyne: J. & P. Bealls, 1966), p. 8.

[127]Gryson, "Commentaires patristiques," p. 484 (my translation). In the introduction to his critical text Gryson is even more definite: "The commentary on the Apocalypse is the first of the Scriptural works of Bede" (CCL 121A:153; my translation).

[128]Bede *Expositio*, preface (CCL 121A:231).

guided by the rules of Tyconius, serve as a kind of exercise for the interpretation of the whole of Scripture.

The acquisition of many books by Benedict Biscop and Ceolfrith gave the library of Wearmouth and Jarrow an unusual richness and extent of manuscript materials for its time. From this fact alone we might surmise that Bede had at his disposal a broad array of sources in his commentary writing.[129] The most important source is without question Tyconius, the fourth century Donatist interpreter of the Revelation. Bede speaks of Tyconius with uncommon praise and respect. In the introductory letter he calls Tyconius "a man of very great learning" (*viri inter suos eruditissimi*) among the Donatists. Moreover, Tyconius had understood the Revelation with penetrating insight (*vivaciter intellexit*) and had expounded it "truthfully and in a sufficiently catholic sense" (*veridice satisque catholice disseruit*). Of course, certain aspects of Tyconius's commentary were unacceptable, namely those passages in which he claimed that the Revelation had foretold the sufferings of the Donatists. However, as Bede explicitly states, "in the present work we have followed the interpretation of this author," for he is a man of great learning who flourished "as a rose among thorns."[130] Indeed, a considerable portion of the letter to Eusebius consists of a summary of the seven rules of Tyconius that will guide the commentary of Bede. In his commentary itself Bede will cite Tyconius by name at least ten times, as Gryson notes, "more often than Augustine, Gregory and Jerome combined."[131] By way of comparison we may also note that Bede cites Primasius by name on only one occasion, and this only for a matter of interpretative detail.[132] The importance of Bede for research into Tyconius and his commentary has long been recognized. In the judgment of Gryson Bede is probably "the most faithful witness" to the text of Tyconius and is decisive when one wishes to determine the *ipsissima verba* of Tyconius.[133]

In terms of sheer frequency and quantity of use, however, the commentary of Primasius of Hadrumetum (sixth century) takes pride of place. Bede often incorporates the views of Primasius, yet without naming him and often with minor changes of language. Many of the earliest manuscripts of Primasius come from monasteries founded by English or Irish monks, so it is not surprising that Bede had a copy of Primasius and used him extensively.[134] Yet, despite the significance of Primasius as a source of his commentary, Bede makes no mention of him in the introductory letter to Eusebius and mentions him but one time in the commentary. Bonner's evaluation seems correct: "Bede would seem to have valued

---

[129]For the sources used in Bede's commentary see especially Gryson (CCL 121A:153-78); also Gryson, "Commentaires patristiques," pp. 484-86; Bonner, *Saint Bede*, pp. 3-11.

[130]For these statements concerning Tyconius, see Gryson (CCL 121A:223, 231-33).

[131]Gryson (CCL 121A:154).

[132]Bede introduces Primasius's interpretations of the number of the beast in Rev 13:18 (CCL 121A:415).

[133]Gryson (CCL 121A:154). In Bonner's view "Bede's qualitative debt to Tyconius is greater than his quantitative debt to Primasius" (*Saint Bede*, p. 11). For a listing of passages quoted directly from Tyconius or strongly influenced by him, see Steinhauser, *Apocalypse Commentary on Tyconius*, pp. 267-316.

[134]Noted by Bonner, *Saint Bede*, pp. 7-8. For the text of Primasius used by Bede, see also Gryson (CCL 121A:160-61).

Primasius rather as a quarry for material than as a guide to understanding."[135] The third commentary that Bede used in the writing of his own is that of Victorinus, although in the later recension of Jerome indicated by the letter Φ.[136]

In addition to the three commentaries of Tyconius, Primasius and Victorinus-Jerome, Bede cites or makes use of a significant number of other writers. Most important, as one might surmise, are Augustine, Gregory the Great and Jerome. Bede cites Augustine at the end of the introductory letter to justify the division of his commentary into three books, and he refers to Augustine by name four times in the commentary itself. It seems certain that Bede was familiar with the seven rules of Tyconius from Augustine's *On Christian Doctrine* and not directly from the *Regulae* of Tyconius himself. Moreover, Bede seems to have had possession of Augustine's *City of God* and to have used it independently from the use made of it by Primasius. No figure was more important to the early history of the English church than Pope Gregory the Great. Bede names him three times in the introductory letter to his commentary and in the commentary itself he makes use of Gregory's *Moralia in Job* and most likely also his commentary on Ezekiel. Bede seems to have also possessed Jerome's commentary on Daniel and perhaps the commentary on Isaiah. Bede apparently makes use of Jerome's *On Illustrious Men* in citing the letter of Ignatius of Antioch to the Romans and of Jerome's *Life of Paul* when citing words from Letter 56 of Cyprian.

Among other sources cited by Bede we may mention the *Etymologies* of Isidore of Sevilla, a verse by Fortunatus, a verse by Arator and the Latin translation by Rufinus of the *Ecclesiastical History* of Eusebius. In the long and complex commentary concerning the twelve jewels that adorn the New Jerusalem, Bede used a variety of sources including a Latin translation of Epiphanius's treatise on gems and Irish/Celtic lapidary traditions. Finally, we should mention the high probability that in his commentary Bede incorporated interpretations received from Irish/Celtic masters and teachers.[137]

Bede has divided his commentary into three books (*in tres libellos*), as he writes in his introductory letter, "to give relief to the mind."[138] The First Book (*liber primus*) encompasses the commentary on Revelation 1:1–8:1; the Second Book (*liber secundus*) comprises the commentary on Revelation 8:2–14:20; the Third Book (*liber tertius*) contains the commentary on Revelation 15:1–22:21. As he describes it in the first portion of the letter to Eusebius, Bede further divides his commentary into seven sections (*septem periochis*). This division allows Bede to interpret the Revelation according to a pattern based

---

[135]Bonner, *Saint Bede*, p. 13. Gryson believes that Bede did not give adequate credit to Primasius by reducing him to the status of mere go-between (CCL 121A:161-62).

[136]There is no evidence that Bede was aware of the homilies of Caesarius of Arles.

[137]For the commentary on the twelve jewels, see Gryson (CCL 121A:173-77). For Irish antecedents to Bede's Apocalypse commentary, see Joseph F. Kelly, "Bede and the Irish Exegetical Tradition on the Apocalypse," *Revue bénédictine* 92 (1982): 393-406.

[138]CCL 121A:233. Here Bede quotes a passage from Augustine's *Against the Adversaries of the Law and the Prophets* 1.53, where Augustine says that the completion of a book renews the mind of a reader just as a hotel restores the strength of a traveler.

on the six-day creation of the world. The seven sections are as follows: in the First Book are sections one (Rev 1:1–3:22) and two (Rev 4:1–8:1); in the Second Book are sections three (Rev 8:2–11:18) and four (Rev 11:19–14:20); in the Third Book are sections five (Rev 15:1–17:18), six (Rev 18:1–20:15) and seven (Rev 21:11–22:21). In commenting Bede cites the Biblical text, sometimes in its fullness, sometimes with a few words of the text followed by *et cetera*. He then comments on the quoted passages in a manner simple and direct and without learned discussion. For as we learn from the conclusion of the introductory letter, Bede is not writing for the learned scholar but for the poor and uneducated people of the Angles.

Some sixty-five manuscripts dating from the eighth to the fifteenth century exist. Some twenty of these are Carolingian.[139] The translation of this volume is based on the critical edition of Roger Gryson.[140] In the translation we have noted the division of the commentary into three books. Although Bede apparently divided his commentary into some thirty-eight chapters (*capitula*), there remains some uncertainty about the *capitula lectionum* of Bede.[141] In his critical edition Gryson notes this division into *capitula* by bold Roman numerals. While this procedure might be helpful and of interest to some, it seemed best for the purposes and readership of this volume not to confuse the division of the text by using a system no longer known or used. Therefore, the present translation is divided into chapters and verses corresponding to the standard divisions in contemporary Bibles.

Bede's Exposition on the Revelation: Theology and Method

Bede himself gives us the primary clues to his interpretation of the Apocalypse of Saint John. In the introductory letter to Eusebius Bede clearly lays out the principles by which he interprets the Scriptures, the division of the text of the Apocalypse that gives structure to its meaning and the general thesis of the Apocalypse.

As we have noted, the guiding authority behind Bede's interpretation of the Apocalypse is Tyconius. The Donatist church, of which Tyconius was a member, was the conscious heir of the strict eschatological understanding of the Apocalypse. This interpretation regarded virtually all scenes of the Apocalypse as prophecies of the final, end-time struggle of the church. The prophecy of John was primarily of a future time when the antichrist would come, the final persecution would be endured and the first resurrection

---

[139]See Gryson, "Commentaires patristiques," p. 486. Gryson notes that most manuscripts of Bede exist on the European continent, not in England. The reason for this is the Viking raids which destroyed some of the most ancient exemplars and made the production of new copies impossible. This explains why Bede was much used by Carolingian scholars such as Alcuin and Haimo of Halberstadt.

[140]Roger Gryson, *Bedae Presbyteri Expositio Apocalypseos* (CCL 121A; Turnhout: Brepols Publishers, 2001). The text given in Migne (PL 93) is not satisfactory and should not be consulted if the Gryson text is available.

[141]See the discussion in Steinhauser, *Apocalypse Commentary of Tyconius*, pp. 109-15; Gryson, "Commentaires patristiques," pp. 487-89. In the introductory letter to Eusebius Bede mentions this division for the sake of those who wish more easily to locate discussion (*ut facilior quaerentibus inventio redderetur*).

to the earthly bliss of the millennial kingdom would commence. Upon its completion, the second resurrection of all flesh would occur, followed by judgment either to eternal condemnation or to eternal joy in heaven. The seven rules of Tyconius undercut the assumptions of this paradigm. The second rule, "concerning the bipartite body of the Lord," for example, argued against the separatist idea of Donatism that already in this world a separation of the good from the evil occurs. Tyconius argued that in this age the church was a "mixed church" (*ecclesia mixta*) in which the holy and the hypocrite lived. Who were the true Christians was an invisible reality that only God knew. The separation would then occur only at the last judgment. Indeed a clear and perceptible division of times was equally impossible, for throughout time and in all places God has been at work in grace and judgment. The effect of this understanding was to deconstruct the millenialist conviction of the last days as a temporal period. Rather, the death and resurrection of Christ has ushered in the last days so that the millennial period was nothing other than the time of the church which stretches from his birth to his second coming.

The Revelation of John, therefore, is a vision of the spiritual realities at work as the church sojourns in this world on her way to her consummation. It is a sojourn replete with temptations and dangers, within and without. It is precisely this understanding of the theme of the Revelation that Bede states at the very beginning of his letter to Eusebius: in the Revelation of Saint John "God has considered it worthy to reveal by words and figures the internal wars and struggles of his church."[142] Thus, Bede interprets the name Ephesus to mean either "great fall" or "my will in it," since the letter to that church blames some in the church and praises others. To interpret the Revelation as a revelation of present spiritual realities heightens the impact and the relevance of the Revelation. While the eschatological interpretation might be effective in exhorting to endurance in view of a yet outstanding end-time drama, the ecclesiological interpretation of Tyconius and his followers makes the Revelation into a spiritual template of the present life and struggle of every person who bears the name Christian. In the one view the Revelation concerns what will be, in the other view the Revelation concerns what is. In the one the hearer or reader is positioned in what is not yet and so, as it were, stands outside the events (or at least most of them) of the text. In the other the hearer or reader is positioned, as it were, in the text and perceives through the vision of John the drama of which he is already an actor. If we keep this in mind, we can see the practical importance of Bede's intention to speak clearly for the people of the Angles who have been "lax in the cultivation of the faith."[143]

Second, in his letter to Eusebius Bede states that the Revelation is to be divided into seven sections. This division of the text was not accidental or due to a mere literary analysis. It corresponded to the view that the time of the world was by God divided into six

---

[142]CCL 121A:221.
[143]CCL 121A:233.

ages even as the world had been created in six days.[144] The sixth age extended from the birth of Christ to his second coming for judgment and the resurrection of all the dead. The seventh age is the eternal Sabbath rest of the New Jerusalem and the new creation. We, therefore, presently live in the sixth age that will come to its conclusion with the coming of the antichrist. However, the signs of the end of this sixth period are obscure and not readily discerned.

Thus, the Revelation concerns the present life of the church and is divided into seven sections that correspond to the seven ages of the world. This hermeneutical stance allowed for and perhaps even demanded the interpretative strategy of recapitulation. As Bede explains it, it is the custom (*consuetudo*) of the Revelation to narrate unto the number six. At this point, however, the prophet recapitulates by returning to events already narrated and skipping the narration of that which is seventh. The seventh age, which is that of the New Jerusalem, cannot properly be narrated until all that which pertains to the present life of the church is depicted. Thus, Bede notes that the letter to the church at Philadelphia is in sixth place since the letter speaks of penultimate things such as the final humiliation of the Jews and the conversion of some of them to the church. In the seventh place is the letter to the church at Laodicea, for that church is tepid and lukewarm and so indicates that state of humankind when the Lord comes for final judgment. To this point Bede quotes Luke 18:8: "When the Son of man comes, do you think that he will find faith on earth?"

There are three great commentaries on the Revelation that come from the eighth century. That of Beatus of Liébana (c. 780) fully incorporated the commentaries of Tyconius, Victorinus-Jerome, Primasius and Apringius. However, Beatus is little known in the Carolingian and medieval periods and hardly at all outside of Spain. It is the historical significance of Bede's commentary and that of Ambrose Autpertus (d. 781) to have become the principal means by which the traditions of Tyconius, Augustine, Victorinus and Primasius came to Carolingian interpreters such as Alcuin and Haimo and through them became the common stock of Apocalypse interpretation in the Middle Ages.[145]

---

[144]Bede most likely inherited this view from Augustine *City of God* 22.30.

[145]For the critical text of Aupertus, see CCL 27A (*continuation mediaevalis*); for Beatus, see Henry A. Sanders, *Beati in Apocalipsin Libri Duodecim*. Papers and Monographs of the American Academy in Rome, vol. 7 (Rome: American Academy in Rome, 1930).

VICTORINUS OF PETOVIUM
Commentary on the Apocalypse

REVELATION 1

1. At the beginning of the book he promises blessedness to the one who reads and to the one who hears and to the one who keeps what is written, so that by attending to the reading one might learn good works and safeguard that which it commands. "Grace to you and peace from God who is and who was and who is to come."[1] He was because he made all things with the Father and did not acquire a beginning from the Virgin. To be sure, he is going to come for judgment.[2] "From the sevenfold Spirit." We read in Isaiah, "a Spirit of wisdom and understanding, of counsel and strength, of knowledge and piety, a Spirit of the fear of the Lord."[3] These seven gifts are of one Spirit, that is, they are gifts of the Holy Spirit.

"And from Jesus Christ who is the faithful witness, the firstborn from the dead." When he assumed human nature, he gave forth a witness to the world, and by suffering in the world "he released us from sin by his blood," and when hell was conquered,[4] he arose as the first from the dead, and "death will no longer have dominion over him."[5] Rather, since he is now reigning, the kingdom of the world is destroyed. And "he has made us a kingdom and priests," that is, the whole church of the faithful, as the apostle Peter says: "a holy nation, a royal priesthood."[6] "Behold, he is coming with the clouds, and all peoples will see him." He who first came in a hidden way when he assumed the flesh will after a little while come openly in majesty and glory for judgment.

2. It says that "in the midst of golden lampstands there was one walking similar to a son of man." It says "similar" because death had been destroyed. For when he had ascended into heaven and when his body was united to the Spirit of glory that he received from the Father,[7] henceforth he could be called as though Son of God but no longer as son of man.[8] He is "walking in the midst of golden lampstands," that is, in the midst of the churches, as he spoke through Solomon: "I walk in the paths of the just."[9] By the "whiteness on the head" is shown his antiquity and immortality and the source of his majesty, for "the head of Christ is God."[10] [In the white hairs there is a figure of those who have been made white.[11] It is similar to wool, because they are sheep; it is similar to snow because of the innumerable multitude of those made white by grace from heaven.[12] "His eyes were

---

Revelation 1   [1]Victorinus is the first Western witness for the reading "from God." He attributes the three predicates to Jesus, thereby making a strong claim to the divinity of Jesus. Tertullian had already attributed the three phrases to Christ (*Against Praxeas* 17.4 [ANF 3:613]). [2]The recension of Jerome reads at the beginning "he is because he continually exists" (*permanet*). [3]Is 11:2-3. "Fear of the Lord," as in MS A (so read by Dulaey, SC 423:46). Hausleiter reads "fear of God," following MSS from the Jerome recension (CSEL 49:18). [4]Here *infernus* is personified, and the descent of Christ into hell is depicted as a battle between him and hell. [5]Rom 6:9. [6]1 Pet 2:9. [7]See 1 Pet 1:21. [8]Victorinus seems to say that on his ascension Christ assumed his divine sonship and so the title Son of man was no longer adequate. Now he is "similar" to a son of man. [9]Prov 8:20. [10]1 Cor 11:3. [11]The words in brackets appear in the margin of MS A, taken from the Jerome recension. However, Jerome has *multitudo*, not *similitudo*. Those made white refers to the baptized, here expressed by *albati*, not the more usual *candidati* that is used in the second mention of those made white. [12]The image of sheep recalls that Christ is their shepherd. The snow suggests the heavenly origin of their spiritual condition.

as a flame of fire." This refers to the commandments of God that give light to those who believe but fire to those who not believe.]

3. "The brightness of the sun was in his face." His face was his appearance by which he conversed with people face to face.[13] For although the glory of the sun is less than the glory of the Lord, yet because of the rising and setting of the sun and its rising again, the Scripture uses this figure and says that his face was like the glory of the sun, because he was born and suffered and rose again.

4. The one like a son of man was "in priestly garment." This clearly indicates his flesh which was not corrupted by death and which possesses through his death that eternal priesthood that was given to it. His breasts refer to the two Testaments, and the golden girdle represents the chorus of the saints who, as gold, have been proved through fire.[14] Alternatively we might say that the words "a golden girdle was tied to his breast" suggest that a vibrant knowledge and a pure spiritual understanding have been given to the churches.

The phrase "a sharp two-edged sword issued from his mouth" shows that it was he who earlier gave to the whole world knowledge of the law through Moses but who now gives the blessings of the gospel.[15] And since by the same word every human race will be judged, whether of the Old or of the New Testament, he is called a "two-edged sword." For a sword arms a soldier, a sword kills the enemy, and a sword punishes the deserter. And that he might show the apostles that he was announcing judgment, he said, "I have not come to send peace, but a sword."[16]

And when he had fulfilled all the parables, he said to them, " 'Have you understood all this?' And they said, 'Yes.' And he said, 'Therefore, every scribe who has been trained for the kingdom of heaven is like a householder who brings out of his treasury what is new and what is old.' "[17] By the "new things" he means the words of the gospel, and by the "old things" he means the law and the prophets.[18] That these had come from his own mouth he told to Peter, "Go to the sea and cast a hook, and take the first fish that comes up, and when you open its mouth you will find a shekel—that is, two denarii. Give that for me and for you."[19] And David spoke in a similar way through the Spirit: "Once has God spoken, twice have I heard this,"[20] meaning that the Lord once decreed from the beginning what was going to be to the end.[21] Therefore all of these things are the two Testaments which, according to an understanding of time, are called either two denarii, or new things and old things or a sharp two-edged sword. And finally, since he has been established as judge by the Father, he wishes to show that people will be judged by the word of his preaching, and so he said, "Do you think that I will judge you on the last day? The word that I have spoken to you, that will judge you on the last day."[22] And Paul wrote to the Thessalonians in view of the antichrist, "Whom the Lord will kill by the breath of his mouth."[23] This is, therefore, the two-edged sword that issues from his mouth.

5. "His voice was as the sound of many waters." The many waters are understood to be the people, but they are also the gift of baptism that he sent down[24] so that by his command it would be

---

[13]His *apparition* refers to the incarnation, for in this way God conversed with people "face to face" (see Ex 33:11). [14]This comment about the breasts and the girdle follows the reading of Dulaey. [15]As the Word of God, Christ speaks in both Testaments; therefore the fundamental unity of both Testaments. See Irenaeus *Against Heresies* 4.12.3 (ANF 1:476). [16]Mt 10:34. [17]Mt 13:51-52. [18]A traditional interpretation found already in Irenaeus *Against Heresies* 4.9.1 (ANF 1:472). [19]Mt 17:27. [20]Ps 62:11 (61:12 lxx). [21]According to Dulaey, this is the first use of this psalm text for the unity of the two Testaments (SC 423:158). [22]Jn 12:48. [23]2 Thess 2:8. [24]Reading *demisit* with MS A (Dulaey, SC 423:52). Baptism comes from above. Hausleiter follows Jerome and reads *emisit*, emphasizing the extension of baptism to the whole world (CSEL 49:26).

extended through the apostles for the salvation of humankind.[25] "His feet were like burnished bronze refined in a furnace." He is speaking of the apostles, because refined through suffering they preached his word. For those through whom the proclamation walks[26] are properly called feet. And the prophet understood this beforehand in saying, "Let us worship where his feet have stood,"[27] because where the apostles as the first stood and established the church, namely, in Judea, there all the saints will come together and worship their God.[28]

6. "There are seven stars in his right hand." We have said that the Holy Spirit with its sevenfold energy was given into his power by the Father, as Peter exclaimed to the Jews, "Therefore, having been exalted to the right hand of God and having received the Spirit from the Father, he poured out this which you have seen and heard."[29] Also John the Baptist had anticipated this by saying to his disciples, "For he does not give the Spirit in measure. The Father loves the Son and has given all things into his hand."[30] These are the seven stars.

7. He mentions seven churches by the explicit use of their own names to which he has sent letters. He does this not because they are the only churches, or even the most important of the churches, but because what he says to one, he says to all. For it makes no difference whether one speaks to a cohort, in number only a few soldiers, or whether one speaks through it to the entire army. Whether in Asia or in the whole world, Paul taught that all of the seven churches that are named are one catholic church.[31] And therefore, that he

might preserve this understanding, he did not exceed the number of seven churches, but he wrote to the Romans, to the Corinthians, to the Ephesians, to the Thessalonians, to the Galatians, to the Philippians and to the Colossians. Later he wrote to individual persons, lest he exceed the number of seven churches, and to give a brief summary of his preaching, he said to Timothy, "That you might know how you ought to behave in the household of God, which is the church of the living God."[32]

We read that this type was announced by the Holy Spirit through Isaiah, who spoke of seven women who seized one man.[33] However, this one man is Christ, who was not born of seed. And the seven women are churches who received their own bread and wear their own clothes but who ask that their reproach be taken away and that his name be invoked over them. The "bread" is the Holy Spirit, who nourishes to eternal life.[34] It is "their own" because it has been promised to them through faith, and "their own clothes" refers to the promises that have been made to them and by which they wish to be covered, as Paul says: "It is necessary that this corruptible be clothed with incorruption and that this mortal be clothed with immortality."[35] And the words "that their reproach be taken away" refer to that first sin that is taken away in baptism when each person begins to be called a Christian, which is the meaning of the words "your name will be invoked over us."[36] In these seven churches, therefore, we are to think of the one church.

8. For the sake of the quality of their faith and election, he has written either to those who

---

[25]See Mt 28:19. [26]The Latin is *ambulat*. Victorinus is preserving the image of the feet. [27]Ps 131:7 LXX. [28]Apringius also gives this interpretation. This is apparently a belief of early Jewish Christianity that continued among Christians of chiliastic persuasion. [29]Acts 2:33. [30]Jn 3:34-35. [31]That in writing to seven churches John and Paul were speaking to all churches of the one catholic church is a common idea. It appears in the Revelation commentaries of Apringius, Primasius and Bede and can be found already in the Muratorian Canon (c. 200). [32]1 Tim 3:15. [33]Is 4:1. [34]Dulaey claims that this is an allusion to Jn 6:51. The Holy Spirit is communicated to us in the eucharistic bread. See also Irenaeus *Against Heresies* 4.38.1 (ANF 1:521) and Origen *Homilies in Genesis* 16.4 (SC 7:382). [35]1 Cor 15:53. [36]Perhaps referring to the invocation of the trinitarian name in baptism.

live and work in the world by the honesty of
their own labor but who are patient when they
see some in the church who are destructive
squanderers and bear with them, lest there be
division—yet he admonishes them concerning
love, in which faith resides, that they might
repent; or, he has written to those who live
in places of cruelty among persecutors, that
they might remain faithful; or, he has written
to those who have been taught humility and
have courageously persevered in the faith; or,
to those who under the pretext of mercy have
allowed in the church unlawful sins and teach
others to do them; or, to those who are at ease
in the church; or, to those who are wholly
negligent and are Christians in name only; or,
he accuses those who study the Scriptures and
labor to know the mysteries of the preaching
but do not want to do the work of God, which
is mercy and love. To all, he declares penitence;
to all, he announces judgment.

REVELATION 2

1. In the first letter, John says, "I know your
work and toil and your patient suffering"—I
know that you work and toil, and I see that you
are patient; lest you think that I will remain
a long time away from you—"and that you are
not able to bear evil persons and those who
call themselves apostles you have found to be
liars, and you have suffered patiently for the
sake of my name." All of these things are in
view of praise, and no ordinary praise. And yet
it is good that such persons and such a class of
people and such elect persons be admonished in
every way, lest they be robbed of those blessings
that are their due. But he said that he had a few
things against them. "You have forsaken your
first love," he said. "Remember from where you
have fallen." When someone falls, he falls from

a height, and therefore he says "from where,"
since even to the very end works of love must be
practiced, for this is the principal commandment.[1] And, therefore, unless this is done, he
threatened to "move the lampstand from its
place," that is, to scatter the people.

However, they hate the works of the Nicolaitans, which also he hates, and this is deserving of praise. "Works of the Nicolaitans" refer
to the fact that before that time there were
factious and troublesome people who as ministers made for themselves a heresy in the name
of Nicolaus, so that what had been offered to
idols could be exorcised and eaten and that
anyone who had committed fornication might
receive the peace on the eighth day.[2] And,
therefore, he praised those to whom he wrote
and promised to such great people the tree of
life, which is in the paradise of their God.

2. The next letter shows the following manner
of life and habit of another group. And so he
says, "I know you that you are poor and labor,
but you are rich." For he knows that for such
persons there are hidden riches with him. And
he knows the slander of the Jews, whom he de-
nies that they are Jews, but rather a synagogue
of Satan, for they are gathered together by the
antichrist.[3] That they might persevere even to
death, he says to them: "Whoever will persevere, will not be harmed by the second death,"
that is, he will not be punished in hell.

3. The third class of saints are persons who
are strong in the faith and are not frightened
by persecution. But since there are even among
them some who are inclined toward illicit
indulgences, he says, "I will fight with them by
the sword of my mouth," that is, "I will say what
I will command, and I will tell you what you are
to do." For there are some "who have taught the

Revelation 2   [1]See Mt 22:38.   [2]Victorinius is the sole witness to give us these details about the Nicolaitans: that they exorcised meat
that had been consecrated to demons and that they were lax in matters of penance.   [3]According to Victorinus, during the last days the
Jews will collude with the antichrist.

doctrine of Balaam and have placed a stone of stumbling before the eyes of the sons of Israel, to eat what is sacrificed to idols and to commit fornication." And this was known a long time ago. For he gave this advice to the king of the Moabites that in this way he had scandalized the people.[4] "So," he says, "you have some among you who hold to this teaching," and under the pretext of mercy you corrupt others.

"Whoever conquers," he says, "I will give to him from the hidden manna." The hidden manna is immortality; the "white stone" is the adoption as a son of God. The "new name" is that of Christian.[5]

4. The fourth class indicates the nobility of the faithful who do good works every day and who do greater works. But even among these the Lord shows that there are persons who too easily grant an unlawful peace and pay attention to new prophecies,[6] and he urges and admonishes the others, to whom this is not pleasing, who know the iniquity of the adversary. And for these evils and deceptions he seeks to bring dangers on the head of the faithful. And therefore he says, "I do not place on you any further burden"—that is, "I have not given to you the observations and duties of the law," which is another burden—"but hold fast to that which you have, until I come. And to him who conquers, I will give power over the nations"—that is, "he will be established as judge among the rest of the saints"—and "I will give to him the morning star," that is, Christ promises the first resurrection. For the morning star drives the night away and announces the light, that is, the beginning of the day.

REVELATION 3

1. This fifth class, group or manner of saint refers to those persons who are negligent and

behave in a manner other than what they ought in the world, who are vacuous in works and who are Christian only in name. And therefore he exhorts them so that in some way they might reverse themselves from this dangerous negligence and be saved. "Strengthen," he says, "that which is in danger of death. I have not found your work perfect before my God." For it is not sufficient that a tree live but yet not give fruit. Neither is it sufficient that one be called a Christian, confess himself to be a Christian and yet not do the works of a Christian.

2. This sixth class represents the highest manner of life of the elect saints, namely, of those who are humble in the world and are untutored in the Scriptures but hold steadfastly to the faith and in no way withdraw from the faith out of fear. To these he says, "I have set before you an open door," and he further says, "For you have kept the word of my patience"—with such little strength—"and I will save you from the hour of temptation." And that they might know his glory in this manner, he does not permit them to be handed over into temptation.

"He who conquers," he says, "will become a pillar in the temple of God." A pillar is a decoration of a building, and so he who perseveres will obtain nobility in the church.

3. This group, the seventh class, speaks of those wealthy persons who are believers placed in positions of dignity and who believe in the manner of wealthy people. Among them the Scriptures are interpreted in their bedchamber, while the faithful are outside and the Scriptures are understood by no one. That is, they boast and say that they know all things and possess a confidence in the learning of letters, yet they are empty when it comes to

---

[4]Num 25:1-2. [5]The manna, the stone and the name are blessings given in baptism. [6]"New prophecies" refer to the claim of new spiritual revelations by the Montanists.

works. And so, the Lord says to them that they are neither cold nor hot, that is, that they are neither unbelieving nor believing, for they are all things to all people. And since one who is neither cold nor hot must of necessity be lukewarm, he produces nausea. And the Lord says, "I will vomit him from my mouth." For nausea is hateful and is hidden to no one, and it is the same way with such persons when they are thrown out. But because there is time for repentance, he says, "I counsel you to buy from me gold refined by fire." That is, if in some way you should be able to suffer something for the name of the Lord. And the Lord says, "Anoint your eyes with eye salve." That is, what you freely know through the Scriptures, it is necessary that you desire to do this. And since such persons would be of great benefit not only to themselves but to many were they in some way to return away from a great destruction to a great repentance, he promises to them no small reward, namely, to sit on the throne of judgment.

REVELATION 4

1. "There was," he says, "an open door in heaven." John sees the preaching of the New Testament, and it is said to him, "Come up here." When it is shown that the door was opened, it is clear that previously it had been closed to humankind. However, it was sufficiently and perfectly opened when Christ ascended in the body to the Father in heaven. When he says that the voice that he heard was the voice that spoke with him, without any doubt this proves to the stubborn unbelievers[1] that he who comes is the same as he who spoke through the prophets. For John was from the circumcision, and that entire people had heard the preaching of the Old Testament and had been edified by that voice. For "that voice," he says, "which I heard, it said to me, 'Come up here.'" This is Jesus Christ whom a little before he said that he had seen as a son of man among the golden lampstands. And now he recalls that which had been foretold in the law by means of similitudes, and through this Scripture he joins together all the previous prophets and opens the Scriptures. And since our Lord later summons to heaven all who believe in his name, he immediately poured out the Holy Spirit who will bear every person to heaven. And he says, "Immediately I was in the Spirit." And because the mind of the faithful is opened through the Holy Spirit, what was already foretold to the ancients is revealed to them.

2. Significantly, there was a "throne set" in heaven, which is the seat of judgment and of the king, and over this throne he says that he saw something similar to jasper and carnelian. Since jasper has the color of water and carnelian that of fire, it was manifested that these two Testaments have been placed over the tribunal of God until the consummation of the world. And of these judgments one has already been accomplished through water, while the other will be accomplished through fire.[2]

And the rainbow around the throne had a vibrant color. The rainbow is called a "bow," and God had already spoken to Noah and his sons about this, lest they fear that a deluge of water might again take place. "I will place," he said, "my bow in the clouds,"[3] that you no longer fear water, but fire. And "before the throne there was, as it were, a sea of glass similar to crystal." This is the gift of baptism, which he poured out through his Son during the time of

---

Revelation 4   [1]Translating *contumaces*. Victorinus may have in mind the Jews who did not believe that Christ is the Word who spoke through the prophets and who in his incarnation and death fulfilled them. Or, as Hausleiter suggests, he may have in mind the Marcionites, who believed that the Old and New Testaments were derived from distinct deities and so rejected the unity of the two Testaments (CSEL 49:44).   [2]See 2 Pet 3:6.   [3]Gen 9:13.

repentance, before he should begin the judgment. And, therefore, it is "before the throne,"[4] that is, before the judgment. And since it says "a sea of glass similar to crystal," it shows that it is pure water, smooth, not made rough by the wind or like a river flowing downhill, but given as an immoveable gift from God.

3. The four animals are the four Gospels. "The first," he says, "was similar to a lion, the second similar to a calf, the third similar to a man and the fourth similar to an eagle in flight. And they had six wings all around and eyes within and without, and they did not cease to say, 'Holy, Holy, Holy, Lord God Almighty.'"[5] And there were twenty-four elders who had twenty-four tribunals. These are the books of the prophets and of the law, which give the testimonies of the judgment. However, these twenty-four fathers are also the twelve apostles and the twelve patriarchs. That the living creatures were different in appearance has this explanation.[6]

4. The animal similar to the lion is the Gospel according to John. For while all the Evangelists proclaim that Christ was made man, he proclaims that he was God before he came down and assumed the flesh, saying, "The Word was God,"[7] and since he cried out, roaring like a lion, his preaching took on the appearance of a lion. The likeness of a man refers to Matthew, who strives to tell us the genealogy of Mary, from whom Christ took his flesh. And, therefore, since he numbers the family of Mary from Abraham to David and from David to Joseph,[8] he speaks as though of a man, and for this reason his

Gospel receives the image of a man. And Luke narrates of the sacerdotal service of Zechariah, who offered a sacrifice for the people, and of the angel who appeared to him, and on account of the sacerdotal service and the sacrifice,[9] this narrative bears the image of a calf. As the interpreter of Peter, Mark remembered what he had taught publicly and wrote, although not in order,[10] and began with the word of prophecy proclaimed by Isaiah.

And therefore, the Gospels begin in the following ways. John says, "In the beginning was the Word, and the Word was with God, and the Word was God"[11]—this is the face of a lion. Matthew says, "The book of the generation of Jesus Christ, the Son of God, son of David, son of Abraham"[12]—this is the face of a man. Luke says, "There was a priest by the name of Zacharias, of the order of Abia, and his wife was from the daughters of Aaron"[13]—this is the image of the calf. Mark begins, "The beginning of the gospel of Jesus Christ, as was written in Isaiah,"[14] and so he begins with the Spirit in flight and so possesses the image of a flying eagle. However, it is not only the prophetic Spirit but also the very Word of God the Father Almighty, who is his Son, our Lord Jesus Christ, who bore the same images during the time of his coming to us. Indeed, he had been proclaimed as a lion and as a lion's whelp.[15] For the salvation of humankind he was made man for the defeat of death and for the liberation of all.[16] Because he offered himself as a sacrifice to God the Father for us, he is called a calf. And because, when death was conquered, he ascended into the heavens and held out his wings to cover his people, he is called an eagle in flight. And although there are four proclama-

---

[4]*Ante solium.* Victorinus interprets *ante* in a temporal sense, not a spatial sense. [5]As both Hausleiter (CSEL 49:48) and Dulaey (SC 423:66) claim, the original text seems to have read both in the Greek and in the Latin: ἅγιος ἅγιος ἅγιος *sanctus, sanctus, sanctus.* This would suggest that still at the end of the third century the Trisagion was sung in Greek in the liturgy of Petovium. [6]Victorinus follows Irenaeus in his interpretation of the four creatures (*Against Heresies* 3.11.8 [ANF 1:428]). [7]Jn 1:1. [8]Mt 1:1-16. [9]Lk 1:8-13. [10]Victorinus takes this information about Mark from Papias (in Eusebius *Ecclesiastical History* 3.39.15). [11]Jn 1:1. [12]Mt 1:1. [13]Lk 1:5. [14]Mk 1:1-2. [15]Gen 49:9. [16]Victorinus is thinking of Gen 49:11. He who is as a lion "washes his garments in wine and his vesture in the blood of grapes." The lion is the figure not merely of royalty, but of a royalty that suffers for the freedom of its people.

tions, yet there is really but one proclamation, because it proceeds from one mouth, just as the river in paradise was from one source yet was separated into four streams.

5. And these animals had eyes within and without. This refers to the preaching of the New Testament. It indicates the spiritual foreknowledge[17] that sees into the secrets of the heart and those things which are going to happen, that is, things within and without.

The wings are the testimonies of the Old Testament, that is, of the twenty-four books, the same number as the elders on the tribunals. For just as an animal cannot fly unless it has wings, neither can the preaching of the New Testament acquire faith unless its testimony is seen to correspond to those foretold in the Old Testament, through which it rises from the earth and flies. For it is always the case that when something spoken in the past is later found to have happened, that creates an undoubting faith.[18] On the other hand, if the wings do not attach to the animal, they have no source from which to draw their life. And so, unless that which the prophets foretold had been fulfilled in Christ, their preaching would be empty. And therefore the catholic church believes both that which was previously foretold and that which afterward was fulfilled, and rightly then flies and is lifted from the earth, as though a living animal. Those heretics, however, who make no use of the prophetic testimony are as animals who do not fly, because they are of the earth.[19] And likewise the Jews, who do not accept the preaching of the New Testament, are like wings that have no life, for they offer empty prophecies to people, not allowing the fulfilling deeds to correspond to the words of prophecy.

The books of the Old Testament that are received are those twenty-four that we find in the epitomes of Theodore.[20] However, as we have said, the twenty-four elders are the patriarchs and apostles who will judge the people. For when the apostles asked and said, "We have left everything and followed you. What shall we have?" our Lord answered, "When the Son of man shall sit on the throne of his glory, also you will sit on twelve tribunals, judging the twelve tribes of Israel."[21] But it was said also of the patriarchs that they would judge, for the patriarch Jacob said, "And he will judge his people among his brothers, as one of the tribes of Israel."[22]

6. And "lightning and voices and thunder come from the throne of God, and there are seven torches." These things signify the proclamations and the promises that come from God, as well as his threats. The "lightning" represents the coming of the Lord; the "voices" represent the proclamations of the New Testament; the "thunder" represents words that are from heaven; and the "torches of burning fire" signify the gift of the Holy Spirit[23] that the first man lost on a tree but is now regained through the wood of Christ's passion.

7. And when these things occurred, he says, "All the elders fell down and worshiped the Lord, when the animals gave him glory and honor." That is, when the gospel—namely, both the actions and the teaching of the Lord—had fulfilled that word previously foretold by them, the prophets worthily and properly exulted, knowing that they had rightly ministered the word of the Lord. And finally, because he had come who would conquer death and would alone be worthy to take the crown of immortality, as many as possessed crowns

---

[17]Translating *providentiam spiritalem.* [18]A common claim of early Christian apologetics. See Justin Martyr *1 Apology* 31-42 (ANF 1:173-77). [19]Victorinus is referring to the followers of Marcion, who rejected the Old Testament. [20]This work is unknown. [21]Mt 19:27-28. [22]Gen 49:16. [23]There are seven torches, signifying the sevenfold gifts of the one Holy Spirit.

because of the glory of his most excellent deed "threw them under his feet," that is, on account of the greatness of the victory of Christ they threw their victories under his feet. And Christ fulfilled this in the gospel by his speaking.[24] For when at the end our Lord came to Jerusalem to suffer, the people came out to him in the way,[25] some strew on the road palm branches that they had cut down, others laid down their own tunics. And this shows the two peoples, one of the patriarchs and the prophets, of the great men, who had whatever palms of their victories against sin, and threw them under his feet.[26] However, the palm signifies the same thing as the crown, for it is not given to anyone but to the victor.

REVELATION 5

1. "In the hand of him who is seated on the tribunal there is a book written within, sealed by seven seals." This signifies the Old Testament, which was given into the hand of our Lord, who received the judgment from the Father. "A herald cried out," he says, "whether there was anyone worthy to open the book and to loose its seals, and no one was found worthy, neither in heaven, nor on earth nor under the earth." However, to open the Testament is to suffer and to conquer death for humanity. No one was found worthy to do this, neither among the angels in heaven, nor among people on the earth nor among the souls of the saints who are at rest; only Christ, the Son of God, whom he says that he saw as though a lamb slain, having seven horns. What had been prophesied of him, whatever the law had mediated of him through oblations and sacrifices, it was necessary that he fulfill. And because he was the testator who had conquered death, it was just that he be appointed God's heir, so that he might possess the property of the one who was dying, that is, the human race.[1]

2. It says that he is "the lion from the tribe of Judah who has conquered, the root of David." We read in Genesis of the lion from the tribe of Judah, for the patriarch Jacob says, "Judah, your brothers praise you; and you will sleep and rise up as a lion and a lion's whelp."[2] He is called a "lion" because he was to conquer death; but because he was to suffer for humankind, he "was led as a lamb for the slaughter."[3] Therefore, he opens and unseals the testament that he had sealed. And Moses the lawgiver knew that it was necessary for the testament to be sealed and hidden until the coming of his passion, and so he covered his face and in that way spoke to the people, revealing that the words of preaching were veiled until the time of Christ's coming.[4] For when he had read this law to the people, he took wool soaked in calf's blood and water and sprinkled all the people, saying, "This is the blood of the testament, concerning which the Lord had commanded you."[5] Therefore, the diligent person ought to be attentive to the fact that the totality of preaching comes together into a unity. For it was not sufficient that it was called "law," since it was also called a testament. For no law is called a testament, nor is anything called a testament, except that which is made by one who is about to die. And

---

[24]MS A, followed by Hausleiter (CSEL 49:58), reads *supplevit Christus dicendo*. The MSS of the Jerome recension, followed by Dulaey (SC 423:72), read *supplevit Spiritus ostendendo*. We have followed Hausleiter, although the choice is uncertain. *Dicendo* is difficult, since the context of Jesus' entry into Jerusalem does not contain a discourse. However, Christ has been the referent of Victorinus's comments to this point, and Christ is the one who fulfills the patriarchs and prophets. [25]Mt 21:8. [26]The Latin is *unum patrum et prophetarum, magnorum virorum, qui . . .* Victorinus does not identify the second people, unless the world *alium* is to be assumed before the words *magnorum virorum*, in which case the "great men" are the second group. Jerome edits, *unum partum et alium prophetarum*, making the patriarchs one people and the prophets the other. **Revelation 5** [1]*Substantia morientis*. The idea that Christ receives the human race as his inheritance is also found in Irenaeus (*Against Heresies* 5.9.4 [ANF 1:535]). [2]Gen 49:8-9. [3]Is 53:7. [4]Ex 34:33; 2 Cor 3:7-18. [5]Ex 24:8; Heb 9:19-20.

whatever is within the testament is sealed until the day of the death of the testator. But since he conquered death and overcame the work of the executioner, it is said that he was "as though slain." And therefore rightly it is unsealed by the Lamb slain who, as a lion, destroyed death and fulfilled that which had been foretold of him and had freed humankind, that is, flesh, from death, and had received as a possession the property of him who was dying, namely, of the human race. For as through one body all people had come into the debt of death, so through one body all who believe might rise to eternal life.[6] Now the face of Moses is uncovered; now it is revealed, and therefore the apocalypse is called a "revelation"; now his book is unsealed; now the sacrifices of the victims are understood; now the offerings and the duties of the Anointed, the building of the temple and the prophecies are clearly understood.

3. "The twenty-four elders and the four animals had harps and bowls and were singing a new song." The preaching of the Old Testament joined with the New reveals the Christian people singing a new song, that is, the proclaiming of their public confession.[7] It is new that the Son of God became man; it is new that he was given over into death by people; it is new that he rose again on the third day; it is new that he ascended in the body into heaven; it is new that he gives the forgiveness of sins to people; it is new that people are sealed with the Holy Spirit; it is new that they receive the priestly service of supplication[8] and await a kingdom of such immense promises.

The harps, whose strings are stretched on its frame, signify the body of Christ, that is, the flesh of Christ bound to his passion.[9] The bowls represent the confession of faith and the extension of the new priesthood. The praise is "of many angels," indeed, it is of all who bring the thanksgiving of all the elect to our Lord for the deliverance of the human race from the destruction of death.

REVELATION 6

1. The breaking of the seals, as we said, is the disclosing of the prophecies of the Old Testament and the foretelling of those things that will happen at the end of time. Although our prophetic writing expresses the events to come by way of the individual seals, it is not until all of the seals have been opened that the announcement is able to run its course. When the first seal was opened, he says that "he saw a white horse and a rider who was crowned and who had a bow"—for this is what happened at first. For after our Lord ascended into heaven, he opened all things and sent forth the Holy Spirit. Through preachers the words of the Holy Spirit penetrate into the human heart as though they were arrows, and they conquer unbelief.[1] The crown on the head is promised to the preachers by the Holy Spirit. The other three horses clearly signify the famine, wars and pestilences that the Lord foretold in the Gospel.

And therefore, he said, "one of the living creatures," because all four are one. "Come and see."[2] "Come" is spoken to one who is invited to faith. "See" is spoken to one who has not seen. And therefore, the white horse is the word of preaching that was sent into the world by the Holy Spirit. For the Lord has said, "This gospel will be preached in all the world as a witness to the nations, and then the end will come."[3]

2. The black horse signifies famine.[4] For, the Lord said, "And there will be famine in many

---

[6]1 Cor 15:21; Rom 5:12. [7]The new song is essentially the christological portion of the baptismal creed. [8]That is the priestly service of intercession, perhaps thinking of 1 Jn 2:1-2. [9]This is the first occurrence of this interpretation. **Revelation 6** [1]Victorinus interprets the rider on the white horse to be the Holy Spirit. [2]The text followed by Victorinus has "come and see," corresponding to Jn 1:46. [3]Mt 24:14. [4]Unlike the text of the Revelation, Victorinus mentions the black horse before the red horse.

places."[5] However, this passage is also properly extended to the time of the antichrist, that is, to that time when there will be a great famine and people will be injured. The balance in the rider's hand is the book of inquiry that shows the merits of each person. A voice says, "Do not harm oil and wine." That is, do not weigh down the spiritual person with plagues. This is the black horse.[6]

"And there was a red horse, and he who sat on it had a sword." This passage signifies those wars that will occur in the future, as we read in the Gospel: "For nation will rise against nation, and kingdom against kingdom, and there will be earthquakes on the earth."[7] This is the red horse.

3. "And there was a pale horse, and he who sat on it had the name of death." The Lord had foretold these very things, along with other catastrophes.[8] For when he said, "And hell follows him," he was speaking of the devouring of the souls of many of the impious. This is the pale horse.

4. "And he saw the souls of the slain under the altar," that is, under the earth. For both the heaven and the earth are called "altar." And so, the law, prefiguring by way of images the form of the truth, presented two altars, one that is gold within and one that is bronze without.[9] And we understand that this altar is called "heaven," since this testimony was given to us by our Lord. For he said, "When you offer your gift on the altar"—to be sure, our gifts are the prayers that we ought to offer—"and there should remember that your brother has

anything against you, leave there your gift,"[10] and most certainly prayers ascend to heaven. And so, heaven is understood to be that altar that was gold within—for even the priest, who had the command of Christ, entered into the temple to the golden altar once a year.[11] The Holy Spirit was signifying that Christ was going to do this, that is, that he would suffer once for all.

And parallel to this, the bronze altar is to be understood as the earth, under which exists Hades, a region removed from pains and fire, a place for the repose of the saints, in which to be sure the just are seen and heard by the impious, but these cannot go across to those.[12] He who sees all things willed that we know that these, that is, the souls of the slain, await the vindication of their blood, that is, of their body, from those who dwell on the earth. However, since at the end of time the eternal reward of the saints and the condemnation of the impious will come, they are told to wait. And for a consolation of their body they received, it says, white robes, that is, the gift of the Holy Spirit.[13]

REVELATION 7

1. "I saw an angel descending from the rising of the sun."[1] He is speaking of Elijah the prophet, who was to come before the time of antichrist to restore and to strengthen the churches from the intolerable persecution. We read of these things in the opening of the book both of the Old Testament and of the new preaching. For through Malachi the Lord said, "Behold, I send to you Elijah, the Thesbite, to

---

[5]Mt 24:7. [6]The words concerning the balance and the voice do not appear in MS A but are in the recension of Jerome (Dulaey, SC 423:80). [7]Lk 21:10-11. [8]See again Lk 21:11. [9]See Ex 27:2; 30:3. [10]Mt 5:23-24. [11]See Heb 9:7. [12]See Lk 16:26. Dulaey notes that Victorinus interprets the souls under the altar to be those of the saints in general, not the souls of the martyrs, which is a more common interpretation (SC 423:179). [13]See also Irenaeus *Against Heresies* 3.23.5 (ANF 1:457). The white robe as the gift of the Holy Spirit is most likely influenced by baptismal symbolism. The commentary of Victorinus on Rev 6 concludes at this point. For commentary on the rest of Rev 6, Dulaey uses the Jerome recension (SC 423:82-84), while Hausleiter adduces passages from other Western commentators such as Primasius and Beatus (CSEL 49:76-80). **Revelation 7** [1]The text of Victorinus appears to have read "descending," not "ascending." Elijah can "descend," because he was, according to ancient understanding, taken directly to paradise. See also Irenaeus *Against Heresies* 5.5.1 (ANF 1:530-31).

turn the hearts of the fathers to their children and the heart of man to his neighbor,"[2] that is, to Christ through penitence. "To turn the hearts of the fathers to their children," that is, at the time of the calling to recall the Jews to the faith of that people who follow them. And therefore he shows the number of those from the Jews who will believe and the great multitude of those from the Gentiles.[3]

REVELATION 8

1. We read in the Gospel that the prayers of the church are offered from heaven by an angel and that they are received and poured out against wrath and that the kingdom of antichrist is extinguished by the holy angels. For he says, "Pray, that you may not enter into temptation. For there will be a great anguish, such as has not been from the beginning or from the origin of the world, and unless the Lord had shortened those days, no flesh on the earth would be saved."[1] Therefore, he sends these seven great archangels to strike against the kingdom of the antichrist. For the Lord said in the Gospel, "Then the Son of man will send his angels and will gather his elect from the four winds, from one end of heaven to the other."[2] And before that he said, "Then there will peace in our land, when in it seven shepherds will arise and eight attacks of men and they will encircle Asshur, that is, the antichrist, in the trench of Nimrod,"[3] that is, at the damnation of the devil. And similarly Ecclesiastes says, "When the keepers of the house tremble."[4] And the Lord spoke as follows: "When the servants came to him and asked him, 'Lord, did you not sow good seed in your field? How then has it weeds?' He answered them, 'An enemy has done this.' They said, 'Do you want us to go and pluck

them out?' He said to them, 'No, let both grow together until the harvest, and at that time I will tell the reapers to gather the weeds and throw them into the fire, but to gather the wheat into the barn.' "[5] Here the Revelation reveals that these reapers and laborers are the archangels.

2. The "trumpet" is the word of power. And although there is a repetition of scenes by means of the bowls,[6] this is not spoken as though the events occurred twice. Rather, since those events that are future to them have been decreed by God to happen, these things are spoken twice. And therefore, whatever he said rather briefly by way of the trumpets he said more completely by way of the bowls. Nor ought we pay too much attention to the order of what is said. For the sevenfold Holy Spirit, when he has passed in revue the events to the last time, to the very end, returns again to the same times and supplements what he had said incompletely. Nor ought we inquire too much into the order of the Revelation. Rather, we ought inquire after the meaning, for there is also the possibility of a false understanding.

And therefore, those things written concerning the trumpets and the bowls are either the devastation of the plagues sent to the world, or the madness of the antichrist himself, or the blasphemies of the peoples, or the variety of the plagues, or the hope for the kingdom of saints, or the ruin of cities or the ruin of Babylon, that is, of the city of Rome.

3. "And there was an eagle flying in midheaven." This passage signifies the Holy Spirit who through two prophets proclaims that a great wrath of plagues is imminent. This occurs so that, although it is at the end of time, someone might in some manner still be saved.

---

[2]See Mal 4:5-6. [3]The 144,000 represent the Jews who will believe, while the innumerable multitude represents the Gentiles who will come to faith. **Revelation 8** [1]Mt 26:41; 24:21-22. [2]Mt 24:31. [3]See Mic 5:5. Asshur and Nimrod were traditional figures for the antichrist or the devil. See Gen 10:8, 10. [4]Eccles 12:3. [5]Mt 13:27-30. [6]See Rev 15:7–16:20.

REVELATION 10

1. And by this "mighty angel" he signifies our Lord, as we explained above.[1] It says that it "had come down from heaven, wrapped in a cloud—and there was a rainbow over his head and his face was as the sun and his feet were as columns of fire—and having in his hand an open book, and he placed his feet on the sea and on the earth." By the words "his face was as the sun" he indicates the resurrection. By the "rainbow was over his head" the seer indicates the judgment, which has occurred or will occur. The "open book" is the Revelation that John received. As we explained earlier,[2] "his feet" are the inspired apostles. That he walks on both the sea and the land signifies that all things have been placed under his feet. He speaks of him here as an "angel," that is, a messenger of the almighty Father, for he is called the "messenger of great counsel."[3] That he "cried out with a loud voice" signifies that great voice of heaven that announces the words of the almighty God to people that when the time of repentance is closed there will afterward be no future hope.

2. "The seven thunders uttered their voices." The Spirit of sevenfold power announced through the prophets all things that were to come and by his voice has given witness in the world. But since he said that he was going to write whatever the thunders had said, that is, whatever had been obscurely foretold in the Old Testament, he was forbidden to write but told to keep it sealed. For he was an apostle, and it was not fitting that the grace of the second rank should be given to the person of the first rank, "for the time is already near."[4] For the apostles overcame unbelief by

powers and signs and wonders and mighty deeds. And after them the comfort of having the prophetic Scriptures interpreted was given to the churches that were confirmed in faith. And these interpreters the apostle calls "prophets," for he says, "And he has appointed in the church first apostles, second prophets, third teachers," and following.[5] In another place he says, "Let two or three prophets speak, and let the others weigh what is said."[6] And he says, "Any woman who prays or prophesies with her head uncovered dishonors her head."[7] When, however, he said, "Let two or three prophets speak, and let the others weigh what is said," he was not speaking of catholic prophecy of some unheard of and unknown kind but of that prophecy that has been foretold.[8] They weigh what is said to ensure that the interpretation conforms with the witness of the sayings of the prophets. It is clear that John, armed as he was with a superior power, had no need of this, while the church, which is the body of Christ, is adorned by her own members and ought to respond from her own rank.[9]

3. That he "received the little scroll and ate it" indicates that he committed to memory what had been shown to him. "And it was sweet in the mouth." The fruit of preaching is very sweet to the speaker and to those who hear, but through suffering it becomes very bitter to the preacher and to those who persevere in the commandments. "It is necessary that you again preach," that is, to prophesy, "among peoples and tongues and nations." When John saw this revelation, he was on the island of Patmos, having been condemned to the mines by Caesar Domitian. There, it seems, John wrote the Revelation, and when he had already

---

Revelation 10 [1]Apparently referring to his comments in *Commentary* 1.3, on Rev 1:16. [2]In his comments on Rev 1:15, in *Commentary* 1.5. [3]Is 9:6. [4]Rev 1:3; 22:10. [5]1 Cor 12:28. [6]1 Cor 14:29. [7]1 Cor 11:5. [8]The Christian prophet does not give new prophecy but interprets the prophecies of the Old Testament. [9]The man who speaks with head uncovered is the apostle; the woman who speaks with head covered is the church speaking through her interpreter prophets.

become aged, he thought that he would be received into bliss after his suffering. However, when Domitian was killed, all of his decrees were made null and void. John was, therefore, released from the mines, and afterward he disseminated the revelation that he had received from the Lord. That is what it means when it says, "You must prophesy again."

REVELATION 11

1. And "he received a measuring rod like a staff, that he might measure the temple of God and the altar and those who worship in it." In this passage he speaks of that authority that John afterward exercised in the churches after his release. For he later also wrote a Gospel. And when Valentinus and Cerinthus and Ebion and other sects of Satan had spread throughout the world, bishops from the neighboring cities gathered to him and persuaded him to write his testimony concerning the Lord.[1] The "measure" of the faith,[2] however, is the commandment of our Lord, namely, that we must confess the Father almighty, as we have been taught, and his Son, our Lord Jesus Christ, who was spiritually begotten from the Father before the beginning of the world, who was made man, and when he had conquered death was received with his body by the Father into heaven, holy Lord and pledge of immortality; he was foretold by the prophets, he was described by the law and through the hand of God and the word of the Father almighty he is also the creator of the whole world.[3] This is the rod and measure of the faith, so that no one might worship at the holy altar except him who confesses this, "the Lord and his Christ."

2. "The court on the inside leave outside." The court is called an atrium, an open area between walls. He commands that such as these are to be thrown out of the church, for they are unnecessary. Because, it says, "it is given over to be trampled by the nations." This means that such persons are to be trampled either by the nations or with the nations. He mentions then again the destruction and the slaughter of the last times and says, "and they will trample the holy city for forty-two months. And I will give my two witnesses, clothed in sackcloth, to preach for one thousand, two hundred and sixty days," that is, for three years and six months. This one thousand, two hundred and sixty makes forty-two months. Their preaching, therefore, is for three years and six months, and the kingdom of the antichrist again as much. With the words "from the mouth of these prophets comes forth fire against their foes," he speaks of the power of the word. For all the plagues that will come from the angels will be sent by their voice.

3. Many think that it is either Elisha or Moses who is with Elijah. However, both of these died. But the death of Jeremiah was never discovered. Our ancients have handed over the opinion that he [the other witness] was in every respect Jeremiah.[4] For the very word that was given to him is witness of this: "Before I formed you in the womb of your mother, I knew you; and I appointed you prophet to the nations."[5] However, he was never a prophet among the nations, and so, since the two words are divine, it is necessary that what God promised, that he also demonstrate, namely, that he be a prophet among the nations. He

---

Revelation 11 [1]This tradition concerning the writing of John's Gospel is similar to that in the Muratorian Canon (c. 200). There we are told that "when his fellow disciples and bishops urged him," John told them to fast for three days. On that evening it was revealed to Andrew that while all the disciples were to take part in the gospel, John was to write everything down in his own name. Jerome is aware of the same tradition (*On Illustrious Men* 9.1 [FC 100:19]). [2]Victorinus takes *mensura* to be the equivalent of *regula* (*fidei*). [3]Jerome's rendering of Victorinus has *hunc esse manum dei et verbum patris*, identifying Christ to be the "hand of God and the Word of the Father." [4]For the view that Jeremiah would return to earth at the end of time, see 2 Esd 2:17-18 (with Isaiah) and Pseudo-Tertullian *Carmen adversus Marcionem* 3.179-89 (CCL 2.1439; on Elijah, 3.149-50). [5]Jer 1:5.

says that these are "two lampstands" and "two olive trees." And therefore he has encouraged you, that you might understand here what you perhaps did not understand when you read it elsewhere, for in Zechariah, one of the twelve prophets, it is written:

4. "These are the two olive trees and the two lampstands that stand in the presence of the Lord of the earth,"[6] that is, in paradise. It is necessary that after many plagues have come to the world these be killed by the antichrist, who, it says, is "the beast that ascends from the bottomless pit." That he will ascend from the pit is attested by many witnesses. For Isaiah says, "Behold, Assyria is a cypress on Mount Lebanon."[7] "Assyria" is a deeply rooted "cypress," high and full of branches, that is, Assyria possesses a numerous people. It is "on Mount Lebanon," that is, a kingdom among kingdoms. It is "beautiful in its offshoots," that is, it is strong in its armies. "Water nourishes it," it says;[8] that is, there are many thousands of persons who will be submitted to it. "The abyss increased him," that is, it vomited him forth. For Ezekiel often speaks in such words.

Paul also gives witness that the antichrist is in a kingdom among kingdoms and was among the Caesars. He writes to the Thessalonians, "If only he restrains, who is seen to be restraining, until he be taken from the way. And then he will appear whose coming is like the activity of Satan with signs and deceptive works."[9] And that they might know that he was to come who was then emperor, he adds, "he is already working the mystery of wickedness."[10] That is, he is working in a mysterious way that wickedness that he will do. But he will not be aroused to this work by his own strength or by that of his father but by the command of God. And for this reason Paul said, "Therefore, since they did not receive the love of God, God sends on

them a spirit of error, that all of them might be persuaded by delusion, who were not persuaded by the truth."[11] Isaiah says, "Darkness arose on them who were awaiting the light."[12]

5. The Revelation shows that these prophets are killed by him. Yet, they will rise on the fourth day lest anyone be found to be equal to God. However, because of the deeds of a persecuting people, he calls Jerusalem "Sodom" and "Egypt." Therefore, it is important that we follow diligently and with the greatest attention the prophetic announcement and understand that the Holy Spirit announces and anticipates and moves through to the end of time in a disconnected way. The Spirit repeats what occurred in former times, and he presents as though it occurred at several times that which will occur at the same time. You will fall into a profound confusion unless you understand that what is said several times will not occur in the future several times. Therefore, the interpretation of the following passages will consist in the attempt to understand not so much the sequence of the sayings as the sequence of their meaning.

6. That "the temple of God that is in heaven was opened" signifies the appearance of our Lord. For the temple of God is his Son, as he said: "Destroy this temple, and in three days I will raise it up." And when the Jews said, "It was built in forty-six years," the Evangelist said, "He was speaking of the temple of his body."[13] The "ark of the covenant" is the preaching of the gospel and mercy for sins and everything whatsoever that has come with him. That, he says, appeared.

REVELATION 12

1. "A woman clothed with the sun, with the moon under her feet, having a crown of twelve

---

[6]See Zech 4:11-14. [7]Ezek 31:3. Victorinus wrongly attributes this passage to Isaiah. [8]Ezek 31:4. [9]2 Thess 2:7-9. [10]2 Thess 2:7. [11]See 2 Thess 2:10-12. [12]See Is 59:9. Victorinus is the first to cite this text in relation to the coming of antichrist. [13]Jn 2:19-21.

stars, and giving birth in her anguish." This is the ancient church of the patriarchs and the prophets and the holy apostles. For they experience the groans and torments of their desire until that which was long since promised was fulfilled out of their own people and according to their own flesh.[1] That the woman was "clothed with the sun" signifies the hope of the resurrection and the promise of glory. The "moon" refers to the death[2] of the bodies of the saints on account of their debt to death, although the moon can never fully disappear. For just as the life of people is diminished and so again is increased, so also the hope of the sleeping is never utterly extinguished, as some think, but in their darkness they will have light as of the moon. The "crown of twelve stars" indicates the crown of the fathers[3] from whom the Spirit[4] was to assume flesh, according to the birth of the flesh.

2. "The red dragon stood expecting to devour her son when she had delivered him." This is the devil, namely, that fugitive angel[5] who thought that the destruction of all people could be equally accomplished through death. However, he who was not born from seed owed no debt to death, and for this reason the devil was not able to devour him, that is, to subject him to death. For indeed, the devil had come to him intending to tempt him as man. But when he had discovered that he was not whom he thought, "he departed from him," it says, "until an opportune time."[6]

3. "And he was caught up to the throne of God." We read of this in the Acts of the Apostles. For as he was speaking with the disciples, he was caught up into heaven.[7] "And he

is to rule all nations with a rod of iron," which is the sword. For under the subterfuge of the antichrist all the nations are going to be arrayed against the saints. By the sword, it says, both will fall.

It says that the dragon was the color of red, that is, of scarlet, for the fruit of his work has given him such a color. For he was a murderer from the beginning,[8] and everywhere he has oppressed the whole race of people, not so much by the debt of death as through all kinds of miseries.

The "seven heads" are the seven Roman kings from whom the antichrist comes, as we will mention in due course. The "ten horns" are the ten kings at the end of time, and we will expound on them more fully there.

4. "The woman flew into the desert with the assistance of the wings of a great eagle," that is, of two prophets. This is the whole catholic church, in which at the end of time 144,000 will come to faith through Elias the prophet. There at the coming of our Lord, Jesus Christ, he will find another, second people. To be sure, the Lord Christ says in the Gospel, "Then let those who are in Judea flee to the mountains,"[9] that is, as many as have been gathered in Judea, let them go to that place that has been prepared "that they might be nourished there for three years and six months from the presence of the devil." The "wings of a great eagle" are two prophets, Elias and the prophet who will be with him.

5. "The water that the serpent sent from his mouth" signifies that at his order an army will follow him. However, that "the earth opened its mouth and devoured the water" shows that the

---

Revelation 12   [1]According to Victorinus, this woman is the church of the old covenant, which lived expectantly for the fulfillment of the promise. [2]Translating *casus* that refers to an accident, usually a misfortune. [3]Presumably the twelve patriarchs. The Christ would come from Israel. [4]MS A and the recension of Jerome, adopted by Dulaey (SC 423:100), read "Christ." "Spirit" is to be adopted as the more original and primitive reading. It does not refer to the Holy Spirit but to the deity of Christ, the divine Son incarnate. The reading "Christ" arose, most likely, for reasons of orthodox clarity. [5]Translating *angelus refuga*. [6]Lk 4:13. At the temptation in the desert, Satan learned of Christ's true identity (also Irenaeus *Against Heresies* 5.21-22 [ANF 1:549-50]). [7]Acts 1:9. [8]Jn 8:44. [9]Lk 21:21.

woman has been delivered from her persecutors. Although it shows her giving birth and after the birth shows her fleeing, these things did not occur at one time. That Christ was born we know, and that times have intervened, but that she should flee from the presence of the dragon, to the present time this has not happened.

6. Then it says, "There was war in heaven. Michael and his angels fought with the dragon, and the dragon and his angels fought, and there was found for him no place in heaven. And the great dragon was thrown out, that ancient serpent, and he fell to the earth." This is the beginning of the coming of the antichrist. However, beforehand Elijah must preach, and there must be peaceful times. And when the three years and six months of the preaching of Elijah is ended, the dragon[10] along with all the apostate angels is to be thrown out from heaven, where he had the power of ascent until that time. And that the antichrist is to be aroused from hell, also Paul the apostle says: "Unless the man of sin shall come first, the son of perdition, the adversary, who will exalt himself over everything that is called and is worshiped as God."[11]

7. That "the tail of the dragon swept down a third of the stars" may be understood in a twofold way. Many understand this to mean that he was able to seduce a third of the believers. However, this may be more truthfully understood to mean that he seduced a third of the angels who were subordinated to him while he was yet prince and that they fell when he toppled from his position. Therefore, to return to that which we were speaking about above, the Revelation says, "He stood on the sand of the sea."

REVELATION 13 AND 17

1. "And I saw a beast rising out of the sea, like a leopard." This passage indicates that the kingdom of that time, the kingdom of the antichrist, will be commingled with a variety of nations and peoples. "Its feet were like the feet of a bear," that is, they were of a strong and utterly filthy beast. He speaks of the leaders of this kingdom as his "feet." And "its mouth was like the mouths of lions." This means that the beast is armed by teeth intended for blood.[1] For the "mouth" is his command and his tongue, which proceed only for the purpose of the shedding of blood.

2. "The seven heads are seven mountains on which the woman is seated," that is, the city of Rome. "They are also seven kings, five of whom have fallen; one is, the other has not yet come, and when he comes he must remain only a little while." "And the beast that you saw belongs to the seven but is an eighth." This must be understood in terms of the time when the Apocalypse was written, for Domitian was Caesar at that time. However, before him there was Titus, his brother, and Vespasian, their father, also Otho, Vitellius and Galba.[2] These are the five who have fallen. "One is," it says. This is Domitian, in whose reign the Apocalypse was written. "The other has not yet come." This refers to Nerva, who, "when he comes, he must remain only a little while," for he did not complete even two years as Caesar.

"And the beast that you saw," it says, "belongs to the seven." This refers to Nero, who reigned before these kings. "But it is an eighth," it says, since when he will afterward arrive, he assumes the eighth position. And

---

[10]MS A, adopted by Hausleiter (CSEL 49:114) reads "antichrist." Hausleiter defends the reading by remarking that the devil could be identified with the antichrist. However, the recension of Jerome reads *eum* ("him"), clearly referring to the great dragon of Rev 12:7-9. Dulaey follows Jerome and rightly says that for Victorinus the dragon is the devil (SC 423:104, 193-94). [11]2 Thess 2:3-4. **Revelation 13 and 17** [1]Adopting the reading of Dulaey (SC 423:104, 194). Hausleiter reads "armed and wet with blood" (CSEL 49:116). [2]Victorinus does not give the correct order of these three short-lived emperors. Jerome corrects the order: Vitellius, Otho, Galba.

since with his coming the consummation will occur, it adds, "and it goes to perdition." For "ten kings have received royal power." When Nero moves from the east, these will be sent[3] by the city of Rome with their armies. He calls these "ten horns" also "ten diadems." And Daniel also gives this revelation, "three of the first will be rooted up," that is, three of these chieftains will be killed by the antichrist. And the remaining seven will give him "glory and honor and kingdom and power." Concerning these it says, "these will hate the harlot," speaking here of the city, "and they will devour her flesh with fire."

3. "One of its heads was mortally wounded, but its mortal wound was healed."[4] He is referring here to Nero. For it is a well-known fact that when the army sent by the Senate was following him, he cut his own throat.[5] And he is the one whom, when he has been brought to life again, God will send as a king worthy of those who are worthy of him, namely, the Jews and those who persecute Christ, and he will send him as a christ such as the persecutors and the Jews deserve. And since he will bear another name, he will also undertake another life, so that they [the Jews] might receive him as the Christ.[6] For Daniel said, "he will not know the desire of women"—he who himself is the most impure!—"and he will know no god of his fathers."[7] To be sure, he would not be able to seduce the people of the circumcision were he not to pose as a defender of the law. Finally, he will urge the saints, if he proves able to seduce them, to accept nothing other than circumcision. And so at last he will create a trust in himself, so that he will

be called "Christ" by them. That he will come forth from Hades, we have already mentioned through the words of Isaiah, "water nourished him, and the deep set him on high."[8] Nonetheless, whoever should come having changed his name, the Holy Spirit says, "his number is six hundred and sixty-six."[9] This number must be interpreted according to the Greek letters.[10]

4. "Another great beast rose out of the earth." This is the false prophet who will do signs and portents and false prodigies before him in the presence of people. It says that he has "horns like a lamb" because he has the form of a righteous man and that he "speaks like a dragon" because he is full of the malice of the devil. He will perform his works in the presence of people, so that even the dead seem to rise again, for through apostate angels even magicians do such things in front of people. And he will even see to it that a golden image of the antichrist is placed in the temple at Jerusalem, and the apostate angels will enter there and from there issue voices and oracles.

And he himself will cause "both slave and free to receive a mark on their foreheads or on their right hands"—namely, the number of his name—"so that no one can buy or sell unless he has the mark." Daniel had already spoken of this destruction of people and this contempt of God and this abomination, saying, "And he will place an image in his temple between the mountain of the sea and the two seas,"[11] that is, at Jerusalem, and then he will place here his golden image, just as King Nebuchadnezzar had done.[12] And the Lord recalls this to all the churches when he speaks of the last times: "When you see the

---

[3]All MSS have the singular. Both Hausleiter and Dulaey emend to the plural; the ten kings will be sent by Rome. [4]Victorinus reads *occisum*, not *quasi occisum*. He believed that Nero had once died but was to be revived in the future. [5]See Suetonius *Nero* 49. [6]The Jews will mistake the antichrist for the expected Christ because he will promote circumcision and the law. [7]Dan 11:37. [8]Ezek 31:4. [9]MS A does not have the number. Both Hausleiter and Dulaey adopt it from the Jerome recension. Victorinus makes no attempt to give a name to the number 666. The later recensions of Jerome, however, include certain traditional guesses: Teitan, Antemos, Diclux. [10]For early reflections on the number, see Irenaeus *Against Heresies* 5.30.1, 3 (ANF 1:558-60); Hippolytus *On the Antichrist* 50 (ANF 5:215). [11]Dan 11:45. [12]See Dan 3:1. In erecting an image of himself, Nebuchadnezzar became a type of the antichrist.

contempt of turning away[13] spoken of by the prophet Daniel, standing in the holy place, where it ought not, let the reader understand."[14] It is said to be "contempt" when God is provoked because idols are being worshiped. On the other hand, it is said to be a "turning away" when unstable people, seduced by false signs and wonders, are turned away from their salvation.

REVELATION 14 AND 17

1. The "angel flying in midheaven" which he said that he saw we have above[1] interpreted to be that very Elijah who precedes the kingdom of the antichrist. By "another angel who was following" he indicates that prophet who was his companion in preaching. And because, as we have said, the lieutenants of the antichrist conspire together in order to capture this city, the great Babylon, he has testified of its downfall.

2. He says, "Come, I will show you the damnation of the harlot who is seated on many waters. And I saw," it says, "a woman drunk from the blood of the saints and from the blood of the witnesses of Jesus Christ." For all the saints have suffered martyrdom because of a decree of the Senate of this city,[2] and although tolerance is proclaimed, it is she who has given to all nations every law against the preaching of the faith.

I saw "a woman is seated on a scarlet beast." This is she who is responsible for murders, and she has the image of the devil. And there also are these "heads," which we have already mentioned and explained. Because of the dis-

persion of the peoples, in the Apocalypse she is called "Babylon," as does Isaiah.[3] However, Ezekiel calls her "Sor."[4] And if one would compare what is said of Sor and what the Apocalypse and Isaiah say about Babylon, one would discover that they are the same.

3. When it says, "Put in your sharp sickle and gather the clusters of grapes,"[5] it speaks of the nations that are going to perish at the coming of the Lord. To be sure, here it shows this through many images, but the end of the kingdom of the antichrist and the appearance of the kingdom of the saints will occur at the same time at the coming of the Lord.[6]

REVELATION 19

1. It shows "a white horse and him who sat on it," namely, our Lord coming with his celestial army to establish his kingdom. At his coming all the nations will be gathered and will be slain with the sword. Those among them who are more noble will be preserved in order to serve the saints,[1] and it will be necessary that these at the end of time, when the kingdom of the saints is ended, before the judgment and when the devil is again released, be killed. The prophets prophesy about all these things in a similar manner.

REVELATION 20

1. Everyone should know that the "scarlet devil" and all of his rebellious angels are shut up in the Tartarus of Gehenna[1] at the Lord's coming, and after one thousand years they are

[13]Translating *aspernationem eversionis* (cf. *Vetus Latina*). [14]Mt 24:15. **Revelation 14 and 17** [1]Apparently referring to his comments on Rev 12:7. [2]Victorinus is probably referring to the persecution under Decius. See also Commodian *Carmen Apologeticum* 823, 851. [3]Is 21:9. See Gen 11:9. Babylon is taken to be derived from "Babel," the confusion of tongues. [4]Ezek 26–28. "Sor" (LXX Σορ) is the Hebrew name for Tyre. [5]Rev 14:18. [6]Hausleiter notes that the comments of Victorinus on Rev 14 and Rev 17 end at this point and that his comments on Rev 15 are also missing (CSEL 49:134, 136). The recension of Jerome contains comments on Rev 14:19-20 and on Rev 15:1-2 (see Hausleiter, CSEL 49:135, 137; Dulaey, SC 423:112 **Revelation 19** [1]See Is 60:10; 61:5; Irenaeus *Against Heresies* 5.35.1 (ANF 1:565). **Revelation 20** [1]See 2 Pet 2:4-5. The phrase "Tartarus of Gehenna" is a redundancy, Tartarus coming from Greek mythology and Gehenna coming from the Hebrew.

released because of the nations who will have served the antichrist so that they alone might perish who will have merited such a punishment. Thereupon the universal judgment will occur. And therefore it says, "The dead who are written in the book of life came to life, and they will reign with Christ a thousand years. This is the first resurrection. Blessed and holy is he who shares in the first resurrection.[2] Over such the second death has no power." Concerning this first resurrection he says, "And I saw the Lamb standing and with him—that is, standing with him[3]—144,000."[4] He is speaking of those from among the Jews who will come to believe at the end of time through the preaching of Elijah and who, the Spirit testifies, are chaste not only in body but also in their speech.[5] And therefore, it is mentioned above that the twenty-four elders had said, "We give thanks to you, Lord God, that you have begun to reign, and the nations have become enraged."[6]

2. At the time of this first resurrection will also be that future, beautiful city that this writing has described. Also Paul spoke in this manner to the church in Macedonia concerning this first resurrection: "For this we declare to you," he says, "by the word of God, that at the trumpet of God the Lord himself will descend from heaven to arouse the dead from sleep. And the dead in Christ will rise first; then we who are alive shall be caught up together with them in the clouds to meet the Lord in the air, and so we shall always be with the Lord."[7] We have heard that he speaks of a trumpet. We observe that in another place the apostle mentions another trumpet. He says to the Corinthians, "At the last trumpet the dead will rise"—they become immortal— "and we shall be changed."[8] He says that the

dead will rise immortal in order to suffer their punishments; however, it is clear that we will be changed and clothed in glory. When, therefore, we hear that there is a "last trumpet," we must understand that there has also been a first trumpet. Now these are the two resurrections. Therefore, however many shall not rise previously in the first resurrection and reign with Christ over the world—over all the nations—they will rise at the last trumpet after the thousand years, that is, at the final resurrection among the impious, the sinners and those guilty in various ways. Rightly, then, does the passage continue by saying, "Blessed and holy is he who shares in the first resurrection; over such the second death has no power." Now, the second death is damnation in hell.

REVELATION 21

1. At the time of the kingdom and of the first resurrection, the holy city will appear, which, it says, will come down from heaven. It will be foursquare and decorated with jewels of different value, color and kind, and it will be like pure gold, that is, clear and transparent. It says that its street is paved with crystal and that the river of life flows through the middle, as do fountains of the waters of life. The tree of life produces different fruits each month. There will be there no light from the sun, since there is a more outstanding glory. For, it says, the Lamb—that is, God—will be its light.

2. Each of its gates are from a single pearl. There are three gates on each side, and these gates are not closed but open. The Scripture shows extensively that the kings of every region and nation, who are its servants, will bring their wealth into the city. It is speaking of

---

[2]See also Irenaeus *Against Heresies* 5.34.2 (ANF 1:564). [3]The word *standing* in the vision of the 144,000 convinces Victorinus that it is a vision of the resurrection of the saints from the dead. [4]Rev 14:1. [5]Victorinus is commenting on Rev 14:4-6. [6]See Rev 11:17-18. [7]1 Thess 4:15-17. [8]1 Cor 15:52.

the subduing of the last nations, of which we have already spoken. However, "city" is not to be understood in a manner such as we know. For without a guide we are unable to conceive of anything grander and larger than what we have heard and seen. But here "city" refers to every region of the eastern provinces that were promised to the patriarch Abraham. It says, "Look into the heaven from the place in which you are now standing"—that is, "from the great river Euphrates to the river of Egypt"—"all the land that you see I will give to you and to your seed."[1] Then the Holy Spirit said, "He shall have dominion from sea to sea"—that is, from the Red Sea, which is in Arabia, to the Sea of the North, which is the Sea of Phoenicia—"and to the ends of the earth,"[2] that is, the regions of great Syria. Therefore, it is manifest that all of these regions will be made level[3] and cleansed at the coming of the Lord, and that when the splendor comes down from heaven as a cloud, they will be covered all around with a light from above that surpasses the splendor of the sun.

3. For the Holy Spirit also spoke through Isaiah the following words: "As with bright smoke in a flaming fire it will be covered with all glory."[4] And in another place he says, "Shine, O Jerusalem, for your light has come, and the glory of the Lord has risen on you. For the sun shall not shine on you by day nor the moon by night. For the Lord, your God, will be your everlasting light."[5] And David said, "There will be a strong support on the earth on the tops of the mountains, and its fruit will be exalted beyond that of Lebanon, and they will blossom forth from the city like the grass of the earth."[6] Moreover, Daniel said that the stone cut out without hands had struck the statue made up of four elements—that is, gold and silver, bronze and iron and at its extremity

clay—and that, after it had reduced the statue to dust, the stone had itself become a great mountain and filled all the earth.[7] And Daniel interpreted the dream for the king and said, "You are the head of gold, you and your house. Another kingdom shall arise, inferior to you; and there will be a third kingdom that will rule over all the earth. And there will be a fourth kingdom, very strong and powerful as is iron that subdues all things and cuts down every tree. And at the end of time, even as clay is mixed with iron, people will be mixed together and will not be in harmony or be of the same mind. And in these times the Lord God will raise up another kingdom, which the saints of the Most High God will receive. And no other people shall overcome this kingdom. For God will smite and overcome all the kingdoms of the earth, but this kingdom will remain forever."[8]

4. Also Paul makes mention of this kingdom when he says to the Corinthians, "He must reign until he has put his enemies under his feet."[9] In this kingdom the saints are going to say, "I have rejoiced!" just as we have heard.[10] And in this same kingdom one will find those who preserve an intact faith, those of whom he says, "they stand on the sea of glass, with harps and bowls."[11] That is to say, they are firmly established on their baptism, and with their confession in their mouth, they shall rejoice there.

5. In this kingdom Christ promised to his servants, "Whoever shall have left father or mother or brother or sister for my name's sake, he will receive as a reward a hundredfold now, and in the future he will possess eternal life."[12] In this kingdom those who have been defrauded of their goods for the name of the

---

Revelation 21   [1]Gen 13:14-15; 15:18. [2]Ps 72:8 (71:8 LXX). [3]See Is 40:4. [4]Is 4:5. [5]Is 60:1, 19, 20. [6]Ps 72:16 (71:16 LXX). [7]Dan 2:32-35. [8]See Dan 2:32-45. [9]1 Cor 15:25. [10]See Ps 48:8 (47:9 LXX); Rev 19:7. [11]Rev 15:2. [12]Mt 19:26. See also Irenaeus *Against Heresies* 5.33.2 (ANF 1:562).

Lord,[13] also the many who have been killed by every kind of crime and imprisonment—for before the coming of the Lord, the holy prophets were stoned, killed and cut in half[14]—will receive their consolation, that is, their crowns and celestial rewards. In this kingdom the Lord promised that he would compensate for the years in which the grasshopper and locust and corruption destroyed.[15] In this kingdom the whole of creation will be preserved and reestablished and will, by the command of God, bring forth good things within it. Here the saints will receive "gold for bronze and silver for iron and precious stones."[16] In this kingdom "he will give over to them the wealth of the sea and power of the nations."[17] In this kingdom "they will be called priests of the Lord and ministers of God," just as they were called impious.[18] In this kingdom "they will drink wine and be anointed with oil and be given over to joy."[19]

6. Before his passion, the Lord made mention of this kingdom when he said to the apostles, "I shall not drink again of the fruit of this vine, until I shall drink it new with you in the future kingdom."[20] This is the "hundredfold," which is ten thousand more or less. And when he says that there will be stones that are different in kind and color, he is speaking of people, but he is also indicating the very precious variety of faith that exists in each person. The gates made of pearl refer to the apostles. And they will not be closed, it says, for through them grace has been given that will never be closed. In this kingdom they will see face to face,[21] and "one has not inquired after another."[22] And the names of the patriarchs and of the apostles shall be on the walls and the gates. We have already discussed and interpreted the twenty-four elders. And of those who will have reigned in this kingdom it is said, "They shall judge the world."[23]

---

[13]A common millenarian view. See Irenaeus *Against Heresies* 5.32.1 (ANF 1:561). [14]See Heb 11:36-37. [15]The millennial kingdom will be one of abundance and prosperity. [16]See Is 60:17. [17]See Is 60:5. [18]See Is 61:6. [19]See Amos 6:6; Is 25:6-7. [20]Mt 26:29. Irenaeus also applies this passage to the millennial kingdom (*Against Heresies* 5.33.2 [ANF 1:562]). [21]1 Cor 13:12. [22]See Is 34:16 LXX. [23]1 Cor 6:2.

APRINGIUS OF BEJA

Explanation of the Revelation by the Most Learned Man, Apringius, Bishop of the Church at Pax [Julia]

The weakness of our humanity cannot explain the twofold history of the divine law and expound it by the mystery of the twofold sacrament[1] unless it employ the mode of speaking and the language of expression from the author of the law himself, the Lord Jesus Christ. Therefore, as I undertake to interpret the Revelation of Saint John, I call on the Holy Spirit who dwelled in him that he who willed to reveal to him the secrets that were concealed might open to us the door of our inner mind, so that we might without fault discourse on that which is written and, God teaching us, truthfully draw out the meanings.

REVELATION 1

[1:1] The beginning of the book that now concerns us is written as follows: *The revelation of Jesus Christ, which God gave him to show to his servants what must soon take place.* From this we learn that this book is called an apocalypse, that is, "revelation," which manifests those secrets that are hidden and unknown to the senses, and that unless Christ himself reveals them, he who perceives the revelation will not have the strength to understand what he sees. And what does it say? "The revelation of Jesus Christ, which God gave him," that is, to John, the most blessed of the apostles. "To show to his servants": that he might explain those things that he had learned and that he might reveal those things that he had explained. "What must soon take place." He signifies that the inner meaning of the times and that which

is intelligible to the senses will be completed by a rapid movement.

And he made it known through his messenger[1] to his servant John. The revelation is not grasped by thought, nor is it written by some false-speaking poets, but it comes "through a messenger," an envoy of his truth, "to his servant," John, the most tested and most holy of all the apostles.

[1:2] *Who bore witness to the Word of God.* This is to say that he who proclaimed the Son of God and maintained his divinity also gave testimony concerning our Lord, Jesus Christ, whatever he had seen in him and had heard from him. And so in his letter he writes, "What we have seen and what we have heard and what our hands have touched concerning the Word of Life, and the Life was present among us, and so we have made it known to you."[2]

[1:3] *Blessed is he who reads and he who hears the words of the prophecy and keeps those things which are written in it.* He wishes to make clear that the reading does not accomplish the obedience of the commandments, nor does the hearing display the completion of an accomplished deed. Rather, this alone is perfection, that you perform with understanding what you read and what you hear. *The time*, it says, *is short.* For those who accomplish these things, he does not prolong the time of recompense, but it says that the gift of the divine reward is near.

Introduction   [1]The Latin reads *duplici sacramenti mysterio.* The twofold sacrament that guides the explanation of the Revelation is the mystery of the divine and human natures of Christ.   **Revelation 1**   [1]"Messenger" translates the Latin word *angelus.*   [2]See 1 Jn 1:1-2.

[1:4] Then he begins his discourse and says, *John to the seven churches which are in Asia.* Could such a great man have desired to reveal the mystery of the divine revelation to one province only and not to all the nations, and so have directed his writings to such a small number of churches in one province? For "from the rising of the sun to its setting, the name of the Lord is worthy of praise."[3] And "in every place a pure offering is sacrificed and offered."[4] And of what importance are the people of Asia that they alone deserve to receive the apostolic revelation? However, there is a mystery in the number and a sacrament in the name of the province. First, let us discuss the meaning of the number, because both the number six and the number seven are always used in the law with a mystical meaning. "For God made heaven and earth in six days, and on the seventh day he rested from his works, and on it," it says, "they shall again enter into my rest."[5] The number seven, therefore, signifies the period of the present life, so that the apostle is not merely writing to seven churches or to that world in which he was then present, but it is understood that he is giving these writings to all future ages, even to the consummation of the world. Therefore, he mentions the number in a most holy manner, and he names Asia, which means "elevated" or "walking," indicating that celestial fatherland that we call the catholic church. For exalted by the Lord and always moving toward the things that are above, it is the church that advances by spiritual exercises and is always desirous of the things of heaven.

Grace to you and peace from him who is and who was and who is to come. As he declared his own name at the beginning of the writing, where he said, "John to the seven churches which are in Asia," so in a similitude of words he confirms most evidently that he is John by saying, "who is, who was, and who is to come." For in God there is always being. Therefore it was said to Moses, "I am who am,"[6] and the apostle himself says in the Gospel, "In the beginning was the Word, and the Word was with God, and the Word was God; he was in the beginning with God."[7] By this he indicates that the Word exceeds every beginning because he was in the beginning, nor does he have a beginning because he was with God, nor will he receive an end because he was God. Rather, he will remain forever because he was in the beginning with God, and he indicates that it is this one who is to come.

And from the seven spirits who are before the throne. Here is that mystery of the number seven that is everywhere indicated. Here the seven spirits are introduced, which are one and the same Spirit, that is, the Holy Spirit, who is one in name, sevenfold in power, invisible and incorporeal, and whose form is impossible to comprehend. The great Isaiah revealed the number of its sevenfold powers when he wrote: "the Spirit of wisdom and understanding"—that through understanding and wisdom he might teach that he is the creator of all things—"the Spirit of counsel and might"—who conceived these things that he might create them—"the Spirit of knowledge and piety"—who governs the creation with piety by the exercise of his knowledge and whose purposes are always according to mercy—"the Spirit of the fear of the Lord"—by whose gift the fear of the Lord is manifested to rational creatures.[8] This is itself the sacred character of the Spirit who is to be worshiped that includes ineffable praise and does not indicate any form of nature.

[1:5] *And from Jesus Christ, who is the faithful witness, the firstborn of the dead and the ruler of the kings on earth.* Since earlier he had recalled that Word who, before the assumption of the

---

[3]Ps 113:3 (112:3 LXX). [4]Mal 1:11. [5]Apringius gives a conflated quotation from Ex 20:11; Heb 4:4-5; see also Gen 2:2. [6]Ex 3:14. [7]Jn 1:1-2. [8]Is 11:2-3. Victorinus of Petovium also refers to this passage of Isaiah to claim that the sevenfold spirits are the one Holy Spirit.

flesh, was with the Father in glory, he of necessity adds the humanity of the assumed flesh when he says, "And from Jesus Christ, who is the faithful witness." For through the humanity that he had assumed, he gave a faithful testimony to his divinity, and by his passion and blood he interceded for our sins and cleansed us from all unrighteousness. And so, for the sake of our frailty and weakness he brought a faithful witness to God the Father "with whom there is no variation or shadow due to change."[9] He is "the firstborn of the dead" because he rose as the first from the dead, since death could not hold him. For this reason the apostle also says, "Christ the first-fruit, then those who are of Christ at his presence."[10] That is, then we who have been named "Christian" through baptism shall rise from death, being brought to life again at his second coming. And therefore he is called "firstborn" or "first-fruit of the dead," because he himself, as the first, returned to heaven, having conquered the lower regions. He is "the ruler of the kings on earth," because he is the King of kings and the Lord of lords.[11]

Who loved us, for we did not receive the recompense of God's love by loving God, but "he himself first loved us,"[12] that for the sake of our weakness he might become man and receive the form of a servant.[13] *And he has washed us from our sins by his blood.* He indicates the effect of his love and charity, for although there was in him no cause of death, nor did he possess a mortal nature, yet he willed to die for us, and for this reason it says "he washed us from our sins by his blood."

[1:6] *And he made us a kingdom, priests to his God and Father.* Because he suffered and rose from the dead for us, he made us to be a kingdom that we might merit to be priests of God the Father. For he makes us to be a kingdom,

since he suffered and rose again. *To him be glory forever and ever. Amen.* He offers eternal praise and everlasting glory to God, the creator of all things.

[1:7] *Behold, he is coming with the clouds of heaven, and every eye will see him, even those who pierced him.* The seer has mentioned his death and the results of his death and the cleansing of sins, as well as his resurrection and the restoration of all things through him and the glory and praise given to God the Father almighty. Therefore he now speaks of his second coming that will be in the same form and in the same body in which he suffered, died and rose again. But he will come in divine power, and not as before in human weakness, and he who showed himself for the witness of the true man that he assumed will appear to be seen by his persecutors. As Zechariah said, "They shall look on him whom they have pierced, and they shall mourn for him, as over an only child."[14] So also, here it says *all tribes of the earth will wail on account of him. Even so. Amen,* which means "certainly" or "truly." And this is said to show the one person of both God and the assumed man.

[1:8] And since the substance of his humanity has been made plain, he announces the glory of his divine substance and speaks the words of the Lord himself, saying, *"I am the Alpha and the Omega, the Beginning and the End," says the Lord God, who is and who was and who is to come, the Almighty.* Although our authorities have nicely and usefully explained this matter by noting that it was in the form of a *peristera*,[15] that is, of a "dove,"[16] in which the Holy Spirit is said to have appeared when the Lord was baptized in the Jordan by John, son of Zacharias—the word *peristera* in Greek reckoning gives the number 800, which is the

---

[9]Jas 1:17. [10]1 Cor 15:23. [11]See Rev 19:16. [12]1 Jn 4:19. [13]See Phil 2:7. [14]Zech 12:10. [15]Apringius transliterates the Greek word περιστερά ("dove"). [16]Here Apringius uses the Latin word *columba* ("dove").

value of Omega; and the word moves toward Alpha which has the value of one; and so the word suggests the deity of the Holy Spirit in the unity of the Trinity—may the Holy Spirit himself look with favor on us, that also we might be worthy to add something to our authorities. We ought with wisdom to consider why it is that the Truth himself mentions these letters from the alphabet.

For the figure of the letter A itself, both in the Greek and in the Latin, is formed by three marks drawn in equal length. And so, our commentators have reasonably claimed that this suggests the unity of the deity. In Greek, the Ω is written with three curved marks that lie along the bottom and in part are raised. In the Latin, the letter is closed in the roundness of a circle.[17] Now, both in this enclosure of the circle and in that raising of what lies at the bottom, that divinity is declared that contains and protects all things. And so, regarding the explanation of these letters, they are the beginnings of knowledge and a certain means for leading the foolish to wisdom. Therefore, the A is the beginning of wisdom and reveals Wisdom himself, Christ, the Son of God. The Ω, which is at the end of the Greek alphabet and among us possesses a certain middle position,[18] signifies that the Lord Jesus Christ is himself the beginning and the end and the middle of wisdom, the mediator of God and humankind.

That he adds "the Beginning and the End" refers not only to the previous letters of the alphabet but also teaches the power of his greatness. For he is himself the Beginning of all things, and in him the destiny of all things is determined, because also through him that which is yet to be completed and that which is already completed is believed to be restored.

Just as he gave a beginning to the beginnings, so he might provide an end to our consummation itself. In this way the end itself might possess an ending and the consummation itself might possess a consummation. And so, in all things he might be what he always is, as the present Scripture says: "The Lord God says, who is and who was and who is to come, the Almighty."

Saint John wrote this at the beginning of his Revelation. Now another beginning begins, so that he might attain to the very order of the revelation by referring to the why, how, where, when and on which day all that which was spoken by the Lord shall be revealed. He declared what had been said to him and what Lord he had seen with manifold understanding, yet he does this in few words.

[1:9] And so he writes the beginning of the holy Revelation, so that he might address those to whom he speaks, saying, *I, John, your brother, who shares with you in Jesus the tribulation and the kingdom and the patient endurance, was on the island called Patmos on account of the word of God and the testimony of Jesus.* The ecclesiastical writers have taught that at the time of Claudius Caesar, when that famine that the prophet Agabus had announced in the Acts of the Apostles[19] would come in ten years time was at its height, that during that difficulty this same Caesar, impelled by his usual vanity, had instituted a persecution of the churches. It was during this time that he ordered John, the apostle of our Lord Jesus Christ, to be transported into exile, and he was taken to the island of Patmos, and while there he confirmed this writing.[20] That he might present the trials of suffering that he was bearing at that time, he

---

[17]Latin has no letter that strictly corresponds to the Greek omega. In Latin the omega is written with the letter O, hence the "roundness of a circle" of which Apringius speaks.   [18]In the Latin alphabet the letter O lies in the middle, while in the Greek alphabet the omega lies at the end. Apringius makes use of this relation between the omega of the Greek and the O of the Latin to claim that Christ is the end and the middle of wisdom.   [19]Acts 11:28.   [20]The last of the Julio-Claudian dynasty, Claudius was emperor of Rome during A.D. 41–54. The famine foretold by Agabus is usually dated to the year 45. According to the tradition of the "ecclesiastical writers," John was exiled to Patmos about 45, dating the Revelation much earlier than is usually the case. Apringius does not name the ecclesiastical writers.

recalls that he was a participant in suffering, and he then adds the kingdom to the suffering of tribulation, and because of the kingdom to be received he further adds patient endurance that he bore for the sake of Jesus. Then he makes known the place to which he had been exiled when he says, "I was on the island called Patmos." And by the words "on account of the word of God and the testimony of Jesus," he indicates the reason why he received this condemnation. He thus indicates that he had been deported to such sufferings of exile on account of the proclamation of the gospel and for the sake of a faithful witness that he had given to the people concerning the deity of our Lord.

[1:10] And while he was on that island, he says, *I was in the spirit on the Lord's day.* He says that he was taken up in the spirit, that is, that he was raised up to the secret things of God, in order that he might see those things that he was to speak. Moreover, he says that he did not enter into the heights of heaven in a bodily manner but that he entered in the spirit, recalling this word, "No one has ascended into heaven except he who has descended, namely, the Son of man, who is in heaven."[21] The holy apostle Paul says that he was taken up, but in what way? He says, "Whether in the body or out of the body, I do not know, God knows."[22] He writes that he had been taken up into ecstasy, in the spirit. But since the day of the Lord is mentioned in this passage, when he says that he had been taken up in the spirit, he is indicating that he had been cleansed of any work of a profane kind. For on the Lord's day the apostle could only devote himself to divine things and holy duties.

[1:11] *And I heard behind me a loud voice like a trumpet saying, "Write what you see in a book."* Concerning the preachers of the gospel, it is written, "Cry aloud, do not cease, lift up your voice as a trumpet."[23] And concerning the words "behind me" the prophet said, "And they shall hear a voice from behind of one teaching."[24] Let all humanity be exalted to whatever degree of sanctity, in comparison with the holy acts of God and with the divine words, it can by no means ever stand as an equal before his presence and face. But our flesh, weighed down by a certain weakness, is instructed, as it were, from behind by the words of God. Therefore, in saying "behind me" he indicates the weakness of his human nature. He heard "a loud voice like a trumpet." By its sound the divine speech teaches a certain greater wisdom, and by a fuller understanding it teaches a greater virtuousness and resonance.

"Write what you see in a book." From this it is understood that, while the divine speech is heard and the mysteries of the kingdom are penetrated, it is not only the ears that are opened but also the eyes, so that they might see that which is hidden and might behold that which is spiritual.[25] And whatever he sees, he is commanded to write down in a book. The Lord spoke of this book through the prophet, saying, "After those days, says the Lord, I will put my laws in their minds and I will write them on their hearts, and I will be their God and they shall be my people. And no longer shall each man teach his neighbor and each his brother, saying, 'Know the Lord' for they shall all know me, from the least of them to the greatest, for I will forgive their iniquity, and I will remember their sins no more."[26] This is the book in which the apostle is admonished to write what he sees, to impress on the hearts of the hearers or to retain in his own memory. Of this book the most blessed teacher of the Gentiles says, "You are our letter, written on your hearts, which is known and read by all men."[27]

---

[21]Jn 3:13. [22]2 Cor 12:2. [23]Is 58:1. [24]Is 30:21. [25]"Spiritual" translates the Latin *intellecta*, literally, that which is comprehended by the mind. [26]Jer 31:33-34. [27]2 Cor 3:2.

And whatever he will write, he is commanded to *send to the seven churches*. We have already said that he addressed one church that exists during the time of the whole world, that is, from that time when he spoke to the consummation of the world. Since he now mentions the names of these churches specifically, let us see what meanings they have. It says, *To Ephesus and to Smyrna and to Pergamum and to Thyatira and to Sardis and to Philadelphia and to Laodicea*. Did the perfection of the Christian religion only appear in these churches? Does not "their voice go out throughout the whole earth, and their words to the ends of the world"?[28] But there is a mighty mystery in the names, which we will examine and discuss to the extent that God allows.

Ephesus means "my will" or "my counsel." He wills that we know that the whole reality of our faith and the dignity of the catholic church is not to be ascribed to human merit, but they are the will of God and the disposition of the divine purpose.

Smyrna means "their song." And what else is the song of the perfect if not the celestial doctrine and the preaching of the gospel and the advance of the Christian religion, or the melodious confession of the catholic church?

Pergamum means "to him who divides their horns." This refers either to the insolence of the powers of the air or to the arrogance of the heretics. And he teaches that the pride of the powers is always to be separated and divided from the congregation of the church, for the horns are either power or arrogance.

He writes to Thyatira, that is, "enlightened." This signifies that, after the expulsion of heretical pride and after the defeat of temptations from the powers of the air, the holy church is deserving of the light of righteousness.

Sardis means the "beginning of beauty."

The church is seized by the sun of righteousness and is illumined by the light of truth, so that she might have the beginning of beauty, the Lord Jesus Christ, and might always shine in perpetual light.

Philadelphia means "preserving devotion to the Lord." After possessing the sun of righteousness, after the illumination of holiness, after the comeliness of holy beauty, the church rightly is devoted to the Lord and preserves herself by an inviolable observation of devotion.

Laodicea means either "a tribe beloved of the Lord" or, as some would have it, "a birth is expected." Both are meaningful, for she [the church] who has merited the beauty of faith and the sun of righteousness and knows that through faith the Lord cleaves to her might also be a tribe whom the Lord loves, who is both loved by the Lord and preserved by the Lord. Furthermore, the church might well await her own birth, either the regeneration of baptism or the glory of the resurrection, whenever she preserves herself in humility and patience.

The names of the church are divided by these stages; nor were the names of the cities written by the prophecy without purpose. For why would he, who has spoken to the whole world, write only to seven churches? It is so he understands that whenever he speaks, the Lord, by a sign of the celestial mystery, intends that by these seven elect names the church of the whole world is contained, and that he might make known both the mystic number and the dignity of the whole church.[29]

[1:12] *And I turned to see the voice that was speaking with me.* Human weakness, strengthened by divine teachings, turns its face. But he does not say "that I might see the face of him who is speaking with me," but he says "that I might see the voice," that is, that I might com-

---

[28]Ps 19:4 (18:5 LXX); Rom 10:18.   [29]Primasius gives the same spiritual meanings to the names of the seven cities (CCL 92:12-15).

prehend the mystery of the voice. For in the Lord mysteries are comprehended, but his face is not perceived.

And having turned, I saw seven golden lampstands. When I had comprehended the mystery of the voice, after the very first form of my turning, I saw seven golden lampstands. Resting on three arms, a lampstand raises the body of a single shaft, and on this shaft there is placed a lamp of light. "For no other foundation can any one lay than that which is laid, which is Jesus Christ,"[30] says the apostle, "from which the whole body, joined and knit together by every joint with which it is supplied, makes bodily growth and upbuilds itself in love, according to the work and ability of each member."[31] This is that branch of which it is said: "There shall come forth a branch from the stump of Jesse."[32] On this branch a light is placed, that is, the light of the catholic church is made ready, so that seized by the truth of his light, she might herself bring forth perpetual light, and marked by the manifestation of one faith, she might be exalted by the light of the divine majesty. That he speaks of "seven" indicates either that she possesses the sevenfold grace of the Holy Spirit or that she remains during the seven days of the world. That he mentions that the lampstands are gold signifies either the strength of the faith that is colored by the blood of Christ or the faith of the martyrs in the church, who were dipped in the red blood of suffering.

[1:13] *And in the midst of the seven golden lampstands, one like a son of man, clothed with a long robe.* Our Lord, Jesus Christ, dwells in signs and power in the midst of the lampstands, that is, in the midst of the churches in the form of his own manhood, which he willed to assume from the holy virgin for the sake of our weakness. "Clothed with a long robe," that is, with the robe of the priest-

hood, for as the apostle says, he is himself the "chief shepherd,"[33] and concerning him the teacher of the nations said, "For it was fitting that we should have such a high priest, holy, blameless, unstained, separated from sinners, exalted above the heavens."[34] *And with a golden girdle around his breast.* The breasts of the Lord are the holy teaching of the law and the gospel. This girding is a sign of the passion, concerning which the Lord spoke to Peter: "When you are old, another will gird you and lead you where you do not wish."[35] The "golden girdle" is his everlasting power, washed in the blood of the Lord's passion. There is a variety of this girdle in the diversity of powers, yet there is one power behind the multitude of wonders. Another interpretation: The golden girdle is the chorus of the saints, tested as gold through fire. Another: The golden girdle around the chest is the fervent conscience and the pure spiritual understanding refined as though by fire, and so it was given to the churches.

[1:14] *His head and his hair were white as white wool and as snow.* The head of Christ is God,[36] and he himself is white on account of the brightness of the purity of the Unbegotten and on account of the unmixed light of the Only-Begotten and on account of the pure radiance of the Holy Spirit and the immaculate glory of his righteousness. And not without reason is he called white, because he is compared with white wool and with snow on account of his tenderness, which he gives without ceasing to sinners. As it is written: "Though your sins are like scarlet, they shall be as white as snow; and though they are red as crimson, they shall become as wool."[37]

His eyes were like a flame of fire. On account of the ineffable foreknowledge of the judge and the unavoidable light of his eyes, he is rightly called a flaming fire. For it is written: "Our

[30]1 Cor 3:11. [31]Eph 4:16. [32]Is 11:1. [33]1 Pet 5:4. [34]Heb 7:26. [35]Jn 21:18. [36]1 Cor 11:3. [37]Is 1:18.

God is a consuming fire,"[38] that is, he is one who judges with certainty and looks into the heart. Here is another interpretation: The eyes of the Lord are the commandments of God that give light to those who believe but are a burning fire to those who do not believe.

[1:15] *His feet were like burnished bronze, as in a fiery furnace.* The feet are his human nature, which he possessed and which he assumed out of mercy for our salvation. For just as when copper ore is refined in a furnace there is no accretion or rusty buildup on the outside, so the most pure and perfect flesh of the assumed man, taken up by deity and remaining in deity, continues without any defect of human nature, without any guilt of the parent. Another interpretation: The feet are his apostles, who, forged by sufferings, have preached his word. For those through whom the preaching comes are rightly called "feet." And prophecy anticipated this by saying, "We will worship where his feet have stood."[39] And since they first stood where they also established the church, that is, in Judea, there all the saints are going to be gathered, and there they are going to worship their Lord.

And his voice was like the sound of many waters. The greatness of his teaching, the elegance of his voice and the blessed sweetness of his precepts are likened to the multitude of cascading waters. Concerning these waters it is written: "Thunder from a multitude of waters, the clouds gave forth a voice."[40] Therefore, we understand this water to be the divine decrees and the ordinance of the sacred law. Concerning these waters the most wise one said, "If the clouds are full of waters, they will pour them out on the earth."[41] This means that if the teachers have received the divine words, they will certainly dispense them to the people.

[1:16] *In his right hand he held seven stars.* His right hand is that multitude of whom it is written: "But the souls of the righteous are in the hand of the Lord."[42] He mentions seven and signifies without doubt those saints who from the beginning of this world and throughout the seven days in which the world exists until the consummation have stood steadfast and will stand steadfast in the right hand of our God and Lord. *From his mouth issued a sharp two-edged sword.* The apostle spoke about this sword: "The sword of the Spirit, which is the word of God."[43] And in another place: "The word of God is living and active, sharper than any two-edged sword, piercing to the division of soul and spirit, of joints and marrow, and discerning the thoughts and intentions of the heart."[44] Therefore, the sword of God is understood to be the commandments of his law and the divine teaching.

And his face was like the sun shining in full strength. His face is likened to the sun. However, often examples of lesser things are cited for the contemplation of greater things. For as the brightness of the sun, which does not come from itself but is made and continues by the divine direction, sends the ray of its splendor everywhere, so the face of God, although receiving nothing from outside, yet by the translucent power of its virtue possesses nothing dark, nothing obscure. Another interpretation: The brightness of which he spoke was his appearance, by which he spoke to people face to face. However, the glory of the sun is less than the glory of the Lord. Yet, because of the rising and setting and rising again of the sun, the Scripture makes an analogy between his face and the glory of the sun, since he was born and suffered and rose again.

[1:17] *When I saw him, I fell at his feet as though dead.* He mentioned earlier that he had turned, not to see a form but to see a voice. Here, having

---

[38]Heb 12:29. [39]Ps 131:7 LXX. [40]Ps 76:17-18 LXX. [41]Eccles 11:3. [42]Wis 3:1. [43]Eph 6:17. [44]Heb 4:12.

beheld the full majesty of the deity and carried by a certain leaving of the mind, "I fell," he says, "at his feet as though dead." Thoroughly terrified by fear of his weakness, insignificance and inferiority, he fell down, not falling only to some degree, wholly giving himself over to the Lord in humility and faith.

And, therefore, the Lord also felt compassion in view of this most pious devotion. *He laid his right hand on me, saying, "Fear not."* Here he both rewards faith and strengthens the faithful, who is terrified not by unbelief but by an awe-filled wonder, and he urges John not to fear. And he expressed his affection in this manner so that he might turn him to the contemplation of his power and transform the awe and wonder of his faith into the love of Christ.

[1:18] The Lord comforts the humble man and says, *I am the first and the last, and the living one; I died, and behold I am alive forevermore, and I have the keys of death and Hades.* If you have grasped the spark of my love, and "love never fails,"[45] rise up, with your fear now gone, and recognize him before whom you were awestruck. "I am the first," that is, before every creature, "before the earth was formed."[46] I am myself the beginning and the end. In me the end of all things consists, because through me all things are going to be restored at the end. "And I am the living one; I died, and behold I am alive," that is, he accepted death for our salvation while remaining without defect. "And behold I am alive forevermore," that is, behold I now exist in the eternity of God. "And I have the keys of death and Hades," so that I shall shut whenever I will, and when I will, I shall open again, and what was locked in by death I will lead into the open light by the resurrection. Concerning this key the prophet Isaiah taught us, saying, "And I will place on his shoulder the keys of

the house of David; he shall open, and none shall shut; and he shall shut, and none shall open."[47] For the key is the Lord Jesus Christ himself, who both opened the door of life and destroyed the coming of death.

[1:19] *Write, therefore, what you see, both what is and what is to take place hereafter.* Behold, he reveals that he will speak concerning not only present realities but also of things past, and the Lord commands him to address those in the future and equally to speak to those who will be born at the end of time.

[1:20] Then he explains the vision that he showed. *The mystery of the seven stars that you saw in my right hand and the seven golden lampstands. The seven stars are the seven angels of the churches, and the seven lampstands are the seven churches.* We spoke of this above. The stars placed in the right hand of God are the souls of the saints, or, what is the same thing, the entire congregation of the blessed who have been and who will be until the consummation of the world. In a similar way, we have said that the seven lampstands are the one, true church that has been established during the seven-day period of this world, which is founded by faith in the Trinity and which is made strong by the sacrament of the heavenly mystery.[48]

Having explained these things, he begins again with the churches and teaches the apostle what he should write to the churches themselves, saying,

REVELATION 2

[2:1] *To the angel of the church in Ephesus write.* He indicates the number of all the saints under the name of one angel. By the name Ephesus, that is, "my will" or "my counsel," he speaks, as we mentioned above, of the catholic

---

[45]1 Cor 13:8. [46]Prov 8:23. [47]Is 22:22. [48]That which founds the church is faith in the Trinity confessed at baptism; the church is strengthened by its continual partaking of the Lord's Supper, "the sacrament of the heavenly mystery."

church, to whom he reveals that which he is now to speak. *These things he says who holds the seven stars in his right hand, who walks among the seven golden lampstands.* This refers to him who holds in his hand the souls of the saints and walks in the midst of his churches by means of wonders and miracles and lives with them by the greatness of his power.

[2:2] And to the same church he says, *"I know your works, your toil and your patient endurance."* He says that he knows the exercise of their good work and the concern and patience of their toil and spiritual zeal, through which the church withstands and conquers temptation. And with a judgment of truth he praises the purity of his church. Concerning this church Isaiah said, "Sing, O barren one, who did not bear; sing forth with praise and hymn, you who have not borne, for the sons of the abandoned one will be more than those of her who has a husband."[1] And concerning the toil of this church, it is said, "Blessed are they who mourn, for they will be comforted."[2]

[2:3] Therefore, in this passage the Lord says, *"And that you cannot bear evil men but have tested those who call themselves apostles but are not, and you have found them to be false. And you are bearing patiently and are bearing them for my name's sake, and you have not grown weary."* We understand this passage to be clearly about the heretics, for they put themselves forward as teachers of the truth, but they are teachers of a deceitful lie. They claim that they are good, but they are proven to be perverters along with the demons. But the catholic faith discovers their lie and perversity and with patience restrains the many evils brought into it by them. And all of this happens for the name of Christ, and his faithfulness does not falter. Indeed, through the prophet it is said to the church concerning the

heretics, "Every weapon made against you shall not find its target, and you shall judge every tongue that resists your judgment."[3]

[2:4] *But I have this against you, that you have abandoned your earlier love.* He receives every sinful person who is in the catholic church and is guilty of all kinds of sins, and he shows that he pleads with them, because having abandoned the prior charity of their faith, they have become ensnared by many delinquencies.

[2:5] Therefore, he admonishes them and exhorts them, saying, *Remember then from where you have fallen. Repent, and do your first works.* The Lord spoke in the same way through the prophet: "Put me in remembrance, let us judge together; put forth your cause, that you might be proven right."[4] For although he wishes that we remember those instances in which we have badly fallen, he exhorts that we might not fall again. And that our faults that we have committed might be cleansed, he shows a way by which one might come to pardon when he says, "Repent." That is, wash away your sins with tears, just as "that sinful woman," as a type of the church, "washed the feet of Jesus with her tears and wiped them with her hair."[5] And he exhorts and commands what one should do after repentance: "Do your first works," either by an extraordinary goodness or do those works that you had done in the earnestness of your first conversion.

However, if not, I come to you, and I will move your lampstand from its place, unless you repent. What is it to remove the lampstand if not to turn away his face and to take away his protection? For without the consideration of the Most High, without the protection of God, our faith would have no strength to remain strong. And therefore it is said through the prophet, "You have made a wide place for my steps under me, and my footsteps were not

---

Revelation 2   [1]Is 54:1. [2]Mt 5:5. [3]Is 54:17. [4]Is 43:26. [5]Lk 7:38, 44.

---

weak."[6] And before that the psalmist said, "You have placed my arms as bronze bows, and you have given to me the shield of salvation."[7] And he also says, "Unless the Lord had judged me, my soul would soon have dwelt in Hades."[8] Therefore, he moves the lampstand of our faith and extinguishes the light of our confession when he turns his face from us. And he says, "unless you repent." What repentance can the flesh perform unless it receives assistance from the creator? What watery tears can flow from the dryness of the flesh, unless the coming of the Holy Spirit makes moist that heart pricked by the mercy of the Lord? Repentance occurs, therefore, only if one is urged and given repentance.

[2:6] Yet this you have, you hate the works of the Nicolaitans, which I hate. The designation "Nicolaitans" is interpreted as "a pouring out" or "the folly of a fainting church." And this is rightly said of heretics who have been poured out from the container of the truth and have tumbled headlong into the mud of deceit. And concerning this pouring out, it is said in the Law: "You are poured out as water; you will not rise up."[9] Clearly, the foolishness of a fainting church is the perverse teaching of the heretics, for they do not bring healing to the wound of the people, but they afflict on the people the greatest of weaknesses, thinking foolish thoughts about God and being themselves fully taken over by ridiculous ideas. Concerning such persons it is said: "They have restored the sorrow of my people to dishonor, saying, 'Peace, peace,' when there is no peace."[10]

[2:7] Then, to show that he had spoken this mystery for the sake of what is hidden, he says, Whoever has ears, let him hear what the Spirit says to the churches. In the Gospel the Lord also says, "The words that I speak to you are spirit and life."[11] Therefore, whoever has his ear opened to faith, whoever through the good belief of the inner person exhibits the most attentive hearing, that one will be able to hear the words of the divine speech, which the Holy Spirit utters.

To him who conquers, I will give him to eat from the tree of life, which is in the paradise of my God. He has spoken of the toil of the church. He has described the perversity of the heretics. Now to those still in their failures, he exhorts to repentance, and he promises rewards after this toil to those who are victorious, so that, entering into paradise, they might freely eat from the tree of life, for which Adam was expelled from paradise, lest he eat anything from it. And so he says, "which is in the paradise of my God," where, namely, the wind breathes life, where the mysteries give virtue, and he furnishes the fruit of the tree of life, that is, an eternity that does not fade away.

[2:8] And to the angel of the church in Smyrna. "Smyrna" means "their song," that is, of those who have rightly confessed the catholic truth.

[2:9] To these the Holy Spirit speaks, saying, The words of the First and the Last, who was dead and lives: "I know your tribulation and your poverty." He praises the works of his church, for through many tribulations she contends for the kingdom. He mentions explicitly the grace of poverty, because the church despises very much the things of the present time, so that she might acquire future things. But you are rich. You are rich in faith and are filled with an abundance of blessings. And you are slandered by those who say that they are Jews and are not, but are a synagogue of Satan. For the church often sustains much insult from those who claim that they confess God, but do not confess him. Rather, their congregation is bound to the devil as its source.

---

[6]Ps 18:36 (17:37 LXX). [7]Ps 18:34-35 (17:35-36 LXX). [8]Ps 94:17 (93:17 LXX). [9]See Gen 49:4. [10]Jer 8:11. [11]Jn 6:63.

[2:10] For that reason, he exhorts his church not to fear those "who kill the body, but afterward have nothing which they can do,"[12] and so he says, *Fear not what you are about to suffer.* He speaks of those future trials and evils that will come on them from the impious, and he comforts his faithful, that they not be fearful of the tortures of the persecutors. And he indicates what they would be strong enough to suffer and what the enemy would be able to do. *Behold, the devil is about to throw [some of you into prison, that you may be tested,] and for ten days you will have tribulation.*[13] For just as in the early period of the catholic church, after the banishment of the apostle, whose sayings these are, the sufferings continued and many tribulations were inflicted on the church, so we know that also in the future more sufferings will be inflicted when the antichrist arrives, although even now the church often sustains many sufferings in various places and regions from heretics and from the native populations. But he says, "You will have tribulation for ten days." This is to say, should you consider the present evils that you suffer in comparison with the perpetuity of the future blessedness, you will regard these without doubt as small and as quickly transient, as though of ten days' duration. And therefore, the apostle said, "I consider that the sufferings of this present time are not worth comparing with the glory that is to be revealed to us."[14]

Therefore, he comforts the saints and says, *Be faithful unto death, and I will give you a crown of life.* In the Gospel it is said: "He who perseveres to the end, the same will be saved."[15] For it could happen that someone now living in an evil manner will, at the end of time, be forgiven through repentance, and that someone now living in a good way will, at the end of time, be lost through some kind of excess. But

"he who perseveres to the end," that is, he who shall not have injured his soul to death, or he who will have remained in the faith of Christ even to death, "he will be saved," and surely the crown of life will be presented to him.

[2:11] As is customary, he urges that whoever has kept the faithful hearing of the interior person should present attentive ears for hearing, that he might know what the Spirit is saying to the churches. To these it is said: *He who conquers shall not be hurt by the second death.* Whoever either shall have endured in suffering or shall have preserved his faith undiminished to the end shall be granted exemption from the second death.

[2:12] And then he indicates that the Lord himself spoke. *The words of him who has the sword that is sharp on both sides.* This is the two-edged sword that is interpreted to be the word of God and is revealed as coming forth from his mouth.[16] However, he also indicates that the church lives in this world.

[2:13] *I know where you dwell, where Satan's throne is.* They live where temptation does not cease, and death claims many who are accused. But the church is praised because she holds to the confession of the name of Christ, and she *does not deny her faith* and is then adorned with the honor of martyrs. From these a certain Antipas is named as most faithful, who was killed in this age, where Satan, that is, the adversary, is said to live.

[2:14] However, the Lord has a complaint against the church because there are some there *who hold the teaching of Balaam,* which is interpreted "without a people" or "without property." For Balaam is a type of the adversary who does not gather a people for salva-

---

[12]Lk 12:4. [13]The text is unclear here. Gryson edits as follows: *Ecce missurus est diabolus [ex vobis in carcerem, ut temptemini] ··· in profundum, ut temptetur ··· [et habebitis] tribulationes diebus decem* (CCL 107:51). [14]Rom 8:18. [15]Mt 10:22. [16]Eph 6:17; Rev 1:16; 19:15.

tion, nor does he rejoice in the number of the multitude that is being saved. Rather, as long as he destroys all and remains without a people and without any property, then he rejoices. It is he who taught *Balak to put a stumbling block before the sons of Israel.* For Balak is interpreted to mean "throwing down" or "devouring." He has thrown Israel down so that it might be consecrated to the idol, Phogor,[17] and he has devoured them by the eating of pleasure and luxury.

[2:15] In a similar way, he says that the church has some who hold the teaching of the Nicolaitans, that is, they follow the teaching of the heretics.

[2:16] He advises them to turn to the Lord and to repent, lest he should begin to fight with them by the sword of his mouth, for when he comes for judgment, he will inquire of each one concerning his deeds.

[2:17] And also in what follows he says, *To him who conquers I will give the hidden manna, and I will give him a white stone.* The hidden manna is immortality; the white gem is the adoption of the sons of God. The new name written on the stone is the name Christian.

[2:18] Then he says, *The Son of God says these things, who has eyes like a flame of fire and whose feet are like burnished bronze.* "His eyes like flames" signifies his gaze, which discerns all things, and "his feet like burnished bronze" signifies his unstained flesh, which glows, just as bronze in a fire is bright with clarity.

[2:19] *I know your works.* He says that he knows the work, the love, the faith, the service and the patience of his church. *And your latter works exceed the first.* He indicates that at the end of time there will be a greater number of

saints, when, with the coming of the man of sin, the son of perdition, innumerable thousands of saints will be consecrated with their own blood.

[2:20] He explains that he has a complaint against the church. For there was in that church a type of that prostitute, Jezebel, that is, a certain teaching, which instructs the church to eat food sacrificed to idols.

[2:21] And they will receive a time for repentance, but they will think light of it and choose not to repent.

[2:22] The Lord promises that a sickness and a weariness will come to this doctrine, and a weariness of the sickbed, that is, the pleasure of this world. And to those who commit adultery through this teaching, he promises that a very great tribulation will come on them on the day of judgment. For Jezebel is interpreted as "dung heap" or a "flowing of blood." What else is thought to be in the filth of a dung heap or in blood, unless the evil deed and sin that are committed through fault? Therefore, rightly does he foretell a future condemnation for them, unless they strongly repent of their works.

[2:23] For he also mentions that he will damn her sons, that is, her disciples with the second death. *And all the churches shall know that I am he who searches mind and heart, when I will give to each one according to his works. And I will give a judgment concerning the secrets of each one before his face.*

[2:24-25] And to the rest of you who are in the church and do not follow this most evil teaching, and who have not known the deep wickedness of Satan, he says, *I will not send on you any further burden,* as the Scripture

---

[17]The name given to the god Baal on Mount Phegor in Moab. The deity was often associated with licentiousness. See Deut 3:29.

says, "Tribulation will not arise a second time."[18] This means that in addition to the tribulation that you endure in the present time, I will add no future one to you. Rather, he exhorts that each hold what he has and preserve what he has received until such time as the Lord comes.

[2:26-27] He says what he intends to do. God promises that he will give to him power over the nations and kingdoms, so that he might reign over them with an iron rod and destroy them as though they were a clay pot. He refers to the apostate angels who abandoned their own dominion, for they are going to be judged by the saints on the day of judgment and damned and thrown into eternal destruction, as the apostle says.[19]

[2:28] I will give him power, *even as I have received power from my Father.* I think for this reason that John said, "When he appears, we shall be like him."[20] *And I will give him the morning star,* that is, the Lord Jesus Christ, whom evening never overtakes, but who is eternal light, and who is himself always in light. Or, another interpretation: He promises the morning star, namely, the first resurrection; the resurrection is the morning star that causes night to flee and announces the light.

REVELATION 3

[3:1] It indicates that he who has the seven-fold Spirit of God continues to speak to the churches, namely, the Lord, Jesus Christ, in whom rests the Holy Spirit who possesses one and the selfsame substance.[1] In his hand are the seven stars of which we spoke above.[2]

[3:2] And reproving the negligence of many in the congregation of the church, he says, *I know your works, for you have the name of being alive, but you are dead. Be vigilant and strengthen what remains and was about to perish.* He rebukes those idle persons who do not trust in God with the whole mind and keep the right faith only hypocritically. They are Christians in name only. And so they are said to be living, but in fact they are dead For that reason they are rebuked that they might be vigilant and strengthen what remains of that from which they had fallen.

[3:3] And so he urges them, *Remember then what you received and heard, and repent.* He wishes that they remember the apostolic doctrine, and he warns them to preserve that which they received at the beginning of their faith and to repent of their past sins. And so he threatens whomever does not do this: *If you will not be vigilant, I will come like a thief, and you will not know at what hour I will come on you.* The judgment of God will be sudden, and no one knows the secret hour when he intends to come.

[3:4-5] Piety does not punish the wretched completely, but on the contrary gives consolation. *You still have a few names in Sardis, he says, who have not soiled their garments; and they will walk with me in white, for they are worthy.* Everyone who is not soiled with the filth of sin walks with the Lord in white, and he is made worthy so that he might follow the footsteps of the Lamb. Nor will his name be blotted out from the book of life, and Christ will confess him before his Father, who is in heaven, and before his angels.

[3:7-8] *These things speaks the holy one, the true one, who has the key of the house of David,*

---

[18]Nahum 1:9. [19]See 2 Thess 1:9; Rev 12:10; 17:8. [20]1 Jn 3:2. **Revelation 3** [1]An affirmation of the doctrine of the Trinity. The Holy Spirit possesses the divine nature, as does the Lord Jesus Christ. At the time of Apringius the Iberian peninsula was still struggling with the Arianism of the Visigoths. [2]See comments on Rev 1:16, 20.

who opens and no one closes, who shuts and no one opens. I know your works. Behold, I have set before you an open door, namely, the evangelical faith and the preaching of apostolic doctrine, which no one is able to close because you have little power. I know human weakness, and so I have opened to you the door of knowledge and the mystery of faith, so that no one should be strong enough to close what has been opened because of the smallness of your powers. And you have kept my word and have not denied my name. Since he has mentioned the strength deriving from his gifts, he also indicates the work of his grace, because through the gift granted to him, he has preserved his faith and has not denied the eternal name.

[3:9] Behold, I will give those from the synagogue of Satan who say that they are Jews and are not, but lie—behold, I will make them come and bow down before your feet, and they will know that I have loved you. He indicates that all enemies and foes of the catholic church will be judged by the catholic church. As the apostle says, "In the new world, when the Son of man shall come, then you also will sit on twelve thrones and judge the twelve tribes of Israel."[3] Then truly those will come who say that they are Jews, that is, pious but are not, and they will bow down before the feet of the church, and they will know that the Lord loved her.

[3:10] Because you have kept the word of my patient endurance, I will keep you from the hour of temptation that is coming on the whole world to tempt those who dwell on the earth. Behold, he declares with the utmost clarity that he is speaking not only to his own times but also to future ages. Moreover, he promises that he will preserve his church in the last times, when the demon, the enemy of the human race, will come to tempt those who live on the earth.

[3:11] Lest they who live at that time be utterly confounded in that temptation, he says, Behold, I am coming soon; hold fast what you have; let no one take your crown. He foretells the suddenness of his advent and the quick destruction of Satan in the future. Moreover, he says that the future temptation will not be long. And for that reason he admonishes them that the enemy not seize their crown, as also Solomon said: "Lest you give your honor to others and your years to the merciless."[4]

[3:12] He who conquers, I will make him a pillar in the temple of my God. [He speaks in this manner] so that he might set forth both the decoration and the strength of the temple of God, as the apostle Paul says, "James and John, who were reputed to be pillars, gave to me and Barnabas the right hand of fellowship."[5] "In the temple of my God," that is, among the multitude of the blessed. And never will he go out of it, that is, he will never depart from the fellowship of the saints or from the reward and glory of the elect.

And I will write on him the name of my God, and the name of the city of my God, the new Jerusalem, which comes down from my God out of heaven. [I will write on him the name of my God] so that he might be signed with the divine name and be adorned with the glory of immortality and might receive the name of the divine city of Jerusalem, which is the vision of peace, and so fully enjoy the society of perpetual quiet and security. This is that city that descends out of heaven from God, so that the saints might dwell and repose within it. And my new name. In God nothing is old, because he does not grow old with age. But the name of the Lord is always new, always fresh. And if any is named by this name, having been changed by the eternal power, he will obtain eternal life.

---

[3]Mt 19:28. "New world" translates in regeneratione. [4]Prov 5:9. [5]Gal 2:9.

[3:14] He continues to speak of him who is speaking to the church, namely, the faithful and true, *who is the beginning of the creation of God*, not him who has received a beginning but has given a beginning, and he states that he rebukes the lukewarm nature of some and reproaches their wantonness.

[3:15-16] *I know your works; for you are neither cold nor hot. Would that you were cold or hot! But because you are lukewarm, and neither cold nor hot, I will begin to spew you out of my mouth.* He despises those who are deceived by some foolishness, and he assails those who prove themselves to be neither very cold in their iniquity nor diligent in good works. Rather, they are lukewarm in both. And therefore they do not serve up any food of good works to Christ, who desires to be sated in good works,[6] but claim that they are faithful even as they persist in that which pleases them. Therefore, he threatens immediately to vomit them out from his heart and to throw them out.

[3:17] *For you say that you are rich and have prospered and have need of nothing. But you do not know that you are wretched, miserable, poor, blind and naked.* He confounds those who boast in their works and exult so strongly that they have given a single coin to the poor or boast that they have done anything good. Confident in the knowledge and faith that they have assumed so lukewarmly, they confess that they have done nothing amiss. But he censures them as destitute, in need of mercy and weighted down by this poverty of good works. And since they neither see nor consider their own nakedness, they are requited as those who are naked and void of good works.

[3:18] With his customary goodness, he calls them onward to salvation. *I counsel you to buy from me gold refined by fire, that you may be rich and be clothed in white garments and that the shame of your nakedness may not be seen, and salve to anoint your eyes, that you may see.* This is the gold that is promised to the church through the prophet: "Instead of bronze I will bring gold, instead of iron, silver, instead of wood, bronze, and instead of stones, iron."[7] In this way he indicates that the speaking of the Lord and the evangelical, apostolic teaching is gold. With such gold one will be prosperous, and without doubt will be deserving of spiritual riches, and will be well dressed in white garments, that is, in the splendor of good works, and will not be thought confounded by being naked of good works.

He commands eye salve to anoint the eyes, that is, the remorse of the heart and the tears of penance and the healthy sorrow of those who are repenting.

[3:19] He shows that he speaks not as one who is angry and full of hatred, but rather as one speaking out of love, saying, *Those whom I love, I reprove and chasten. Therefore, be zealous and repent.* He arouses those pressed down by the most grievous deed to the repentance of sin, and he invites them to the imitation of the saints.

[3:20] *Behold, I stand at the door and knock; if anyone hears my voice and opens the door, I will come in to him and eat with him, and he with me.* Our salvation, the Lord Jesus Christ, stands and knocks on the door of our heart. Whoever awakens from his serious sins and will cast away the bond of wickedness and the suffocation of the heart, he will without doubt enter and will eat with him, and he will fill him with the delights of righteousness.

[3:21] After this admonition, he indicates that

---

[6]The image of vomiting suggested to Apringius the image of good works as a food. And so he refers to good works as *esca* ("food"), he speaks of "serving up" food (*apponunt*) and Christ being sated with the food (*satiatur*) of good works. [7]Is 60:17.

which he promises for good works. *He who conquers, I will grant him to sit with me on my throne, as I myself have conquered and sit with my Father on his throne.* What is it to sit on the throne of God, unless to repose and to be glorified with God and to stand at his blessed tribunal and to rejoice in the unshakeable felicity of his presence? Here ends the first book.

The Second Book Begins.

REVELATION 4

[4:1] After completing the sevenfold number of the churches, through which he arranged in a mystical manner by the individual names the seven days of this world, he again explains what he saw. *After this I looked, and behold, in heaven an open door.* After the brightness of such an appearance, which he had perceived with the mind of faith, the very secrets of heaven are revealed and disclosed to him. With the mind he peers into the secrets of the divine mystery and contemplates the secrets of God with a faithful deliberation. He sees a door open to him, by which he might, with an eager mind, attain to the knowledge of such majesty.

And he says, *And the first voice that I heard speaking to me was like a trumpet, saying.* He indicates that after the opening of the door of heaven, he heard nothing other than what he had heard before when, while he was still without knowledge, the Lord began to reveal his secrets, until overcome by the vision of his power, he fell at the feet of majesty. Finally, lest we consider the door to be material, he likens the first voice, which he heard, to a trumpet. With a trumpet, the voice is forced inside and the breath collected on the inside, and as long as the voice continues, it makes a sound on the outside. So also the one who receives a word from the Lord understands mentally what he is to speak forth to the outside.

Or, the open door is to be interpreted as the revelation of the mystery of the gospel, and the first voice as the presentation of the Law. For the new things should be in harmony with the old, and that should occur what the psalmist sang: "Once God has spoken; twice have I heard this."[1] For indeed, after the inspiration of minds, after the revelation of the mystery, he heard, *Come up hither, and I will show you what must take place quickly.* This is that which is ordained in the holy Law: "They go from strength to strength, and the God of gods will be seen in Zion."[2] The saint is invited to enter into the holy of holies, where as precursor our Lord Jesus, having become high priest forever, entered through the blood of his passion, in order that he might be entitled already to possess the very presence of the Lord and that he not only might come to know the truth that is past but also might comprehend those things that must happen in the future.

[4:2] *Immediately,* he says, *I was in the spirit.* Who would think that he speaks anything fleshly who reports that he had entered in the spirit? A man so thoroughly tested by his God receives nothing fleshly, nothing earthly. But he was in the spirit, so that he might see the Lord of majesty, whom he perceives in the spirit but does not behold in the flesh. He thereby fulfilled what the apostle said: "Even though we knew Christ according to the flesh, we know him thus no longer."[3]

And then he says, *And lo, a throne was placed in heaven, with one seated on the throne.* The throne that is placed is a kingdom over a kingdom. That is, the power and the truth and the fortitude of God sits within the church.

[4:3] *And he who sat there appeared like jasper and carnelian; and round the throne was a rainbow that looked like an emerald.* The jasper

Revelation 4   [1]Ps 62:11 (61:12 lxx).   [2]Ps 84:7 (83:8 lxx).   [3]2 Cor 5:16.

stone shines with a green and radiant brightness, so that he might know that the flesh of the assumed man, taken up without a hint of sin, shines with the vigor of everlasting sincerity and glows through the indwelling of the divine power. However, the carnelian stone is red and glimmers with a certain darkness, so that you might recognize the integrity of the undefiled flesh assumed from the modest and humble virgin.

"And round the throne was a rainbow that looked like an emerald." He does not yet declare the form of the one seated on the throne, but he indicates what appeared around the throne. For all things that are near to God become green with an unfading light. Indeed, the emerald is resplendent with green light. And the rainbow, which is described as appearing in a circle, is the gospel of the word and the teaching of the apostles and of the prophets. Concerning these things, the prophet said, "With bow and arrows they will enter there, and every mountain that was hoed with the hoe, and the fear of thorns and briars will not come there."[4] Therefore, this preaching, described as similar to a rainbow, always glimmers with a pleasant greenness.

Nor does the pleasantness of the divine Law suffer any dryness; but he says that he saw as always new the likeness of jasper and carnelian.[5] The color of jasper is that of water, while the color of carnelian is that of fire. From this we see that those two judgments decreed for the consummation of the world are revealed over the divine tribunal. Although one of these judgments has already been effected in the cataclysm through water, the other will be effected with fire. The rainbow around the sun has the same colors, and concerning the rainbow, also called an arch, the Lord spoke to Noah and his sons, that they not fear of the work of God. "I have set my bow in the clouds," he says,[6] so that you no longer fear water, but fire.

[4:4] *Round the throne there were twenty-four thrones, and seated on the thrones were twenty-four elders, clad in white garments, with golden crowns on their heads.* Most evidently John has described the chorus of the patriarchs and of the apostles, who sit on the chair of holy doctrine. These he calls "elders," that is, "fathers," and they are clothed in white garments, that is, they are clothed in works of righteousness and in purity. They carry on their heads golden crowns, for they have been made victors in present struggles, since that evil enemy, the devil, has been thrown down, and they have received their crowns from the Lord. Concerning this crown, the vessel of election says: "I have finished the race, I have kept the faith. Henceforth there is laid up for me the crown of righteousness, which the Lord, the righteous judge, will award to me on the day, and not only to me but also to those who love his appearing."[7]

[4:5] *From the throne issue flashes of lightning, and voices and peals of thunder, and before the throne burn seven lamps, which are the seven spirits of God.* He desires that we understand that the entire original preaching of the apostles and indeed the heavenly and sacred doctrine proceeds from the judgment and inspiration of God. We interpret therefore the flashes of lightning to be the words of all the saints, and likewise the thunder to be the voices of the preachers. We confess that all these things come forth from one source, namely, God. Concerning these flashes of lightning and sounds of thunder, it is said: "The voice of your thunder was in the whirlwind; your lightnings lighted up the world."[8] None of these things possesses their own beginning. Rather,

---

[4]Is 7:24-25. [5]The text of this last clause is uncertain. Gryson gives the following: *sed simper novo* [••• *Item aliter*]/*Vidisse se, ait, similitudinem iaspidas et sardini.* [6]Gen 9:13. [7]2 Tim 4:7-8. [8]Ps 77:18 (76:19 LXX).

that which comes forth is shown to come from the throne of God, that is, from the will and power of the Creator, or from his rule. "Before the throne burn seven lamps." This most clearly refers to the sevenfold power of the Holy Spirit, concerning which we have already spoken. They are before the throne, because these powers are granted to them through grace, and they are taught to stand with God, as it is said elsewhere: "Those who approach his feet will receive from his teaching."[9]

[4:6] *And before the throne there is as it were a sea of glass, like crystal.* The sea of glass is like crystal, that is, it is transparent, indicating that it is infused by a certain whiteness and uncommon purity. With good reason we think that this is said of the font of baptism and of the grace of regeneration. For baptism cleanses and illumines those who have received it, and it clothes those who have been led to purity with the splendor of righteousness. These are the waters of which it is written in the prophets: "In those days living waters shall flow out from Jerusalem, half of them to the eastern sea and half of them to the western sea; they shall continue in summer and in winter."[10]

And round the throne are four living creatures, full of eyes in front and behind. The four creatures are the forms of the four Evangelists. They are presented as "full of eyes in front and behind" to indicate either that they contain the past and future mysteries of God or that they are said to speak the secrets of both Laws. They are shown through the contemplation of spiritual things to announce the whole faith of the holy deity and to reveal the mystery of the celestial secrets.

[4:7] Then the form of each is discussed in order. *The first living creature was like a lion.* Most of our interpreters say that this signi-

fies the person of Mark, the Evangelist.[11] And indeed this seems most apt and true, for his Gospel begins in this way: "The beginning of the gospel of Jesus Christ, the Son of God. As it is written in Isaiah the prophet, 'Behold, I send my messenger who shall prepare the way before your face.' "[12] Nor is it strange that here Isaiah is mentioned instead of Malachi, for most certainly this testimony occurs in Malachi. However, Isaiah means "the salvation of the Lord," and Malachi means "angel." And so at the beginning of the Gospel he prefers to speak of the salvation of the Lord, which is Isaiah, rather than of the angel, which is Malachi, in order that through the faith of the gospel he might suggest the immoveable perpetuity of the present and future life. And then, to be sure, he mentions the "messenger," which is "angel," and he adds the words of Isaiah: "Prepare the way of the Lord; make straight the highways of our God,"[13] so that, salvation having been both promised and foretold, he might show the messenger of the truth and might prepare the hearts of humankind for the reception of grace. And the form of the lion is in this, that he reports that John was in the desert preaching and enjoying the desert, as he says: "John was in the desert baptizing and proclaiming the baptism of repentance for the forgiveness of sins."[14]

The words *the second creature was like an ox* introduce Luke. For a bull is representative of the priesthood, as it is said in Isaiah: "Blessed are you who sow on all the waters, letting the feet of the ox and the ass go free."[15] And so at the beginning of his Gospel, he speaks of Zechariah the priest: "In the days of Herod, king of Judea, there was a priest named Zechariah."[16]

The third living creature with the face of a man indicates Matthew, for at the beginning of his book Matthew wished to report the genealogy of the Lord according to the flesh.

[9]Deut 33:3. [10]Zech 14:8. [11]Apringius appears to be following Jerome, who prefers the order man, lion, calf, eagle (*On Ezekiel* 1.1.6-8). Bede follows Augustine. [12]Mk 1:2. [13]Is 40:3. [14]Mk 1:4. [15]Is 32:20. [16]Lk 1:5.

The words *the fourth living creature was like a flying eagle* indicate John. For, at the beginning of his Gospel, John did not speak of the humanity of the Lord or of the priesthood or of John preaching in the desert. Rather, desiring like an eagle to reach toward the height of heaven itself, he left behind all things lowly and spoke properly of him as God: "In the beginning was the Word, and the Word was with God, and the Word was God; he was in the beginning with God."[17]

[4:8] *And the four living creatures, each of them having six wings, are full of eyes all around and within, and day and night they never cease to sing, "Holy, holy, holy, is the Lord God Almighty, who was and is and is to come."* Behold, he describes the four living creatures as protected by six wings, but he does not say as above "before and behind" or "full of eyes," but "around and within." These are the four living creatures that the great Ezekiel says that he saw carrying the throne of God.[18] That "they are full of eyes around and within" teaches us that the divine mysteries are contemplated inwardly by the spiritual mind and are illuminated toward the outside by the sacrament of the mystery, so that the light that is conceived within might shine on the outside. And so, without doubt, it is the throne of God that glows by such a light.

Concerning these living creatures Ezekiel says that "each one walked straight forward."[19] As each approaches the divine presence, he does not look behind but moves ahead rapidly toward that Holy One to whom he is directed. "They walked straight forward," because there is always a reason to be in a hurry and to pass by anything when one approaches God Almighty. Therefore Ezekiel also says, "They did not turn while they walked,"[20] because as they proceed forward they are always attaining to their destination. They are described as having six wings, for during the six days of the present

seven days, in which the world consists, the words of his prophecy are extended.

There are four living creatures that have six wings, that is, two times twelve, namely, the sacred teaching of the patriarchs and the apostles who have instructed the world by the public proclamation of his prophecy. In this very teaching the worship of the Trinity is proclaimed and without rest the name Holy is declared by a threefold repetition. And this worship that is proffered to the one, omnipotent God reveals the Trinity of a single substance. Previously the teaching taught that he was before all ages and through all ages and after all ages, and these voices proclaim that the same one will come again to take charge of the judgment of those from all ages.

[4:9-10] *And when those living creatures gave glory and honor and thanksgiving to him who is seated on the throne, to him who lives forever and ever.* Whenever the fourfold number of the Gospels sing with supernal sounds of the omnipotence of God the Father and of the glory of the Only-Begotten, *the twenty-four elders shall fall down before him who is seated on the throne, and they shall worship him who lives forever and ever.* For now it becomes clear what the authority of the fathers had taught, what the doctrine of the patriarchs and the apostles had prophesied, as the proclamation of the Gospels is opened, as the Lord himself says: "Were you to believe Moses, you would also believe me, for he spoke of me."[21] And that they are said to fall before him who is seated on the throne indicates that that which is written proclaims what has been concealed in the presence and memory of God. Then it is said that the chorus of the fathers worshiped "him who lives forever and ever," while all of the prophecies are repeated and through them the hearts of people prepared, so that the Most High might be worshiped.

---

[17]Jn 1:1-2. [18]See Ezek 1:5-14. [19]Ezek 1:9. [20]Ezek 1:9. [21]Jn 5:46.

[4:11] And let no earthly mind dare to ascribe this to man. *They cast their crowns before the throne of God, saying, "You are worthy, Lord, our God, to receive glory and honor and power, for you created all things, and by your will they existed and were created."* Without doubt he is indicating that the whole course of the Scriptures is to redound to the praise of the Lord and that all honor and power are to be given to God alone, because on account of his will that which is written exists, or all things that have been created in heaven and on the earth continue to exist without doubt through him.[22]

REVELATION 5

[5:1] *And I saw in the right hand of him who was seated on the throne a scroll written within and on the back, sealed with seven seals.* This scroll, which is said to be written on the inside and on the outside, is every creature of all the present world.[1] God perceives the inner thoughts of every creature, and he knows their outer deeds.[2] For, by the virtue of his power he surpasses this world, which is contained by him, and by the clarity of his majesty he searches into the inmost parts. The book is said to be sealed by seven seals, so that the decree and limit of the present seven days, in which the world was made, might be manifested. Another interpretation: This book signifies the teaching of the Old Testament, which was given into the hands of our Lord, who accepted the judgment from the Father. The seven seals are these: First, incarnation; second, birth; third, passion; fourth, death; fifth, resurrection; sixth, glory; seventh, kingdom. These seals, therefore, are Christ.[3] Since he completed all

things through his humanity, he opened and unsealed everything that had been closed and sealed in the Scriptures.

[5:2] *And I saw a strong angel proclaiming with a loud voice, "Who is worthy to receive the scroll and break its seals?"* This strong angel, who is said to cry out and inquire concerning whom is most worthy to open the scroll and break the seals, is to be interpreted as the chorus of all of the Scriptures or of the holy fathers who lived in divine awe and, seeing with the eyes of faith, understand that the disposition of the present times and the order of all things, which have been sealed by the administration of God, have the God of majesty as their creator, and so they proclaim and say, "Who is worthy to understand all things and to open the secrets of the Lord?" For he disposed of the secrets by a marvelous decree in the seven-day creation of the world, and by an ordinance did he establish it, and by wisdom sealed it, and by counsel founded it and by power made it.

[5:3] *And no one in heaven or on earth or under the earth was able to open the scroll or to look into it.* From all the creatures that are in heaven and on the earth and in the depths, not one was found who could either loose the seals or knew what had been ordained or could tell what had been done. Another interpretation: No one was found worthy, not in heaven or on the earth or under the earth, to open the seals. For the sake of humankind, which is conquered by death, no one was found worthy to do this, not among the angels of heaven or among people on the earth or among the souls of the saints at rest, none except Jesus Christ alone, the Son of God.

---

[22]These last words translate *ipso sine dubio auctore persistunt.*   **Revelation 5**   [1]The Latin reads: *Liber hic praesentis est mundi totius creatura.* Apringius seems to identify *liber* and *creatura.*   [2]"Inner thoughts" translates *interiora;* "outer deeds" translates *exteriora.*   [3]The Greek commentator Oecumenius also interprets the seven seals to refer to events in the life of Christ, although his list is somewhat different: (1) incarnation; (2) the temptation and Christ's victory over the tempter; (3) Christ's teaching and miracles; (4) the lashes that Christ received; (5) the chains and scourging of Christ; (6) the second coming and the rewards then given. Apringius' list most probably was influenced by the Eucharistic rite of the Visiogothic liturgy.

[5:4] *And I wept much that no one was found worthy to open the scroll or to look into it.* The saint weeps, aware of the weakness of humanity, for he understood that no one was sufficiently worthy to understand these things or to look on them with knowledge.

[5:5] *Then one of the elders said to me, "Weep not; lo, the Lion of the tribe of Judah, the Root of David, has conquered, so that he can open the scroll and loose its seven seals."*[4] "Then one of the elders." This signifies the message of the holy Scriptures, which, should one read it through, teaches that our Lord Jesus Christ is that very strong lion from the tribe of Judah, about whom it was said: "He rested and couched as a lion."[5] He who is the Root of Jesse and the offspring of David, he has conquered the world and death, and he only is able to open the scroll and to break its seals. For he is the creator of all things and the marvelous arranger of the universe.

[5:6] And then it continues. *And I saw and behold, between the throne and the four living creatures and among the elders, there was a Lamb standing as though it had been slain, with seven horns and seven eyes, which are the seven spirits of God sent out into all the earth.* Here he showed even more clearly our Lord Jesus Christ, whom he declares was not dead but was as though slain because of the suffering and the death that he had undergone. He says that he had seen this Lamb in the midst of the throne, that is, in power and in divine majesty. "And among the four living creatures." This is because he is known in the fourfold order of the Gospels. "And among the elders." By this he indicates the chorus of the law and the prophets, or of the apostles. He testifies that he saw the Lamb there, not slain but as if slain, that is, even he who had conquered death and had trampled on the passion. "And he had seven horns and seven eyes." The horns symbolize power and strength. The number seven represents the condition of the world, which he rules effectively and which he governs with great power. Moreover, he calls the seven eyes the seven spirits of God, and in this way speaks of the Holy Spirit who remains with our Lord Jesus Christ, gloriously by the degrees of the seven virtues. Concerning him the apostle says, "We know that God was in Christ reconciling the world to himself."[6] And again: "The Spirit of him who raised Christ from the dead will also vivify our mortal bodies on account of his Spirit who dwells in you."[7] Since "their sound has gone out into the whole world," he speaks of the Spirit as "those sent," calling to mind the gifts of the Holy Spirit that have been abundantly spread throughout the entire earth.

[5:7] *And he went and took the scroll from the right hand of him who was seated on the throne.* Now, what it is said that he received must be considered and discussed with greatest diligence. To be sure, the Lamb is the assumed man who for our salvation willingly offered himself over to death. Worthily he "received the scroll," that is, the power of all the works of God, and "from the right hand of him who is seated on the throne," that is, he received all things from God the Father, as he himself said: "All that the Father has is mine."[8] Then did he receive this scroll, when rising from the dead he showed the mystery of the Trinity, which had been hidden from the ages, and revealed it to the world.

---

[4]This verse was especially important in the Mozarabic/Visiogothic liturgy for Easter vigil and the week after Easter (octave of Easter). As the priest held the broken host over the chalice, he repeated three times "the Lion from the tribe of Judah, the Root of David has conquered! Allelujah!" To this the people would reply, "He who sits upon the cherubim, the Root of David, Allelujah!" Apringius would have been very familiar with this liturgical use of Rev 5:5. [5]Gen 49:9. [6]2 Cor 5:19. [7]Rom 8:11. [8]Jn 16:15.

REVELATION 18

[**18:6**] *Render to her as she herself has rendered, and repay her double for her deeds; mix a double draught for her in the cup she mixed.*

[**18:7**] *As she glorified herself and was in sins, so give her a like measure of mourning, for she has said in her heart, "I sit as a queen, I am no widow, and mourning I shall never see." So shall her plagues come in a single day, death and mourning and famine, and she shall be burned with fire; for mighty is the Lord God who will judge her.*

[**18:8**] In Isaiah it is said to her: "Come down and sit in the dust, O virgin daughter of Babylon; sit on the ground, for there is no throne for the daughter of the Chaldeans, because you shall no longer be called tender and delicate."[1] And shortly thereafter: "Sit, be silent, go into the darkness, for you shall no more be called the mistress of kingdoms."[2] And again: "You said, 'I shall be mistress forever,' so that you did not lay these things to heart, nor did you remember your name. Now therefore, hear this, you delicate one who dwells in confidence, who says in your heart, 'I am, and there is no one besides me; I shall not sit as a widow or know the loss of children.' These two things shall come to you suddenly, in one day, sterility and widowhood."[3] Who would not understand these things together to be one prophecy and that they were said of one, universal event?

[**18:9**] *And the kings of the earth, who committed fornication with her and lived in her pleasures, shall weep and wail over her when they see the smoke of her burning; they will stand far off in fear of her torment, and say, "Alas, alas, you great city, you strong city, Babylon! For in one hour has your judgment come!"*

[**18:10**] *And the merchants of the earth shall weep and mourn over her, for no one buys any more their cargo.*

[**18:11**] Who does not understand that this is truly spoken of the same city that is ruled by all the kings of the earth and into which the merchandise of the world was imported due to the greatness of its strength and wealth? For also the rest that has been written can easily be understood by all.[4] For the prophet has adopted the lament of the merchants and the kings to make evident the magnitude of her power and wealth, which is going to pass away.

[**18:20**] And when the prophecy has been completely fulfilled, he said, *Rejoice over her, O heaven, O saints and apostles and prophets, for the Lord has given judgment for you against that city.* That is, rejoice, because all of the blood of the martyrs that she poured out to her damnation has been vindicated, and they see the avenging of the saints whom she persecuted. For, indeed, to show that the blood of the saints is to be requited and to demonstrate the image of her ruin, there follows:

[**18:21**] *A mighty angel took up a stone, like a great millstone, and threw it into the sea and said, "With this violence shall the great city, Babylon, be thrown down and shall be no more."* Behold, the coming time of perdition is likened to a stone that is thrown with force.

[**18:22**] *And the sound of harpers and minstrels, of flute players and trumpeters, shall no longer be heard in you.* He mentions one by one the professions of each one of those who give joy and says that they will no longer be heard in her. He inserts the reason for which she will be judged: *In her was found the blood of prophets and of saints, and of all who have been slain on earth.*

Revelation 18   [1]Is 47:1.   [2]Is 47:5.   [3]Is 47:7-9.   [4]Apringius has in mind especially Rev 18:12-19, for which he provides no commentary.

REVELATION 19

[19:1-3] *After this I heard what seemed to be the voice of a great multitude in heaven, saying: "Hallelujah! Salvation and glory and power belong to our God, for his judgments are true and just; for he has judged the great harlot who corrupted the earth with her fornication, and he has avenged from her hands the blood of his saints." And again they said: "Hallelujah! The smoke from her goes up forever and ever."* We notice that the saints exult over the destruction of the traitorous city, and we see that they praise God with the jubilation of praise. What does this describe other than the coming of the retribution of the evildoers and the rewarding of the good? This is that of which Daniel spoke: "Some will rise to everlasting life, and some to everlasting reproach,"[1] so that they might see this forever. For this reason it is said, "The smoke from her goes up forever and ever."

[19:4] Therefore, in order that the exultation of the saints might be described more fully, he adds, *The twenty-four elders and the four animals fell down and worshiped him who was sitting on the throne, saying: "Amen. Hallelujah."* Out of an affection of a good love, the hearts of the saints are turned, and for exultation and joy in the promises that they behold they worship, saying, "Hallelujah!"

[19:5] *And from the throne came a voice, saying, "Praise our God, all you his servants, you who fear him, small and great."* No creature is able to praise the Lord, unless it shall have received the gift of praise from the throne of God and shall have heard the voice of holy inspiration.

[19:6-8] *And I heard what seemed to be the sound of a great trumpet and as the voice of many waters and as the sound of great claps of thunder, saying: "Hallelujah! For the Lord, our God, the Almighty, has begun to reign. Let us rejoice and exult, because the marriage of the Lamb has come, and the Bride has made herself ready; and it was given to her to be clothed with fine linen, splendid and white."* The fine linen is the righteous deeds of the saints. After thanksgiving has been given and after the voice of exhortation has been heard, the praise to God, as though the sound of claps of thunder, is loudly proclaimed by those who rejoice that the marriage feast of the Lamb has come. This will occur when, after the consummation of the world, "every rule and authority will have been destroyed and he will have delivered the kingdom to God the Father, so that God will be all in all."[2] This will occur, that is, when his wife, namely, the catholic church, will be joined to him in the purity of faith. Concerning this the holy apostle said, "For I betrothed you to Christ to present you as a pure virgin to one husband."[3] And so, the fine linen that she [the church] wears does not represent the beauty of a vestment but the righteousness of the saints.

[19:9-10] *And he said to me: "Write: 'Blessed are those who are invited to the marriage feast of the Lamb.'" And he said to me, "These are true words of God." And I fell down at his feet to worship him. But he said to me: "Behold, do not do this; I am a fellow servant with you and your brethren who hold the testimony of Jesus. Worship God. The testimony is the Spirit of prophecy."* Who are those who have been invited to the feast of the Lamb, unless those to whom it is said: "I will not drink from this fruit of the vine until I will drink it new with you in the kingdom of my Father who is in heaven."[4] And again: "Many will come from east and west and will recline at table with Abraham, Isaac and Jacob in the kingdom of heaven."[5] This is to drink the new cup, to prepare the new bodies of those being raised, to keep a new joy and to

---

Revelation 19   [1]Dan 12:2. [2]1 Cor 15:24. [3]2 Cor 11:2. [4]Mt 26:29. [5]Mt 8:11.

repay the sincere righteousness of a true faith. These are the blessed who are prepared for this feast and for this repast.

Then it says, "These are true words of the almighty God." When the royal commands of God were heard, he fell down to worship him who was speaking with him. However, to respect the nature of his own office and to show that God is above all things, he prohibited this, saying, "Do not do this, because I am a fellow servant with you and your brethren who hold the testimony of Jesus." The testimony of Jesus is the true profession of the catholic confession. "For the testimony of Jesus is the Spirit of prophecy." The Spirit of prophecy is truth and judgment and justice, which in their fullness are contained in the catholic faith.

[19:11-13] *And I saw heaven opened, and behold, a white horse! And he who sat on it was called Faithful and True, and in righteousness he judges and makes war. His eyes are like a flame of fire, and on his head are many diadems; and he has a name inscribed that no one knows but himself. And he was clothed in a robe dipped in blood, and his name was called Word of God.* The white horse is the body that Christ assumed. He who sits on it is the Lord of majesty; he is the Word of the most high Father; he is the only-begotten of the unbegotten Father. Therefore, the true character of his person is expressed when he is called Faithful and True. For of God it is said, "God is faithful, in whom there is no iniquity."[6] And "in righteousness he judges and makes war." For concerning him it is written, "God is a judge, just, strong and patient."[7] He makes war by freeing us from the adversity of sin; he is patient by enduring the sins we commit; he is called strong because he repels whatever opposes him.

"His eyes are like a flame of fire." As fire penetrates everything that contains it and leaves no portion untouched by the force of its burning heat, so the eyes of the Lord cannot be avoided, for they are everywhere and pervade all things, and seeing all things that people do, they investigate them with a holy scrutiny. "And on his head are many diadems." There are many diadems because he brings to God, who gathers all, all the glory of the saints and all the honor of the blessed. And these do not remain quiet but bring forth praise and thanksgiving.

That he might declare his majesty more openly, he adds, "Having a name inscribed that no one knows but himself." For even Jacob said to one who asked, "Why is it that you ask my name? For it is wonderful."[8] And so, no one comprehends the name of God, which cannot be known or heard, except he himself. "And he was clothed in a robe dipped in blood." Of this Isaiah said, "Who is this that comes from Edom, in crimsoned garments from Bozrah? He is glorious in his apparel, marching in the greatness of his strength."[9] In the present passage he is shown wearing a robe dipped in blood, while in that passage he is said to be wearing crimsoned garments. However, a single meaning is intended by these different manners of speaking. "And his name was called Word of God," it says. Since his name was above said to be unknown by all and incomprehensible, but known to him alone, he is said to be Word of God for the profession of our faith, for salvation and for the hope of a perfect regeneration.

[19:14] *And the armies, which are in heaven, clothed in fine linen, white and pure, followed him on white horses.* We interpret the armies of heaven to be the bride herself, who above was said to be prepared for the marriage of the Lamb. When it says that they were "on white horses," it is speaking either of the purity of

---

[6]See Deut 32:4. [7]Ps 7:12 LXX. [8]Gen 32:29. [9]Is 63:1.

faith, or it is alluding to the members of our bodies made new through the resurrection. "Clothed in fine linen, white and pure." We noted above that this refers to the righteous works of the saints.

[19:15-16] *From his mouth issues a sharp sword to smite the nations with it, and that he might rule them with a rod of iron and that he might tread the wine press of the fury of the wrath of God Almighty. And on his robe and on his thigh he has written, King of kings and Lord of lords.* The sharp sword that issues from his mouth is the authority of the law and the severity of the judge. It remains sharp for justice, so that he might separate all things and reckon the deeds of every person. Then it says, "so that he might smite the nations with the sword." To smite means to strike, to determine, to free, to damn, to justify, to rescue, to save. "And he might rule them with a rod of iron." The rod of iron is the discipline of power by which he will make right all nations, equally changing and judging them. "And he might tread the wine press of the fury of the wrath of God Almighty." The wine press is hell, and the wine is the judgment by which those are restrained and subdued on whom the righteous anger of God will have come.

"And on his robe and on his thigh he has a name written, King of kings and Lord of lords." Christ is the basis and the foundation on which Paul builds as an architect. Christ is the good Shepherd "who gives his life for his sheep."[10] Christ is the head of every dominion and power.[11] He is the head of the church, wherefore it is said, "the head of man is Christ,"[12] because he is the head of the church. He is the father, because by him through baptism all the nations of the earth are born again. His thigh, on which his name is written, are the believers whom the Son of

God, that is, Christ, has willed to name "sons" through the adoption of faith. His robe is the assumed man, and because there is one person of two substances, we recognize his divinity in his robe, that is, in the sacrament of the Lord's body. On the vestment of his body it is said that his name was written, "King of kings and the Lord of lords." Indeed, it is written also on his thigh, because all who are called "sons" through faith witness with an unswerving confession that he is the King of kings and the Lord of lords.

[19:17-18] *And I saw an angel standing in the sun, and with a loud voice he called to all the birds that fly in mid-heaven: "Come, gather for the great supper of God, that you may eat the flesh of kings and the flesh of captains and the flesh of mighty men and the flesh of horses and their riders and of all men, free and slave, small and great."* He again makes a certain apostrophe and leaving out the nature of the judgment jumps by a kind of leap of the prophetic speech again to the end of time.

He saw an angel standing on the sun. The sun on which this angel is standing is the Faith of the catholic church.[13] Concerning this angel also Daniel spoke as follows: "At that time shall arise Michael, the great prince who stands before the sons of your people."[14] For just as then this holy archangel stood in the sight of God on behalf of the sons of the ancient people, so now he unceasingly intervenes for the people of the whole catholic church. "And there shall be a time, such as never has been since there was a nation till that time."[15] In the Revelation the holy John says that in that time the birds of the earth shall gather to consume the bodies of the impious.

[19:19] *And I saw the beast and the kings of the earth and their armies gathered to make*

---

[10]Jn 10:11, 15. [11]Col 2:10. [12]1 Cor 11:3. [13]By *Faith* Apringius refers to the creed that the church confesses. [14]Dan 12:1. [15]Dan 12:1.

war against him who sits on the horse and against his army. So also here, if you compare the words of the blessed Daniel, you will find one and the same thing. "He will come with a great multitude so that he might exterminate and destroy many."[16] However, in the Revelation it is said that, when the kings of the earth and their armies are gathered together, they will war against him who sits on the horse, that is, against Jesus Christ, and against his army, that is, against all saints who follow him.

[19:20] *And the beast was captured.* Also Daniel says, "No one will help him."[17] When the Lord fights against him, no one is able to bring assistance to him. *And with it was captured also the false prophet who did signs before him.* These words refer to that unclean spirit who performed wondrous deeds before him in order to cause people to fall. *Who deceived those who received the mark of the beast.* Those who were led astray by these persuasive falsehoods are all those who believed in the antichrist and therefore received the mark of the enemy and *who worshiped its image. These two were thrown alive into the lake of fire that burns with sulphur.* [The two thrown into the fire were] the devil, the leader of every evil being, and that one who is most wicked, who is called the antichrist.

[19:21] *And the rest were slain by the sword of him who sits on the horse, the sword that issues from his mouth; and all the birds were gorged with their flesh.* All who have believed the beast will be killed by the judgment of our Lord Jesus Christ and by the breath of his mouth, and their flesh will be put out for the birds of the air and for the beasts of the earth.

REVELATION 20

Likewise the Explanation of Bishop Apringius Concerning the Binding of the Devil During the Same Thousand Years[1]

[20:1] We must entreat the Lord more earnestly here, lest we consent in error concerning the number of the thousand years or through our own excess nurture error. Rather, let us entreat the Lord that he who is called "Faithful" and "True" might keep our faith safe. The Lord himself said at the beginning of this book, "I am the first and the last, am the living one although I was dead; and I have the keys of death and of Hades."[2] By the key it speaks of him who bears the office of ministry, so that he might open the pit of the abyss. The great chain is the unbreakable bond of the divine commandment. It is in his hand, which means that he exercises it by work and deed.

[20:2] And he *seized the dragon,* the enemy of the human race, *who is called the devil and Satan. And he bound him for a thousand years.* In Greek letters, one thousand is designated with an alpha. In the alpha we have the beginning, which is Christ; in the name of Christ we have the cross,[3] which is our victory and the destruction of the evil enemy. Therefore, both by the cross of Christ and by the authority of the cross he bound the enemy of the world who deceived those who dwell on the earth. For to that eternity no time is added, and the eternity of his time will be enclosed by no end, nor will there ever be an end to the number of years.

[20:3] And so by the sovereignty of the Lord through the power of the cross he bound him in the abyss *and sealed it over him,* that is,

[16]Dan 11:44. [17]Dan 11:45. **Revelation 20** [1]The manuscript of Apringius has inserted after Revelation 19 and before Revelation 20 material from Jerome's recension of Victorinus. This subtitle reflects that preceding material, indicating that the commentary of Apringius on the same subject matter will now begin. For discussion of the manuscript, see CCL 107:17-20. [2]Rev 1:17-18. [3]Apringius is thinking of the X in the name Χριστός.

placed on it the bolt of the cross so that he might never regain his strength, nor any more seduce the nations, whom the resurrection will restore and make better.

However, what comes next seems in opposition to this explanation. "Until the thousand years shall be ended. After that he must be loosed for a little while." However, one can understand this to mean to the extent that the will of our Lord, Jesus Christ, and his authority allow. "For a little while," that is, in a moment of time and by the power of the one who commands, Satan is dissolved into nothing and at the same time disappears. For if he is loosed so that he might be free, how then does he say, "I saw thrones?" This is similar to the most holy Daniel, who speaks in the same sense as follows: "In that day your people shall be saved, every one whose name shall be found written in the book. And many of those who sleep in the dust of the earth shall awake, some to eternal life, and some to disgrace, that they might eternally see."[4] For, how is he released from chains if the resurrection is already celebrated and if the seats of judgment are seen?

[20:4] *And they sat on them and judgment was given to them* that they might judge concerning every person and the saints might scatter all the nations of the earth. *And I saw the souls of those who had been beheaded for the name of Jesus and for the Word of God, and who had not worshiped the beast or its image and had not received its mark on their foreheads or on their hands. And they came to life and reigned with Christ a thousand years.* The souls of all the martyrs and of all the Christian faithful who rise again and awaken from the dust of the earth shall reign, it says, with Christ for a thousand years. That is, they will reign by the sign of the cross and by the pre-eminence of the Lord's passion.

[20:5] *The rest of the dead did not come to life.* He did not say, "They did not arise again," but that they did not come to life, because without joy and happiness, and without the reward of eternity, in their torments they shall be regarded as though dead. *Until the thousand years were ended,* that is, until such time as the sacrament of the faith and the mystery of the cross is perfected in them and that those who are beginning to flourish might appear in their eternal blessedness. *This is the first resurrection.* That is to say, the happiness of the saints and their reward; for it is said to be the "first" because of its splendor and of its preeminence.

[20:6] And therefore it is said: *Blessed and holy is he who shares in the first resurrection. Over them the second death has no power.* He indicates that those over whom the second death has power did not come to life. To be sure, they have been resurrected to the second death, that is, they have been damned to the lake of fire, even as it is stated in the Psalms: "As though living he swallows them as in anger."[5] Indeed, concerning those over whom the second death has no power, it says, *they shall be priests of God, and they shall reign with him a thousand years.* All those who shall have been in the congregation of the saints shall be called saints, and they shall be priests of Christ our God, and they shall reign with him in the strength of the cross and in the sovereignty of his might.

[20:7] This interpretation presents to us a second difficulty, because it said: *And when the thousand years are ended, Satan will be loosed from his prison and will go out to deceive the nations which are at the four corners of the earth, that is, Gog and Magog.* We must inquire how it is that when the thousand years have ended, the enemy is given his freedom and the nations

---

[4]Dan 12:1-2. [5]Ps 57:9 (57:10 LXX).

continue to live on the earth within that infinity [which occurs after the end]. For indeed, after the resurrection, when the judgment of the living and the dead has been rendered, all things everlasting are given, and those who reign with Christ, namely, the saints, will come with God's aid to the eternal blessings themselves, that is, to the very reality of eternality itself. Moreover, they will be rewarded with the contemplation of him who is the Beginning, and possessing the presence of a vision of such a majesty they will be established in its bliss. When the rewards of all the blessed have been consummated and perfected, and all things have been brought to the one headship of our Lord Jesus Christ and in him all things are held together,[6] "Satan will be loosed from his prison." Then the nether regions themselves will be freed of him, at the same time the author of darkness will be dissolved and disappear "and go out" into eternal perdition. "And he will deceive the nations which are at the four corners of the earth, that is, Gog and Magog." In this passage "to deceive" means to scatter or to spoil, that is, to drag the nations along with him into condemnation, namely, all the wicked whom he has deceived in every part of the earth. And he will cause those who have been gathered together with him in one single condemnation to be delivered over to eternal torments.

For Gog means "roof" and Magog means "out of the covering" or "out from the roof." Everyone whom he has brought out and led to the collapse of his own arrogance, or those whom he supported by the roof of pride, or those who will be recognized as coming from the same cover and height of his arrogance, all these persons will be taken at the same time in one condemnation and by an eternal fire. When it says *he will gather them for battle*, it describes as something future what is in the past, for in some manner this battle is the hostility that the wicked have toward good works. And since those who are wicked are many and numerous, he adds, *whose number is like the sand of the sea.*

[20:8] *And they ascended on the height of the earth[7] and surrounded the camp of the saints.* Lifted up by their arrogance, the impious ascended into the heights, but their earthly arrogance holds them back. They are wise in nothing heavenly, nor do they fear the power of celestial greatness. "They surrounded the camp of the saints." This means that they wished to exist in common with the saints, but of them the prophecy is fulfilled that says, "They shall return at evening and be hungry as a dog and go around about the city."[8] In the present passage he calls the city "beloved," saying, *they shall surround the camp of the saints and the beloved city.*

[20:9-10] *And fire came down from God out of heaven and consumed them; and the devil who had deceived them was thrown into the lake of fire and sulphur where the beast was and the false prophet, and they will be tormented day and night forever and ever.* This is that dissolution whereby the seducer perishes along with those whom he has seduced.

However, another interpretation may be given concerning the thousand years, so that the present passage may be confirmed and the signs of the future times might be shown. In those thousand years of which the Apocalypse speaks are contained the seventy-seven weeks of which Daniel speaks, and the sixty-two and one weeks add up to 980 years.[9] The twenty that are omitted in the book of Daniel are either reserved for the preparation of the evil that is coming, or they have been left out because of the magnitude of that evil. For as

---

[6]See Col 1:17. [7]The text of Apringius and Caesarius of Arles reads *ascenderunt super altitudinem terrae*, not *super latitudinem* as in the text of Primasius and Bede. [8]Ps 59:6 (58:7 LXX). [9]See Dan 9:24-27.

the Lord taught in the Gospel, it is necessary at the coming of the enemy that there be the beginning of the sorrows and the presence of great tribulations.[10] The half week, that is, the three and a half years in which "offering and sacrifice shall cease"[11] refers to that time of the accursed one when "he will sit in the temple of God," that is, in the church, "showing himself as though he were himself God," as the apostle says.[12] And at that time no one of the faithful will offer any offering or sacrifice to the Almighty God when "he will see the desolating sacrilege,"[13] that is, the image of the antichrist. These are, I think, the thousand years of which the Apocalypse speaks, because through faith all the saints will have risen with Christ. After the beginning of the oracle, Daniel heard that those who had died in sins will rise up as also those who were holy and approved people.

Concerning these persons the book of the Maccabees says many things. At the time of Antiochus, who assumed the form of that most perverse antichrist, many are reported to have become martyrs.[14] Also at the coming of our Lord Jesus Christ, all who shall have risen through faith in Christ and the grace of baptism also reign with Christ, as long as the world remains. For the world too reigns, in heretics and schismatics[15] and pagans, and gathering together the multitude of their perversity, they daily fight against the holy church, until that final evil shall come that is full of every error. And then offering and sacrifice shall cease "in order that those who are approved may be manifested"[16] and the faith of the saints appear more clearly.

Moreover, the sword that issues from the Lord's mouth is said to have slain those whom we mentioned above,[17] namely, the impious people who believed the antichrist. For they received the mark of the beast and by believing evil announce his coming for judgment, and

they worshiped his image and added that perfidy to their own wickedness. The birds, that is, the demons are called to the great banquet of God and devour these persons by an unholy eating frenzy. Concerning these it is written, "The dragon that you did make to play in it, all look to you so that you may give them food in due season."[18]

In my opinion, after these years the enemy of humankind, who tempted those who dwell at the four regions of the earth, Gog and Magog, will be set free from his prison. Concerning these the prophet Ezekiel speaks, saying, "The word of the Lord came to me, saying, 'Son of man, set your face toward Gog and Magog.'"[19] He has taught us here the locations of the nations, so that from the names of the places he might reveal to us those peoples against whom he was speaking. These are the regions of the Scythians, and therefore he also says, "prince of the head of Meshech and Tubal,"[20] so that he might indicate the beginning of Europe. For Meshech indicates Cappadocia, and Tubal signifies Spain, so that in these two places he might indicate the whole of Europe at the same time. And now I will briefly comment on the meaning contained in these names. Gog means "roof" or "ceiling" and Magog means "from the roof." Meshech means "of the head," while Tubal means "the one taken away." And so you may recognize in the "roof" him who is exalted to the height of pride, and in "from the roof" you may understand those who partake of him and are compatriots of his disgraceful folly. And therefore Meshech, that is, "of the head" follows because he always brings souls to death so that he might possess them. Furthermore, Tubal, which means "he who takes away" or "he who is taken away," is understood to be he who always brings on evil or who is led away to death. Nor is it in vain that we read all these things that are in the

---

[10]Mt 24:8. [11]Dan 9:27. [12]2 Thess 2:4. [13]Mt 24:15. [14]See 2 Macc 5:11-14. [15]Translating *dogmaticis*. [16]Dan 9:27; 1 Cor 11:19. [17]See Rev 1:16; 19:15. [18]Ps 104:26-27 (103:26-27 LXX). [19]Ezek 38:1-2. [20]Ezek 38:3.

holy Scriptures, if we recognize that something else is indicated by the significance of the names. For the Lord himself threatens that he himself will oppose him, and not through some spiritual minister of God, saying, "Behold, I am against you, prince of the head of Meshech and Tubal; and I will turn you about, and put a bridle into your jaws."[21] The author of arrogance deserves to have the Lord himself as an opponent, even as it was also said of the king of the Assyrians, "I will put my ring in your nostrils and my bridle in your mouth."[22] And in the psalm it is read, "With bit and bridle restrain their jaw so that they do not come near to you,"[23] so that the pride of the adversaries might be destroyed because the Lord himself is restraining them. "And I will bring you forth and all your army, horses and horsemen all of them clothed in full armor, a great company of those who wield spear and shield and sword."[24] We read of this also in Daniel, "The king of the north shall come as a tempest with chariots and horsemen and with many ships; and he shall come into countries and over run them and pass through."[25] And if one should investigate and compare, he will discover that these very passages announce the presence of the antichrist. As in Daniel it says that he will come with many ships and a great army, so here in Ezekiel it says, "I will bring you forth and all your army, horses and horsemen all of them clothed in full armor, a multitude of those who wield spear and shield and sword."[26]

And to indicate more clearly that all of this is written about the antichrist, it adds, "Persians, Ethiopians and Libyans with them."[27] For Persia means "tempter," and what is demonstrated in the enemy if not the force of its temptation? The Ethiopians signify "shadows" or "darkness," because that enemy will advance surrounded by shadows and darkness. The Libyans symbolize "those who are coming."

The shadows, the darkness, the temptation always are coming, but they are unable to arrive at their goal. They always go forth to kill everyone. David says, "He sits with the rich in hidden places so that he might kill the innocent. But God will not hand them over into his hands, nor will the Lord condemn the just when he is brought to judgment."[28] All who come with him are described as bearing shields and helmets. He wears the helmet of wickedness, and he clothes himself with the shield of arrogance. What kind of persons come with him are indicated by the words "Gomer and all his hordes."[29] Gomer is interpreted as "consummation," for with him comes the end, devastation and ruin and everything that pertains to death. "Beth-togarmah, from the uttermost parts of the north."[30] In Jeremiah we read, "Out of the north all evil will break forth on the face of all the earth."[31] Togarmah means "exiled" and signifies the complete forced wandering and utter exile of the enemy.

[20:12] *And books were opened.* What is this book that God has if not that the works of each person are declared by the authority of the one who is judge? God is said to have a book, which is not a physical book but a spiritual book, that is, the eternal memory in which the names of the elect are kept. And so the psalm says, "The righteous shall be in everlasting remembrance."[32] *And another book was opened, which is the Book of Life.* The Book of Life, and Life itself, is the Lord Jesus Christ. Then it shall be opened, that is, made manifest to every creature, when he will render to each according to his work. *And the dead were judged by what was written in the books, by what they had done.* "God has spoken once, and I have heard these two things," it says.[33] And what these two things are he makes clearer when he says, "The kingdom is the Lord's, and

---

[21]Ezek 38:3-4. [22]Is 37:29. [23]See Ps 32:9 (31:9 LXX). [24]Ezek 38:4. [25]Dan 11:40. [26]Ezek 38:4. [27]Ezek 38:5. [28]Ps 9:29 LXX; Ps 37:33 (36:33 LXX). [29]Ezek 38:6. [30]Ezek 38:6. [31]Jer 1:14. [32]Ps 112:6 (111:6 LXX). [33]Ps 62:11 (61:12 LXX).

he is the governor of the nations."[34] There he heard of the kingdom; here he has beheld the book. There he heard two things; here he has also seen another book. And what is contained in these two books he says there, "the power of God is also yours, O Lord, and mercy."[35] The power is in the judging and the mercy in the giving of recompense. "And the dead were judged by what was written in the books, by what they had done." And so he says there, "for you will recompense everyone according to his works."[36] O, what a great likeness this is of what was spoken! Anyone who investigates with wisdom, to that extent the saint will not flee from the truth.

[20:13] *And the sea gave up the dead who were in it, and death and Hades gave up the dead who were in them.* Lest anyone say that those who have died at sea or have been drowned by water or have been eaten by beasts or have been destroyed by fire cannot be raised again, it says that they gave up their dead. And since no one will escape the judgment of God, it adds, *and all were judged by what they had done.*

[20:14] Lest anyone should think that after the resurrection there follows a death of the body, an opinion that is profane to believe and even to mention, he added, *Then Hades and death were sent into the lake of fire.* This is to show that since death has been overtaken no one will die again. Moreover, since the nether region has been condemned, hell will find no one further whom it might receive.

[20:15] *And whoever is not found written in the Book of Life is thrown into the lake of fire.* Whoever did not believe during life and did not open his mouth in confession of our Lord Jesus Christ shall be destroyed along with death and hell because he failed to receive life.

Nevertheless, we do not confess that everyone will die or come to punishment. Rather, that will be fulfilled which we read in Daniel: "Some shall rise to everlasting life, and some to everlasting contempt, so that they might always behold."[37] And what shall they always behold, if not that they are tormented but others are glorified?

REVELATION 21

[21:1] *And I saw a new heaven and a new earth; for the first heaven and earth had passed away, and the sea was no more.* These things occur just as they are described by the witness of Isaiah who, speaking from the word of the Lord, says, "Behold, I create a new heaven and a new earth; and the former things shall not be remembered or come into mind. But you will be glad and rejoice forever on the day which I create."[1]

[21:2] *And I saw the holy city, new Jerusalem, coming down out of heaven, prepared as a bride adorned for her husband.* The heavenly Jerusalem is the multitude of the saints who will come with the Lord, even as Zechariah said: "Behold, my Lord God will come, and all his saints with him."[2] These are being prepared for God as a fine dwelling, namely, those who will live with him. "As a bride adorned for her husband." Adorned with holiness and righteousness, they go to be united with their Lord and shall remain with him forever.

[21:3-4] *And I heard a loud voice saying, "Behold, the dwelling of God is with men; and he will live with them, and they shall be his people, and God himself will be with them as their God. And God will wipe away every tear from their eyes, and death shall be no more, neither shall there be mourning nor sorrow, nor crying,*

---

[34]Ps 22:28 (21:29 LXX). [35]Ps 62:11-12 (61:12-13 LXX). [36]Ps 62:12 (61:13 LXX). [37]Dan 12:2. **Revelation 21** [1]Is 65:17-18. [2]Zech 14:5.

because the former things have passed away. The Lord gives witness to himself, for the multitude of the saints will become his temple, so that he might dwell with them forever and that he might be their Lord and they might be his people. He will take away all weeping and every tear from the eyes of those whom he rewards with eternal gladness and whom he makes bright with perpetual blessedness.

[21:5] *And he who sat on the throne said, "Behold, I make all things new."* The promise of the Most High is accomplished for the saints, so that they might be renewed in all things and might shine with every splendor. Therefore, the apostle says, "and the dead will rise incorruptible,"[3] and they will change into glory.

[21:6-8] *And he says, "Write, for these words are most trustworthy and true." And he said to me, "It is done!"* He declares that the matter is completed with such quickness so that it might be regarded as though it had already happened. Therefore, all these things are promised to those who conquer, so that the one who conquers might be called "son of God."

[21:8-9] *But as for the unthankful, the faithless, murderers, idolaters, fornicators, sorcerers, and liars.* The lake of fire and sulphur, which is called the "second death," is promised for the punishment of evildoers.

[21:10-11] Then he is led by an angel *in the spirit to a great and high mountain.* That is, he is elevated to the height of faith, so that he might behold the bride of the Lamb. *And he showed the holy city Jerusalem coming down out of heaven from God, having the glory of God.* We read of this very city in the prophets: "The sun shall be no more your light by day, nor shall the brightness of the moon give you light.

But the Lord will be everlasting light, and your God will be your glory."[4]

And its light was like that of a precious jewel, as jasper, like crystal. As the brilliance of a stone shines neither in itself nor from the outside but is translucent by the clarity of its nature, so this city is described as illumined by no radiance of the stars but as invisibly illumined by the light of God alone. The shining clarity of the crystal signifies that in the city the grace of baptism shines with a reddish hue.[5]

[21:12] *And it had a great, high wall.* Zechariah said, "For I will be," says the Lord, "a wall of fire round about."[6] What is so great and high as the Lord of majesty, who with the protection of his presence surrounds the holy city? *And it had twelve gates and at the gates twelve corners,*[7] *and the names of the twelve tribes of the sons of Israel were written on the gates.* In the Gospel we read that the Lord spoke concerning himself: "I am the door; if anyone enters by me, he will enter and will find pasture."[8] Therefore, Christ is the door. However, the ancient people of our faith are named together not as doors, but their names are written on the gates, that is, on the doors. Thus our Lord shows to all the saints that he is the door of truth and freedom. This shows that the whole band of the patriarchs belonged to the faith in our Lord, Jesus Christ.

The twelve corners of the gates and the twelve gates and the twelve foundations on which the names of the apostles and of the Lamb are written yield the number of thirty-six. It is clear that this is the number of hours that our Lord, Jesus Christ, lay in the grave after his passion. This demonstrates that the host of leaders who came beforehand and the chorus of apostles who came afterward had been redeemed by the one faith and passion

---

[3]1 Cor 15:52. [4]Is 60:19. [5]Baptism is into the death of Christ. [6]Zech 2:5. [7]The text of Apringius reads *angulos* ("corners"), not *angelos* ("angels"), as does the text of Caesarius of Arles and Bede. [8]Jn 10:9.

of the Lord and that they have come to the knowledge of the omnipotent God through the one entrance of faith in Christ, who is the door. For also the names of the apostles are said to be written on the twelve foundations, because Christ is the foundation, as Paul says: "For no other foundation can anyone lay than that which is laid, which is Jesus Christ."[9] And he himself is in each, and each is in him. The Lord says, "You are Peter, and on this rock I will build my church."[10] And it is written in the words of the most blessed Paul that "the rock was Christ."[11] Therefore, it is Peter to whom the Lord spoke: "On this rock I will build my church."[12] That is, the church is built on the faith in the incarnation, passion and resurrection of the Lord.[13]

[21:13] Then it indicates that the gates are divided into four groups: *on the east three gates, on the north three gates, on the south three gates, and on the west three gates.* This signifies that the four parts of the world have accepted the mystery of the Trinity. That the names of the patriarchs are inscribed demonstrates that the ancient faith has been fulfilled.

[21:15] *And he who talked with me had a measuring rod of gold to measure the city and its gates and walls.* The wall of fire surrounding it is the Lord, as we have already said. The golden measuring rod is the faith concerning the Lord's incarnation, for on account of its purity and sinlessness his body is revealed to be clearer and more brilliant than any metal. He alone is the one through whom the measure of the faith and the integrity of the holy city is established, and he only is recognized as the measure of its gates and the height of its wall.

[21:16] *And the great city lies foursquare.* That

is, the city persists in the faith of the fourfold gospel. It is said that its length is the same as its breadth, so that one might see that in its faith there is nothing disproportionate, nothing that has been added and nothing that has been taken away. *And he measured the city with his rod, twelve stadia; its length and height and breadth are all equal.* He measured the city with his rod, which we understand to be the body of Christ, and it was twelve stadia. For the faith in Christ and the integrity of the holy people are recognized by means of these twelve stadia, that is, by means of the teaching of the apostles and the faith of the ancient fathers. "For the length and the breadth were the same." All things are equal, for nothing is found in the saints that is superfluous or that comes from the outside, nor is anything inferior found within them.

There are twelve stadia, which are the length of one thousand paces and five stadia. Let us consider what mysteries this number contains for our understanding. We read in the Psalms concerning the law of the Lord: "The words that you commanded for a thousand generations."[14] In this number, therefore, there is reckoned that which is full and complete,[15] so that he might show that all the fullness of the saints is made strong in faith by the sevenfold form of the Holy Spirit. This form consists not in thought but in the virtues. For the Spirit is said to be of wisdom and understanding; he is said to be of counsel and might; he is said to be of knowledge and piety; and he is said to be the Spirit of the fear of the Lord.[16] Moreover, one stadium is 143 paces in length, and therefore each stadium contains in the number one hundred the perfection of the saints and the faith of those on the right side.[17] In the number forty we are to understand that the perfect fullness of the ten words of the law

---

[9]1 Cor 3:11. [10]Mt 16:18. [11]1 Cor 10:4. [12]Mt 16:18. [13]It seems most likely that Apringius is summarizing the content of the Christian creed, rather than referring to that personal faith that believes in the incarnation, passion and resurrection of Christ. [14]P 105:8 (104:8 LXX). [15]That is, the number thousand. "That which is full and complete" translates *plenitudo*. [16]Is 11:2. [17]See Mt 25:33-34.

are contained in the fourfold teaching of the Gospels.[18] In the number three is the mystery of the Trinity.

The five stadia that remain—so that we might complete the twelve—indicate that under this mystery of the number, that we have mentioned, the understanding of rational minds are able to agree with the discipline of the dominical faith, so that in the measuring of the city of God it can be reckoned. Likewise, the five stadia, which are 715 paces in length,[19] possess seven hundreds. By this it is shown that the precepts of the perfect persist in the seven days of the present world, for "in six days God made heaven and earth, and on the seventh day he rested from his works."[20] And we believe that the world is established in seven days, for in the Gospel the Lord says concerning the last day, "Pray that your flight may not be in winter or on a sabbath."[21] This number represents the fact, as is shown when the seven hundred is considered, that in the seven days, in which the world exists, the full completion of the saints increases and grows strong in the mystery of the faith that we have mentioned.

The three fives that remain signify that, as the apostle teaches, the fullness of deity dwells bodily in our Lord Jesus Christ.[22] Moreover, the number fifteen can be divided into three parts. It shows that beyond all human thoughts, beyond all human comprehension <***> that our Lord Jesus Christ remains the assumed man, lest anyone dare think that in him there is a limitation of the flesh similar to us.[23] Rather, you ought recognize that his flesh shines brightly beyond the body of even the most worthy, beyond the understanding of the saints, because in him exists the fullness of deity, as he said: "I am in the Father, and the Father is in me."[24] Indeed, in him all power exists; nothing is coequal with mortals.

Although it might be said that due to the assumption of the flesh he was made our equal, he must be believed to be beyond all flesh, for the apostle says, "Even though we knew Christ according to the flesh, we now no longer know him in that manner."[25] We must certainly not think that he can be regarded as a common human person.

[21:17] Now we must consider the measure in the wall itself, for the wall of this city is our Lord Jesus Christ. That it was measured by the measure of a man indicates that the assumed man is beneficial for the protection of the saints and for the safeguarding of all bliss. This measure of a man is said to be that of an angel because he is himself the angel of the covenant of whom it is said, "The Lord whom you seek will suddenly come to his temple; the messenger of the covenant whom you desire."[26] And again it is said, "His name will be called Wonderful Counselor, Mighty God, Everlasting Father, Prince of Peace."[27]

Let us see what mystery is contained in the fact that its height is measured to be 144 cubits. One hundred, composed of ten tens, passes to the right side, and from this it is most wonderfully shown that the full plenitude of the saints and all righteousness that is perfected in the fulfillment of the Decalogue and the proclamation of the gospel is held in the right hand of our Lord Jesus Christ. However, the forty-four when divided into four tens and the remaining four ones indicates similarly that the fourfold truth of the gospel and the perfection of every heavenly doctrine remain in his power. Moreover, the number twenty-four itself is the sum of two equal parts so that it might show that the fullness of the ancient law and the power of the gospel rest in him and come from him. We know that this is

---

[18]Ten (the Decalogue) times four (the four Gospels) equals forty. [19]Above Apringius noted that a stadia consists of 143 paces. Five stadia, therefore, equal 715 paces. [20]See Ex 20:11. [21]Mt 24:20. [22]Col 2:9. [23]A lacuna makes this statement uncertain. [24]Jn 14:10. [25]2 Cor 5:16. [26]Mal 3:1. [27]Is 9:6.

a figure of the apostles of the Lamb and of the patriarchs and is the very image of the twenty-four elders. This number [i.e., twenty-four] multiplied six times teaches that in the six days of this present week in which the world exists, the entire congregation and multitude of the saints is included, even as in our Lord Jesus Christ there is every perfection and in him the full righteousness of all the saints is shown to be safeguarded.[28]

However, every measure of the city that is mentioned in this book contains also a number of the times, for certainly in these times the perfect righteousness of the saints has made advance. For the twelve stadia, that extend to 1715 paces, when the 144 cubits of the height [of the wall] are added, become 5289 cubits. Indeed, the Evangelists testify that our Lord Jesus Christ, who is the completion of truth and righteousness and in whom the highest perfection of all things is contained, was born from the virgin Mary in this age of the world, that is, in the six thousandth year. Therefore, he said, "The last hour has come."[29] In saying this, he shows that he even now at the end of times offers salvation, that he proffers to people, and, before the day of judgment itself comes, he does not refuse the mercy of his own love.

[21:18] *And its wall was built from jasper.* Jasper glimmers with a certain faint greenness and so shows the modest face of virginity. This is so that you might understand that our Lord Jesus Christ is joined to every building of the city and that that body taken from the flesh of the Virgin rises up for the protection of the whole wall. *The city itself was pure gold, pure as glass.* In this most pure gold, which is purified by the heat of fire and so is proven, we perceive the chorus of the saints who have

been tested in the furnace of suffering and by the heat of temptation and so have been made pure through the power of the Lord. They are compared with pure glass to indicate the transparent and pure brightness of the holiness that is in them.

[21:19] *The foundations of the wall of the city were adorned with every precious jewel.* These foundations of the city are understood to be the apostolic faith and the preaching of the apostles, on which our Lord Jesus Christ constructs his city. For he who is the Foundation of foundations is himself the builder who on the faith in his own most blessed name builds the holy church, which consists of those who were the very first and of those who follow after them until the end of the world, which is unknown to us. The various precious stones signify the apostles because in each of them shine the gifts and miracles that belong to the Holy Spirit. Moreover, that the brightness of the unified light is seen within them indicates that what shines outward from them never ceases to exist within.

[21:21] *And the twelve gates were twelve pearls, each of the gates from a single pearl.* It is one thing to speak of each of the pearls; it is another thing to speak of the one pearl from which they come. For when it speaks of each pearl, it is shown that in each pearl one pearl is shining forth and that this one pearl is our Lord Jesus Christ. And when the pearls are related to a single pearl, we are taught that the apostolic teaching possesses already the light of righteousness that it has received from him. Just as Christ is the door, so also the apostles are the doors through which we are taught and enter into the faith.

The following words reveal the difference

---

[28]The two equal parts of twenty-four, that is twelve and twelve, represent the twelve patriarchs and the twelve apostles. Multiplied, 12 x 12 = 144. Similarly, 24 x 6 = 144. In both instances the number of cubits of the height of the wall.   [29]1 Jn 2:28. Although the letter of John seems to be quoted, the sense of the passage indicates that Jesus is the speaker.

of merit that exists within the very beatitude of the saints. For above it was said that the entirety of the city was like pure gold, clear as glass.[30] Now it says that *the streets of the city are pure gold, transparent as glass.* These are the saints of the city that are of lesser merit. Nonetheless, gathered together into one congregation, it is indicated that they do not shine with a lesser light.

[21:22] *And I saw no temple in the city. The Lord God Almighty is its temple.* God established the temple so that the people gathered within the walls of the temple might call on him whom neither the world nor the temple can contain. In this way their minds might obtain through the work of faith what cannot be seen of God. However, where he openly manifests himself to the faithful there a temple is neither desired nor existent, for he who sanctifies the temple is known in the sight of all.

[21:23] *And the city had no need of sun or moon to shine in it, for the glory of God gives it light.* What an image there is in these words, that the city, which has no need of a temple, has no need of the brightness of the heavenly luminaries! And what is the reason for this? Because the glory of God gives it light. The glory of God, that is, the presence of his majesty, about which it is said: "We shall see him as he is."[31] Therefore, why would those who shall see God have need of sun or moon?

[21:24-26] *And its lamp is the Lamb, and by its light shall the nations walk, and the kings of the earth shall bring their glory and honor into it. And its gates shall not be shut by day, for there shall be no night in it. And the nations shall bring their glory and honor into it.*

[21:26] By the light, the Lamb is clearly shown to be the city's lamp, and the kings and the nations will walk in his light. The prophet knew this and said: "In your light we shall see light."[32] The apostle also spoke concerning this light: "The night is far gone, the day is at hand."[33] The Evangelist also writes in a similar way: "The life was the light of people, and the light shines in the darkness, and the darkness did not comprehend it."[34] This is to say, what the nature of our weakness had concealed and what the shadow of our humanity had rendered dark was made clear by the assumption of the Lord's body. And while God, who is light, inhabits the lot of our flesh, he enlightens the whole by the greatness of his glory. For this reason the honor and the glory of the kings and the nations are given to him, because all have been made glorious through him, and the darkness of night shall not overcome his faithful, whom the presence of the Lamb and the Word of the ineffable, unbegotten Father illuminate.

[21:27] *Nothing unclean shall enter it, nor what touches uncleanliness and falsehood. None shall enter into it, except those who are written in the Lamb's book of life.* It is true that no one enters into that communion of the saints who either refuses to be cleansed of former sins and from the guilt of their parents, or having become filthy after purification refused to be cleansed by the washing of humility and the shedding of tears. Indeed, Judas committed such an abomination, and so does a heretic who worships God deceitfully. However, those are said to enter who are written in the Lamb's Book of Life, namely, those whom the heart of a true faith and a firm hope embrace.

REVELATION 22

[22:1] *And he showed me the river of the water of life, bright as crystal, flowing from the throne of God and of the Lamb.* The living water is the

---

[30]See Rev 21:18. [31]1 Jn 3:2. [32]Ps 36:9 (35:10 LXX). [33]Rom 13:12. [34]Jn 1:4-5.

Lord Jesus Christ. Of this water he spoke to the Samaritan woman: "If you knew the gift of God and who it was who says to you, 'give me to drink,' you would rather ask from him, and he would give to you the living water."[1] He was speaking of the knowledge of his deity and the fullness of a holy faith. For concerning him it is said: "For with you is the fountain of life."[2] For they are buried with him through baptism, as the apostle says: "For we have been buried with him by baptism into death."[3] Therefore, the living water that is like crystal and is perfectly clear is the washing of the holy font and the resulting brightness of a most blessed faith. It is said to flow from the throne of God and of the Lamb because the cleansing is from him, life is from him, and all righteousness and holiness of baptism flows from and proceeds from him.

[22:2] *In the middle of its street*, it says. Concerning wisdom it is said: "She proclaims outside, she raises her voice in the streets, and she cries out on the top of the walls."[4] And should anyone refuse to come to the marriage of the king, she commands her servants and says, "Go to the streets and byways and invite whomever you meet to the wedding, that my house might be filled."[5] This water of salvation and the cleansing of grace are described as flowing in the streets. *Also on either side of the river the tree of life bearing twelve kinds of fruit, yielding its fruit each month; and the leaves of the tree were for the salvation of the nations.* The two banks of the river are the two Testaments in which the fullness of our salvation is written down. There is the tree of life. There is told the story of our Lord Jesus Christ, who is the tree of life: "Through him we live, move and have our being."[6] The leaves are his words; they are of use for the health of all nations. The twelve months are the apostles of the Lord, because the Lord himself is the "favorable year of forgiveness."[7]

These are the twelve months, each bringing to the many the fruit of unending preaching out of an abundance of knowledge.

[22:3-4] *There shall no more be anything accursed, but the throne of God and of his Lamb, and his servants shall serve him, and they shall see his face and his name shall be on their foreheads.* There will be in that city nothing accursed, that is, no temptation will approach, no profane sin shall be recorded through the rashness of the envious one. Rather, in its midst will be the rule of the divine power and of the Lamb. All will serve him with the great joy of their happiness. They shall rejoice in the vision of his face and in the sweetness of his presence, and they shall bear his name engraved in the sign of his cross on their foreheads.

[22:5] *And night shall be no more; they need no light of lamp or sun, for our Lord shines on them, and they shall reign forever and ever.* Neither the night of sin nor the darkness of unrighteousness will ever appear again. Nor in that bliss will the saints live by the words of any teacher; nor established in such a fullness will they require the light of another's understanding. The Lord himself will give them great understanding and wisdom, for all knowledge that is desired is revealed in the brightness of his countenance. And they shall reign in all wisdom and truth.

[22:6-7] *And he said to me: "These words are most trustworthy and true. And the Lord God, Spirit of the prophets, has sent his angel to show his servants what must soon take place. Behold, I am coming quickly. Blessed is he who keeps the words of the prophecy of this book."* What is so faithful and true as the promise of Christ and the future hope of the saints? He who spoke through his servants and prophets did so that he might be recognized as the Lord of the

---

Revelation 22   [1]Jn 4:10. [2]Ps 36:9 (35:10 LXX). [3]Rom 6:4. [4]Prov 1:20-21. [5]Lk 14:23. [6]Acts 17:28. [7]Is 61:2.

living and be called "the Spirit of the Lord."
For the Spirit is life, and all flesh is made alive
by the Spirit. By the messenger of the truth
the Lord directly reveals "to his servants what
must soon take place." And unless anyone is
in doubt about the expectation of the end, he
indicates that what is to happen will happen
quickly and that he is blessed who keeps the
words of the prophets.

[22:8] *I, John, am he who heard and saw these
things. And when I heard and saw them, I fell
down to worship at the feet of the angel who
showed them to me.* John, the most blessed of
the apostles, says that when he heard these
words he was overcome with fright by the
power of the words and the magnitude of the
vision and fell to the ground because of this.
And he says that he was prostrate that he
might adore the angel of truth "who showed
these things to me."

[22:9] And since there is no pride in the
servant nor any vanity in the saints, the angel
immediately exhorts him, *"You must not do
that! I am a fellow servant with you and your
brethren the prophets, and with those who keep
the words of this book. Worship God."* The angel
proclaims that nothing is equal to the Creator,
and he declares that nothing can be offered to
another that is owed to the Lord God only.

[22:10] *And he said to me, "Do not seal up the
words of the prophecy of this book, for the time
is near."* He says that the time of retribution
and of the end is near. With heavenly words
he indicates the reason why those things that
were commanded and spoken ought not be left
in silence. Rather, they were written for the
admonition of all.

[22:11] *Let the evildoer still do evil, and the
filthy still be filthy.* The angel does not desire
that sinners perish. He rather warns those who
do iniquity so that hearing the sound of a celestial threat, they might wish to abstain from
evil works. Moreover, that the righteous might
be made even better, he says, *Let the righteous
still do right, and the holy still be holy.* He says
this that they might realize the imminent
coming of the Lord and that they might more
easily keep themselves from sin and from that
time forward always devote themselves to holiness and righteousness.

[22:13] *I am the Alpha and the Omega, the
first and the last, the beginning and the end.*
Concerning this enough has already been sufficiently said in the previous sections.

[22:14] Blessed *are those who wash their robes,
that their power might be in the tree of life and
they might enter the city through the gates.* He
calls those blessed who either wash their nup-
tial garment in the blood of the Lord's passion
through the washing of regeneration that they
receive or who through the sorrow of their
heart and with tears accomplish the washing
away of sins committed at the present time.
He indicates that without doubt these will
have the right to possess the tree of life.[8] This
is that right, that they see the face of our Lord
Jesus Christ, who is true life, and rejoice, and
that they desire to be admitted to his presence
through the gates, that is, through the doctrine
of the apostles and the prophets, which they
worked to fulfill.

[22:15] *Outside are dogs and sorcerers and
fornicators and murderers and idolaters, and
everyone who loves and practices falsehood.*
Those who are outside the congregation of the
saints will be manifestly thrown out of the ark
of blessedness.

---

[8]Apringius's text reads *super lignum vitae potestatem.* I have translated *potestas super* to suggest the idea of a right granted for the possession of something.

[22:16] He moreover declares by whose authority these things have been shown or said to John when he continues, *I, Jesus, have sent my angel to witness to you in the churches. I am the root and the offspring of David, the bright Morning Star.* This is that star of truth by which the magi themselves were led to his salutary presence. For our exposition can bring forward nothing more clearly than do the very words of this book.

[22:17] *The Spirit and the Bride say, "Come."* The Holy Spirit and the church call all to come to salvation. *He who hears, let him say, "Come."* And whoever keeps the words of this prophecy and hears him whom the Lord himself has commanded to speak, he is worthy to be taught. *And he who thirsts, let him come, and he who desires, let him receive the water of life without price.* Salvation is given without any price and without any barter. Rather, he who desires to be saved, he will enter and will either receive free of charge the regeneration of baptism, or he will receive the remedy of repentance without cost or charge. The prophet spoke in a similar manner: "All who thirst, come to the waters; and you who have no money, hasten, come, buy and eat."[9]

[22:18-19] *I warn everyone who hears the words of the prophecy of this book: if anyone adds to them, God may add to him the plagues described in this book. And if anyone takes away from the words of the book of this prophecy, God may take away his share in the tree of life and in the holy city and in those things described in this book.* This does not imply that the words that he had spoken were not to be explained. Rather,

around that very time in which the saint had his vision, the error of various teachers and heretics began to emerge and to take their rise. Therefore, in order that no one promoting error might through the usual deceit of their error intend either to add or to subtract from his words and in that way seek to confirm their views by the witness of this most holy man, he determined to conclude his book with this warning.

[22:20] And that no one might think that what he said was merely a human opinion, he now mentions the Lord Jesus Christ, who is the author of these things. *He who testifies to these things says,* that is, the very same Lord Jesus Christ who commanded me to write these things: *Surely, I am coming soon.* He makes known the certainty and the quickness of his coming. And already certain of his own blessedness, this saint fervently declares, *Come, Lord Jesus.*

May the almighty Jesus Christ grant to us that as we earnestly await his coming we might, with his protection, keep ourselves from every grave sin, and that when our desire is fulfilled, he find nothing in us worthy of punishment. But should there be anything to pardon, may he nevertheless have mercy on the accused and not condemn the sinner. May he with whom the blessed One lives and reigns forever grant this. Amen.

The Exposition of the Revelation is completed which the Lord Bishop Apringius has made.

I give thanks to God, now that this labor is ended.

---

[9]Is 55:1.

CAESARIUS OF ARLES
Exposition on the Apocalypse

EXPOSITION ON THE REVELATION OF SAINT JOHN

[In the reading of the Revelation of the holy apostle John, dearest brethren, we direct our minds and will take care to explain, the Lord granting it, the reading according to its anagogical meaning.[1] For the revelation of Jesus Christ makes itself wide for our ears, so that those heavenly realities that are hidden might be manifested to our hearts.

"The Revelation of Jesus Christ, which God gave him to make clear to his servants," that is, to manifest to his servants, "what must soon take place, signifying it," that is, showing it, "to his servant John." John is interpreted as the grace of God, and he writes these things "to the seven churches that are in Asia." Asia means "elevated," and through it the human race is indicated. These seven churches and the seven lampstands are to be seriously considered, because they represent the sevenfold grace that is given by God through Jesus Christ, our Lord, to us of the human race who have believed. For he himself promised to send to us the Spirit Paraclete from heaven, whom he also sent to the apostles who were seen to be in Asia, that is, in the prideful world, where he also gave the sevenfold grace to the seven churches, that is, to us, through his servant

John. "Grace to you and peace be multiplied from God the Father and from the Son of man," that is, from Christ.][2]

Dearest brothers, that which is contained in the Revelation of Saint John seemed to some of the ancient fathers to signify, either in the totality of the reading[3] or certainly in its greatest part, the day of judgment or the coming of the antichrist. Those, however, who have more diligently commented on the Revelation understand that what is contained in this Revelation had begun immediately after the passion of our Lord and Savior and therefore was to be fulfilled to the day of judgment. As a result, only a small period of time remained for the times of the antichrist. Therefore, whatever you shall hear in the recitation of the reading, whether it is of the Son of man or of stars or of angels or of lampstands, or of the four living creatures or of the eagle flying in midheaven, understand that these and everything else are reality in Christ and in the church. Or if you will, recognize that these realities have been declared by way of their types.

On account of the sevenfold Spirit of grace,[4] we are to recognize the one catholic church in the seven churches in Asia to which the Evangelist Saint John wrote. It speaks of "the faithful witness," that is, of Christ, "who gave witness under Pontius Pilate."[5] "He made us,"

Exposition [1]In general, the anagogical sense was that which leads the mind "upward." It leads the mind from the visible to the invisible, from the earthly to the heavenly, from the purely historical to the eschatological. It is important to know that the anagogical meaning was based on the conviction that in the coming of Christ the final purposes of God began to be disclosed. See esp. Henri de Lubac, *Medieval Exegesis*, vol. 2: *The Four Senses of Scripture* (Grand Rapids: Eerdmans; Edinburgh: T&T Clark, 2000), pp. 179-226. For Caesarius, the "heavenly things that are hidden" are especially the spiritual dynamics at work in the earthly lives of people and in the life of the church. [2]Most manuscripts have this *exordium*, or beginning. Only MS C begins as below. [3]Caesarius speaks of a *lectio* that seems to suggest that the text of the Revelation was read to the brothers of the monastery, or perhaps to other members of the clergy. Below he explicitly speaks of "reading the *lectio* out loud" (*in ipsa lectione recitari*). [4]See Is 11:2. [5]See 1 Tim 6:13.

it says, "to be a kingdom and priests to God." When it speaks of priests to God, it refers to the whole church, as Saint Peter said: "You are an elect people, a royal priesthood."[6] "And I saw," it says, "seven golden lampstands." The church is signified by these seven lampstands. "And in the midst of the lampstands was one like a Son of man," that is, Christ.[7] Whether it is the Son of man or the seven lampstands or the seven stars, it is the church together with Christ her head that is to be recognized. It says that this one "was gird with a golden girdle around his breasts." He who is gird signifies Christ the Lord. By the two breasts understand the two Testaments, which receive from the breast of our Lord and Savior as though from a perennial fountain and from which the Testaments nourish the Christian people to eternal life. The golden girdle is the chorus or the multitude of saints. For just as the breast is bound by a girdle, so the multitude of the saints is bound to Christ, so that as the two Testaments are encompassed as two breasts, the saints are nourished by them as by holy paps.

"His head and his hair," it says, "were as white wool, as snow." The white hair is the multitude of those made white, that is, he is speaking of the neophytes who come forth from baptism. He speaks of wool because they are the sheep of Christ. He speaks of snow because just as snow falls freely from heaven, so also the grace of baptism comes apart from any preceding merits.[8] For those who are baptized are Jerusalem, which each day comes down from heaven as though it were snow. Jerusalem, that is, the church, is said to descend from heaven because that grace is from heaven through which it is both freed from

sins and joined to Christ, who is her eternal head and heavenly spouse. But the beast is said to ascend from the abyss, that is, an evil people that is born from an evil people. For just as by descending humbly Jerusalem is exalted, so the beast, that is, that prideful people that arrogantly ascends, is cast down.

"His eyes were like a flame of fire." When he speaks of the eyes of God, he means the commandments, as it is written: "Your word, O Lord, is a lamp to my feet,"[9] and "Your speech has been tested as in a fire."[10] "His feet were like burnished bronze refined as in a furnace of fire." In the feet refined as by fire we are to perceive the church, for as the day of judgment looms nearer, she is tested by a great number of trials and is proved by fire. And since the feet are at the furthest extremity of the body, it is said that the feet are refined as by fire. In this manner the feet represent the church of the end times as a church being tested by many tribulations as gold in a furnace. And whoever considers the matter carefully sees that this is already occurring through a multitude of evils. And so it likens the church to bronze that is brought to the color of gold by the additions of much air and fire and other elements. In a similar manner the church is rendered purer by tribulations and sufferings. The golden girdle that girds round the breast can also be interpreted to be the spiritual knowledge and pure understanding that is given to the church.

"From his mouth issued a sharp two-edged sword." This signifies Christ, who now sends to the whole world the blessings of the gospel and who earlier had sent through Moses the knowledge of the law. David spoke of him in a similar way: "Once God has spoken, two

---

[6]1 Pet 2:9. [7]The *exordium* unique to MS C concludes at this point. [8]Caesarius was the leading participant at the Council of Orange (529), which set out to settle issues of free will, sin and grace occasioned by the theology of Augustine of Hippo. Canon 13 of the Council of Orange states, "Concerning the restoration of free will. The freedom of will that was destroyed in the first man can be restored only by the grace of baptism, for what is lost can be returned only by the one who was able to give it. Hence the Truth himself declares, 'So if the Son makes you free, you will be free indeed'" (Jn 8:36). [9]Ps 119:105 (118:105 LXX). [10]Ps 118:140 LXX. The Latin of Caesarius reads *ignitum eloquium tuum*, corresponding to the πεπυρωμένον τὸ λόγιόν σου σφόδρα of the LXX.

things I have heard."[11] These things are the two Testaments that according to the understanding of the time are called either the new or the old or the sharp two-edged sword.

"His voice was like the sound of many waters." The many waters are understood to be peoples. The voice is the preaching of the apostles. What was said above, that "his feet were like bronze, as though smelted in a furnace," may also be interpreted as referring to the apostles, for they preached his word after the suffering of the Lord. Through them the proclamation walked,[12] and so they are rightly called feet, as the prophet said: "How beautiful are the feet of those who proclaim peace, who proclaim good news,"[13] and in another passage, "Let us worship in the place where his feet have stood."[14]

It says, "In his right hand he held seven stars." By this image it intends to designate the church, for on the right hand of Christ is the spiritual church, which is placed at his right and to whom he says, "Come, blessed of my Father" and following.[15] The seven stars, therefore, are the church, for we have said that the Spirit of sevenfold power has been given to her by the Father, as Peter said to the Jews concerning Christ, "Exalted to the right hand of God, he has poured out the Spirit whom he received from the Father."[16] However, he does not mention the seven churches that he calls by name because they alone are churches. Rather, what he says to one, he speaks to all.[17] Therefore, whether in Asia or in the whole world there are altogether seven churches but one catholic church. As Paul says to Timothy, "How you ought to behave in the house of God, which is the church of the living God."[18] And in Isaiah we read of seven women who have taken hold of one man.[19] The seven women signify the church, which is also one.

The man we understand to be Christ, and the bread of the women is a figure of the Holy Spirit who nourishes us to eternal life.

In order that what has been said might be more firmly impressed on us, we wish to give a recapitulation of them. The seven churches to whom Saint John writes are understood to be the one catholic church because of the sevenfold grace. When it speaks of the faithful witness, it speaks of Christ. The seven lampstands are the catholic church. The one in the midst of the lampstands who is like a Son of man is Christ in the midst of the church. When it speaks of him who is girded about the breasts, we understand the breasts to be the two Testaments that receive spiritual milk from the breast of Christ so that they might nourish the Christian people to eternal life. Indeed, the golden girdle is the chorus or the multitude of the saints who while they persevere together in reading and in prayer are tested to remain close to Christ. For now let this suffice for your charity. By a holy conversation among yourselves, consider what you have heard, until such time as, the Lord granting it, you are able to hear that which still remains. May he deem it worthy to perform this work.

THE CONTINUATION OF THE EXPOSITION OF THE REVELATION (HOMILY 2)

Dearest brothers, the lampstand of which you heard as the Revelation was being read we interpret to be the people. The words "I will move your lampstand" mean "I will scatter the people because of their sins." "And I will fight them with the sword of my mouth." This means that I will make known my commandments through which your sins or transgressions are revealed. The words "his face was shining like the sun in all its bril-

---

[11]Ps 62:11 (61:11 LXX). [12]Caesarius writes *ambulat praedicatio*, remaining faithful to the image of feet. Clearly he means that through the apostles the gospel was extended. [13]Is 52:7; Rom 10:15. [14]Ps 131:7 LXX. [15]Mt 25:34. [16]Acts 2:33. [17]Each of the seven churches represents the church universal. [18]1 Tim 3:15. [19]Is 4:1.

liance" refers to the coming or the presence of Christ because his person is manifested and made known by way of the face. One could also interpret this as a reference to the church, to whom Christ promised that brightness of which he said, "Then the righteous will shine like the sun in the kingdom of their Father."[1]

The "morning star" refers to the first resurrection that occurs through the grace of baptism. The morning star causes the night to flee and announces the coming light, that is, it takes sin away and imparts grace, should however good works follow on the grace received. For it is no great thing if a tree is alive and yet does not produce fruit. So also, there is no advantage if one is called a Christian and yet does not possess Christian works. And for this reason it says, "I counsel you to buy from me refined gold," that is, strive so that you might suffer something for the name of the Lord. "And anoint your eyes with salve," that is, strive so that what you gladly learn from the Scriptures, you might complete by deeds.

"There was an open door in heaven." John, the preacher of the new testament, is given a vision,[2] and there is said to him, "Come up here." When something is shown to be open, it is clear that beforehand it had been closed to humankind. "There was a throne placed in heaven," which is the seat of a judge, and on the throne he saw "one like jasper and carnelian." Jasper has the color of water and carnelian has the color of fire, and in these two stones we recognize the two judgments. The one judgment is that which has already occurred through water in the flood. The other judgment is that which will occur through fire at the consummation of the age. In this passage it is also possible that the two stones indicate the life of the servants of God. For in a way similar to water and to fire, sometimes all the saints experience the prosperity of life and sometimes experience the adversities of life.

The sea of glass is the gift of baptism, and it is said to be "before the throne" because baptism is given before the coming of judgment. After this[3] it says, "I have the keys of death and Hades."[4] It says this because one who believes and is baptized is freed from death and Hades. Just as the church possesses the keys of life, so too does she possess the keys of Hades. To church it was said, "To whom you shall remit sins, to him they are remitted; if you shall retain his sins, they are retained."[5]

Wherever in the Revelation it has mentioned the angel of a man, it is referring to the man himself. So also the churches and their angels cannot be interpreted in the same figure, unless the angels are either the bishops or the leaders of the churches. Since it commands the angels to repent,[6] it is altogether clear that in the person of the angels the catholic churches are intended. For the angels in heaven have no need of repentance, but human beings do have such a need, since they are unable to live without sin. An angel may also be interpreted as a messenger. For whether one is a bishop or a presbyter or even a layperson, whoever frequently speaks for God, he is rightly called an angel of God. Therefore, since no one can live without sin, it is said to the angel, that is, to man, that he must repent. And whoever considers these matters carefully knows that I am not simply speaking of the laypeople. For also priests ought not allow one day to go by with repentance. Just as not one day goes by during which anyone is able to live without sin, so no day should go by without the remedy of satisfaction.

Whether we consider seven lampstands or one lampstand, in both we recognize the sevenfold church. And therefore whatever the

---

Homily 2   [1]Mt 13:43. [2]Translating *vidit* ("he sees"); PL 35:2419. [3]Although Caesarius has been making some comments on Rev 4, he now returns to his interpretation of the final passages of Rev 1. [4]"Hades" translates the Latin *inferni*, which strictly means "the lower regions." [5]Jn 20:23. [6]"Repent" translates the Latin *paenitentiam agere*, which strictly means "to do (perform) penance."

vision shows is spoken to the seven churches, this is spoken likewise to the one church that is spread throughout the world, for in the number seven the perfect fullness is indicated. Therefore, when he mentions the angels he is speaking of the church. It shows that in the church there are two parts, that of the good and that of the wicked. For this reason the Lord gives not only praise but also admonition, directing his praise toward the good and his admonition toward the wicked. In a similar way, in the Gospel the Lord spoke of the entire body of those placed in front of him as one servant who is both blessed and rejected, whom, when "the Lord himself comes, he will divide" into pieces.[7] How can this happen that one servant is divided, when no one can live if divided into pieces? However, by the one servant he indicates the whole Christian people. Were that people completely good, it would not be divided. However, since this people contains not only the good but also the wicked, it must be divided. Then the good will hear, "Come, blessed of my Father, receive the kingdom." But the thieves and adulterers, who practiced no mercy, will hear, "Depart from me, you accursed, into everlasting fire."[8]

That which he addressed to individual churches in the Revelation, dearest brothers, corresponds to various persons who together exist in the one church. "This he said who holds the seven stars in his hand." He holds you in his hand means that he possesses you and governs you by his power. "He who walks in the midst of the golden lampstands." By this it means that he walks in your midst, since these lampstands symbolize the Christian people. "And I will move your lampstand from its place, unless you repent." Note that he did not say that he "takes away" but that he "moves." For the lampstand signifies the one Christian people. Therefore, he says that this lampstand is to be moved not taken away so that we

might understand that in the one and selfsame church the evil people are moved but the good are confirmed. Moreover he means that by the hidden but nonetheless just judgment of God, that which is taken from the evil is given as increase to the good. This fulfills that which is written: "He who has, it will be added to him; but to him who has not, even that which he has shall be taken from him."[9]

And it says, "To him who conquers I will give to eat of the tree of life." That is to say, from the fruit of the cross. "Which is," it says, "in the paradise of my God." By paradise he refers to the church, for in this symbol all things have been accomplished. When he says "I know your works and your tribulation and your poverty, yet you are rich," he is speaking of the whole church, which although poor in spirit yet possesses all things.[10] When he says, "For ten days you will have tribulation," by these ten days he is referring to all the remaining time, for the number ten is perfect. And during this time the Christian people, as the apostle says, will enter the kingdom of heaven through many tribulations.[11]

He says to the angel of the church at Pergamum, "I know where you dwell, where the throne of Satan is." In saying this he is speaking to the whole church in the name of this one, individual church, for Satan dwells everywhere by means of his body. The body of Satan consists of those persons who are prideful and wicked, just as the body of Christ consists of those who are humble and good. "To him who conquers I will give to eat from the hidden manna," that is, from the bread that comes down out of heaven. The manna in the wilderness was merely a figure of this manna, for, as the Lord said, although many ate of this manna, "they died."[12] And even now whoever eats of this manna unworthily "eats judgment on himself."[13] Likewise this bread is also the tree of life. By this manna we are able

---

[7]Mt 24:51. [8]Mt 25:34, 41. [9]Mt 25:29. [10]See Mt 5:3. [11]See Acts 14:21. [12]Jn 6:49, 58. [13]1 Cor 11:29.

to receive even immortality. "And I will give him a white stone," that is, a body made white by baptism. "And on the stone is written a new name," that is, the knowledge of the Son of man. "Which no one knows except him who receives it." That is, no one knows it except through revelation, and for that reason it is said of the Jews, "For had they known, they would not have crucified the Lord of glory."[14]

He says to the angel of the church at Thyatira, "I have this against you, that you tolerate the woman Jezebel." In these words he is speaking to the leaders of the churches who fail to impose the severity of ecclesiastical discipline on the extravagant and the fornicators and those who do whatever other kind of evil. It is possible that this also refers to heretics. "Who calls herself a prophetess," that is, a Christian, for many heresies flatter themselves with this name. "You have not learned the deep things of Satan," that is, unlike the heretics, you have not adopted the teaching of Satan. "I will not lay on you any further burden," that is, any burden beyond that which you are able to bear. "However, hold fast what you have, until I come. To him who conquers and preserves my works until the end, I will give him the nations and he shall govern them[15] with a rod of iron, and they will be dashed to pieces as a clay pot." "Even as I myself have received power from my Father." In Christ the church possesses such power, as the apostle says, "With him he has given all things to us."[16] It speaks of an iron rod on account of the severity of righteousness, for by means of this rod the good are corrected and the wicked are crushed.

AGAIN, A CONTINUATION OF THE REVELATION (HOMILY 3)

Dearest brothers, we have just heard the blessed John rebuke sinful people in a terrible way. Therefore, with a sincere fear let us consider and with trembling let us fear what is now said. "I know your works; you have the name of being alive, but you are dead." No one dies except for the person who has become guilty of a mortal sin, and this is in accord with what is written: "The soul that sins, it will die."[1] What is worse, many are known to carry about dead souls in their living bodies. "Be vigilant, and strengthen that which is about to die."

"These are the words of him who is holy and true, who holds the key of David," that is, the royal power.[2] "He who opens and no one shuts, and who shuts and no one opens." It is evident that Christ would open the door to those who knock, but to the hypocrites, that is, to those who live in deception, he closes the door of life. "Behold, I have set before you an open door." This was said so that no one could say that anyone was able to close, even partly, the door that God has opened for the church throughout the whole world. It continues, "I know that you have but little strength." It is a praiseworthy work of God that he opens the door to the little faith of the church. "I will write on him the name of my God," clearly meaning that name by which we are signed Christian.[3] "And the name of the city of my God, the new Jerusalem that comes down from heaven." By the new Jerusalem he means the celestial church that is given birth by the Lord. He calls it new, because of the newness of the Christian name and because we are made new from that which is old.[4]

"You are neither cold nor hot," that is, you are useless.[5] We may interpret this to refer to those persons whose riches are sterile. They possess abundance and means,[6] yet they do no

---

[14]1 Cor 2:8. [15]Caesarius uses *pascere*, which means "to feed, to supply, to maintain." [16]Rom 8:32. **Homily 3** [1]Ezek 18:20. [2]Caesarius does not note that he has begun comment on the letter to the church at Philadelphia. [3]Most likely Caesarius is referring to the naming of the Trinity and the giving of the sign of the cross at the time of baptism. [4]Translating *ex veteribus*. Behind this language is the Pauline distinction between the old man and the new man. [5]Caesarius does not note that he has begun comment on the letter to the church at Laodicea. [6]Translating *facultates*.

works of mercy from this abundance. They are not poor, because they have great abundance; yet they are not wealthy, because they do not use their riches for good works. "I counsel you to buy from me gold." That is, by doing works of mercy and by living in good works you might yourself be made gold, that is, you might receive understanding from God and through your good behavior you might merit to suffer martyrdom.

"And behold," it says, "in heaven an open door." The open door is Christ, because he is the door.[7] By heaven it refers to the church, where the concerns of heaven are carried out and transacted.[8] As the apostle says, "To perform all things that are in heaven and that are on earth."[9] Here heaven refers to the primitive church of the Jews, while the earth indicates the church from the Gentiles. It continues, "Come up here, and I will show you." This is appropriate not only for John, but for the church and indeed for every believer. For whoever beholds the open door in heaven, that is, whoever believes that Christ was born and suffered and was resurrected, he ascends into the heights and sees the things of the future.

"And behold, a throne was placed in heaven," that is, in the church. "And he who sat on it was similar in appearance to the jasper and carnelian stones." These comparisons are proper for the church. The jasper has the color of water, and the carnelian has the color of fire. As we said before, by these colors the text wishes to indicate two judgments. The first judgment through water has already occurred in the flood; the other judgment through fire will occur in the future. "Round the throne I saw twenty-four thrones, and on the thrones sat twenty-four elders." The elders represent the whole church, as Isaiah said: "For he was glorified in the midst of his elders."[10] The twenty-four elders represent both the leaders

of the church and the people. The leaders are represented in the twelve apostles, while in the other twelve we are to recognize the rest of the church. "And from the throne issued flashes of lightning and voices." On the one hand, heretics have gone out of the church, for "they went out from us."[11] There is another meaning to this passage as well. The flashes of lightning and the voices represent the preaching of the church. In the voices we recognize the words, and in the flashes of lightning we recognize the miracles.

"Before the throne there was a sea of glass." The sea of glass symbolizes the font of baptism, and it is said to be before the throne because it is before the judgment. At times one may interpret a throne to represent a holy soul, as it is written: "The soul of the just is the seat of wisdom."[12] At other times the throne represents the church in whom God has his throne. "And in the midst of the throne were four living creatures," that is, the Gospels are in the midst of the church. "And they were full of eyes in front and in back," that is, on the inside and on the outside. The eyes are the commandments of God, and they are "in front and in back" because they comprehend both that which is past and that which is future. The first living creature, which is like a lion, reveals the fortitude of the church, and the ox represents the suffering of Christ. The third living creature, which is like a man, signifies the humility of the church, for she flatters herself in no way so that she might assume a posture of pride, but she holds fast to the adoption of sons. The fourth living creature refers to the church. It is "like an eagle," that is, it is flying and free and also raised up from the earth, elevated as though by the wings of the two Testaments or guided by the rudders of the two commandments.[13] For when John the Evangelist looked within these living

---

[7]See Jn 10:7, 9. [8]Translating *ubi caelestia geruntur.* [9]See Eph 1:10. [10]Is 24:23. [11]1 Jn 2:19. [12]See Prov 12:23 LXX. [13]By the two commandments Caesarius probably has in mind the commandments to love God and to love the neighbor as oneself.

creatures, he saw that the fourfold mystery had been fulfilled in Christ, namely, he saw a man being born, an ox suffering and a lion reigning, and then he saw also an eagle returning to the celestial heights. "Each of the living creatures had six wings all around." In the living creatures we recognize also the twenty-four elders, for the total of six wings on each of the four creatures is twenty-four wings. Moreover, he saw the living creatures around the throne, where he said that he had seen the elders. But how can a creature with six wings be similar to an eagle that has two wings, unless the four creatures, who have twenty-four wings and in whom we recognize the twenty-four elders, are one creature, that is, the church, which is like an eagle? We may also interpret the six wings to be the testimonies of the Old Testament. For just as a creature cannot fly unless it has wings, so also the preaching of the New Testament cannot produce faith unless its has the prophetic witnesses of the Old Testament by which it rises from the earth and flies. For when something future has been prophesied beforehand and afterward is discovered to have happened, it produces an unshakeable faith. Therefore, unless the prophets had foretold what was to be fulfilled in Christ, their preaching would have been without effect. And so, the catholic church maintains both of these, that which was proclaimed beforehand and that which was afterward fulfilled.[14] The church, therefore, is properly said to be a living creature that flies and is lifted up into the heavens.

"And they never rest." The living creatures are the church that never rests but praises God without ceasing. We may also interpret the twenty-four elders to be either the books of the Old Testament or the patriarchs and the apostles. The flashes of lightning and the thunder that comes forth from the throne may be regarded as the preaching and the promises of the New Testament. "They lay their crowns before the throne." They do this because the saints attribute to God whatever honor and dignity they possess. In a similar manner, according to the Gospel the people threw palms and flowers under his feet,[15] that is, they accredited to him every victory that they had won.

"For you created all things, and by your will they existed and are created." They were, according to the nature of God, by whom all things are possessed before they come into being. They are created, however, in order that they might be seen by us, as Moses said to the assembly: "Is he not your Father, who made you and possessed you and created you?"[16] He possessed all things in his foreknowledge; he made all things in Adam; he created all things from Adam.[17]

A CONTINUATION OF THE REVELATION (HOMILY 4)

"And I saw in the right hand of him who was seated on the throne a scroll written within and without." This refers to both Testaments; the Old Testament was written on the outside, and the New Testament was written on the inside because it was hidden within the Old Testament. "And it was sealed," it says, "by seven seals." This means that the plenitude of all mysteries lay hidden within the book, since until the passion and resurrection of Christ it had remained sealed. For nothing is ever called a testament unless those who are about to die make it, and it is sealed until the death of the testator, and after his death, it is opened. And so, after the death of Christ every mystery was revealed.

"And I saw a strong angel proclaiming with

---

[14]Caesarius possibly has in mind the heresy of Marcion, who rejected the Old Testament. [15]Mt 21:8. [16]See Deut 32:6. [17]This represents Caesarius's understanding of three verbs in his text of Deut 32:6: *fecit, possedit, creavit. Fecit in Adam* seems to refer to the original creation; *creavit ex Adam* perhaps refers to the continuing creation.

a loud voice, 'Who is worthy to open the scroll and to loose its seals?'" When at first the seals are loosed, then the scroll is opened. However, there is a certain meaning to this, because Christ at that time began to open the scroll when in his conception and birth he initiated the work of his Father's will. And he loosed the seals of the scroll when he died for the human race. "And no one in heaven or on earth or under the earth," that is, no angel or any creature on the earth or anyone of the dead, "was able to open the scroll or to look into it." That is to say, no one was able to behold the splendor of the grace of the New Testament. "And I wept much because no one was found worthy to open the scroll and to look into it." Here John is a symbol of the church, for she is weighed down and burdened by sins and pleads for her own redemption. "And behold, one of the elders." In this elder we are to recognize all the prophets,[1] for the prophets gave comfort to the church as they announced that the Christ would be "from the tribe of Judah, the Root of David." And they called him this because he conquers every sin in us, and whatever goodness anyone possesses, he has received it from him.

"And I saw, and behold, in the midst of the throne and of the four living creatures and in the midst of the elders was a Lamb standing, looking as though it had been slain." The throne, the creatures and the elders are the church, and the Lamb that appeared as though it were slain is the church together with her head, for she dies for Christ so that she might live with him. However, the martyrs of the church may also be indicated by the Lamb that appears as though slain. "It had seven horns and seven eyes," it said, "which are the seven spirits of God sent out

into all the earth." From this passage it is clear that no one can possess the Spirit of God outside the church. "He came and took the scroll from the right hand of him who was seated on the throne." We interpret the one sitting on the throne to be the Father and the Son and the Holy Spirit. The Lamb takes the scroll from the right hand of God; that is, the church[2] receives from the Son the task of bringing to pass what is in the book. As he himself said, "As the Father sent me, also I send you."[3] By this he means that he will complete in them what he has given.

"Each of the creatures and the elders had a harp," that is, they were singing songs of praise.[4] "And they were holding golden bowls." These are the vessels in the house of the Lord in which it is the custom to offer incense. Therefore, in this image the prayers of the saints may well be recognized. "And they were singing a new song," that is, the New Testament. In singing this new song they were openly offering their declaration of faith.[5] And to be sure, it is new that the Son of God became man, that he died and rose again, that he ascended into heaven and gives to people the remission of sins. A harp consists of strings stretched out tight on a wooden frame, and this symbolizes the flesh of Christ bound to his passion. The loosening of the seals is the opening of the Old Testament.

"Then I saw and heard the voice of many angels." By these angels he refers to those persons who are also called the sons of God. They sang, "Worthy is the Lamb, who was slain, to receive power and wealth and wisdom" and the rest. This is not said of his Godhead, "in which are all the treasuries of wisdom,"[6] so that he should receive wisdom. Rather, this is said of his assumed manhood, that is, concern-

---

Homily 4 [1]Caesarius writes *totum corpus prophetarum* ("the whole body of the prophets"). This image is at once highly visual and indicates the unity of the prophetic message. [2]Caesarius has just interpreted the Lamb slain to be the church together with her head. The work of Christ continues through the mission of the church, for in her he continues to work. [3]Jn 20:21. [4]Translating *chordas laudum*. A *chorda* is a string on a musical instrument, so "strings of praise." [5]From what follows it seems likely that by the *professio* Caesarius has in mind the creed. [6]See Col 2:3.

ing his body, which is the church. Or, it might be said of his martyrs who were slain for his name. For the church receives all things in her Head, as the Scriptures say: "He has given us all things with him."[7] The Lamb receives, as he said in the Gospel, "All authority in heaven and on earth has been given to me."[8] However, he receives this authority according to his humanity, not according to his divinity. "I heard all creatures saying," it says, " 'To him who sits on the throne,' that is, to the Father and the Son, 'and to the Lamb,' that is, to the church with her Head, 'blessing and honor and glory forever.' " To whom[9] is honor and glory and the kingdom forever and ever. Amen.

THE CONTINUATION (HOMILY 5)

As you have just now listened as the divine reading[1] was being read, so now listen to what Saint John says. "And behold, a white horse, and its rider held a bow; and a crown was given to him, and he went out conquering." The white horse is the church, and its rider is Christ. This horse of the Lord with the bow made ready for war was promised beforehand by Zechariah. "The Lord God will visit his flock, the house of Israel, and he will arrange him as a goodly horse in war, and from him he will look, and from him he will arrange the battle order, and from him came the bow in anger, and from him will come out every oppressor."[2] And so we interpret the white horse to be the prophets and the apostles. In the rider who is crowned and has a bow we recognize not only Christ but also the Holy Spirit. For after the Lord ascended into heaven, he opened all mysteries and sent the Holy Spirit. Through preachers the words of the Spirit, as though they were arrows, went out to the hearts of people and conquered their unbelief.

The crown on the head are the promises made through the Holy Spirit.

"And when the Lamb opened the second seal, I heard the second living creature say, 'Come and see.' And out came a red horse, and its rider was given power to take peace from the earth so that humans should slay one another; and he was given a great sword." The red horse comes out against the victorious and conquering church. That is, there comes an evil and wicked people, made bloody from its rider, the devil. This is just as we read in Zechariah concerning the red horse of the Lord, except that there it is red from his own blood, while here it is red from the blood of others.[3] "And to him a great sword was given, to take peace from the earth." This refers to the peace of the earth, for the church possesses an eternal peace that Christ left behind for himself. As we noted above, the white horse is the church, and its rider is Christ or the Holy Spirit in whose hand is a bow that sends forth his commandments, as though they were powerful, sharp arrows, throughout the whole world both to kill sins and to enliven the hearts of the faithful. The crown on his head is the promise of eternal life. Here, the red horse is an evil people whose rider is the devil. It is said to be red because it has been made red with the blood of multitudes. And a sharp sword was given to it to take peace from the earth. This means that with the devil's connivance and influence evil people join together and do not cease to incite among themselves strife and dissension, even to death.

In the black horse we recognize an evil people who works in concert with the devil. "He had a balance in his hand" indicates that while evil persons feign to have the scales of

---

[7]Rom 8:32. [8]Mt 28:18. [9]Caesarius writes, *cui est honor. . . .* Since Caesarius has just mentioned "the church with her Head," the dative *cui* apparently refers to the antecedent. In this case, the church is included in the doxology to God. **Homily 5** [1]Caesarius uses the term *lectio divina*, which referred to the sequential reading of the biblical text, perhaps accompanied by commentary. However, the basic idea is that in the reading of the text the Holy Spirit is speaking, inviting the hearer to join in the speaking of the text within the heart. One might say that *lectio divina* is the prayerful reading and hearing of the text. [2]Zech 10:3-4. [3]Zech 1:8.

justice, they deceive many. And it says, "Do not harm the wine and oil." The wine is to be interpreted as the blood of Christ, and the oil as the unction of chrismation. The whole church is in the wheat or barley, whether this distinction is among the great or among the less important or more likely among the leaders and the people.

In the pale horse we perceive evil people who never cease to incite persecutions. And these three horses are one, who came out after the white horse and against it. They have as their rider the devil, who is death. And so, the three horses are interpreted to be war, famine and pestilence. For in the Gospel, the Lord foretold these things, and they have already occurred, and as the day of judgment draws nearer they will occur even more.

When it says that he saw "under the altar the souls of those who had been slain," it is referring to the martyrs. And it says that there was a great earthquake, by which it means the final persecution. It says also that the sun turned black and the moon turned to blood and the stars fell from the sky. The sun and the moon and the stars all refer to the church that is spread throughout the earth. When it says that the stars fell, it does not mean that all of them fell but all of a certain portion of them fell. For in persecutions those who are good persevere, while the wicked fall from heaven, that is to say, from the church. Then there follows, "like a shaken fig tree drops its unripened fruit when shaken by a wind." In such a manner the wicked fall from the church whenever they are thrown into confusion by any tribulation. And it says that "the sky receded like a scroll," meaning by this the church separated from the wicked that is as a scroll rolled up that contains in

itself divine mysteries known to itself.

Then it says, "the kings of the earth fled and hid themselves in the caves of the earth." This signifies that the whole world among the good and the saints will take refuge in the church and, made firm under its protectiown, they will be able to attain to eternal life, with the help of our Lord Jesus Christ, who lives and reigns forever and ever. Amen.

THE CONTINUATION (HOMILY 6)

"And I saw another angel ascending from the rising of the sun." By this other angel he is referring to the same catholic church. "From the rising of the sun," that is to say, from the passion and resurrection of the Lord. "The angel was calling to the four angels of the earth." "He called with a loud voice to the four angels who had been given power to harm the earth and the sea." "You will not harm the earth or the sea." He received a sword. We may interpret this generally to mean that it was given to him to kill those who are alive or that he persuades some to quarrel among themselves concerning temporal affairs even to death.

Concerning the third seal he says that "a black horse came out, and its rider had in his hand a balance." He had in his hand, it says, a balance, that is, he had the measure of equality and justice[1] because although he feigns to maintain justice, in fact he injures by simulation and falsification. It is said "do not harm" in the midst of the living creatures, that is, in the midst of the church in order to show that those who are spiritual do not possess the power for destruction among the servants of God unless they receive such power from God. "Do not harm the wine and oil." In the wine and oil we recognize the anointing with oil and the blood of the Lord, while in the wheat and barley he speaks of the church, whether

---

Homily 6 [1]Caesarius writes *examen aequitatis*. An *examen* was the tongue of a balance at the ends of which were placed the weights. The image suggests that the angel was measuring whether the capacity and responsibility of good works was equaled by the performance of good works.

this distinction is among the great Christians or among the lesser Christians or between the leaders and people of the church.

Concerning the fourth seal it says, "A pale horse and its rider had the name of death, and Hades followed it, and power over a fourth part of the earth was given to it, to kill with the sword, by famine and death and the beasts of the earth." These three horses are one and they came out after the white horse and against the white horse. Together they have one rider, namely, the devil, who is death. From the sixth seal it is clear that the rider is the devil together with his followers, for it is said that the horse gathered together for the final war. And, therefore, we understand the three horses to be famine and wars and pestilence, as the Lord foretold in the Gospel. The white horse is the word of preaching that goes out into all the earth. In the red horse and its rider are symbolized wars, those that lie in the future but also those that are even now occurring, since even now people rise up against people. In the pale horse and its rider a great pestilence and mortality is signified.

"And Hades followed him," that is, it was intent on the destruction of many souls. "When he opened the fifth seal, I saw under the altar of God the souls of those who had been slain." Although it is true that the souls of the saints are in paradise, nonetheless because the blood of the saints was poured out on the earth, they are said to cry out from under the altar. This is according to the saying, "The blood of your brother cries out to me from the earth."[2]

When he opened the sixth seal, "there was a great earthquake," that is, the last persecution, "and the sun became black as sackcloth, and the full moon became like blood, and the stars fell to the earth." Whether it is the sun and moon or also the stars, the church is in view, although a part is understood from the whole.

For it is not the whole church that falls from heaven, but rather those in the church who are evil. The text speaks of the whole since the last persecution will occur throughout the lands of the earth. At that time those who are righteous will remain firm in the church as though they were in heaven. However, those who are full of avarice, the unrighteous and the adulterers will have consented to give sacrifice to the devil. Moreover, at that time those who call themselves Christians but are so only in name will fall from heaven, that is, from the church, as though they were stars. "As the fig tree sheds its fruit when shaken by a mighty wind." The church is compared with a tree shaken by the wind, for the strong wind refers to persecution. The fruit refers to evil people, who will be cut off from or will leave the church.

"The sky vanished like a scroll that is rolled up." Also in this passage it speaks of the church as the sky that recedes from evil persons and within itself alone contains the revealed mysteries, as though it were a scroll rolled up which the iniquitous neither wish to comprehend nor indeed are they able. "And every mountain and island was moved from its place." Whether it is the sky or, as here, the mountains and islands, they all refer to the whole church, which, when the final persecution occurs, will have moved from its place. This will occur either among the good who will flee persecution, or it will occur among the evil who will fall from faith. The passage is an apt description of either part, for also the good part is moved from its place when it flees, that is, it loses that which it possesses, as it was said: "I will move your lampstand from its place."[3] "Then the kings of the earth and the powerful"[4] will hide. We understand the kings to be powerful persons, for persons from every rank and condition have turned to Christ. In addition, those who will be kings at that time, with the exception of him who is persecutor,

---

[2]Gen 4:10. [3]Rev 2:5. [4]Caesarius uses the word *magistratus*, which indicates those who hold an office of importance.

"will hide themselves in the caves and rocks of the mountains." In the present age all flee to the faith of the church and are concealed in the hidden mystery of the church. "And they call on the mountains and rocks, 'Fall on us,' that is, cover us, 'and hide us,'" that is, so that the old man might be hidden from the eyes of God. Another interpretation is possible. Those who consider the coming day of judgment are converted to the mountains, that is, to the church, so that in the present age their sins might be hidden through repentance, lest they be punished in the future age.

"Until we have sealed the servants of our God on their foreheads." He is threatening[5] the church and says to evil persons, that is, to the left part that is doing the harm, "Do not harm!" This is the voice that in the midst of the four living creatures says to him who was sent to harm, "Do not harm wine and oil." In the wine and oil we understand all who are righteous whom neither the devil nor evil persons will be able to harm, except for those occasions when from time to time God permits it for their testing. "Do not harm," it says, "wine and oil." The Lord commands his spiritual servant[6] not to harm any of the earth until such time as all of his servants are sealed.

"And I heard the number of the sealed, a hundred and forty-four thousand sealed out of every tribe of the sons of Israel." The 144,000 represent the fullness of the church. "After this I looked, and behold a great people which no one could number, from all nations and tribes and peoples and tongues." He did not say, "After this I saw another people," but "I saw a people," that is, the selfsame people he had seen in the mystery of the 144,000, which he now sees as a people without number from every tribe and tongue and nation. For by believing, all nations have been engrafted into the root. In the Gospel the Lord showed forth in the figure of the twelve tribes the whole church both from the Jews and from the Gentiles. He said, "You will sit on twelve thrones, judging the twelve tribes of Israel."[7] By the white robes he means the gift of the Holy Spirit. "And all the angels stood round the throne." It speaks of the church in terms of angels, for it has not been describing anything other than the church.

"Then one of the elders addressed me and said, 'These who are clothed in white robes, who are they?'" The elder who spoke indicates the office of the priests, for they teach the church, that is, the people in the church, who are the recompense of the labor of the saints. "And he said, 'These are they who have come from the great tribulation, and they have washed their robes in the blood of the Lamb.'" These are not, as some think, only martyrs, but rather the whole people in the church. For it does not say that they washed their robes in their own blood but in the blood of the Lamb, that is, in the grace of God through Jesus Christ, our Lord. As it is written, "And the blood of his Son has cleansed us."[8]

"And he who sits on the throne dwells on them." Those on whom God dwells in his church are themselves his throne. "The sun nor any heat will strike them." As Isaiah speaks concerning the church, "She will be in shade away from the heat."[9] "And he will guide to springs of living waters" and following. All of this comes already in the present time to the church spiritually, since when our sins have been forgiven, we arise, and having been stripped of the mourning of our previous life and of the old man, in baptism we have put on Christ and been filled with the joy of the Holy Spirit.

"And when he opened the seventh seal, there was silence in heaven," that is, in the church, "for about half an hour." The half-hour shows the beginning of the eternal rest. "Then

[5]Translating *denuntiat*. Some MSS read *adnuntiat* ("he addresses" the church). [6]Caesarius writes *suam spiritalem*. [7]Mt 19:28. [8]1 Jn 1:7. [9]Is 25:4. Caesarius writes *erit in umbra ab aestu*.

I saw seven angels who stand before God." In the seven angels he is speaking of the church. "Who received seven trumpets." This means that they received the completed and perfected proclamation, as it is written: "Lift up your voice as a trumpet."[10] "And another angel came and stood before the altar." This other angel of whom it speaks does not come after those seven angels, for this angel is the Lord Jesus Christ himself. "He had a golden censer," and by this censer it refers to his holy body. For the Lord himself was made a censer from which God received the odor of sweetness, and this became even more gracious for the world since he bore himself in the odor of sweetness. "Then the angel took the censer and filled her with fire from the altar." The Lord received his body, that is, the church, and he filled it with the fire of the Holy Spirit in order that the will of the Father might be fulfilled. "And there were voices and thunder and lightning and earthquakes." All of these things are the spiritual proclamations and mighty deeds of the church.

"And the seven angels who had the seven trumpets made ready to sound the trumpets." This means that the church prepared herself for preaching. "The first angel blew his trumpet, and there was hail and fire, mixed with blood." This event represents the wrath of God that bears within itself the death of many. "It fell on the earth, and a third part of the earth was burned up, and a third part of the trees, and all green grass was burned up." Here the earth as well as the trees and the grass are human persons. Indeed, in the green grass we are to understand flesh, which is bloody and dissolute,[11] according to the passage, "All flesh is grass."[12]

"The second angel blew his trumpet, and something like a great mountain, burning with fire, was thrown into the sea, and a third part of the sea became blood." The mountain burning with fire is the devil, and what the third part of the earth and trees are, that also is the third part of the sea.[13] It says that a third part of the living creatures died to indicate those who are physically alive but spiritually dead. "And a third part of the ships were destroyed." The teaching of the heretics corrupt those who find common cause with them.

"And the third angel blew his trumpet, and a great star fell from heaven, blazing like a torch." It is speaking of haughty and impious persons who fall from the church. It speaks of a great star because it refers to persons of great power and wealth. "The name of the star is Wormwood, and a third part of the waters became wormwood." A third part of humankind was made like the star that fell on it. "And many died of the waters, because it was made bitter." People died from the waters. This can manifestly be interpreted to refer to those who are rebaptized.

"The fourth angel blew his trumpet, and a third part of the sun was struck, and a third part of the moon and a third part of the stars." The sun, moon and stars are the church, a third part of which was struck. In this third part we recognize all evil persons. It is said to be struck because such persons have been given over to their own wickedness and lusts, and at the proper time they will be made known, since their sins abound and become ever greater. "And I looked, and I heard the voice of an eagle flying in midheaven, saying, 'Woe, woe, woe to those who dwell on the earth.'" The eagle is the church, which is said to be flying in midheaven because it moves about in the midst of its own members and with a loud voice proclaims the plagues of the end time. For whenever the priest announces the day of judgment, the eagle flies in midheaven.

---

[10]Is 58:1. [11]Caesarius uses the terms *sanguineam* and *luxuriosam* for the flesh. *Luxuriosus* can mean "excessive," "immoderate" or "dissolute." [12]Is 40:6. [13]Below Caesarius interprets more clearly that this refers to impious and wicked people.

As we noted above,[14] the other angel that was said to arise from the rising of the sun is the church rising up from the rising of the sun, that is, from the passion and resurrection of the Lord. It says, "Do not harm the earth or the sea." This is what the church proclaims to evil persons as it preaches every day. "Do not harm wine and oil," it says. The wine and oil represent all those in the church who are righteous and whom no one can harm unless God permit this for their testing. The text also mentions the 144,000 who have been sealed, and by this number signifies the whole church. And it says that he also saw a great people that no one could number, and in this great people it indicates the same church. It says that they were clothed in white robes because they had received the gift of the Holy Spirit. The angels standing before the throne are likewise the church, since the text was describing nothing other than the church. The elder who answers and says, "Who are these, and from whence did they come?" represents the office of the priests who teach the people in the church. When it says that they "have washed their stoles," it speaks of the whole church, not only of the martyrs. It does not say that they washed their robes in their own blood but "in the blood of the Lamb," which, to be sure, is fulfilled in the sacrament of baptism.

"He who sits on the throne dwells on them," for these are themselves the throne, and on them God has his dwelling. "The sun shall not strike them, nor any heat, and he will guide them to springs of living water" and the following. In the present age and in these days all of these things already come spiritually to the church, since she is so protected by the grace of God that she is made strong by the persecutions of this world rather than being conquered by them. When it says that "there was silence in heaven for half an hour," it means in the church and signifies the beginning of

the eternal rest. In addition, it speaks of seven angels who blow their trumpets. The angels represent the church, and the trumpets represent the preaching of the church. There was another angel which, it says, stood before the altar; this angel is the Lord Christ. "He held a golden censer," that is to say, his holy body through which God the Father accepted the incense of his passion, the odor of sweetness.

When it says that "there were voices, flashes of lightning and thunder," it is speaking of the church's spiritual proclamations. "The seven angels who made ready to blow their trumpets" are the church, in which there is a spiritual preaching against every sin and transgression throughout the entire world. When the first angel blew his trumpet, "a third part of the earth was burned up." This signifies haughty persons who have been given over to their desires and whom by his just judgment God permits to be consumed by the fire of wantonness and lust. When the second angel blew his trumpet, "a burning mountain fell into the sea." This mountain is the devil, and the sea is this world. As we already said above, the "third part of the sea" is wicked and impious people. When the third angel blew his trumpet, "a great star fell from heaven." This star symbolizes people of status[15] who by evil habits and iniquitous acts fall from the church as though it were from heaven. When the text says that "many persons died of the waters, because the waters had become bitter," we may recognize this to be about those who are rebaptized.

When the fourth angel blew his trumpet, "a third part of the sun and of the moon and of the stars was struck." The church is recognized also in this passage, for every day in her those who are evil and false listen to the devil and are cut in the soul with the wounds of sins. It says that there was an eagle flying in midheaven and crying out "Woe, woe, woe." In this too the seer intends the church to be recog-

---

[14]Caesarius begins here his summary recapitulation of this homily. [15]Translating *homines magni*.

nized. For in the constancy of her preaching she flies in the midst of heaven, that is, in the midst of her members, and announces to them the plagues of the last times. For whenever in the church the priest preaches concerning the day of judgment, the eagle flies in the midst of heaven. It is according to divine compassion[16] that when priests are constantly diligent in their preaching and the people faithfully fulfill that which is preached to them, they together merit to advance toward that which is eternal. May the Lord Jesus Christ, who lives, fulfill this.

THE CONTINUATION (HOMILY 7)

Dearest brothers, as the Revelation was being read, we have just now heard that when the fifth angel blew his trumpet, a star fell from heaven on the earth. This singular star is the body of those many persons who have fallen through sins. "And he was given the key of the pit, of the abyss."[1] The star, the abyss, the pit are human persons. For this reason it says that a star fell from heaven, because a sinful people have fallen from the church. "And he received the key of the pit, of the abyss." That is, he received the power of his own heart, so that he might open his own heart in which the devil, although bound, is not constrained so that he might do his will.[2] "He opened the pit of the abyss." This means that the devil revealed his own heart, which sins without any fear or shame. "And smoke rose from the pit," that is, it rose from a people that covers and obscures the church, so that it is said that "the sun and air were darkened with the smoke of the pit." It says that the sun was darkened, not that it perished. For the sins of evil and prideful persons, which are constantly being committed throughout the world, obscure the sun, that is, obscure the church and sometimes cause

darkness for the saints and the righteous. For the number of evil persons is so great that it is often difficult for the good people among them to become evident. "As of a great furnace," it says. "Then from the smoke of the pit came locusts on the earth, and they were given power like the power of scorpions of the earth," that is, to harm by means of poison.

"They were commanded not to harm the grass of the earth or any tree, but only humans, but they were not allowed to kill them." There are two parts in the church, one part of those who are good and one part of those who are evil. The one part is struck down in order that it might be corrected; the other part is given up to its own desires. A part of those who are good is handed over to humiliation that they might know the righteousness of God and might remember penance, as it is written: "It is good that you have humbled me, that I might know your righteous deeds."[3] "They were not allowed to kill them but to torture them, and their torture was like the torture of a scorpion, when it stings a man." The torture like a sting of a scorpion occurs when the devil draws near through the poison of transgressions and sins.

"And men will seek death." To be sure, death has been called a rest. And so they seek death, however a death from evil things, that is, from sufferings, so that they themselves might rest, while the evils perish.[4] "On the heads of the locusts," it says, "were what looked like crowns of gold." In an earlier passage the church was described in the twenty-four elders who had crowns of gold. Those here, however, have crowns similar to gold. That is because they are the heretics who merely imitate the church. "And they had hair like the hair of women." In the image of the hair of women it intends to indicate not only the inconstancy characteristic of women,[5] but indeed that of

---

[16]Translating *divina pietas*. *Pietas* means dutiful conduct or activity proper to one's station and character. **Homily 7** [1]It is clear that Caesarius understands the star, and not the angel, to have received the key to the pit. [2]Although the devil is bound by the work of Christ, in the hearts of his followers the devil is not constrained, and so they do the devil's will. [3]See Ps 119:71 (118:71 LXX). [4]Caesarius is following Tyconius, who, however, interpreted the evils here as the vices (TS 2 7:105-6). [5]Translating *fluxum effeminatum*.

both sexes. "They had tails like scorpions, and stings in their tails." By the tails it means the leaders of the heretics, as it is written: "The prophet who teaches lies is the tail."[6] These are false prophets who carry out the cruelties ordered by kings.[7] "They have as king over them the angel of the bottomless pit," that is, the devil, who is the king of this age. The bottomless pit is a people [who follow the devil]. "His name in Hebrew is Abaddon, and in Greek he is called Apollion, and in Latin Perdens.[8]

One woe has passed; behold, two woes are yet to come, and after this the sixth angel blew his trumpet." From this point on the final preaching of the church begins. "And I heard one of the four horns of the golden altar that is in the sight of God saying to the sixth angel who had the trumpet, 'Release the four angels who are bound at the great river Euphrates.'" In the altar that is in the sight of God we are to understand the church. In the time of the last persecution she will dare to despise the words and commands of that most inhumane of kings and will separate from those who have submitted to him. "Release the four angels who are bound at the great river Euphrates." By the river Euphrates it refers to that sinful people in whom Satan and his will are bound. The Euphrates is a river in Babylon, and it was in the midst of Babylon that Jeremiah tossed his book into the Euphrates.[9]

"And the four angels were released." This indicates that the persecution had commenced. "They had been held ready for the hour, the day, the month and the year, to kill a third of humankind." These are the four periods of time that make up the three and a half years.[10] "And the number of the army of the beast," it says, "was thousands of thousands. And I heard their number." However, it does not say how many of thousands. "To kill a third of humankind." This is the third part of the haughty from whom the church had separated. "And I saw horses in the vision, and their riders had breastplates of fire and hyacinth and sulphur." It speaks of human persons as horses, and by the riders it has in mind evil spirits, and they are armed with fire and smoke and sulphur. "And the heads of the horses were like those of lions," that is, they are for the purpose of rage and violence in persecution. "And from their mouth issued forth smoke and fire and sulphur." The smoke, fire and sulphur from their mouths are the blasphemies that come forth from the mouths of those who are against God. "Their tails are like serpents." The leaders of the heretics we call "tails," and the rulers of the world we call "heads." It is through these that the devil does his harm, and without these he is not able to do harm. For either irreligious kings do harm by an evil exercise of authority, or impious priests do harm by teaching badly.

"And I saw," it says, "another mighty angel coming down from heaven, clothed in a cloud, with a rainbow," that is, a bow, "over his head, and his face was like the sun." In the angel clothed in a cloud we recognize the Lord clothed with the church, for we read that the saints are clouds, as Isaiah said: "Who are these who fly as clouds?"[11] Therefore, interpret the one who is clothed with a spiritual cloud, that is, with a holy body, to be Christ. "And a rainbow over his head." This refers either to the judgment that is now occurring and that is in the future, or it refers to the promise that continues. And in the description of the Lord we ought also to recognize the church,[12] for

---

[6]Is 9:15. [7]Caesarius may have in mind certain Visigothic kings who were Arian. [8]Caesarius adds to the text the Latin equivalent of the name in the Hebrew and the Greek. [9]See Jer 51:63. [10]Translating *haec sunt quattuor tempora triennii et pars temporis*, literally "these are the four times of a three year period and part of a time." Caesarius probably intends something similar to the comment of Primasius: "He indicates by an apt expression the four times during which the persecution will be continuing, that is, three years and six months . . . since a day is gradually filled with hours, and months with days, and finally years with months" (*Commentary on the Apocalypse* 9.15; CCL 92:153-54). [11]Is 60:8. [12]Translating *ecclesiam enim describit in domino.*

it says "his face was as the sun." It is speaking of the resurrection, for he appeared as the sun when he rose again from the dead. "And his feet were as pillars of fire." It refers to the apostles as feet, for through them his teaching has gone into all the world. Perhaps, however, since the feet are at the extremity of the body, it is speaking of the church and the brilliance of the saints after the future fire of the last persecution.

"And he set his right foot on the sea, and his left foot on the land." This indicates that the church is to preach across the sea and to every land of the earth. "And he called out with a loud voice, like a lion roaring," that is, this preaching will be strong and vigorous. "When he called out, the seven thunders sounded their voices." These are the same as the seven trumpets. "And I heard a voice from heaven saying, 'Seal up what the seven thunders have said, and do not write it down.'" This command is because of those who have become dull, so that what the thunders said would not lie open and be accessible to just anyone of the impious. Therefore, in another passage there is a command on behalf of his servants, "Do not seal up the words of this prophecy."[13] And we learn for whom there was a command to seal up the words of the book and for whom there was a command not to seal up the revelation. "He who perseveres in evil," it says, "let him do evil, and he who is filthy, let him still be filthy," that is, because of these things I will speak to them only in riddles. But "he who is righteous, let him do yet more righteousness, and likewise let him who is holy do that which is more holy."[14] That is, "blessed are your eyes, for they see, and your ears, for they hear."[15] To such as these the words of the book are not sealed, but to the evil they are sealed up. "The angel swore that there will be no more time, but that in the days of the seventh angel when he shall begin

to blow his trumpet." The seventh trumpet proclaims the final persecution and the coming of the Lord, and therefore the apostle said that at the final trumpet the resurrection will take place.[16]

As we said above, when the fifth angel sounded his trumpet, another star fell from heaven.[17] And again, this star represents the totality of all those stars that have fallen from heaven,[18] that is, of all those people who have fallen from the church, and so this star represents a haughty and impious people. "And he was given the key of the abyss." That is, he was abandoned to the power of his own heart, so that he might open his heart to the devil and do all manner of evil without any piety or reverence. "And smoke arose from the pit," that is, from an evil people. The smoke darkened the sun and the moon. It says that the sun was obscured, not that the sun ceased to shine. It speaks in this fashion because the sins of evil and haughty people seem to darken the sun, while from time to time through many tribulations they cause darkness for the saints and the righteous. However, they are not able to extinguish their light because they cannot bring the righteous to consent to evil.

It says that from the smoke of the pit came out locusts and that they received the power of torture, but they were not allowed to kill. The text is referring to the two parts that exist within the church, namely, that part that consists of those who are good and that part that consists of those who are evil. The one part is tormented in such a way that it is corrected, while the other part is abandoned to its own desires. When it says that "their torture was like the torture of a scorpion when it stings a man," we recognize that this occurs whenever like the poison of a scorpion the devil draws near to dissipate people through faults and sins. "On their heads were what appeared to

---

[13]Rev 22:10. [14]See Rev 22:11. [15]Mt 13:16. [16]1 Cor 15:52. [17]At this point Caesarius begins his summary recapitulation of this homily. [18]Translating *corpus multarum stellarlum de caelo*.

be crowns of gold." The twenty-four elders, in whom the church is represented, had crowns of gold. These locusts, however, have crowns that only appear to be of gold, for they represent the heretics who merely imitate the church. They had the hair of women, it says, and by this it does not merely wish to show the inconstancy characteristic of woman, but also that of both sexes.

Their tails were similar to those of scorpions, and in these tails we are to recognize the rulers and leaders of the heretics. As it is written, "The prophet who teaches a lie is the tail."[19] "They had over them the king of the pit." This refers to the devil, and by the pit that evil people is symbolized whose lord is the devil.

By the golden altar that it says is in the sight of God, it is referring to the church, for as gold that is purified she will dare to despise the commands of that most cruel king at the time of the final persecution, and she will separate itself from those who comply with them. The text mentions "the four angels who are bound at the river Euphrates." The river Euphrates represents a sinful people in whom Satan and his will is bound. The Euphrates is a river in Babylon, which interpreted means "confusion." And for this reason anyone who effects works characterized by confusion belongs to this river.

And it says that he saw horses and "the riders wore breastplates of fire and hyacinth and sulphur." By these horses it is referring to arrogant persons, and their rider is the devil and his angels. And when it says that "the heads of the horses were like lions' heads," it is suggesting the violent persecution at the hands of evil persons. "From their mouth came out smoke of fire and sulphur," that is, blasphemies against God came out of their mouth. As we have already noted above, the tails that were like serpents are the rulers and leading men of the heretics through whom the devil is accustomed to wreak his harm. For either sacrilegious rulers harm by issuing evil commands, or sacrilegious priests do harm by evil preaching.

The angel that it says was wrapped in a cloud is our Lord and Savior, for he is wrapped in the cloud of the church, as it is written: "Who are these who fly like a cloud?"[20] It says that "his face was like the sun" because of the resurrection of the Lord, for when he arose from the dead, he appeared as the sun. "His feet were like pillars of fire." The feet represent the apostles through whom Christ's teaching has run throughout the whole world. "He set his right foot on the sea," and by this he signified that his preaching would go across the sea and into all the world. "He called out, like a lion roaring," that is, he preached with power and strength. A voice said, "Seal up what the seven thunders have said." This was spoken on account of the dull and uncomprehending concerning whom it is said in the Gospel, "Do not give to dogs what is holy."[21] This means that the word of God ought not be made accessible indiscriminately to just any impious persons. And, therefore, in another passage he spoke on behalf of his servants, "Do not seal up the words of this prophecy."[22] And so it shows those for whom he orders a sealing and those for whom he orders that there not be a sealing. Namely, on the one hand, it speaks of those who do evil continuing to do evil and those who are filthy continuing to be filthy.[23] For such persons as these the word of God is sealed. However, in a similar manner it speaks of those who are righteous continuing to do right and those who are holy doing that which is more holy.[24] For such persons the word of God is not sealed. Let us pray that for the sake of his own compassion[25] the Lord might deem it worthy to fulfill this also in us. For he lives and reigns with the Father and the Holy Spirit. Amen.

---

[19]Is 9:15. [20]Is 60:8. [21]Mt 7:6. [22]Rev 22:10. [23]Rev 22:11. [24]Rev 22:11. [25]Translating *pro sua pietate*.

THE CONTINUATION (HOMILY 8)

The "voice from heaven" is the reign of God, who touches the heart of the church and commands her to receive that future peace that he preached to the church when the book was opened. "I went to the angel so that he might give me the book." The church is saying this in the person of John,[1] since she is desirous to be more thoroughly taught. "And the angel said to me, 'Take it and eat'" That is to say, Open wide your inmost parts and imprint the words of God on the wideness of the heart. "It will make your stomach bitter, but in your mouth it will be sweet as honey." This means that when you have received the word of God, you will delight in the sweetness of the divine eloquence. However, when you begin to speak and to act according to what you have come to understand, then you will experience bitterness. As it is written, "On account of the words of your lips, I have maintained the difficult ways."[2] There is another possible interpretation. "It will be sweet as honey in your mouth," it says, "but bitter in your stomach." By the "mouth" we are to understand the good and spiritual Christians, while by the "stomach" we understand the carnal and dissolute. And so it is that when the word of God is preached, it is sweet to those who are spiritual, but to the carnal, whose "god is the belly" as the apostle says,[3] it seems bitter and harsh.

"Then I was given a measuring rod similar to a staff, and the angel said, 'Rise and measure the temple of God and the altar and those who worship in it.'" When the angel says "Rise," he is rousing the church for action, for John did not hear these things while sitting down.[4] "Measure the temple and the altar and those who worship in it." He is ordering the church to be placed under review and to be prepared for the end time. "And those who worship in it." However, not everyone who seems to be worshiping is in fact a true worshiper. And for this reason it says, "The court that is outside the temple, leave that out, and do not measure it." Those persons are the court who appear to be in the church but are really outside of it, whether they are heretics or catholic Christians whose lives are evil. "For it is given over to the nations, and they will trample the holy city for forty-two months." Both those who are excluded as well as those to whom the court is given to trample will trample the court.[5]

"And I will grant to my two witnesses," that is, to the two Testaments, "and they will prophesy for one thousand two hundred and sixty days." He has indicated the number of the final persecution and the number of the future peace and of the whole time from the passion of the Lord, since both times have the same number of days, as we will mention at the right place.[6] "The two witnesses were clothed in sackcloth," that is, in a coarse garment. The sackcloth refers to confession, and therefore to be clothed in sackcloth indicates that they were established in confession,[7] because it says that they were clothed in sackcloth from their attitude of humility. The text then indicates who these two witnesses are, saying, "These are the two olive trees and the two lampstands which stand in the sight of the Lord of the earth." These are they who are standing, not those who will stand. The two lampstands represent the church, although it speaks of two because of the two Testaments. In the same

---

Homily 8 [1]Translating *ex persona Iohannis*. In this passage John represents the figure of the church. [2]Ps 16:4 LXX. [3]Phil 3:19. [4]The person of John in the text continues to represent the church. Caesarius received this interpretation from Tyconius. [5]From the context those who are excluded seem to be the heretics, while those to whom it is given to trample appear to be the wicked Christians. Tyconius, whose interpretation Caesarius is following, also includes in the nations those who have never heard the gospel. [6]Caesarius appears to have in mind his comments on the thousand years mentioned in Rev 20:4. [7]Caesarius uses two words for confession. First, he uses *in exomologesi*, which is a transliteration of the Greek; second, he writes *in confessione*. In both cases the reference is to the confession of one's sins.

way because of the number of the corners of the earth he said that the four angels are the church, even though there are seven.[8] So too the whole church is indicated by the seven lampstands, whether the text mentions one or more because of their locations.[9] For Zechariah saw a single sevenform lampstand and the two olive trees,[10] that is, the two Testaments that pour oil into the lampstand, that is, into the church. So also in the same way the seven eyes, that represent the sevenfold grace of the Holy Spirit, are in the church and take notice of the whole earth.

"And if anyone would harm them or kill them, fire will come out from their mouth and will consume their foes." This means that should anyone harm the church or wish to harm her, through the prayers of her mouth he shall be consumed by a divine fire either in the present age for his correction or in the future age for his damnation. "They have power to shut the sky, that no rain may fall during the days of their prophesying." It says "they have," not "they will have." It speaks in this manner because it signifies the time which even now is occurring. Moreover, the sky is spiritually closed, lest he send forth showers, that is, lest by the hidden yet just judgment of God any blessing from the church fall on the unfruitful earth. "And when they have finished their testimony, the beast that ascends from the bottomless pit will make war on them." It reveals plainly that all of these things occur before the final persecution, for it says, "when they have finished their testimony," at least that which they will present until the revelation of Christ. "And he will conquer them and kill them." He will conquer in those who will have succumbed; he will kill in those who will have confessed God.

"And their body will be thrown in the streets of the great city." It has spoken of one body of the two. At other times it mentions their bodies, and so it preserves both the number of the Testaments and the one body of the church. Of this one body we read, "You have cast my words behind you."[11] "In the streets of the great city," that is, in the middle of the church. "For three days and a half," that is, for three years and six months, "men from the peoples and tribes and tongues will gaze on their body." It mingles the time, now speaking in the present, now in the future, as also the Lord did when he said, "The hour will come when whoever will kill you will think he is offering an obedience to God."[12] Such an hour is both now present and will also come. "And they will not allow their bodies to be placed in a tomb." The text speaks both of their intention and of their hostile activity. Certainly they will not have the capacity to accomplish their intention; otherwise the church would be lost to memory. As it is said, "You neither enter yourselves nor allow others to enter,"[13] so even while many will be entering the church, they continue to work against this and for this reason do not allow the bodies of the witnesses to be placed in a tomb.

"And those who dwell on the earth will rejoice over them and make merry and exchange presents." This has always occurred, and also at present they exchange presents, and at the end time they will rejoice and make merry. For as often as the just are afflicted, the unrighteous rejoice and make merry. "For these two prophets had tormented them." The prophets had tormented them through plagues that torment the human race on account of its contempt for the Testaments of God. For this reason, even the sight of the righteous is grievous for the unrighteous, as they themselves attest: "Even the sight of him is a burden to us."[14]

---

[8]The text of Morin and of Migne reads, *siciut quattuor angelos dixit ecclesiam, cum sint septem pro numero angelorum terrae.* The ninth-century MS A (Egerton 874) reads *angulorum* instead of *angelorum.* This variant seems to make more sense in the context. [9]The one lampstand, that is, the church, may also be mentioned as the seven churches of Asia Minor. [10]Zech 4:1-3. [11]Ps 50:17 (49:17 LXX). [12]Jn 16:2. [13]Mt 23:13. [14]Wis 2:15.

However, they will rejoice because they will have nothing that they experience impatiently, although the righteous have been mistreated and killed and their inheritance confiscated.

"But after the three and a half days a breath of life from God entered them." We have already spoken of the days. The angel speaks of the future, but the future of which he hears, he speaks of as though it were accomplished. "And they stood up on their feet, and great fear fell on those who saw them. Then I heard a loud voice from heaven saying, 'Come up hither!' And they went up to heaven in a cloud." The apostle spoke of this when he said, "We shall be caught up in the clouds to meet Christ."[15] It is written that this cannot happen to anyone before the coming of the Lord, "Christ the beginning, then at his coming those who belong to Christ."[16] This suffices to exclude every false idea of those who think that these two witnesses are two men who ascend to heaven on clouds before the coming of Christ. For how could those who dwell on the earth rejoice at the death of two men if they had died only in one city? And how would they exchange presents if after a period of three days those who beforehand had rejoiced at their death were troubled by their resurrection? And what kind of feasting and enjoyments could there be in the streets of those feasting, if along with the feast there was the stench of human cadavers dead already for three days? From this may the Lord deign to free us![17]

THE CONTINUATION (HOMILY 9)

In the reading just recited, we have heard, dearest brethren, that "at that hour there was a great earthquake." In this earthquake we recognize persecution that the devil is in the habit of arousing through wicked people. And it says, "a tenth of the city fell; seven thousand people were killed in the earthquake." The number ten and the number seven are perfect numbers, and even were this not the case, the whole would have to be understood from the part. For there are two structures in the church. One is built on the rock; the other is built on sand. That which is on the sand is said to topple to the ground.[1] "And the rest were terrified and gave glory to God." Those who were built on the rock gave glory to God, and they were not able to fall down with those who were on the sand. And for this reason it says "they were terrified," because when the righteous person sees the death of a sinner he becomes even more ardent in obedience to the commandments. As it is written, "He will wash his hands in the blood of the sinner."[2]

"Then," it says, "God's temple in heaven was opened." This means that the mysteries of Christ's incarnation were manifested in the church, since we have shown that heaven indicates the church. "And the ark of his covenant was seen within his temple." It is understood that the church is the ark of the covenant. "And there were flashes of lightning and peals of thunder and an earthquake." All of these are the powers of the preaching and of the trembling and of the struggles of the church.[3]

"And a great sign was seen in heaven, a woman," it says, "clothed with the sun, with the moon under her feet." It says that the church has a part, that is, the hypocrites and the evil Christians under her feet. "And on her head a crown of twelve stars." These twelve stars can be interpreted as the twelve apostles. That the woman is clothed with the sun signifies her hope in the resurrection. For this reason it is written, "Then the righteous will shine like the sun in the kingdom of their Father."[4] The great red dragon is the devil, who seeks to devour anyone who is born of the church. "And the

---

[15]1 Thess 4:17. [16]1 Cor 15:23. [17]The comments of Caesarius on Rev 11:9-12 follow very closely those of Tyconius. See TS 2 7:163-66.
Homily 9 [1]See Mt 7:24-27. [2]Ps 57:11 LXX. Throughout these comments Caesarius continues to follow Tyconius (TS 2 7:166-71).
[3]Translating *virtutes praedicationis et coruscationis et bellorum ecclesiae.* [4]Mt 13:43.

devil has," it says, "seven heads and ten horns." The heads are kings, and the horns are clearly kingdoms, for in the seven heads it speaks of all kings, and in the ten horns it speaks of all kingdoms of the earth. "His tail swept down a third of the stars of the heaven and cast them to the earth." The tail symbolizes the evil prophets, that is, heretics who threw down to earth those stars of heaven who joined them through a repeated baptism.[5] They are under the feet of the woman. Many believed that these are persons whom the devil made his companions since they were of the same mind as he. Many believe that these are angels who were thrown down with him when he fell.[6]

"The woman cried out in pangs of birth that she might deliver." Every day throughout all time the church is giving birth, whether in time of prosperity or in time of adversity. "And the dragon stood before the woman who was about to bear a child, that he might devour her child when she brought it forth." In her misfortunes the church is always bringing forth Christ through her members, and the dragon is always seeking to devour the one who is being born. "And the woman brought forth a male child," that is, Christ. For this reason the church is the body of Christ, because she always is bringing forth members of Christ. And it says that it was a male child, because he is victor against the devil.[7] "And the woman fled into the wilderness." With good reason we understand the wilderness to be this world, where to the end Christ guides and feeds the church. Through the help of Christ the church also in this world tramples and treads under foot haughty and impious persons as well as all the power of Satan, as though they were scorpions and vipers.

"Now war arose in heaven," that is, in the church. "Michael and his angels fought with the dragon." We understand Michael to be Christ and his angels to be holy persons. "And the dragon and his angels fought." This refers to the devil and to those persons who submit to his will. For it would be senseless to believe that the devil with his angels had dared to fight in heaven, when he had not even dared to tempt Job on earth until he had requested permission from the Lord to harm Job.[8] "But they did not prevail, and there was found no longer any place for them in heaven," that is, among the saints. Those who believe have fully expelled the devil and no longer receive his compatriots, so that, as Zechariah said, the idols are utterly removed and no longer receive any place.[9]

"And the great dragon was thrown down, the ancient serpent, who is called the devil and Satan, and his angels with him." The devil as well as every unclean spirit with their leader were expelled from the hearts of the saints to the earth, that is, to persons who are wise only in earthly things and have their entire hope in earthly things. "And I heard a loud voice from heaven, saying, 'Now is accomplished the salvation and the power and the kingdom of our God!'" He speaks of the salvation of the church. It is showing in which heaven these things occurred. For with God the power and the kingdom and the authority of his Son always existed, but it says that salvation in the church was accomplished through the victory of Christ. Seeing this salvation, those of whom the Lord said, "Many righteous and prophets longed to see what you see,"[10] said, "Now is accomplished the salvation of our Lord, for the accuser of our brethren," and the following. If, however, as some think, the voice is of angels in the higher heaven and not that of the saints

---

[5]"The stars of heaven" apparently refer to those Christians who consented to a second baptism. Heaven here continues to refer to the church. [6]Caesarius does not say whom he has in mind. However, Victorinus of Petovium expresses the opinion that Caesarius mentions (CSEL 49:116). [7]Caesarius is following Tyconius, who says that through the victory of Christ "the devil, who had conquered a woman, ceased to be a conqueror" (TS 2 7:188-89). [8]See Job 2:5. [9]See Zech 13:2. [10]Mt 13:17.

in the church, they would not have said "the accuser of our brethren" but "our accuser." Nor would they have said that "he accuses" but that "he accused." If the angels in heaven called the righteous on the earth their brethren, there would be no joy, since the devil would have been sent to the earth and the saints there would have to endure his vexation even more now that he was with them on the earth than were he still in heaven, as it is claimed.[11] And therefore they curse the earth, saying, "Woe to you, O earth and sea," that is, you who are not heaven, "for the devil has come down to you in great wrath, because he knows that his time is short." It says "he has come down" to preserve the allegory. As all are in "heaven," that is, in the church, which is rightly called heaven, when the devil is thrown out of the saints, he "comes down" to his followers who are the "earth" because of their earthly affection. He is said to be thrown out of heaven, not so that he might come to those who have already been made heaven but because of who they now are, not what they might become. For the saints cannot become heaven unless the devil has been expelled. Therefore, he calls those among whom the devil can find no place "heaven," not according to the primary meaning of the word but according to its second meaning. From this danger may the Lord design to free us and place us under his protection.

THE CONTINUATION (HOMILY 10)

We have heard just now, dearest brethren, that "when the dragon saw that he had been thrown down from the saints[1] to the earth," that is, from heaven to sinners, "he pursued the woman who had borne the male child." The more that the devil is thrown out of the saints, the more he persecutes them. "And there was given to the woman," that is, to the church,

"two wings of a great eagle that she might fly from the serpent into the wilderness, to her place where she is nourished for a time and times and half a time." A time is understood to be both a year and a hundred years. The two great wings are the two Testaments of the church, which she accepts and by which she evades the serpent. "To the desert, to her place," it says, that is, into this world where serpents and scorpions dwell, for to the church it was said, "Behold, I send you out as sheep in the midst of wolves."[2] And to Ezekiel it is said, "Son of man, you dwell among scorpions."[3] "The serpent sent water like a river out of his mouth after the woman." It refers to the violence of the persecutors. "But the earth came to the help of the woman and opened its mouth and swallowed the river." This refers to that sacred earth, that is, the saints, for each day persecutions are inflicted on the church, and by the prayers of the holy earth, that is, by the prayers of all the saints, the persecutions are either removed or ameliorated. For indeed our Lord Jesus Christ, who intercedes for us, also removes these persecutions, since this very earth sits at the right hand of power.

We might also interpret the woman who flew into the desert to be the same catholic church in which the synagogue will come to believe at the end of time when Elijah comes. In this case, the two wings of the great eagle are the two prophets, namely, Elijah and whoever it is that will come with him. The water that comes forth from the mouth of the dragon signifies the multitude of those who persecute the church. That the water has been swallowed up indicates that the church has been set free from its persecutors.

"Then the dragon was angry with the woman and went off to make war on the rest of her offspring." This means that when the

---

[11]Caesarius is arguing against the interpretation that this passage speaks of the devil's expulsion from highest heaven to the earth. According to Caesarius, "heaven" refers to the church and "earth" to sinners. Therefore, there can be joy among the saints, for the devil has been expelled from their midst. **Homily 10** [1]"From the saints" is an interpretive insertion by Caesarius. [2]Mt 10:16. [3]Ezek 2:6.

86

dragon saw that the persecutions that he was in the habit of initiating through the pagans were no longer able to continue, because they had been made to cease by the mouth of the holy earth, that is, by the prayers of the saints, he began to stir up heresies.[4] "And he stood on the sand of the sea," that is, on the multitude of the heretics.

"I saw a beast rising out of the sea," that is, out of an evil people. That he was "rising out" means that he was coming into existence, even as the blooming flower[5] comes forth from the root of Jesse. In the beast coming forth from the sea he signifies all impious persons, who are the body of the devil. "And the beast that I saw was like a leopard, and its feet were like a bear's, and its mouth was like a lion's mouth." The beast was like a leopard because of the variety of nations; he was like a bear because of his maliciousness and madness; he was like a lion because of the strength of his body and the haughtiness of his mouth.[6] At the time of the antichrist his kingdom will be as a leopard, for it will contain a commixture of various nations and peoples; it will have feet as a bear in its leaders, and its commanding authority will be as the mouth of a lion. "And the dragon gave him his power." We see how the heretics, who have the power of the devil, are powerful in this world. For just as formerly it was the pagans who devastated the church, so now it is the heretics.

"And I saw one of its heads wounded as though to death, but this mortal wound was healed." That which "seemed wounded" are the heretics who hypocritically seem to confess Christ but yet they blaspheme, since they do not believe as the catholic faith has it. They prophesy that he who was wounded is also raised again, "for even Satan himself transfigures himself into an angel of light."[7] Another

interpretation might be that heresies are slain by the catholics, for they are suppressed by the testimonies of the Scriptures. Yet, as though a wound of Satan they are nonetheless revived and accomplish the works of Satan and do not cease from blaspheming and attracting whomever they can to their teachings. "And the whole earth followed the beast with wonder. And they worshiped the dragon, for he had given his power to the beast." To be sure, the heretics possess power, most especially the Arians.[8] "And they adored the beast, saying, 'Who is like the beast, and who can fight against it?'" To be sure, the heretics flatter themselves that no one believes better than they and that no one can conquer their people who are marked by the name of the beast. And such power was given to him by the devil, although with God's permission, that he should speak haughty things and blasphemies, as the apostle says: "There must be heresies in order that those who are genuine among you may be manifested."[9]

"And it was allowed to exercise authority for forty-two months." The forty-two months are to be interpreted as the time of the last persecution. "Then it opened its mouth to blaspheme against God."[10] It is clear that this refers to those who have left the catholic church, for while earlier they seemed to be within the church as though they held the right faith, in time of persecution they openly blasphemed God with the mouth. "And they blasphemed his dwelling and those who dwell in heaven." The dwelling of God is among the saints who are contained within the church, which is called "heaven," because they are indeed the habitation of God.

"Also it was allowed to make war on the saints and to conquer them. From the whole we understand the part that was able to be

---

[4]Caesarius may well have in mind the Visigoths, who became Arian Christians when they converted from paganism. [5]Translating *flos in bonam partem*. [6]Caesarius received these interpretations from Tyconius. [7]See 2 Cor 11:14. [8]Caesarius probably has in mind the Arian Visigoths who ruled in south Gaul. [9]See 1 Cor 11:19. [10]Bede (CCL 121A:405) explains that *ad deum* ("to God") means *adversus deum* ("against God").

conquered, for it is not the good Christians who are conquered but those who are bad. "And power was given to it over every tribe and tongue, and all who dwell on earth will worship it." It speaks of all, namely, of those who dwell on the earth, not of those who dwell in heaven.[11] "Whose name has not been written in the book of life of the Lamb." It is speaking of the devil or of his people, whose name has not been written in the book of life. "Sealed from the beginning of the world." In the foreknowledge of God the church was beforehand foreordained and sealed. He will bring this to pass.

THE CONTINUATION (HOMILY 11)

In the reading that was just now recited, dearest brethren, we heard Saint John say, "Then I saw another beast that rose out of the earth." Earlier it was from the sea; now it is from the earth. "It had two horns like a lamb." That is, it had two testaments in a way similar to the Lamb, which is the church. "And it spoke like a dragon." This is that which manifests the Lamb by way of the Christian name alone, just as the poison of the dragon comes in secretly. For this is the church of the heretics. It would not be an imitator of the likeness of the Lamb if it would speak openly. For it feigns Christianity so that it might more easily deceive the incautious. For this reason the Lord said, "Beware of false prophets,"[1] and the following.

"And it makes the earth and its inhabitants to worship the first beast, whose mortal wound was healed. It works great signs, even making fire come down from heaven to earth." Since the church is "heaven," what is this fire that falls from heaven other than heresies that fall from the church? As it is written, "They went out from us, but they were not of us."[2] For fire falls from the church whenever heretics, who leave the church as though fire, persecute the

church itself. Therefore, the beast with the two horns causes the people to worship the image of the beast, that is, the devices of the devil.

"That it might give to them a mark on their right hand or on their forehead." It is speaking of the "mystery of lawlessness."[3] For the saints who are in the church receive Christ on the hand and on the forehead. The hypocrites, however, receive the beast under the name of Christ. "Those who do not worship the beast or its image, nor receive the mark on the forehead or on the hand will be slain." It is not inconsistent with the faith that the beast be understood as the city of the impious itself, that is, as the congregation or conspiracy of all those who are impious or filled with hubris. This city is called Babylon, which is interpreted as "confusion," and to it belong all who desire to work that which is worthy of confusion. He himself is the citizenry of unfaithful persons who are the opposite of the faithful people, that is, of the city of God. His image is an imitation, that is, it is among those people who confess the catholic faith but live the life of infidelity. For they feign to be what they are not, and they are called Christians, not by way of the true Image but by way of a false image. Of such persons the apostle wrote, "holding the form of religion but denying the power of it."[4] Not a small number of such persons are within the catholic church. However, the righteous do not worship the beast, that is, they do not assent to him, nor do they submit to him, nor do they receive his mark, the mark of sin, on their forehead, on account of their confession, and on their hand, on account of their works.

They work in this way "so that no one may buy unless they have the mark or the name of the beast or the number of its name. This calls for wisdom. Whoever has understanding, let him reckon the number of the beast, for it is the number of a man." That is, it is the number of the Son of man, Christ, whose name the

[11]Caesarius continues to think of heaven as the church.   **Homily 11**   [1] Mt 7:14. [2]1 Jn 2:19. [3]See 1 Thess 2:7. [4]2 Tim 3:5.

beast takes for himself among the heretics. Let us, then, consider the number that is spoken, so that having learned and comprehended the number, we might discover a name or a significance to it. "Its number is," it says, "six hundred and sixteen."[5] Let us consider the matter according to the Greek letters, especially since John wrote to Asia. He also said, "I am the A and the Ω." In Greek letters the number 616 becomes χις.[6] When these marks are given a value, it is a number. However, when they are rendered as a monogram, they are a symbol and a name and a number. It is understood to be a sign of Christ and shows a likeness of him that the church in reality holds in reverence. In their opposition the heretics make something similar to this sign for themselves. When they persecute Christ spiritually, they nonetheless seem to be glorified by the sign of the cross of Christ. For this reason, therefore, it is said that the number of the beast is the number of a man.

"Then I looked, and lo, on Mount Zion there was a lamb standing, and with him a hundred and forty-four thousand who had his name and the name of his Father written on their foreheads." It was revealed what signs were on the forehead by way of imitation, while it now says that both God and Christ were written on the foreheads of the church. "And I heard a voice from heaven as of many waters," that is, of the hundred and forty-four thousand. "And a sound like that of loud thunder; and the voice I heard was like the sound of harpers playing on their harps," and the following. When it says, "These are those who have not defiled themselves with women," we do not understand the "virgins" of this passage[7] to be only those who are chaste in the body. Rather, we have especially

in mind the whole church, which holds to the pure faith, as the apostle says, "I betrothed you to one husband, to present you as a pure virgin to Christ."[8] For she is not corrupted by any adulterous commixture of the heretics, nor to the end of her life is she hindered by the alluring yet deadly desires of this world or by an infelicitous perseverance in them without the remedy of penance. He continues after these things, saying, "And in their mouths no lie is found." He does not say no lies "were" found, but no lie "is" found.[9] Whatever kind of person the Lord finds when he calls him from this world, such is the person whom the Lord also judges. For whether through baptism or through penance we are able in the interior of our being to be made both chaste and without guile.[10]

There occurs now again a recapitulation of the narrative. "Then I saw," it says, "another angel flying in midheaven." This is to say that there was preaching going on throughout in the midst of the church. "The angel had an eternal gospel to proclaim to those who dwell on earth, saying, 'fear the Lord,'" and the following.[11] Some want to interpret this angel who flies in the middle of heaven to be Elijah, and the angel that follows it to be an associate of Elijah who will preach at the same time. "Another angel followed," that is, the preaching of the future peace. "Saying, 'Fallen, fallen is Babylon, she who is great.'" By Babylon he means that impious city that is the congregation of the devil, as we noted above. It is that people that grants its consent to him and in that destruction that comes to him and to the entire human race seeks every kind of lust and corruption. For just as the city of God is the church and every heavenly manner of life, so on the contrary the city of the devil is the

---

[5]Caesarius is reflecting an ancient reading. Already Irenaeus knew of manuscripts that read 616, although he ascribed this reading to the error of copyists (*Against Heresies* 5.30.1). [6]The MSS that the Migne edition followed has χιστ' (PL 35:2437). [7]The Greek text refers to οἱ παρθένοι, the virgins. [8]2 Cor 11:2. [9]The text of Caesarius read *non est inventum mendacium*. Caesarius notes that *est* is used, not *fuit*. [10]Translating *et virgines et sine mendacio*. [11]The text of Caesarius reads "fear the Lord," rather than "fear God."

Babylon that exists in all the world. As the Lord said, "Behold, I place Jerusalem as a stone that crushes for all nations."[12] Therefore, it is the church that says, "Fallen, fallen is Babylon, she who is great." She speaks as though that were perfected which is yet in the future, just as is also the case in this passage, "They divided my garments among them."[13]

"She gave all nations to drink from the wine of her fornication." All nations are the city of the world, that is, all who are haughty and impure, no matter whether they exist outside the church or within the church. "Then I looked, and lo, a white cloud," or a bright cloud,[14] "and seated on the cloud one like a son of man," that is, Christ. He is describing the church in her glory, especially since she is white after the flames of persecution. "He had a golden crown on his head." The gold crown is the elders with their golden crowns. "And a sharp sickle in his hand." The sickle in his hand is that which separates the catholics from the heretics and the saints from the sinners, just as the Lord speaks concerning the reapers. But if we are to think especially of Christ as the reaper who is seen on the white cloud, who is that vintager who comes after him? Unless it is Christ yet in the form of his body the church. Perhaps we would not be far wrong were we to understand those three angels who come out[15] to represent the threefold sense of the Scriptures, namely, the historical, the moral and the spiritual senses. The sickle would then be the difference between them.

"And the angel sent into the wine press of the wrath of God something great." He did not send into a great wine press, but he sent into the wine press every haughty person.[16] "And the wine press was trodden outside the city," that is, outside the church. For whenever discord

has happened, every person of sin shall be outside. The treading of the wine press refers to the retribution against the sinners. "And blood flowed from the wine press, as high as a horse's bridle." Vengeance shall flow out even to the leaders of the peoples, for at the time of the last struggle the vengeance of blood poured out shall come to the devil and his angels. "For one thousand six hundred stadia." The blood will flow through all four parts of the world. For that which is fourfold is quadrupled, as in four fourfold planes and wheels.[17] For four times four hundred is one thousand six hundred.

THE CONTINUATION (HOMILY 12)

In the reading that was recited, dearest brethren, Saint John said that he saw "another sign in heaven, great and wonderful, seven angels," that is, the church, "having seven plagues, which are the last, for with them the wrath of God is ended." He calls these the last plagues, because the wrath of God always smites a contumacious people with seven plagues, that is, completely, as God himself frequently says in Leviticus: "And I will smite you sevenfold for your sins."[1] "And I saw what appeared to be a sea of glass." He speaks of the font of baptism because of its clear transparency. And it was "mingled with fire," that is, it was mingled with the Holy Spirit or with temptation. "And those who had conquered the beast were over the sea of glass," that is, in baptism. And they "had harps of God," that is, the heart of those singing were consecrated to God. "And they were singing the song of Moses, the servant of God, and the song of the Lamb," that is, both Testaments. They sang, "Great and wonderful are your works," and the following. That which those mentioned above were singing is in each of the two Testaments.

---

[12]Zech 12:3. [13]Ps 22:18 (21:19 LXX). [14]Caesarius uses *alba* for white and *candida* for bright. *Alba* is the color white, while *candida* has the connotation of dazzling or bright. [15]That is, in Rev 14:15, 17, 18. [16]An interesting example of Caesarian interpretation. Caesarius cites the biblical text, *et misit in torcular irae dei magnum.* However, he does not want to take *magnum* with *torcular.* Rather, he wants to interpret *magnum* to refer to *superbum quemque.* [17]Translating *quaternitas enim est conquaternata, sicut in quattuor faciebus quadriformibus et rotis.* The text is difficult and uncertain. MS *μ* represented in Migne reads *totis* at the end (PL 35:2438). **Homily 12** [1]Lev 26:24.

He repeats what he had presented before, saying, "After these things I looked, and behold, the tent of witness in heaven was opened." We have already asserted that the temple is to be interpreted as the church, and the angel who "came out of the temple and gave command to him who was seated on the cloud,"[2] was said to be the rule of God. For the command went out, just as the Evangelist said: "A decree went out from Caesar Augustus."[3] The seven angels "were robed in pure and bright linen and their breasts girded with golden girdles." In these seven angels he is manifestly symbolizing the church, for this is the manner that he described the church in Christ at the beginning of the Revelation, "having a golden girdle on the breast."[4]

"And one of the four living creatures gave to the seven angels seven golden bowls full of the wrath of God." These bowls that the elders and the living creatures carry with their odor are the church, as are the seven angels. And the odor is sometimes that of the wrath of God and sometimes that of the word of God. All of these things give life to those who are good, but they inflict death on those who are evil, as this passage expresses it, "to some a fragrance of life to life but to others a fragrance of death to death."[5] For the prayers of the saints are a fire that comes out of the mouth of witnesses and are works of wrath to the world and to the impious. This is because to the proud and wicked it does not suffice to love and to imitate those who are holy. Rather, wherever possible they persecute them. All of these plagues are spiritual and occur in the soul. For at that time the whole people of the impious will be unharmed by any plague of the body, because

they were undeserving to be chastised in the present age, and it was as though they had received all the power of causing pain. However, spiritually all who are impious and haughty are going to suffer, for their sins of will and their mortal sins are sores in their souls.

"The second angel poured his bowl on the sea," and so on. The sea, the rivers and fountains of water, the sun, the throne of the beast, the river Euphrates, the air, all of these on which the angels pour their bowls are the earth and the human race.[6] It was commanded of all the angels to pour their bowls on the earth. These plagues are to be understood in terms of their opposite.[7] For a plague is without cure, and it is a great wrath, especially among the saints, if one accepts the opportunity of sinning and is not corrected. However, it is an ever greater wrath if one gives assistance to unrighteousness by the encouragement to error. These plagues and the wounds they inflict strike whomever takes pleasure in their sins and is self-satisfied in their sins. The prosperity of the wicked, therefore, is a wound on their souls, while the adversity of the righteous is a payment toward eternal joys. In the third angel and in the changing of the waters into blood, recognize all the angels of the peoples, that is, all persons of the earth[8] who bleed in their souls.

"The fourth angel poured his bowl on the sun, and people were scorched with a great heat." This is the fire of Gehenna that still remains in the future. For in the present age, although he may kill his own friends[9] in their souls, the devil does not destroy their bodies by fire but rather, to the extent that he is permitted, gives them glory. Such glory and

---

[2]See Rev 14:15. [3]Lk 2:1. [4]See Rev 1:13. [5]2 Cor 2:16. [6]Caesarius is summarizing the pouring out of the bowls in Rev 16:2, 3, 4, 8, 10, 12, 17. [7]Caesarius is reflecting on the paradox that in the world the righteous often suffer, while the wicked often prosper. However, in view of their final effects, suffering and prosperity bring their opposites. Suffering prepares the righteous for eternal bliss; prosperity hardens the hearts of the wicked and advances them toward eternal suffering. [8]Translating *interiores homines*. *Interiores* usually refers to the inhabitant of a place, one who lives within it. The MSS evidence is uncertain. Other readings are *infirmiores homines* ("weaker persons") and *interioris homines* ("persons who bleed within, in the soul"). [9]The Latin is *amatores suos* ("his own lovers"). Caesarius is thinking along the lines of Augustine. As one may have love for God, so one may also have love for the devil (*amor dei, amor diaboli*).

happiness the Holy Spirit defines as plagues and sorrows. "And they blasphemed the name of God who had power over these plagues, and they did not repent." Since these plagues from God do not strike them in the body but in the soul, they do not give thought to the Lord but progress toward even greater evil and for that reason blaspheme God and persecute his saints. "The fifth angel poured his bowl on the throne of the beast, and its kingdom was put in darkness." The throne of the beast is his own church, that is, the congregation of the proud and haughty, that is blinded by plagues of this sort. "They gnawed their tongues from their anguish." This shows that in their blaspheming they were harming themselves from the wrath of God, for those who were struck believed themselves to be happy. "And they did not repent." Indeed, they had been made obdurate by their pleasure. "The sixth angel poured out his bowl on the great river Euphrates," that is, on the people. "And its water was dried up," as was said previously, "the harvest of the earth was dry,"[10] that is, it was prepared to be set on fire. "That the way of those who are from the rising of the sun," that is, from Christ, "might be prepared." When these things have come to pass, the righteous begin to advance toward Christ.

THE CONTINUATION OF THE REVELATION (HOMILY 13)

Dearest brethren, as he was speaking of the bowls or plagues of the seven angels, Saint John briefly recapitulates from the beginning, as is his habit, leaving out for the moment the seventh angel. He says, "I saw coming out from the mouth of the dragon and from the mouth of the beast and from the mouth of the false prophet three foul spirits like frogs." In fact, he saw one spirit. However, for the whole and in view of the distinction within the one reality, he says that there were three. For the dragon,

who is the devil, and the beast, who is the body of the devil, and the false prophet, who is the leaders of the body of the devil, is one spirit. They were "like frogs," and "they are the spirits of demons who perform signs." In addition to their ugly appearance, frogs are unclean also in the places of their habitation. Although they seem to be natural residents of the waters and native to them, they cannot endure it when the waters recede and dry up, and they roll around in the waters themselves and in the mud and filth of the waters. The hypocrites likewise do not spend their time in the waters, as they seem to, but in filthy acts that those who believe lay aside in the water. Similar to frogs are such persons who are not ashamed to wallow in sins and vices, which others put aside through penance or baptism. Whenever someone converts to God and repents that he had been arrogant, adulterous, drunken or lustful, such a person imitates these sins that another has relinquished by confessing and thinking to himself says, "I do what I want, and later I will do penance as that one has done penance." But suddenly the last day overtakes him, and any confession is lost and his damnation remains. Such is that person who wishes to imitate others, not in that which is good but in that which is evil, and like frogs they cover themselves and roll around in that muck and mire from which others have been liberated. Frogs, therefore, signify the spirits of demons who do signs and wonders.

"They go out to the kings of the whole world, to assemble them for battle on the great day of the Lord." By the great day he is referring to the whole time from the passion of the Lord. This day is to be interpreted variously according to the passage. Sometimes it refers to the day of judgment, sometimes to the last persecution under the antichrist that is yet in the future, sometimes to all of time. As Amos the prophet says, "Woe to those who desire the

---

[10]See Rev 14:15. Caesarius writes *aruit messis terrae*, hence dry, not merely ripe.

day of the Lord. And what is this day of the Lord to you?"[1] and the rest that follows there. All these things in this life are the day of the Lord to those who experience the darkness of the Lord. These are they who desire the day of the Lord, that is, those who delight in this world and for whom this world is easy and pleasant. Such persons work in the world with pleasure and luxury and receive advantage and gain from it. They believe that religion is an opportunity for acquisition, and so it is said to them, "Woe to you who are now full."[2] It is not these of whom it is said, "Blessed that they that mourn."[3]

He now again recapitulates from the same persecution, saying, "And there were flashes of lightning and peals of thunder, and a great earthquake such as had never been since people were made, and that great city was divided into three parts." This great city is to be understood as in general every people that is under heaven. This people will fall into three parts when the church will be divided into three parts. At that time, the Gentiles will be one part, all heretics and false Christians another part and the catholic church the third part. The text continues and shows what the three parts are, for it says, "The cities of the nations fell, and God remembered that great Babylon to give to her the cup of the wine of his wrath. And every island fled away, and no mountain was to be found." The cities of the nations are the nations; Babylon is the abomination of desolation; the mountains and islands are the church. It says that in the cities of the nations every defense and surety and every hope of the nations has fallen. It is not that cities have been separated from the Christians, for there are good cities as well as evil cities that exist within the human race. Therefore, Babylon is said to fall or to drink of the wrath of God

then, when it has assumed power against Jerusalem, that is, against the church. "And the islands were no longer to be found," that is, they had not been overcome and conquered. "And a hailstone as large as a talent dropped on people from heaven." This hailstone represents the wrath of God, just as all of the plagues were figures of spiritual plagues. "And people cursed God for the plague of the hailstone, since the plague of the hailstone was so great."

And now again he recapitulates, saying, "Then one of the seven angels said to me, 'Come, I will show you the damnation[4] of the great harlot who is seated on many waters, with whom the kings of the earth have committed fornication.'" The kings of the earth are all those who are born of the earth.[5] "And he carried me away in the Spirit into a wilderness, and I saw a woman sitting on a beast." The beast symbolizes the whole body of those people who are evil, and the woman represents the corruption of that people. It says that the woman sits on the beast in the desert because she sits on the impious, those who are dead in their souls and who have been deserted by God. He was led away "in the Spirit," it says, because a desertion by God of this kind cannot be seen unless one is in the Spirit. The woman is said to be arrayed in a sumptuous manner because she wears the raiment of her luxury.

As we have already noted,[6] the beast on which the woman sits is a people, and this people is also the many waters, as the text explains. "The waters that you saw, where the harlot is seated, are peoples and multitudes and nations and tongues." It says that she who sits on the peoples in the desert is thoroughly corrupted. The harlot, the beast and the desert are all one thing. As we noted already, the beast is the body of the devil that stands against the Lamb. In this body we may at times

---

Homily 13   [1]Amos 5:18.   [2]Lk 6:25.   [3]Mt 5:4.   [4]Caesarius uses the term *damnationem*.   [5]Caesarius may have in mind the distinction between "being born of the earth" and "being born from heaven" (see Jn 3:31). In this case, he is distinguishing between the unbelievers and hypocrites and those who are baptized and have remained true to their baptism.   [6]Caesarius begins a recapitulation of his exposition.

recognize the devil and at times the heretics who are indicated in the head that seems to be killed. These seem to be glorified through the death of Christ but here are interpreted alone to be a haughty people, who as a whole indicate the city of Babylon.

In the three spirits that come out of the mouth of the dragon in the shape of frogs we recognize one to be the devil, another to be the false prophet or the leaders of the heretics and the third to be the body of the devil, that is, all those hypocritical, prideful and impious Christians who make up such a large number of the church.[7] Finally, they are depicted in such a form because in the manner of frogs they roll around in every kind of uncleanness and in the filth of luxury. Indeed, those persons are similar to frogs who are not ashamed to be polluted by sins and evils that others have put off through penance or baptism. And they say to themselves, "For the present I will fulfill my desires, and afterward as those have converted I also will turn to God." And suddenly, as death overtakes them, the time for confession passes and damnation remains. When it says that people are gathered to the great day, by the great day it refers to the entire span of time from the passion of the Lord to the end of the world. This day is pleasant to those who serve their lusts and their greed and become wealthy in it. But they will come into great misery, for in them that will be fulfilled what was spoken by the prophet: "Woe to those who desire the day of the Lord."[8] Through a false and transitory sweetness they prepare for themselves an eternal bitterness. It is possible that in this passage the great day refers to that desolation when Jerusalem was besieged by Titus and Vespasian when, with the exception of those

who were led into captivity, 110,000 were said to have died.[9] When it says that "he assembled them at the place called Armageddon," it refers to all the enemies of the church. Therefore later a passage follows and says, "They surrounded the camp of the saints and the holy and beloved city,"[10] that is, the church.

There were peals of thunder and a great earthquake, and that great city was divided into three parts. The great city is all people taken together, one part referring to the pagans, another to the heretics and the third to Christians among whom are also the hypocrites. When the good Christians will have been separated from this third part, then those who have only feigned to be in the church will be joined to those other two parts and receive the judgment of God, which to be sure to some extent is already fulfilled in the present age. Babylon falls at that time when the wicked receive power and use it to persecute the good who are of the church. The great hailstone that is the size of a talent and falls from heaven represents the wrath of God. This wrath comes on the impious and the haughty even before the day of judgment, for it enters spiritually into their souls. He sees in the Spirit a woman, a harlot, who is sitting on a beast in the desert. He says that she is in the desert because she is sitting on the impious, that is, she is sitting on the souls of the dead and those forsaken by God. And he says "in the Spirit" because no one can see such a forsakenness unless it is spiritually perceived, for it occurs within the soul. The whore, the beast and the desert are one thing, and altogether they represent Babylon. As we have already said, the beast is the body of the impious that is arrayed against the Lamb. At times in this body we recognize the

---

[7]A clear indication of the pastoral difficulties in sixth-century Gaul.   [8]Amos 5:18.   [9]Caesarius mentions the same carnage in his *Sermon* 127:2: "We read in history that three million Jews were then gathered in Jerusalem; eleven hundred thousand of them are read to have been destroyed by the sword or hunger, and one hundred thousand young men were led to Rome in triumph" (FC 47:222). In the *Sermon* Caesarius compares Jesus to Eliseus and Titus and Vespasian to the two bears which "are said to have torn to pieces forty-two boys for deriding blessed Eliseus." The Jews who cried out, "Crucify him! Crucify him!" are compared to the boys in their derision of "the true Eliseus."   [10]Rev 20:9.

devil. Sometimes we recognize the head that is wounded to death and that signifies the perfidy of the heretics, who gather together and persecute the church of Christ even though they wish to be regarded as glorified by the death of Christ. But it is not only the heretics and the pagans, but also the evil catholics, that is, the proud and the impious who persecute the gentle and humble whom they see in the church. As we are able, we beseech the mercy of God that he might amend even such persons from their evil deeds and bring them to that which is good, and that he might graciously grant to us a blessed perseverance in good works for the sake of his own compassion, who with the Father and the Holy Spirit lives and reigns into the ages of ages.[11] Amen.

THE CONTINUATION (HOMILY 14)

In the divine reading that was just now read, dearest brethren, we heard Saint John say that he saw "a woman sitting on a scarlet beast," that is, she was defiled by the blood of her sins. Moreover, she was "full of blasphemous names." He shows that there are many forms[1] in the beast, that is, in the body of wicked people, as we have already said. "It had seven heads and ten horns." This means that the beast possessed the kings and the kingdom of the world, with whom the devil was seen in heaven. "The woman," that is, the whole multitude of the proud, "was arrayed in purple and scarlet and was bedecked with gold and a precious stone." This means that she was deceptively imaging all the allurement of the truth. And then he explains what was in fact within this beauty, saying, "And she was holding in her hand a golden cup full of abominations and the impurities of her fornication." The golden cup full of impurities symbolizes her

hypocrisy. Indeed, there are those who appear outwardly to others as though they are righteous, but within they are full of every kind of uncleanness.

"And on her forehead a name was written, mystery, Babylon the great, mother of fornicators and of the earth's abominations." There is no false religion that would place a sign upon the forehead unless that of hypocrisy. What pertains to the Spirit is written on the forehead. And who would bear such a title openly? He said that it was a mystery, and he interprets it, saying, "I saw the woman, drunk with the blood of the saints and with the blood of the martyrs of Jesus." There is one body that opposes the church within and without. For within the church there are false Christians, and outside the church there are heretics and pagans. And although this body might seem to be separated in terms of place, yet when it persecutes the church there is working a unity of spirit. For it is impossible for a prophet perish from that Jerusalem that persecutes the prophets.[2] That is to say, it is impossible for good Christians to suffer any persecution without evil Christians.[3] And so the descendants of their ancestors are accused of consenting to the stoning of Zachariah, even though they themselves did not do it.[4]

"The beast was, and is not, and is going to be; it will ascend from the bottomless pit and will go to perdition." We understand this to mean that the beast will be born out of an evil people. And so we can say the beast comes out of the beast and the abyss out of the abyss. And what does it mean that the beast comes out of the beast and the abyss out of the abyss, unless an evil people is born out of an evil people? This is so because wicked children imitate their wicked parents. And it ascends

---

[11]From this concluding doxology it appears that in the words "mercy of God" Caesarius has Christ in mind. We beseech the mercy of Christ, our God.   **Homily 14**   [1]Translating *multa nomina*, literally "many names." A name is that by which something is called or known. Caesarius says that the beast, the body of wicked people, is known by many forms of sin.   [2]See Lk 13:33-34.   [3]Jerusalem is the church, and the good Christians are persecuted by evil Christians. That is, good Christians are persecuted in Jerusalem.   [4]Mt 23:35.

and is present and goes into perdition, even as did their ancestors from whom they ascended. And they are not, since while some are dying, others are succeeding to them. Therefore, those who from the beginning have always plotted against the church are never lacking, whether they are few or many, whether they are hidden or manifest.

When it says that the woman was sitting on a scarlet beast, it is referring to a sinful and bloody people.[5] And when it says that she was arrayed in purple and scarlet and was adorned in gold and a precious stone, it symbolizes a people of proud and impious persons who are sated with every allurement of a truth that they only simulate. The golden cup that she holds in her hand and is filled with abominations and every filth of her fornication symbolizes the hypocrites, that is, those who only feign to be Christians and appear outwardly to be righteous but who on the inside are full of every uncleanness. She had written on her forehead "Babylon, the mother of fornicators." For there is no false religion that would place an image on the forehead other than hypocrisy, for hypocrites give the appearance of being good, although they are wicked. It says that the woman was inebriated with the blood of the saints and of the martyrs of Jesus, and by this it refers to that unified body of the wicked that always arranges itself against the church both within and without. For within the church there are the hypocritical Christians and outside the church there are the heretics and the pagans. And although this body might seem to be separated from time to time, yet when it persecutes the church they are joined in one mind. "The beast was, and is not, and is going to ascend from the bottomless pit." We understand this to mean that an evil people is born out of an evil people. And so we can say the beast comes out of the beast and the abyss out of the abyss. And what does it mean that

the beast comes out of the beast, unless an evil people is born out of an evil people? This is so because wicked children imitate their wicked parents. And this occurs since while some are dying, others are succeeding to them. Therefore, those who from the beginning have always plotted against the church are never lacking, whether they are few or many, whether they are hidden or manifest. And although in this world we can never be separated from having some contact with them, let us beseech the mercy of God, that we might be so separated in our conduct that we do not go with them to an eternal punishment. Rather, when they hear, "Depart from me, you cursed, into the eternal fire," may we be worthy to hear, "Come, blessed of my Father, inherit the kingdom."[6]

THE CONTINUATION (HOMILY 15)

In the reading that has been recited, dearest brethren, he has called those kings who persecute Jerusalem, and these are the wicked peoples who persecute the church. They are said to be "as kings," since they rule as though in dreams. For every evil person who persecutes one who is good does this as though in a dream, because the cruel deeds of those who are wicked will not endure but will dissipate as do dreams. As Isaiah said, "The wealth of all the nations will be as one who dreams in a dream."[1] "These have one mind," that is, they are of one spirit when they persecute those who are good. And he said "they have," not "they will have," because the persecution by those who are evil will be not only when the day of judgment comes, but it does not even cease to exist in the present age. "They will give their power and majesty to the devil." He says this because impious people seem to give power to that one through whose urging they do evil. "These make war on the Lamb." Until the end when at last the saints shall receive all rule, they oppose the church. "And the Lamb will conquer them."

---

[5]Caesarius begins his recapitulation of the material. [6]Mt 25:41, 34. **Homily 15** [1]Is 29:7 LXX.

This is certainly because God will not permit those[2] to be tempted beyond what they are able. Therefore, he says, "And the Lamb will conquer them, for he is Lord of lords and King of kings, and those with him are called and chosen and faithful," that is, the church. He said "called and chosen," because not all are called and chosen, as the Lord said: "Many are called, but few are chosen."[3]

"And the angel said to me, 'You saw where the woman is seated, these are a people and multitudes and nations and tongues. And the ten horns that you saw, they hold the harlot in hatred.'" That is, they hate that woman. The harlot is the life of luxury that is lived by plunder and pleasures. It says that they would hate the harlot, for dissolute persons who are also proud, lustful and arrogant not only persecute the saints but also hold themselves in hatred. And in another way do those hate themselves in whom the word of Scripture is fulfilled: "Those who love iniquity hate their own soul."[4] The text continues, "And they will make her desolate and naked." Through the wrath of God and his just judgment by which they are abandoned by him, they themselves will make the world a desert, since they have been given over to it and use it unrighteously. "And they will devour her flesh." This is so, because as the apostle says, "They will bite and eat one another."[5] And therefore he also adds the cause, saying, "For God has put it into their hearts to carry out his purpose." This means that God has summoned those plagues that he has by right and by merit determined to inflict on the world. "And they will give their royal power to the beast, until the words of God shall be fulfilled." This indicates that the wicked will submit to the devil until the Scriptures will have been fulfilled and the day of judgment will have come. After this the text continues, "The woman that you saw is the great city that has dominion over the kings of the earth." That is, she has power over all wicked and impious people. But of the church the following is said: "Come, I will show you the wife of the Lamb, and he showed me a city coming down out of heaven."[6]

"After this I saw another angel coming down from heaven having great authority; and the earth was made bright with his splendor. And he called with a mighty voice, saying, 'Fallen, fallen is Babylon, she who is great! It has become a dwelling place of demons and haunt of every foul and hateful bird.'" Can the ruins of a single city contain every unclean spirit or every foul bird, or at the time when a city falls, is the whole world made devoid of impure spirits and birds so that they inhabit the ruins of a single city? There is no city that contains every unclean soul except the city of the devil, in which every uncleanness dwells in wicked persons throughout the whole earth. Those whom it calls "kings" because they persecute Jerusalem are evil people who persecute the church of God.

THE CONTINUATION (HOMILY 16)
Whenever you hear the name Babylon, dearest brethren, do not think of it as a city made of stones, for "Babylon" means "confusion," as we have often said. Rather, understand that the name signifies those people who are arrogant, robbers, dissolute and impious, and who persevere in their wickednesses. On the other hand, whenever you hear the name Jerusalem, which refers to the vision of peace, understand that it refers to persons who are holy before God. Since Babylon bears the image of evil people, they are described like this in the following verses: "For all nations have drunk the wine of her impure passion, and the kings of the earth have committed fornication with her." This means that the kings of the earth fornicated with each other. For it would be impossible for all kings to commit fornication with a single harlot. Rather,

²That is, the saints. ³Mt 22:14. ⁴Ps 10:6. ⁵Gal 5:15. ⁶Rev 21:9-10.

97

since the evil and profligate, who are members of the harlot, corrupt each other, they are said to commit fornication with the harlot, that is, by a sinful manner of life. Then it says that "all the merchants of the earth were made rich by the wealth of her wantonness." Here it speaks of those who were wealthy in their sins. For excess in luxury makes for poverty of the soul rather than for wealth.

"And I heard another voice from heaven saying, 'Come out from her, my people, lest you take part in her sins, lest you suffer in her plagues.'" We see from this passage that Babylon is divided into two parts. For as long as God allows, the wicked are converted to the good, so that Babylon is divided, and that part that departs from it is the making of Jerusalem. For as long as some are moved from Babylon to Jerusalem and others are seduced from Jerusalem to Babylon, so long are the wicked converted to the good and those who seem through hypocrisy to be good are openly revealed to be wicked. And, therefore, through Isaiah Scripture speaks to the good: "Go out from their midst and touch no unclean thing; go out from their midst and be separated from them, you who bear the vessels of the Lord."[1] The apostle also mentions this separation, saying, "The firm foundation of the Lord remains; and the Lord knows those who are his, and let every one who names the name of the Lord depart from iniquity."[2] "Lest you take part in her sins," it says, "and lest you suffer in her plagues." Although it is written, "Whatever righteous person shall be taken by death, he will be at rest,"[3] how can a righteous person, whom the fall of the city affects along with the impious, partake of sin? Except perhaps in this way. When the good leave the city of the devil, that is, abandon a profligate and impious life, should any one of them choose to remain and to enjoy the pleasures of Babylon, such a one would certainly share in its plagues. But when-

ever it says "Come out," do not understand this in a bodily sense but in a spiritual sense. For one comes out of Babylon whenever one abandons an evil manner of life. Babylonians are with Jerusalemites in each house and in the one church and in each city. Nonetheless, as long as the good do not consent with the wicked and the wicked do not convert to the good, Jerusalem is recognized in the good and Babylon is recognized in the wicked. Although they live together in the body, they are far from each other in the heart, for the life of the wicked is always in the things of the earth, for they love the earth and place their entire hope and the entire intention of their soul in the earth. But according to the apostle, the mind of the good is always in the heavens, since they are wise in that which is on high.[4]

"Come out from her, my people," it says, "lest you take part in her sins, lest you suffer in her plagues. For her sins have ascended even to heaven, and God has remembered her iniquities. Render to her as she has rendered to you, and repay her double for her deeds; in the cup she mixed, mix for her a double portion. As she glorified herself and played the wanton, so give to her a like measure of torment and mourning." All of this God speaks to his own people, to the good Christians, to the church. "Render to her as she herself has rendered," for both visible and invisible plagues have gone out from the church into the world. "For Babylon says in her heart," that is, the people of all the wicked or prideful, "'I sit as a queen, and I am no widow, mourning I shall never see.' Therefore, her plagues shall come in a single day, death and mourning and famine, and she shall be burned with fire." If she will die and be consumed with fire in one day, who will remain beyond these things and bewail the dead? Or, how great can the famine be that occurs in only one day? However, by one day it means

Homily 16   [1]Is 52:11.   [2]2 Tim 2:19.   [3]Wis 4:7.   [4]See Col 3:2.

the short period of time of their present life in which they are afflicted both in the spirit and in the body. Those who are proud and who have been given over to pleasures suffer greater plagues in their souls than they do in their bodies. And they will suffer a greater plague when they glory in their own iniquities and so by the just judgment of God are permitted to do evil, so that they do not even merit to be scourged among the children of God. Then in them that which is written in the Scriptures will be fulfilled: "They are not in the troubles of other people, and they shall not be stricken with other people; therefore, pride has taken hold of them."[5] "For mighty is the Lord God who will judge Babylon."

"And the kings of the earth, who committed fornication with her, will weep and wail over her." What kings would lament a city that is destroyed, if it were the kings who destroyed it? But what the city is, that is also the kings who lament it. With this repentance, the kings are not bewailing the evil of wealth, because they sinned with the harlot. Rather, they recognize that they are losing the prosperity of the world through which they became subject to its pleasures. Or, since those things in it were beginning to come to an end that because of their luxury were previously pleasing to them, these profligates fight and consume one another, as though smoke from a fierce fire.[6] "And they stand far off," it says, "out of fear of her punishment." They are said to stand afar off, not physically but in their souls, since each one will fear for himself when he sees what another suffers through the maliciousness and power of the haughty. "They say, 'Alas, alas, thou great city, Babylon, thou mighty city! In one hour has your damnation come.'" The Spirit speaks the name of the city. Indeed, they lament the world, which is overtaken by punishment in such a short time and all of whose industry has come to an end so violently.

"The merchants of horses and chariots and slaves, who gained wealth from her, will stand far off weeping and mourning, saying, 'Alas, alas, the great city.'" Whenever the Spirit says that they were made rich from her, he is indicating the abundance of their sins. "She was clothed with fine linen, in purple and scarlet, and bedecked with gold, with a precious jewel and with pearls." Can a city be dressed in fine linen and purple, rather than people? They lament for themselves, since they are despoiled of those riches that are mentioned here. "And every shipmaster and seafaring man, sailors and all whose trade is on the sea, stood far off and cried out as they saw the smoke of her burning." Can all those who are shipmasters and sailors and all who work on the sea be present to see the burning of a single city? Rather, it says that all who loved the world and were the workers of iniquity fear for themselves when they see the ruin of their own hope.

After this it says, "And I saw the beast and the kings of the earth and their armies."[7] The beast signifies the devil, and the kings and their armies symbolize the entire people of the devil. "They were gathered to make war against him who sits on the white horse and against his army." That is, they were gathered to war against Christ and the church. "Then I saw another angel coming down from heaven." He is referring to the Lord Christ in his first coming. "He was holding the key of the bottomless pit," that is, he had authority over evil people, for the bottomless pit represents an evil people. "And a great chain was in his hand," that is, God had given authority into his hand. "And seized the dragon, the ancient serpent, who is the devil and Satan, and bound him for a thousand years." To be sure,

---

[5]Ps 73:5-6 (72:5-6 LXX). [6]Translating *tamquam fumus instantis gehennae*. [7]Caesarius moves quickly to Rev 19:19 and to the beginning of Rev 20.

this concerns the first coming, as the Lord himself said: "Who can enter a strong man's house and plunder his goods, unless he first binds the strong man?"[8] For when he excludes the devil from the people[9] of the believers, he sends him into the abyss, that is, into an evil people. This indeed occurred visibly when Christ cast out demons from certain persons and allowed them to enter into swine, which then cast themselves headlong into the depths.[10] This is fulfilled most especially in the heretics.

THE CONTINUATION OF THE APOCALYPSE (HOMILY 17)

What your charity has now heard from the reading of the Revelation receive, as is your custom, with an attentive soul. For the blessed John the Evangelist said that he saw "heaven opened, and behold, a white horse! He who sat on it was called Faithful and True. His eyes were like a flame of fire, and on his head were many diadems," for in him there is a multitude of those who have been crowned. "And he has a name inscribed that no one knows except himself." That is, no one knows the name except he himself and the entire church that is in him. "He was clad in a vestment sprinkled with blood." The vestment of Christ is the church, and it is she with whom he is clothed. She is splattered with the blood of her many sufferings.

"The name by which he is called is The Word of God. And the armies that are in heaven followed him on white horses." This means that the church imitates him in bodies made white, as it was said above: "These are they who follow the Lamb wherever he goes."[1] "They were arrayed in fine linen, white and pure." This expression refers to the righteous deeds of the saints. "From his mouth issues

a sharp two-edged sword." He is himself this sword, by which the righteous are defended and the unrighteous are punished. "He has this sword to smite the nations, and he will rule them with a rod of iron; he will tread the wine press of the indignation of the wrath of God the Almighty." To be sure, he treads the wine press even now when he permits the wicked to do that which is wicked and abandons them to their own pleasures. But afterward outside the city, that is, outside the church, he will tread the wine press when he gives those who did not repent over to the fires of Gehenna. "On his robe and on his thigh he has a name inscribed, King of kings and Lord of lords." This is the name that the proud do not know. For it is in serving Christ that the church reigns and rules as lord of those who are lords. That is to say, the church conquers its vices and its sins. The thigh symbolizes a person's posterity, as we learn from this passage, "A leader shall not depart from the thighs of Judah."[2] And lest he intermingle his posterity with those of foreign birth, Abraham caused a certain witness to be made between himself and his servant.[3]

"And I saw," it says, "an angel standing on the sun," that is, he saw a preacher in the church. "And with a loud voice he called to all the birds that fly in midheaven." Depending on the context, beasts and birds may represent either those who are evil or those who are good. For example, we read that "the wild beasts will bless me,"[4] or we read of "the Lion from the tribe of Judah."[5] In the present passage the birds flying in midheaven refer to the churches that, being considered as one body, he had said was an eagle flying in heaven.[6] "Come, gather for the great supper of God, to eat the flesh of kings, the flesh of chieftains[7] and of mighty men, the flesh of horses and their rid-

---

[8]Mt 12:29. [9]The text of Morin (p. 264) shows a lacuna here. The Maurists conjectured "from the people," and this appears in their edition (PL 35:2445). [10]See Mt 8:28-34. **Homily 17** [1]Rev 14:4. [2]Gen 49:10 LXX. [3]Gen 24:2-4. [4]Is 43:20. [5]Rev 5:5. [6]See Rev 8:13. [7]Caesarius uses the term *tribuni* ("tribunes").

ers, and the flesh of all people, both free and slave, both small and great." When they come to faith in Christ, all nations are incorporated into the church and are spiritually consumed by the church.

And after this it is said of the devil, "The angel shut the pit and sealed it over him, that he should deceive the nations no more, till the thousand years were ended." The thousand years are to be understood as those that have passed since the coming of our Lord. During these years the Lord prohibited the devil from deceiving the nations, those that beforehand the devil had deceived lest they be reconciled to God, but that are destined for life.[8] "After that he must be loosed for a little while," that is, during the time of the antichrist when "the man of sin shall have been revealed,"[9] when he shall have received the full power of persecution, such as he had not received from the beginning. When he mentions the thousand years, he is speaking of a part in terms of the whole, for here he is speaking of the remaining time of the sixth day of the thousand years in which the Lord was born and suffered.

After this it says, "Alas, alas, that great city, where all who had ships at sea grew rich! In one hour she has been laid waste. Rejoice over her, O heaven, O saints and apostles and prophets." Is Babylon the only city in all the world that persecutes or has persecuted the saints of God, so that when she is destroyed all of them are avenged? Babylon is throughout the whole world in evil people, and throughout the world persecutes those who are good. "The angel took up a stone like a great millstone and threw it into the sea, saying, 'So shall Babylon the great city be thrown down with violence.'" Babylon is likened to a great millstone that is thrown down, for the revolving of times, as though it were a millstone, grinds down

those who love the world, and it sends them in circles. Of these the Scriptures say, "The wicked walk in a circle."[10] Their possessions give them no happiness, and they remain unhappy from the very beginning. "Babylon shall be found no more; and the sound of harpers and minstrels, of trumpeters and flute players, shall be heard in her no more." That is, the joy and happiness of the wicked passes away and is no longer to be found. And it adds the reason for this, saying, "for your merchants were the great men of the earth," that is, they had received good things in their lives. "For all nations were deceived by your sorcery, and the blood of the prophets and the saints was found in her and of all who have been slain by you on the earth." Did the same city kill the apostles that also killed the prophets and all of the rest of the martyrs? Rather, this is the city of all the proud and arrogant, which Cain established by the blood of his brother and which he "named after the name of his son, Enoch," that is, after his posterity.[11] For all the wicked in whom Babylon resides succeed one another and persecute the church of God until the end of the world. In the city of Cain "all the righteous blood" is poured out "from the blood of righteous Abel to the blood of Zechariah," that is, of the people and of the priests, "between the sanctuary and the altar" that is, between the people and the priests.[12] This was said because not only the people but also the priests conspired in the death of Zechariah. It says "between the sanctuary and the altar." The altar represents the priests, and the sanctuary signifies the peoples. There would be no other reason for mentioning these locations. This is the city that killed the prophets and stoned those who were sent to it. This is that city that is built on blood, as the Scriptures say: "Woe to him who builds a city with blood

---

[8]The terseness of Caesarius does not make the thought clear. Augustine's comment on the passage clarifies: "The nations or people freed from the devil's seductions ... are those whom he used to lead astray and hold captive but who now belong to Christ" (*City of God* 20.7 [FC 24:267-68]). [9]2 Thess 2:3. [10]Ps 12:8. [11]Gen 4:17. [12]Mt 23:35.

and founds a city on iniquity."[13]

In the white horse, concerning which we spoke above, we recognize the church, and in its rider we recognize Christ the Lord.[14] It says that "he has a name inscribed that no one knows but himself." To be sure, no one knows the name but he himself and the entire church that is in him. In his vestment splattered with blood we are to recognize the martyrs who are in the church. And his army that is in heaven followed him on white horses, that is, the church followed him in bodies made white. The sharp two-edged sword is the power of Christ by which the righteous are defended and the unrighteous are punished. The rod of iron is the righteousness of God by which the humble are instructed but the proud are broken to pieces as though they were a clay pot. And it says, "He treads the wine press of the wrath of God the Almighty." To be sure, he treads the wine press even now, when he permits wicked people to persecute those who are good and abandons them to their own desires. However, later he will seek repayment, when he sends those into Gehenna who have not repented. We interpret the angel standing in the sun to be the preaching that occurs in the church. And the church is compared with the sun, because it is written of her, "Then the righteous will shine like the sun in the kingdom of their Father."[15]

When the angel calls to all the birds that are flying in midheaven, we understand these birds to be the church. And when it is said, "Come, gather for the great supper, to eat the flesh of kings and the flesh of chieftains," we know that this in fact happens in the church. For when all the nations are incorporated into the church, they are spiritually devoured. Indeed, those who have been devoured by the devil become the body of the devil, while those who have been received by the church are made to be members of Christ. However, of the devil it is said, "The angel shut the pit and sealed it

over him, that he should deceive the nations no more, till the thousand years were ended." These thousand years are those that have passed since the passion of the Lord. During them it is not permitted to the devil to do whatever he wishes, for God does not permit his servants to be tempted beyond that which they are able to endure.[16] However, afterward the devil will be let loose for a little while, namely, the time of the antichrist, and during this time the devil is going to receive a greater power for his fierce rage.

When it is said, "Alas, alas, the great city," we understand it to refer to Babylon. Nevertheless, we ought to know that Babylon is not the only city that persecutes the saints, so that when it is destroyed, all who suffered under it will be vindicated. Babylon exists throughout the whole world in those who are wicked, and throughout the whole world it persecutes those who are good. And an angel threw a great stone like a millstone into the sea, saying, "In like manner shall Babylon be submerged." And he likens Babylon to a millstone, because the revolution of the times grinds fine those who are lovers of the world and sends them in circles. It says, "By your sorcery all the nations were deceived, and the blood of the prophets and of all slain by you was found on the earth." It was not in a single city that the apostles or the prophets or the martyrs were slain. This is rather the city of the prideful that persecutes the saints throughout the entire world. This is the same city that Cain founded on the blood of his brother and that he named after the name of his son, Enoch, that is, after his posterity. For all the wicked, in whom Babylon exists, succeed one another until the end of the world and persecute the church of God. May the Lord through his mercy deign to free us from their persecution, who with the Father and the Holy Spirit lives and reigns into the ages of ages.

---

[13]Hab 2:12.   [14]Caesarius begins a recapitulation of his exposition.   [15]Mt 13:43.   [16]See 1 Cor 10:13.

THE CONTINUATION (HOMILY 18)

In the reading that was just read to you, dearest brethren, the blessed Evangelist John said the following: "I heard the loud voice of many people in heaven saying, 'Hallelujah! Salvation and glory and power belong to our God, for his judgments are true and just; he has judged the great harlot who corrupted the earth with her fornication, and he has avenged on her the blood of his servants.' And once more they cried, 'Hallelujah!'" This is the voice of the church when the separation has already occurred and when all wicked persons have gone out from her to be consumed with eternal fire. "And their[1] smoke goes up forever and ever." Hear, O brothers, and fear and know that Babylon and the harlot whose smoke ascends forever and ever are not to be understood as anything other than lustful, adulterous and arrogant persons. And, therefore, if you wish to avoid these punishments, do not desire to commit such grievous sins. "And their smoke," it says, "goes up forever and ever." Is it the smoke of a burned-out city that is visible and goes up forever and ever, and not rather the smoke of people who remain in their arrogance? It says "it goes up," not "it will go up," for in the present age Babylon is always going into destruction and burning up in part, just as Jerusalem is moving into paradise in those saints who leave the world. The Lord showed this in the story of the poor man and the rich man.[2]

"Then I heard what seemed to be the voice of many people and the sound of many waters like the sound of mighty thunder peals, saying, 'Hallelujah! For the Lord our God the Almighty reigns. Let us rejoice and exult and glorify his name, for the marriage of the Lamb has come, and his bride has made herself ready.'" The bride of the Lamb is the church.

"And it was granted to her to be clothed with fine linen, bright and pure, for the fine linen is the righteous deeds of the saints." It was granted to her to be clothed with her own deeds, as the Scripture says: "Let your priests be clothed with righteousness."[3] "These are all who came to life," it says, "and reigned with Christ a thousand years." That is, who reigned with Christ in the present age. And it says "all" rightly, meaning both those who are still living and the souls of the saints. For, indeed, both those who are still living in this world and those who have already left this life reign with Christ. And they reigned completely and perfectly, as we learn from the passage that says, "They divided my garments among themselves."[4] For it is going to say "they will reign" later.[5] But to demonstrate that these thousand years are the years pertaining to this life, it says, "This is the first resurrection." This resurrection is that by which we rise again through baptism. As the apostle says, "If you have been raised with Christ, seek the things that are above."[6] And again he says, "living as those who have been brought to life from the dead."[7] For sin is death, as the apostle says: "When you were dead to your trespasses and sins."[8] Therefore, just as the first death occurs in this life because of sin, so also the first resurrection occurs in this life through the remission of sins. "Blessed and holy is he who shares in the first resurrection!" This means that that person is blessed who preserves what was received when he was reborn in baptism. "Over such a person the second death has no power," that is, that person will not experience the eternal torments. "And they shall be priests of God and of Christ, and they shall reign with him a thousand years." When the Spirit was writing these things, it was proper that it said that the church shall reign for a thousand years

---

Homily 18 ¹The text of Caesarius reads *eorum* ("their"), not *eius* ("her," as in Bede) or *de illa* ("from her" as in Primasius). ²See Lk 16:19-30. ³Ps 132:9 (131:9 LXX). ⁴Ps 22:18 (21:19 LXX). Caesarius notes the use of the perfect *regnaverunt* and compares it with the same tense of the psalm verse, *diviserunt*. ⁵Rev 20:6. ⁶Col 3:1. ⁷Rom 6:13. ⁸Eph 2:1.

in this age to the end of the world.[9] It is clear that no one ought doubt about the eternal rule when the saints rule even in this present age. For those are rightly said to reign who with God's aid govern well both themselves and others in the temptations of the present world.

"And when the thousand years are ended," it says, "Satan will be loosed from his prison." He speaks of the times having come to an end, but he speaks of a part in terms of the whole. For Satan will be let loose, although the three years and six months, the time of the antichrist and of the final struggle, still remain. "He shall go out to seduce the nations that are at the four corners of the earth." He speaks now of the whole in terms of the part, for all nations cannot be deceived. For only the haughty and the impious will be deceived, while the humble and the true Christians will not be deceived. "Many are called, but few are chosen."[10] "And the devil and his people marched up to the height of the earth,"[11] that is, to the resumption of their arrogance, and "they surrounded the camp of the saints and the beloved city," that is, the church. This refers to what was earlier said about those assembled at Armageddon.[12] However, all of these people cannot be gathered from the four corners of the earth into a single city. Rather, in the four corners of the earth each people will be gathered to besiege the holy city, that is, for the persecution of the church.[13] "And fire came down out of heaven from God," that is, out of the church, "and consumes them." In this passage the fire may be interpreted in two ways. It may symbolize the fire of the Holy Spirit through which they believe in Christ and are spiritually consumed by the church, that is, are incorporated into the church. Or, the fire may indicate the fire of their own sins by which they are consumed and so perish.

"And the devil who had deceived them was thrown into the lake of fire and sulphur where the beast and the false prophets were." The false prophets are either the heretics or the false Christians. From the time the Lord suffered, the beast and the false prophets were dying away and are sent into the fire, until the thousand years from the advent of the Lord should be complete. "And they will be tormented day and night forever and ever. Then I saw the dead, great and small, standing before the throne, and books were opened. And another book was opened, which is the book of the life of each person."[14] The books that are opened are the Testaments of God, for the church will be judged according to both Testaments. The book of the life of each person contains the record of our deeds, and no one could become knowledgeable[15] of the recounting of these hidden acts that the book contains.[16] "And the dead were judged by what was written in the books, by what they had done." The dead were judged from the Testaments, whether they had obeyed the commandments of God or they had not. "And the sea gave up its dead." This speaks of those whom the day of judgment will find yet alive; they are the dead of the sea, for the sea is this world.[17] "And death and Hades gave up their dead." This speaks of those persons whom the day of judgment will find in their tombs. "Then death and Hades were thrown into the lake." It is speaking of the devil and his people. "And

---

[9]The point seems to be that when the Spirit was inspiring the Revelation to be written, the thousand years of rule in this age lay yet in the future. Moreover, Caesarius claims, to understand the matter so does not compromise belief in the eternal reign of the saints with Christ. [10]Mt 22:14. [11]The text of Caesarius reads *in altitudinem terrae*. [12]Rev 16:16. [13]Obviously Caesarius means that in all places throughout the world there will be persecution. [14]The text of Caesarius reads *qui est vitae uniuscuiusque*, which is also the reading of Augustine and Primasius. Bede says that this reading is an *alia editio*. [15]Caesarius uses the term *cognitor*, which was a technical term of a legal advocate, one who had become familiar with the facts of a case. [16]Again, a look at the commentary of Augustine helps to understand the meaning of Caesarius. This book, says Augustine, if considered as an actual book "surpasses all powers of thought for size and length." He asks, "If it contains the entire life record of all people, how much time would it take to read?" (*City of God* 20.14 [FC 24:287-88]). [17]The sea was often regarded as an image of this world with its trouble and turbulence.

if anyone was not found written in the book of life, he was thrown into the lake of fire." This speaks of those who while they were living had been given over to their desires through an investigation in the time of this present age and therefore did not now merit to be judged by God.

"Then I saw a new heaven and a new earth; for the first heaven and the first earth had passed away, and the sea was no more. And I saw the holy city, new Jerusalem, coming down out of heaven from God, prepared as a bride adorned for her husband. And I heard a loud voice from heaven, saying, 'Behold, the dwelling of God is with men, and he will dwell with them, and they will be his people, and God himself will be with them as their God. And he will wipe away every tear from their eyes, and death shall be no more, neither shall there be any mourning.'" He has said all of this concerning the glory of the church such as she will enjoy after the resurrection. "And he said, 'Write this, that these words are faithful and true.' And he said to me, 'I am the A and Ω, the beginning and the end. To the thirsty I will give from the fountain of the water of life without payment.'" This means that to those who desire it, he will give the remission of sins through the font of baptism. "He who conquers shall possess these things, and I will be his God and he shall be my son. But as for the cowardly, the faithless, the polluted, the murderers, sorcerers, idolaters and all liars, their lot shall be in the lake that burns with fire and sulphur, which is the second death."

"He has judged the great harlot who corrupted the earth with her fornication, and he has avenged on her the blood of his servants."[18] This was said above and indicates the voice of the church when all evil persons will have departed from her on the day of judgment to be consumed by the eternal fire. "And their smoke goes up forever and ever." It is not the smoke of a visible city that goes up forever and ever. Rather, it is the smoke of those persons who have persisted in their pride. And when it says that "the marriage of the Lamb has come," it is speaking of Christ and the church. And indeed it says that she was covered in fine linen, because the fine linen symbolizes the righteous works of the saints in which they are clothed. As it is said, "Let your priests be clothed with righteousness."[19] They have reigned a thousand years, it says, meaning the present time during which the saints are rightly said to reign. For with the help of God they reign when they are not able to be overcome by sins. And that he might make this evident, he says later, "This is the first resurrection." This is the resurrection by which we rise again through baptism. For just as the first death occurs in this life through sin, so also the first resurrection occurs through the remission of sins.

"Blessed and holy is he who shares in the first resurrection." This means blessed is he who preserves that which he received when reborn in baptism. And when it says that the church will reign for a thousand years, it refers to this age until the end of the world. It is clear that no one ought doubt about the eternal rule when the saints rule even in this present age. For those are rightly said to reign who with God's aid govern well both themselves and others in the temptations of the present world. When it says of the devil that he deceives the nations that are in the four corners of the earth, it is speaking of a part of the whole, for certainly only the wicked will be deceived. As it is said, "Many are called, but few are chosen."[20]

When it says that the devil and his angels surrounded the camp of the saints and the beloved city, it does not mean that the kings of the earth could be gathered together from the four corners of the earth into one city. Rather, in the four corners of the earth each

---

[18]Caesarius begins here a recapitulation of his exposition. [19]Ps 132:9 (131:9 lxx). [20]Mt 22:14.

people will gather together to persecute the church. We are to interpret the words "fire fell from heaven and consumed them" in a twofold sense. Either they will be consumed spiritually by the fire of the Holy Spirit as they are incorporated into the church, or, should they refuse to be converted to God, they are consumed by the fire of their own sins and perish.

The books that are opened refer to the two Testaments of God, for the church will be judged according to both Testaments. The book that is of the life of each person contains a record of our deeds. For on the day of judgment nothing will remain hidden, and no one will be able to hide his or her sins or transgressions. It says that "the sea gave up its dead." This refers to those whom the coming of Christ will find yet alive in this world. They are called the dead of the sea because the sea represents this world. And then it says that "death and Hades gave up their dead." These are those who will be found in their graves on the day of judgment. "Then death and Hades were thrown into the lake of fire." In this passage death and Hades, the devil and his people, includes those who did not merit to be judged because by a temporal judgment they had been given over to their desires.

After describing the glory of the church, he continues and says, "To the thirsty I will give from the fountain of the water of life without payment." That is to say, I will give to him who desires the forgiveness of sins through the font of baptism. "He who conquers shall have these things, and I will be his God and he shall be my son." May he deign to bring this to pass, who lives and reigns forever and ever. Amen.

THE CONTINUATION (HOMILY 19)

As we have just now heard, dearest brothers, the angel of the Lord spoke to the blessed John and said, "Come, I will show you the bride, the wife of the Lamb." "And in the Spirit he carried

me away on a great and high mountain." By the mountain he refers to Christ. "And he showed me the holy city Jerusalem coming down out of heaven from God." This is the church, the city established on the mountain, that is the bride of the Lamb. The city is then established on the mountain when on the shoulders of the Shepherd[1] it is called back like a sheep to its own sheepfold. For were the church one and the city coming down from heaven another, there would be two brides, which is altogether not possible, for he has called this city the "bride" of the Lamb. Therefore it is clear that it is the church that is described when he says that the city "had the brightness of God, and its radiance was like a most precious jewel." This most precious jewel is Christ.

The city "had a great, high wall, with twelve gates, and on the gates were twelve angels." The twelve gates and the twelve angels are the apostles and the prophets, for, as it is written, we "are built on the foundation of the apostles and the prophets."[2] The Lord also spoke in a similar way to Peter: "On this rock I shall build my church."[3] "On the east three gates, on the north three gates, on the south three gates, and on the west three gates." The city that is described is the church, which is extended throughout the whole world. There are groups of three gates on each of the four sides because throughout the four quarters of the world the mystery of the Trinity is preached in the church. "And the wall of the city had twelve foundations, and on them the twelve names of the apostles of the Lamb." What the gates were, the foundations are as well. What the city was, that is the wall and that which is on it.

"And he who talked with me had a measuring rod of gold." In the golden rod he shows the members of the church, who, although weak in the flesh, are well founded in the golden faith. As the apostle says: "We have this treasure in earthen vessels."[4] "That on the

Homily 19 [1]See Lk 15:5. [2]Eph 2:20. [3]Mt 16:18. [4]2 Cor 4:7.

106

wall and the city were of pure gold, like pure crystal." The church is golden, for her faith has the sheen of gold, and therefore the golden lampstand and the golden altar and the golden bowls all are figures of the church. Glass is a fitting image for the purity of the faith, for what is seen on the outside, this also is within, and there is nothing that is mere appearance, but everything is open to view. This is true also of the saints of the church.

"The foundations of the wall of the city were adorned with every precious jewel. The first foundation was jasper, the second was sapphire, the third was chalcedony, the fourth was emerald, the fifth was sardonyx, the sixth was carnelian, the seventh was chrysolite, the eighth was beryl, the ninth was topaz, the tenth was chrysoprase, the eleventh was hyacinth, the twelfth was amethyst." He mentions the names of the various gems in the foundations so that he might show the gifts of the various graces that have been given to the apostles, as was spoken concerning the Holy Spirit, "who apportions to each one individually as he wills."[5] "And the twelve pearls were single, and each gate was from one pearl." These pearls symbolize the apostles, who are also called "gates" because through their teaching they make known the door of eternal life. The street that is as gold and pure glass represents the church. "The street of the city was pure gold, as transparent as glass." "And I saw no temple in the city, for its temple is the Lord God the Almighty and the Lamb." He saw no temple in the city because the church is in God and God is in the church. "The city had no need for sun or moon to shine in it." The church is not governed by the moon or the elements of the world. She is rather led by Christ, the eternal sun, through the darkness of the world. "For the brightness of God illumines it, and its lamp is the Lamb," as Christ himself said, "I am the Light of the world."[6]

And again, "I am the true Light that enlightens every person who comes into this world."[7] "In his light the nations shall walk" until the end. "And the kings of the earth bring their glory into it." These kings refer to the children of God. "And its gates shall not be shut by day, and there is no night there," even to eternity. "And they shall bring into it the glory and honor of the nations," that is, of those who believe in Christ. "And nothing unclean shall enter it, nor anyone who practices abomination and falsehood, but only those written in the Lamb's book of life."

"Then he showed me a river of water, clear as crystal, flowing from the throne of God and of the Lamb through the middle of the street." This passage shows the fountain of baptism flowing from God and from Christ in the midst of the church. For what kind of honor would there be for this city, were the river to flow through the streets to the hindrance of the inhabitants? "On either side of the river was the tree of life with its twelve kinds of fruit each month, yielding its fruit." It is speaking of the cross of the Lord. There is no tree that bears fruit in every season except the cross. The faithful, who are made wet by the water of the church's river, eat this fruit.[8] And these faithful in turn produce eternal fruit in every season.

"And the throne of God and of the Lamb shall be in it," from now into the ages, "and his servants shall serve him." "And they shall see his face." As he says, "He who sees me, sees also the Father."[9] And also, "Blessed are the pure in heart, for they shall see God."[10] "And his name shall be on their foreheads. And night shall be no more; they shall not work by the light of lamp or by the light of the sun, for the Lord God will be their light, and they shall reign forever and ever." All of this took its beginning from the passion of the Lord.

"And the angel said to me, 'Do not seal up

[5]1 Cor 12:11.   [6]Jn 8:12.   [7]Jn 1:9.   [8]Caesarius is referring to baptism and the Eucharist.   [9]Jn 14:9.   [10]Mt 5:8.

the words of the prophecy of this book, for the time is near. Let the unrighteous do injustice still, and let the filthy still be filthy.'" These words are about those of whom it was said, "Seal up what the seven thunders have said."[11] "Let the righteous do righteousness still, and let the holy be made holy still." These words are about those of whom it was said, "Do not seal up the words of the prophecy of this book." Just as the divine Scriptures are sealed for those who are proud and who love the world more than God, so are they opened for those who are humble and who fear God.

"'Behold, I am coming soon, bringing my recompense, to repay everyone for what he has done. I am the A and the Ω, the first and the last, the beginning and the end.' Blessed are those who do these commandments, that they might have the right over the tree of life and that they might enter the city by the gates." For whoever does not do the commandments and does not enter through the gates, but by another way, for these the book is sealed. Of these he now says, "Outside are the dogs and sorcerers and fornicators and murderers and idolaters, and all who love and practice falsehood." "I Jesus have sent my angel to testify of these things to you in the churches. I am the root and the offspring of David, the bright morning star. The Spirit and the bride say, 'Come,'" that is, the husband and the bride, Christ and the church. "Let him who is thirsty, come; let him who desires take the water of life without price," that is, baptism. "I warn everyone who hears the words of the prophecy of this book; if anyone adds to them, God will add to him the plagues described in this book, and if anyone takes away from the words of this prophecy, God will take away his share in the tree of life and in the holy city, which are described in this book. He who testifies to these things says, 'Surely I am coming soon.'" He says this because of those who would fal-

sify the holy Scriptures, not because of those who speak with simplicity what they think.

The high mountain on which Saint John says that he ascended is the Spirit.[12] The city Jerusalem that he says he saw there signifies the church. And this the Lord demonstrates in the Gospel when he says, "A city set on a hill cannot be hid."[13] When it says that the city has a light like a most precious jewel, we recognize in that jewel the brightness of Christ. According to the words "built on the foundation of the apostles and the prophets,"[14] we recognize the apostles and the prophets in the twelve gates and the twelve angels. Since the city that is being described is the church that is spread throughout the whole earth, there is said to be three gates each on the four sides of the city because of the mystery of the Trinity. In the rod of gold we recognize those members of the church who are weak in the flesh but well grounded with a golden faith. As the apostle said, "Having this treasure in earthen vessels."[15] When it speaks of the city of gold and of the golden altar and the golden bowls, it is speaking of the church on account of its right faith. The purity of her faith is also signified in the glass, and by naming the various jewels in the foundations of the city, he shows the various gifts of grace that have been given to the apostles. In the pearls the text indicates the apostles, who are also called gates because they open the door of eternal life through their teaching.

It says, "I saw no temple in the city, for its temple is the Lord Almighty and the Lamb." There is no need of a temple, for God is in the church and the church is in God. And "the city has no need of sun or moon," because in the darkness of the world the church is illumined not by the visible sun but by the eternal light of Christ. As Christ said, "I am the Light of the world."[16] The kings of the earth are the sons of God, that is, the Christians. In the

---

[11]Rev 10:4. [12]Caesarius begins here a recapitulation of his exposition. [13]Mt 5:14. [14]Eph 2:20. [15]2 Cor 4:7. [16]Jn 8:12.

river of water that is as crystal we recognize the font of baptism that comes from God and from Christ in the midst of the church. The tree on either side of the river that brings forth its twelvefold fruit each month represents the cross. For the cross brings forth fruit for God throughout the whole world, not only every month but every day in those who are baptized. And it says, "The Lord God will enlighten them, and they shall reign forever and ever." This began to occur from the passion of the Lord. When in an earlier part of the book it said, "Seal up that which the seven thunders have said,"[17] it was speaking of those of whom it says, "Let the filthy still be filthy, and let the unrighteous continue to do unrighteous-ness." However, when is says, "Do not seal up the words of this prophecy," it speaks of the saints and the righteous. For, indeed, the divine Scriptures are sealed to those who are proud and who love the world more than they love God. But they are open to those who are humble and who fear God.

And since the Revelation of John the Evangelist concludes with the words, "Behold, I am coming soon," let us pray that the Lord Jesus Christ might deign to come to us according to his promise and through his mercy to free us from the prison of this world and for the sake of his compassion lead us to his blessedness, who with the Father and the Holy Spirit lives and reigns forever and ever. Amen.

---

[17]Rev 10:4.

BEDE THE VENERABLE
The Exposition of the Apocalypse by Bede the Presbyter[1]

A Versicle of Bede the Elder

While an exile, banished from the world of men,
    And forbidden to see the realms of earth,
John, beloved by the Lord, enters triumphantly the courts of heaven
    And joins with praise the choir of the high-throned King.

From here to world below he turns his sacred eyes[2]
    And sees everywhere chariots, scurrying about and tossed,[3]
And Babel and Jerusalem,[4] with intermingled hosts, in conflict joined,
    Now one and now the other takes up sword, or takes to flight.

But the white-robed soldier who follows the gentle Lamb,
    Will with his leader seize the realms of bliss.
While the scaly serpent will plunge by flames, plague and famine,
    His own army in Tartarus's darkness.

Desirous to display this warfare's form and fashion,
    Its order and whatever its skill and array, its victories and battles,
I have wandered through the wide lands where those of old have sown,
    And from those sacred fields I have gathered some few sprouts,[5]
Lest a more copious amount make the feast less welcome,
    Or prohibit a poorer guest to attempt a feast too lavishly prepared.

And so, if what we offer is pleasing to your lips,
    Give praise to him who reigns beyond the stars.[6]
If however what I offer be otherwise, although given with friendly intent,
    Take my verse and with a stone erase it.

Versicle   [1]The Latin reads *Bedae Presbyteri Expositio Apocalypseos*. [2]Translating *sacra lumina*. *Lumen* can mean the light of the eyes, and therefore the eyes themselves. [3]"Chariots" translates *rotas*. Some manuscripts have *rates* which can mean ships. The poem speaks of running about (*currere*) and being tossed by waves (*fluctivagas*). The reading *rates* makes sense of *fluctivagas* but not of running about. The reading *rotas* makes sense of running about but not of being tossed by waves. Gryson reads *rotas* (CCL 121A:218); Migne reads *rates* (PL 93:133). [4]The poem reads *Babel et Solymam*. The latter can be taken as an abbreviation of Jerusalem. The verse expresses the view that the church is a "mixed church," and behind the image is the idea of two cities, Babylon and Jerusalem, the cities of the impious and of the pious. [5]A reference to Bede's use of early Christian authors. [6]Gryson's critical text reads *donanti laudes da super astra deo* ("Give praise to him who gives, to God beyond the stars"; CCL 121A:219). In this instance I have adopted the reading of Migne, *regnanti laudes da super astra deo* (PL 93:133). The language of reign goes better with "beyond the stars."

Prefatory Letter to Eusebius

Bede to my most beloved brother, Eusebius. Greeting.

The Revelation of Saint John, in which God has considered it worthy to reveal by words and figures the internal wars and struggles of his church, seems to me, brother Eusebius, to be divided into seven sections.

In the first section, after a rich introduction that enumerates the sufferings of the Lord and the glories that come afterward[1] for strengthening the faith of the weak, he sees one who is like unto the Son of man robed with the church. When he has recounted what has occurred and what will occur specifically to the seven churches in Asia, the one like a Son of man describes the universal woes and victories of the whole church.[2] And in the sixth place of this list of churches he purposely promised that the Jews will be made subject to the church and that a future temptation will come on the whole world and that he himself will come quickly. Then in the seventh place he places the tepid church at Laodicea.[3] For "when the Son of man comes, do you think that he will find faith on earth?"[4]

In the second section, after the four living creatures on the throne of God and the twenty-four elders have been described, he sees the Lamb who by opening the seven seals of the sealed book discloses the struggles and the triumphs of the church. In doing so and as is the custom of this book he retains the sequence to the number six. Then bypassing the seventh he recapitulates, and as though following the order he concludes the two narratives with the seventh. However, even this recapitulation must be interpreted according to its location. For sometimes he recapitulates from the beginning of suffering, sometimes from a period of time in the middle and sometimes by speaking of the final persecution only or of a short time before it. Nevertheless, this he retains as a fixed constant that he recapitulates from the sixth place.

In the third section he describes the various events of the church under the form of seven angels blowing trumpets. In the fourth section he reveals the struggles and victories of the same church under the figure of a woman giving birth and of a dragon persecuting her, and he repays to each combatant the reward they deserve. During this the words and deeds of seven angels are also reported, although not in the same way as before. For by a mystical ingenuity he retains this number almost everywhere, since indeed in his Gospel and in his letters it is the habit of this John to say nothing frivolous or with excessive brevity. In the fifth section he pours out on the earth the final seven plagues through seven angels. In the sixth section he shows the condemnation of the great whore, that is, of the impious city, and in the seventh he shows the wife of the Lamb beautifully arrayed, that is, the holy Jerusalem that comes down out of heaven from God.

I have also thought that the seven rules of Tyconius, a man of very great learning among those of his own sect, should be briefly mentioned, for those who desire to understand the Scriptures can receive much assistance from them.

The first of these rules is "concerning the Lord and his body." According to this rule there is a transition from the head to the body or from the body to the head yet without any separation from one and the same person. For

---

Prefatory Letter   [1]See 1 Pet 1:11.   [2]"Woes" translates *luctus*, which can refer to sorrow and mourning or to that which causes sorrow and mourning. Hence, *luctus* could refer to the sufferings and persecutions of the church. "Victories" translates *palmas*, which refers to the palm given to the victor in a contest. Hence, *palmas* could refer to the joyousness and celebration of the church in its victory over persecution.   [3]For Bede the number six symbolizes the penultimate, the time before the final events begin. In the sequence of the letters to the seven churches this place belongs to the church at Philadelphia. The number seven is symbol of that which occurs in the final scene of the history of salvation.   [4]Lk 18:8.

it is one person who speaks, saying, "He has placed a miter on me as a bridegroom and has adorned me with ornaments as a bride."[5] Yet it must be understood what of this belongs to the head and what to the body, that is, what to Christ and what to the church.

The second rule is "concerning the bipartite body of the Lord" or rather "concerning the true and false body of the Lord," as Saint Augustine would prefer to call it.[6] For the church says, "I am dark and beautiful, as the tents of Kedar, as the curtains of Solomon."[7] She did not say, "I was dark but am now beautiful." Rather, she said that she is both because of the communion of the sacraments and because of the temporary commingling of good and bad fish within one net.[8] In fact the tents of Kedar belong to Ishmael, who will not be heir with the son of the free woman.[9]

The third rule is "concerning the promises and the law." This rule could be called otherwise "concerning the spirit and the letter" or "concerning grace and the commandment."[10] To Augustine this seems itself to be a great question rather than a rule that may be applied to the solving of questions. For this was the very point that the Pelagians did not understand when they fabricated and fostered their heresy.[11]

The fourth rule is "concerning the species and the genus." For the species is a part, but the genus is the whole of which each species is a part. For example, each city is a part of the whole province, and each province is a part of the whole world. Accordingly, these words are understood by the common people, so that even the uneducated understand what

concerns them particularly and what concerns them more generally in laws established by any imperial decree. This distinction, moreover, obtains also concerning human persons. For example, some things said of Solomon exceed the realities of his own circumstances and become clarified only when they are related to Christ and the church of which Solomon is a part. The species, however, is not always exceeded. Often something is said that quite evidently does correspond to the subject of the words or perhaps to that subject alone. However, when there is a transition from the species to the genus, as though the Scripture continues to speak of the species, on such occasions the attention of the reader must be especially vigilant.

Tyconius advances a fifth rule that he calls "concerning the times," although, it seems to me, it could just as well be called "concerning numbers." The rule is applicable, he says, when the manner of speaking called synecdoche[12] occurs or proper numbers are used. The trope synecdoche allows the whole to be inferred from the part or the part from the whole. By this manner of speaking the question concerning the resurrection of Christ can be resolved. For unless the last part of the day on which he suffered is counted as a full day, that is, the night just past is added to it, and unless the last part of the night in which he rose is reckoned as a full day, namely, the Lord's day that is just beginning to dawn is added to it, one cannot reckon the three days and three nights in which he had predicted that he would be in the heart of the earth.[13] By proper numbers Tyconius means those numbers that the divine

---

[5]Is 61:10 (LXX). [6]In Augustine's words it should be called "concerning the true and the mixed (*permixto*) body or the true and pretended (*simulato*) body of the Lord" (*On Christian Doctrine* 3.45 [FC 2:153]). As in all of his descriptions of the rules of Tyconius, Bede closely follows the discussion of Augustine. [7]Song 1:5. [8]See Mt 13:47-48. [9]See Gal 4:30. [10]These alternative names also derive from Augustine (*On Christian Doctrine* 3.46 [FC 2:154]). [11]According to Pelagius (d. c. 440), the human free will was left intact by sin, and so a person retained the possibility of not sinning. Accordingly, grace was not so much the prevenient creative work of the Spirit, as it was for Augustine, but the natural gift of free will itself and the instruction of the law of Moses and the teaching of Jesus. [12]The Latin reads *tropo synecdoche*. In linguistics a trope is a literary device that uses words in other than their literal meaning. Synecdoche is a figure of speech in which a part is used for the whole or the whole is use for the part. Thus, we may speak of the White House when we are speaking of the executive branch of government. [13]See Mt 12:40.

Scripture most especially mentions, that is, the numbers seven, ten and twelve. Quite frequently these numbers are used to indicate the fullness of time or the perfection of something. For example, "Seven times a day I have praised you,"[14] means nothing other than "His praise is always in my mouth."[15] And they remain of equal value also when they are multiplied by ten, as in seventy or seven hundred, or when they are multiplied by themselves, as ten by ten is one hundred. Thus, in the former instance the seventy years of Jeremiah[16] can be interpreted spiritually to refer to the complete fullness of time when the church is among unbelievers. In the latter case, twelve times twelve renders one hundred forty-four, the number that in the Revelation signifies the full number of the saints.[17]

Tyconius calls his sixth rule "recapitulation." Some things are mentioned in the Scriptures as though they were following a chronological order or were narrated as a sequence of events, when without noting it the narrative in fact returns to previous events that had been omitted. For example, in Genesis it is said, "These are the sons of Noah according to their tribes and tongues, and from these the various and separate nations on the earth have come."[18] Immediately following it is said, "Now the whole earth had one language and the same speech."[19] From this it would seem that at the very time when they were separated all had one and the same language, when in fact by way of recapitulation the narrative is without notice adding how the separate languages came to be.

The seventh rule of Tyconius is "concerning the devil and his body." Occasionally something is attributed to the devil that is not relevant to him but can be recognized as true of his body. When, for example, the Lord explains the deceit and power of his enemy to the blessed Job, among other thing he says, "Will he make many prayers to you or speak to you soft words?"[20] It is not anywhere said of the devil himself that he will be repentant. Rather, it is said of his body that when it is damned at the end of time, it will say, "Lord, Lord, open to us."[21]

Therefore, should anyone take careful thought, he will notice that these rules are applicable not only in the Apocalypse, that is, in the revelation of Saint John the apostle, but also in all of the canonical Scripture and especially in the prophetic books. Tyconius himself understood the Apocalypse in a vigorous manner and expounded it truthfully and in a sufficiently catholic sense. This is the case except in those passages where he endeavors to defend the schism of his own group, that is, the schism of the Donatists.[22] In these passages he deplores the persecutions that they suffered as heretics at the hand of the religious emperor, Valentinian.[23] During these persecutions their churches and congregations and their homes and possessions were confiscated and given over to the catholics, and their bishops were sent into exile. Calling these things martyrdoms, Tyconius boasts that these sufferings were foretold in the Apocalypse.

---

[14]Ps 119:164 (118:164 Lxx). [15]Ps 34:1 (33:2 Lxx). [16]Jer 25:11-12; 29:10. [17]See Rev 7:4; 14:3. [18]Gen 10:32. The Latin reads *ab his divisae sunt insulae gentium upper terram*, literally, "the islands of nations on the earth have been separated." An *insula* is that which stands alone. In the above sentence it is strengthened by the verb *divisae sunt*. I have, therefore, translated "the various and separate nations." [19]Gen 11:1. [20]Job 41:3 (40:22 Lxx). [21]Mt 25:11. [22]After the terrible persecution of Diocletian (303), the view gained strength in northern Africa that those bishops who had given up the holy books (*traditores*) had excluded themselves from the church and were no longer empowered by the Spirit to administer valid sacraments. Moreover, those bishops who remained in communion with an apostate bishop participated in his sin and were also outside the church. The practical result of this Donatist claim was that the true, holy church existed only in Africa within the Donatist communion. The name Donatist comes from the sect's first great bishop, Donatus (d. 355). [23]Valentinian I was emperor of the western Roman empire (364–375). Although he seems to have been a convinced Christian, he is known for his tolerant religious policies. However, the Donatist church was strongly supported by the usurper Firmus, who led a bloody revolt in northern Africa (372–375). When the revolt was crushed, Valentinian passed several severe anti-Donatist laws (373, 375).

In the present work we have followed the interpretation of this author [Tyconius], although for the sake of brevity we have omitted some nonessential things that he included. However, we have been diligent in giving much more discussion to matters that seemed evident or unworthy of investigation to Tyconius, a man of great learning and who, as it is said, flourished as a rose among thorns. As far as we were able, we arrived at our interpretations from the tradition of our teachers or from the recollection of our reading or even from our own understanding. For among the commandments we have also this injunction, that we return to the Lord, with interest, those abilities that we have received.[24]

In some unknown manner, as Saint Augustine says, "the ending of a book renews the interest of the reader, just as a hotel restores the exertion of the traveler."[25] Therefore, to give relief to the mind it seemed good to divide the present work into three books. Nevertheless, in order that those who seek may more readily find, it seemed that the uninterrupted sequence of the chapters should throughout be preserved, which I previously noted in the same book by prefixing marks. Since the idleness of our people, that is, of the Angles, should be kept in mind, I have written in a manner not only to explain the meaning clearly but also to abbreviate my explanations. For it was not long ago, at the time of blessed Pope Gregory, that the Angles accepted the seed of faith,[26] and especially when it comes to reading they have been lax in the cultivation of the faith. For a short explanation that is clear will be better remembered than a verbose discussion.

May you remain strong in Christ, dearest brother, and may you always find Bede worthy of your remembrance.

Here Begins the Tractate of the Elder Bede on the Apocalypse, the First Book

REVELATION 1

[1:1] *The revelation of Jesus Christ, which God gave him to show to his servants.* When the church had been established by the apostles, it was proper that it be revealed by what course the church was to be extended and was to be perfected at the end, so that the preachers of the faith might be strengthened against the adversaries of the world. As was his custom, John refers the glory of the Son to the Father and testifies that Jesus Christ received the revelation of this mystery from God.

Those things that are to happen quickly. That is, those things that are going to happen to the church in the present age.

And he made it known. He constructed this Revelation through mystical words, lest that which is manifested to everyone be regarded as meaningless.

Sending through his angel. The messenger to John was seen in the figure of Christ, as will become more clear in subsequent passages.

To his servant, John. In order that he might make these things public to all of his servants through John, who by reason of his personal chastity deserved more than others to perceive these things.

[1:2] *Who bore witness to the Word of God and the testimony of Jesus Christ, whatsoever he saw.* Lest you doubt concerning the person of John, it was he who gave witness, as he saw it, to the eternal Word of God and to him in his incarnation, saying, "We have seen his

---

[24]See Mt 25:27. "Abilities that we have received" translates *percepta talenta.* A talent was a measure of weight, usually for gold or silver, and therefore a monetary measure. There was no coin called the talent. Bede, of course, is not speaking of money but of his own scholarly capacities that he received as a loan. [25]Augustine *Against the Adversaries of the Law and the Prophets* 1.53 (PL 42:636). [26]Although Christianity was in England at least from the fourth century, Roman Christianity in England is usually dated from the mission of Augustine to King Aethelberht of Kent in 597. Pope Gregory I sent Augustine, a monk in Rome, on this mission.

glory, the glory as of the Only-begotten of the Father."[1]

[1:3] *Blessed is he who reads and he who hears the words of this prophecy.* Both the teacher and the hearers are blessed, because for those who keep the Word of God, joys that are eternal follow this brief period of toil.

[1:4] *John, to the seven churches that are in Asia.* Through these seven churches he writes to the whole church. For it is customary that the whole is indicated by the number seven, since in seven days the entire time of the world is disclosed.

Grace to you and peace from him who is and who was and who is to come and from the seven spirits, and the following. He wishes for the faithful grace and peace from God, the eternal Father, and from the seven-formed Spirit.

[1:5] *And from Jesus Christ.* Grace and peace is also from Jesus Christ, who in his assumed human nature gave witness to the Father. He names the Son in the third place, since most of what he was to say in the following revelation was concerning him. He also names him last, because he is the first and the last. Moreover, he had already named him in the Father when he said "who is going to come."[2]

The firstborn of the dead and the ruler of the kings of the earth. This is what the apostle said: "We have seen Jesus Christ, who on account of the suffering of death has been crowned with glory and honor."[3] And somewhere else, commenting on the shame of the cross, he adds, "Therefore, God has also highly exalted him and bestowed on him the name that is above every name."[4]

[1:6] *And he made us a kingdom and priests to his God and Father.* Since the King of kings and the celestial Priest united us to his own body by offering himself up for us, there is no one of the saints who is spiritually deprived of the office of the priesthood, since everyone is a member of the eternal Priest.

[1:7] *Behold, he comes with the clouds, and every eye will see him.* He who first came in a hidden manner to be judged will then come in an open manner in order to judge. And for this reason does he recount this, that he might strengthen the church in the endurance of her sufferings, for she is now oppressed by enemies, but then she will reign with Christ.

And those who had fought him, and all the tribes of the earth will beat themselves.[5] When they see him as a powerful judge in the same form in which they had judged him as someone insignificant, they will lament for themselves with a repentance that will be too late.

Even so. Amen. Since he knows the future by a most certain revelation from God, he places here an "Amen" to confirm that it will without doubt come to pass.

[1:8] *"I am the Alpha and the Omega, the Beginning and the End," says the Lord God.* He is the Beginning whom no one precedes; he is the End whom no one in the kingdom succeeds.

Who is and who was and who is to come, the Almighty. He had said this same thing concerning the Father,[6] for God the Father has come and will come in the Son.

[1:9] *I, John, your brother, and one who shares in the tribulation.* He indicates the person, the place, the time and the cause of the vision. Moreover, he testifies that he saw the vision in the spirit, lest he be thought to have been deceived by a carnal illusion.

Revelation 1   [1]Jn 1:14. The prophet of the Revelation is none other than the Evangelist of the Gospel of John who in the first verses of the Gospel witnesses to both the divinity and the humanity of the Word.   [2]Bede interprets all phrases of "who is and who was and who is to come" to refer to the Father.   [3]Heb 2:9.   [4]Phil 2:9.   [5]The Latin is *plangent se*. Beating oneself was a sign of lamentation and deep sorrow.   [6]See Rev 1:4.

I was on the island called Patmos, on account of the word of God and the testimony of Jesus. It is known from history that John was banished to this island by the emperor Domitian on account of the gospel, and then he was rightly allowed to penetrate the secrets of heaven while at the same time prohibited from leaving such a small space of the earth.

[1:10] *I was in the spirit on the Lord's day.* He indicates a fitting time for a spiritual vision. For it is customary for the Scripture to indicate the details of the causes, and therefore it often indicates the circumstance of place or of the body or of the air, and so also of time. And so, angels visit Abraham at midday, and they visit Sodom in the evening. In the afternoon Adam became frightened at the voice of the Lord who was walking about, and Solomon received in the night that wisdom that he would not keep.[7]

And I heard behind me a great voice. He is at first admonished by a voice, so that he might direct his attention to the vision.

[1:11] *"Write what you see and send to the seven churches that are in Asia."* The church of Christ was not at that time only in these locations. Rather, the complete fullness consists in the number seven. Asia, interpreted as "elevation," indicates the haughty exaltation of the world in which the church sojourns, and, as is the habit of the divine mysteries, the genus is contained in the species.[8] For the apostle Paul also wrote to seven churches, although not to the same ones as did John. And although these seven locations are a sevenfold figure of the whole church, nevertheless those things for which he rebukes and praises them occurred in each one of them.

[1:12] *And I saw seven golden lampstands.* Here the form of the church is beautifully

described as that which displays the light of divine love in the brightness of a chaste breast. This is according to what the Lord said: "Let your loins be girded and your lamps burning."[9] And he indicates her perfection both within and without through the two parts of the number seven, since the individual members, while consisting of the four qualities of the body, "love the Lord, their God, with all their heart, with all their soul and with all their strength."[10]

[1:13] *And in the midst of the seven lampstands was one like unto a Son of man.* He says that he was like a Son of man, since, having conquered death, he ascended into heaven. For "if we knew Christ according to the flesh, we now know him so no longer."[11] And well does he write "in the midst." It says, "For all who are round about him will offer him gifts."[12]

Clothed in a long robe. The robe, which in Latin is called the *tunica talaris*, is a priestly vestment.[13] It shows the priesthood of Christ by which he offered himself up for us on the altar of the cross as a sacrificial victim to the Father.

And girded around the breasts with a golden girdle. He calls the two Testaments "breasts." By them he feeds the body of the saints that is united to him. The golden girdle is the chorus of the saints that clings to the Lord in harmonious love and embraces both Testaments, "keeping," as the apostle says, "the unity of the Spirit in the bond of peace."[14]

[1:14] *And his head and his hair were white as white wool and as snow.* The antiquity and immortality of majesty is indicated by the whiteness on the head. To this head all the leaders[15] adhere as though hair. On account of

---

[7]For these Old Testament events see Gen 18:1; 19:1; 3:8; 1 Kings 3:5-9. [8]All seven churches are in Asia. Therefore, all the churches in the world live the life of faith in the midst of the arrogance of the world. [9]Lk 12:35. [10]Deut 6:5. [11]2 Cor 5:16. [12]Ps 76:12 (75:12 LXX). [13]A *tunica* was an undergarment worn by both sexes. The word *talaris* has to do with the ankles, and so a *tunica talaris* was a tunic that reached to the ankles. [14]Eph 4:3. [15]Translating *praecipui*, "eminent men," most likely the priests and bishops.

the sheep that will be at the right hand,[16] they are likened to wool, and they are said to glisten as snow because of the numberless multitude of those in white robes, that is, of the elect,[17] who are given from heaven.

His eyes were like a flame of fire. The eyes of the Lord are those who preach. By a spiritual fire they bring light to the faithful but a consuming fire to the unbelieving.

[1:15] *And his feet were like burnished bronze, refined as in a furnace.* The phrase "feet refined by fire" refers to the church of the end time, which will be put to the proof and tested by terrible afflictions. For indeed orichalcum is bronze that is brought to a golden color by a very hot fire and added elements. Another translation renders "like burnished bronze of Lebanon." This indicates that the church in Judea, in which Lebanon is a mountain, will be persecuted, especially at the end time. For even the temple is often referred to as Lebanon, for to it is said, "Open, O Lebanon, your gates and let fire consume your cedars."[18]

And his voice was as a voice of many waters. The voice of confession and of preaching and of praise resounds not only in Judea but also among many peoples.

[1:16] *In his right hand he held seven stars.* In the right hand of Christ is the spiritual church. "At your right hand," it says, "the queen stood in a vesture of gold."[19] And to him who stands at the right hand, he says, "Come, you blessed of my Father, receive the kingdom."[20]

And from his mouth issued a sharp two-edged sword. He who judges things visible and invisible has the power to kill and then also to cast into the gehenna of fire.[21]

And his face was as the sun shining in its full strength. As he appeared to his disciples on the mountain,[22] so will the Lord appear after the judgment to all the saints. For at the judgment the impious will see him whom they pierced.[23] However, all that is here said of the appearance of the Son of man is true also of the church. Since Christ himself has become one nature with the church,[24] he gives to her the priestly honor, and that she might shine as the sun, he gives to her also the power to judge in the kingdom of his Father.

[1:17] *And when I saw him, I fell at his feet.* As a man he trembles at the spiritual vision, but human fear is dispelled by the mercy of the Lord.

"I am the first and the last." He is the first because "all things were made through him."[25] He is the last because all things are restored in him.

[1:18] *"And I have the keys of death and hell."* Not only, he says, have I conquered death by the resurrection, but also I have dominion over death itself. And this he also gave to the church by breathing on her the Holy Spirit, saying, "Whose sins you forgive, they are forgiven to them, and whose sins you retain, they are retained."[26]

[1:19] *"Write therefore what you have seen and what is and what must take place hereafter."* That which you alone have seen make manifest to all, namely, the various labors of the church, and that in the church evil persons will be commixed with the good unto the end of the world.

---

[16]See Mt 25:33. [17]The Latin reads *propter dealbatorum innumerabilem turbam et electorum.* I have interpreted *et* as epexegetical. [18]Zech 11:1. The interpretation of this "other translation" comes from Tyconius, although Bede is also closely following Primasius (see Gryson, CCL 121A:182). [19]Ps 45:9 (44:10 LXX). [20]Mt 25:34. [21]See Lk 12:5. [22]Mt 17:1-8; Mk 9:2-8; Lk 9:28-36. [23]Jn 19:37; Zech 12:10. [24]By one nature Bede probably means the same as one person. Behind Bede's language lies the idea that the church is the body of Christ. [25]Jn 1:3. [26]Jn 20:22-23; cf. Mt 16:18-19.

[1:20] *"The seven stars are the angels of the seven churches."* That is, the rulers of the churches. As Malachi says, "For the priest is the angel of the Lord of hosts."[27]

REVELATION 2

[2:1] *And to the angel of the church of Ephesus, write.* He blames part of this church, and he praises part of this church, according to the quality of its name. For Ephesus may be interpreted as either "great fall" or "my will in it."

The words of him who holds the seven stars in his right hand. That is, he has you in his hand, and he rules and sustains you by his power.[1]

Who walks in the midst of the seven golden lampstands. He who walks about in your midst searches the hearts and the reins of every person.[2]

[2:2] *I know your works and your toil and your patient endurance.* I see that you[3] diligently perform good works, he says, and you endure with equanimity the intolerable injuries of evil persons. In addition, you have diligently examined the words and deeds of the false apostles, and you have determined to concede to them in nothing.

[2:4] *But I have something against you, that you have abandoned your first love,* etc. In some persons you have forsaken the love that was at the beginning, and should they not recover it, I will deprive them of the reward of the promised light. However, in others you have hated the examples of depraved persons, that

is, idolatry and fornication.[4] For these are the deeds of the Nicolaitans, as will become clear in subsequent passages.

[2:7] *He who has an ear to hear, let him hear what the Spirit says to the churches.* He shows that what he writes to the individual churches, he is saying to all churches. For it was not the church of the Ephesians alone that, should she not repent, was to be removed from her place, nor was the seat of Satan in Pergamum only and not everywhere. Likewise, all that will be said of the individual churches is common to every church.[5]

To him who conquers I will give to eat from the tree of life that is in paradise. The tree of life is Christ. By the vision of him holy souls are nourished both in the celestial paradise and in the present body of the church.

[2:8] *And to the angel of the church of Smyrna, write.* To this church he speaks concerning the endurance of persecution, and to this the name also corresponds. For Smyrna may be rendered "myrrh," which signifies the mortification of the flesh.

The words of him who is the First and the Last, who was dead and lives. He who created all things, by dying also restored all things. Since he is going to counsel patience,[6] this is an apt preface.

[2:9] *I know your tribulation and your poverty, but you are rich.* For "blessed are the poor in spirit, for theirs is the kingdom of heaven."[7] Fortunatus put this very nicely in a short verse, saying, "He who is poor in difficult circum-

---

[27]Mal 2:7.   **Revelation 2**   [1]Throughout the seven letters Bede uses the singular pronoun, because John is addressing the church. Here in the commentary Bede uses the plural ("you," *vos*), perhaps referring to members of the church or perhaps to the religious in the monasteries.   [2]The Latin word *renes* refers to the kidneys. In ecclesiastical Latin it referred to the seat of human emotions. See also Rev 2:23.   [3]Here Bede uses the singular pronoun.   [4]The life of the church is lived out concretely in the lives of the individual Christians. Therefore, in some Christians the church is found to be spiritually deficient; in others the church is found to be spiritually strong.   [5]As Bede has noted, the number seven is a symbol of completeness. That John writes to seven churches indicates that he is writing to all churches of every place and time and that what he writes to any of the seven churches is true of all churches of every place and time.   [6]*Patientia* in this context refers to faithful forbearance under tribulation and distress that is caused by others.   [7]Mt 5:3; cf. Lk 6:20.

stances reigns by possessing God."[8]

Those who say that they are Jews but are not. "They profess to know God, but they deny him by their deeds."[9] For the term "Jew" is the name of a controlling conviction.[10] And therefore the apostle also writes, "He is a Jew who is one in secret, and circumcision is of the heart, in the spirit, not in the letter."[11]

[2:10] *Behold, the devil is going to throw some of you into prison, that you might be tested.* These words pertain to the whole church, for the devil is always working his hatred against her, and from this hatred the church cannot escape.

And you will have tribulation for ten days. He signifies the whole time during which the commandments of the Law are necessary. For as long as you follow the light of the divine word, you will of necessity suffer the imprisonment of an enemy who opposes you. Some have understood these words to refer to the ten persecutions of the nations from Caesar Nero to Diocletian.[12]

Be faithful until death, and I will give you the crown of life. He shows how long the ten days extend, for he counsels them to preserve their faith even to death.

[2:11] *He who conquers shall not be hurt by the second death.* He who will remain faithful to the death of the flesh will not fear the eternal death of the soul.

[2:12] *And to the angel of the church of Pergamum, write.* Pergamum may be rendered

"dividing their horns." For by his judgment he distinguishes between the virtue of the faithful and the deceit of the Nicolaitans, so that the horns of the sinners may be broken into pieces and the horns of the just one may be exalted.

The words of him who has the sharp two-edged sword. He has properly mentioned his judicial power first, since he is going to bestow rewards to the victors and punishment to the sinners.

[2:13] *I know where you live, where the seat of Satan is; but you hold my name and did not deny my faith.* To be sure, I approve of your patience that you exercise among the reprobate, who are the throne of Satan, and you do not honor me in name only, being called "Christian," but also by an intact faith, even in times of bloody persecution. But I do not approve of the fact that even among you I notice teachers who lead astray.

Even in the days of Antipas my faithful witness, who was killed among you. Some understand this to refer to a martyr who suffered at Pergamum.[13] Others believe it refers to the Lord Christ who even now is killed by the unbelievers, as far as in them lies.[14]

[2:14] *To eat and to commit fornication.* These are the two principal failings in which the carnal are active, "whose god is their belly, and their glory is in confusion."[15] But, to be sure, every evil deed is an idolatry and a spiritual fornication.[16]

[2:15] *So you also have some who hold the*

---

[8]Fortunatus *Carmina* 8.6 (PL 88:274). Venantius Fortunatus (c. 530–c. 609) was born in Italy and journeyed through Merovingian Gaul (c. 565) eventually arriving at Poitiers. There he found deep spiritual friendship with Queen Radegunda, who had founded a famous monastery at Poitiers, and with Agnes, abbess of the monastery. Around 600 he became bishop of Poitiers. His poetry shows good knowledge of classical Latin, and he is regarded as one of the finest Christian poets of the early medieval period. Most famous of his poems are *Vexilla Regis* ("The Royal Banners Forward Go") and *Pange Lingua* ("Sing, my tongue, the glorious battle"). The Latin of this "short verse" is *pauper in angusto regnat habendo Deum.* [9]Tit 1:16. [10]Bede writes *Judaeus enim religionis est nomen.* A *religio* is that which constrains out of supernatural conviction (from *ligo*, "to bind, to tie"). Hence, a *religio* leads one to certain habits and practices of *cultus* and life. [11]Rom 2:29. [12]See Orosius *Historia* 7.27 (FC 50:325-28); Augustine *City of God* 18.52 (FC 24:174). [13]The Greek commentator Andrew of Caesarea claimed to have read an account of the martyrdom of Antipas. According to tradition, Antipas was a disciple of the apostle John and a bishop of Pergamum during the reign of Domitian. He was powerful against demons and was eventually burned in a bronze bull used to burn incense to the emperor. His death is traditionally dated A.D. 92, and his martyrdom is celebrated April 11. [14]By these others Bede is referring to Primasius (CCL 92:29). [15]Phil 3:19. [16]Every sinful act is to acknowledge someone else or something else as lord and to unite with it.

teaching of the Nicolaitans. The Nicolaitans receive their name from the deacon, Nicolaus, of whom Clement reports that, when he was reproached for jealousy of his very beautiful wife, he responded that whoever wanted might take her as wife. On account of this, the faithless taught that the apostles had permitted to everyone a promiscuous and communal intercourse with women.[17] In addition, the Nicolaitans are said to have proclaimed certain fabulous and virtually pagan ideas concerning the beginning of the world and not to have kept their food separate from that which had been offered to idols.[18]

[2:17] *To him who conquers I will give the hidden manna.* Everyone who will have despised the enticements of the flesh, even though the hypocrites urge them to such behavior, will be filled with the righteous sweetness[19] of the invisible bread that comes down from heaven.

And I will give to him a white stone. That is, the body that now is made white through baptism and then will shine with the glory of incorruptibility.

And on the stone a new name is written. "That we might be called, and in fact be, sons of God."[20]

Which no one knows, except him who receives it. For "he who says that he knows God but does not keep his commandments is a liar."[21] For the hypocrite does not taste how sweet the Lord is.

[2:18] *And to the angel of the church at Thyatira, write.* Thyatira may be translated "for sacrifice." For the saints present their bodies as a living sacrifice.[22]

The words of the Son of God who has eyes as a flame of fire. A little later he explains what is meant by the eyes of flame, saying, "I am he

who searches the minds and the hearts, and I will give to every one of you according to your works."[23]

And his feet were as burnished bronze. Also by these words he explains that the last works of this church are more than the first.

[2:20] *But I have this against you, that you allow the woman Jezebel, who calls herself a prophetess, to teach.* To be sure, in your work and your faith you are praiseworthy, but in this you are worthy of accusation, that you do not reject with sufficient harshness the synagogue of the false apostles that feigns to be Christian. The name Jezebel, which means "a flow of blood," is fitting for these heretics. In particular, this woman is said to have been in the aforementioned church teaching the evil deeds that have been named, and she is a figure of every Jezebel throughout the world, whom indeed he threatens with open revenge.

And you allow her to seduce my servants to commit fornication and to eat food sacrificed to idols. Indeed, under the name of Christ she taught fornication and spiritual idolatry, for how could she openly teach the worship of idols who claimed that she was a prophetess in the church.

[2:22] *Behold, I send her onto a couch.* By the just judgment of God it transpires that she who lay the wretched on a bed of lust is herself laid on the bed of eternal punishment.

[2:23] *And her sons into death.* Here he names the posterity and the works of the woman "sons," and he threatens them not with the temporary death of the body but with the eternal death of the soul.

And all the churches will know that I am he who searches mind and heart. By *mind* he signifies the desires, and by *heart* he signifies the

---

[17]Clement of Alexandria *Stromateis* 3.4 (ANF 2:385). [18]Bede may have gained this information from Augustine (*On the Heresies* 5 [PL 42:26]). [19]Bede writes *iure dulcedine*. The word *iure* suggests that which is rightful and just, according to divine law. [20]See 1 Jn 3:1. [21]1 Jn 2:4. [22]See Rom 12:1. [23]See Rev 2:23.

thoughts. Our works and our words may be made known to people, but what is their intention and what we wish to accomplish through them, only the Lord knows who sees what anyone thinks and in what he takes pleasure. And for what purpose is he who punishes fornication and idolatry, which are manifest sins, said to be one who knows hidden secrets, unless these sins are contained even in the least transgressions? "You will destroy," he says, "all who commit fornication from you."[24] And when he was discussing about false brothers, the same apostle John, who had heard this, ended by saying, "Little children, keep yourselves from idols."[25]

[2:24] *And to the rest of you in Thyatira, I say.* Just as he counsels repentance to the impious by threatening punishment, so also he exhorts the pious to patience with the promise of eternal rewards.

Those who have not known the deep things of Satan. Assuredly, they are approved by the lack of consensus. Just as those who work iniquity do not know God, although they might speak of him, so also God, although he knows everyone, does not take cognizance of the workers of iniquity.[26]

[2:25] *I will not send on you any further burden; only hold fast what you have, until I come.* I will not attempt to test you beyond that which you are able to endure.[27] Another interpretation: "Beware," he says, "of false prophets,"[28] for I will not send to you any new doctrine, but that which you have received, preserve to the end.

[2:26] *For he who will conquer* falsehoods *and will keep* my commandments will be given a suitable reward.

I will give to him power over the nations. In Christ the church possesses this power, just as the body has power in the head. For in him, according to the apostle, God has given all things to us.[29]

[2:27] *And he will rule them with a rod of iron, as when earthen pots are broken in pieces.* He rules the meek with an unwavering justice, so that they might produce more fruit. However, he destroys the stubborn, so that either they may perish eternally or in them all earthly desires and all the dirty deeds of the old person may be destroyed, whatever had been contracted and implanted from the sinful mud.[30]

[2:28] *And I will give to him the morning star.* Christ is the morning star who, when the night of the world has passed away, promises and reveals the eternal light of life to the saints.

REVELATION 3

[3:1] *And to the angel of the church of Sardis, write.* He says that the angel, that is, the priest, exercises insufficient diligence in the correction of evil persons. Nonetheless, he commends him for having some who walk in white garments, and to these the name of Sardis corresponds, namely, "precious stone."

I know your works, for you have the name of being alive, but you are dead. Indeed, you seem to yourself to be alive, but unless you

---

[24]Ps 73:27 (72:27 LXX). [25]1 Jn 5:21. Interestingly, the comment of Bede implies that John received the revelation before writing his first letter. [26]See Mt 7:23. Bede uses two forms of "to know." For God's absolute knowledge, Bede uses *nosco*, which indicates the act of coming to know, the acquisition of knowledge. For God's knowledge at the time of judgment, Bede uses *cognosco*, which indicates recognizing something already known, so to examine and learn more, or in the case of forming an opinion, to take cognizance of. [27]See 1 Cor 10:13. [28]See Mt 7:15. [29]See Rom 8:32. [30]Translating *de peccatore limo*. This language may refer to Adam, created from the dust of the earth yet the primal sinner, whose sin was transmitted to his posterity. Other manuscripts of Bede have *de peccatorum limo* ("from the mud of sins") or *de peccati limo* ("from the mud of sin"), which make less sense of the language of "contracted and implanted."

are vigilant in the correction of the wicked, you will be regarded as already among the dead.

[3:2] *For I do not find your works perfect before my God.* Even though he might seem to people to be guiltless, the works of a teacher[1] are not perfect before God if he does not strive to enliven also others.

[3:3] *I will come to you as a thief.* Just as in the parable of the Gospel,[2] so also here by the example of taking precautions against a thief he forewarns them to be vigilant.

[3:4] *But you have a few names in Sardis who have not soiled their garments.* He did not say a "few" but a "few names." For he who knew Moses by name "calls his own sheep by name"[3] and writes the names of his saints in heaven.

[3:5] *He who will conquer will be clothed thus in white garments.* He calls all to the imitation of those who have preserved the silken robe of baptism without blemish.

[3:7] *And to the angel of the church at Philadelphia, write.* Philadelphia is interpreted "brotherly love," and to that church is opened by right the door of the kingdom, and he promises that she will be loved by the Lord.
The words of the Holy One, the True One, who has the key of David. He speaks of the royal power, either because he was born from the root of David or because the prophecy of David was revealed in the dispensation of Christ.
Who opens and no one shuts, and shuts and no one opens. The secrets of the divine law are made known to the faithful by the power of Christ alone; they are shut to the unbelievers.

[3:8] *Behold, I place before you an open door that no one is able to close.* The door of celestial knowledge, which Christ has opened to his church, is not ever closed by the power or effort of anyone.
For you have but little power and yet you have kept my word. He shows the reason why the church merits these gifts, namely, because she does not trust in her own powers but in the grace of Christ the king. And it is the praiseworthy deed of God, who protects, and of the devotion of the church that the door of victory is opened to a little faith and that a little power is made strong by faith.

[3:9] *Behold, I will give those from the synagogue of Satan, who say that they are Jews but are not.* He promises this to the whole church of that time, for it was not only in Philadelphia that some from the synagogue of the Jews believed, as we learn in the Acts of the Apostles.[4]

[3:10] *Because you have kept the word of my patient endurance, I will keep you from the hour of trial that is coming.* Because you have kept my example in enduring adversaries, I will also preserve you from the impending sufferings. This does not mean that you will not be tempted but that you will not be overcome by your adversaries. And although the church is always struggling against adversaries, it is possible in this passage that the hour of temptation and the humiliation of the Jews at the time of the antichrist are indicated. For just as is often the case in the sixth place in the order of that which follows, so also here in the sixth angel the final persecution may be signified.[5] During this persecution, certainly those of the Jews who are wicked will deceive as well as be deceived, yet others will come to understand the Law

---

Revelation 3 [1]Bede uses the term *rector*, which means one who rules or guides (from *regere*). In ecclesiastical Latin it refers to a church teacher who heads a school. Here it clearly refers to the bishop as teacher. [2]See Mt 24:43-44. [3]Jn 10:3. [4]See, for example, Acts 13:5. The comment comes from Tyconius (*Turin Fragment* 65 [TS 2 7:64]). [5]The letter to the angel of Philadelphia is the sixth out of the seven letters.

spiritually through the teaching of that great prophet, Elijah,[6] and being incorporated with the members of the church, they will believe and courageously conquer the enemy.

[3:11] *Behold, I am coming soon; hold fast what you have that no one take your crown.* Do not grow weary by your endurance, for I will come to your aid quickly, lest it should happen that you falter from lack of steadfastness and someone else receive the reward that was decreed for you. For it is not possible that the number of the saints, which is fixed with God, should become smaller through the perfidy of an increasing number of tares. If, therefore, a crown is lost and given to another, the place of him who lost what he had possessed is not vacant.[7]

[3:12] *He who conquers, I will make him a pillar in the temple of my God, and never shall he go out of it.* Whoever has conquered adversity for my sake will be glorious in the temple of the church and will never fear any further loss from adversity. These pillars, that is, holy persons, now defend the church by supporting her, but then they will adorn the church by their eminence, just as the two pillars at the entrance of Solomon's temple.[8]

And I will write on him the name of my God. That is, because we are called sons of God through adoption.

And the name of the city of my God, the new Jerusalem. He will be joined to the unity of the church, which is born into a new life through a heavenly grace.[9]

And my new name. This is the name Christian, not that this is new to the Son of God who had this distinction before the world was made. However, it is new to the Son of man

who was dead and rose again and is seated at the right hand of God.

[3:14] *And to the angel of the church at Laodicea, write.* Laodicea is interpreted "tribe beloved of the Lord" or "they were in vomit." For there were some there to whom he had said, "I will begin to spew you out of my mouth,"[10] and some to whom he said, "Those whom I love, I reprove and chastise."[11] According to the Greek, Laodicea is interpreted "just people."

The words of the Amen, the faithful and true witness, the beginning of the creation of God. Amen means "truly" or "faithfully." Christ, therefore, who in the essence of his divinity is truth, declares that, through the mystery of his incarnation, he was made the beginning of the creation of God, so that through this he might conform the church to himself for the endurance of sufferings.

[3:15] *I know your works, that you are neither cold nor hot,* and the following. You are neither fervent in faith nor are you wholly unbelieving. Were you until now unbelieving, there would still remain to you the hope of conversion. But since you came to know the will of God, yet now you do not do it, you will be thrown out of the innermost parts of my church.[12]

[3:17] *For you say, "I am rich, I have prospered, and I need nothing,"* and the following. Since you are content with mere faith, in vain do you seek to acquire the riches of righteousness. But should you desire to be truly rich, forsake everything and buy the fervor of love tested by the flame of afflictions, and anoint the eyes of the mind, not with the antinomy of deceitful boasting but with the eye salve of divine knowledge. To anoint the eyes with

---

[6]See Mal 4:5-6 (3:22-23 LXX). [7]This comment can be found in Tyconius (*Turin Fragment* 78 [TS 2 7:69]), and appears also in Augustine (*Admonition and Grace* 13.39 [FC 2:293]) and Primasius (CCL 92:40). [8]See 1 Kings 7:21. [9]A reference to baptism through which the baptized becomes a member of the church through the gift of the Spirit. [10]See Rev 3:16. [11]See Rev 3:19. [12]Translating *de visceribus ecclesiae meae*. The *viscera* are the inner organs of the body.

eye salve is to acquire an understanding of the holy Scriptures through the performance of a good work.

[3:19] *Those whom I love, I reprove and chasten.* Do not flee from the suffering of adversity, since this is a special indication that you are loved by the Lord.

Therefore, imitate and repent. He shows that some were there who had been worthy of imitation and following.

[3:20] *Behold, I stand at the door and knock,* and the following. Indeed, I knock at the door of your heart with the right hand of exhortation, and if you should freely receive me, you will be regarded worthy that I should dwell with you and be co-heir with you.

[3:21] *He who conquers, I will allow him to sit with me on my throne.* He says that a confessor will be a participant with him in power and judgment. "Who has made us to sit with him in the heavenly places in Christ," it says.[13]

As also I have conquered and sit with my Father on his throne. Having conquered, the Lord sat down on the throne with the Father, because after the contest of the passion and after the victory of the resurrection, he declared himself more clearly to all that he was equal with the Father in power. Note that in every church the Lord at first declares his own power and then reviews the works of the church, which are either to be praised or to be reproved, but he always intersperses these comments with admonition. Finally, he assigns to either part the reward that is due it, which may be understood to be both in the present and in the future.

[3:22] When he adds, *He who has an ear, let him hear,* without any doubt we are to understand the ears of the heart for the obedience of the commandments.

REVELATION 4

[4:1] *After this I looked, and behold, an open door in heaven.* After describing the works of the church and what kind of future she would have, he recapitulates from the birth of Christ by speaking of the same things in a different way. For he recounts the whole age of the church by means of the various images in this book.

Behold, it says, *an open door in heaven.* As he was about to ascend, he fittingly sees an open door in heaven, for it had been promised that the heavenly mysteries would be revealed to him. Or, perhaps Christ is the open door, and whoever should believe that he was born and suffered ascends with him to heaven, that is, to the height of the church, and being made spiritual, sees the future things, as he says.

[4:2] *And immediately I was in the spirit, and the first voice that I had heard.* This voice was similar to the first voice that had said, "What you see, write in a book."[1]

And, behold, a throne was placed in heaven, and there was one sitting on the throne. The Lord dwells within the church, which has been positioned in a heavenly way of life. Pope Gregory interpreted the throne of God in the vision of Micah to be the angelic powers by whose minds he who presides on high governs all things below.[2]

[4:3] *And he who is seated appeared like jasper and carnelian.* The color of jasper signifies water and that of carnelian signifies fire, and we know that by these two elements the judgment will be effected. It says, "For as in the days of Noah, so will be the coming of the Son of man."[3]

And there was a rainbow around the throne, in appearance similar to an emerald. The rainbow occurs when the sun shines through

---

[13]Eph 2:6.   **Revelation 4**   [1]See Rev 1:11, 19.   [2]Gregory the Great *Moralia* 2.20 (CCL 143:83).   [3]Mt 24:37.

the clouds. It first appeared after the flood as a sign of propitiation[4] and signifies that the church is protected by the intercession of the saints, whom the Lord illumines. And the rainbow is rightly compared with the emerald, a deep green stone, for while they await with a more perfect faith that inheritance that will not fade away, so they more potently protect also others by prayer.

[4:4] *And around the throne were twenty-four thrones, and seated on the thrones were twenty-four elders.* He had seen the church, which sat on one throne by virtue of its communion in faith. Now on twenty-four thrones he perceives the very same church as that which is born through the twofold testament of the patriarchs and the apostles, and she is seated on account of her judicial dignity in Christ. For all members will sit on thrones and will judge, but in one head and through one head. For how will the saints be able to sit in judgment when they are standing at the right hand of the Judge? And so, the twenty-four elders may also be understood to be those who by the clear preaching of the gospel complete and perfect that work that is indicated by the number six, since four sixes make twenty-four.[5]

And they were clothed in white garments, and on their heads were golden crowns. Clothed in good works, they were seeking by an unfailing recollection of the mind the joys that are above. For it is often customary that the mind be intended by the word *head.*

[4:5] *And from the throne there proceed flashes of lightning and voices and peals of thunder.* This is what Mark said: "And they went forth and preached everywhere, while the Lord worked with them and confirmed the message by the signs that attended it."[6]

And there were seven torches of fire before the throne that are the seven spirits of God. He speaks of the one, sevenfold Spirit,[7] for there is but one Spirit. The sevenfold character of the Spirit, however, suggests its perfection and fullness. And whenever the Holy Spirit is mentioned, it is fitting that the water of baptism follows, in which the same Holy Spirit is believed to be received.

[4:6] *And before the throne there is as it were a sea of glass, like crystal.* By virtue of the trustworthiness of true baptism, he likens it to glass, in which nothing appears on the outside that is not present on the inside. Moreover, the grace of baptism is represented by crystal, which is formed from water pressed into ice and a precious stone.

And in the midst of the throne and around the throne were four living creatures, full of eyes in front and behind. The light of the gospel fills all parts of the throne of God, that is, of the church, with the knowledge of that which is past and that which is future.

[4:7] *And the first living creature was like a lion,* and the following. These living creatures have been interpreted in various ways. The blessed Augustine follows the order in this book and believes that Matthew is intended by the lion, for it is Matthew who narrates the family lineage of the royal dignity in Christ, for he conquered as a lion from the tribe of Judah, for "Judah is a lion's whelp."[8] And in this Gospel, as a king he is feared by a king and is worshiped by the magi.[9] Moreover, in this Gospel a king takes account of his servants, and a king prepares a wedding feast for his son, and at the end a king separates the sheep from the goats.[10] The Gospel of Luke is represented in the calf, which in the Law was a great sacrifice.

---

[4]See Gen 9:12-17. [5]Bede seems to think as follows. There are four Gospels that are preached throughout the world. The number six symbolizes the six-day work of creation, which will be perfected at the end of time. [6]Mk 16:20. [7]See Is 11:2-3. [8]Gen 49:9. [9]See Mt 2:1-12. [10]See Mt 18:23-35; 22:2-13; 25:31-46.

And not only does the Gospel of Luke begin with stories about the temple and sacrifices,[11] but it also ends like this: "And they were in the temple praising and blessing God."[12] The face of a man indicates Mark, who writes nothing about the kingly or priestly power of the Lord but tells in a simple manner what Christ did as a man. The eagle is John, who saw the nativity of the Word with a clarity like that of the risen sun.[13] However, while at times the living creatures signify the Evangelists, at times they signify the whole church. For the fortitude of the church is shown in the lion, her sacrificial life in the calf, her humility in the man and her sublimity in the flying eagle.

[4:8] *And each of them had six wings.* The wings lift the church into the heights by the perfection of their doctrine. The number six is said to be perfect, because it is the first number to be completed by the sum of its parts. For the number one is one-sixth of six; the number two is one-third of six; and the number three is one-half of six; and together they make six. There is another interpretation.[14] The six wings of the four living creatures make twenty-four wings, the same number as there are books in the Old Testament, by which the authority of the Evangelists is supported and the truth of the Evangelists is verified.[15]

And around and within, they were full of eyes. The holy church keeps herself vigilant both before God and before people. The psalmist recognized her eyes within when he said, "All the glory of that daughter of kings is within."[16] And he saw her eyes without when he continued, "Clothed around by a variety of golden fringes."[17] Here is another interpretation. One will always uncover light from the gospel, whether by attending to the letter or by seeking after the allegory. Another translation reads "full of eyes before and behind," for the light of the gospel illumines the shadowy passages of the law, while it pours on the world the brightness of a new grace.[18]

And they do not rest by day nor by night saying, "Holy, holy, holy is the Lord God Almighty." Throughout the whole time of the world the holy living creatures proclaim the one dominion, the deity, the omnipotence and the eternality of the holy Trinity, while the worship of the intelligent creation remains unending in heaven.[19]

[4:10] *The twenty-four elders fall down before the one seated on the throne and worship him.* Whenever the living creatures raise the sound of praise, that is, whenever the Evangelists preach the life and work of Christ,[20] the whole church, which consists of both rulers and people (for this is the meaning of the number twelve times two), falls immediately on its face and worships. . . .

Him who lives forever and ever, and they throw their crowns before the throne. They assign to God whatever power and whatever dignity they possess, for indeed it was he who created all things from nothing.

Revelation 5

[5:1] *And I saw in the right hand of him who was seated on the throne a book, written within and without.* This vision shows to us the mys-

---

[11]See Lk 1:8-23. [12]Lk 24:53. [13]For Augustine, whom Bede follows, see *Tractates on the Gospel of John* 36.5.2 (FC 88:86-87). [14]This other interpretation comes from Primasius (CCL 92:56). [15]Traditionally the Old Testament was divided into three parts: the Law, the Prophets and the Writings (see Lk 24:44). The Law had five books; the Prophets had eight books; the Writings had eleven books. The twelve minor prophets were regarded as a single book. Books such as 1 and 2 Samuel were regarded as a single book. Both Daniel and 1 and 2 Chronicles were listed with the Writings. [16]See Ps 45:12 (44:14 LXX). [17]Ps 45:14 (44:14-15 LXX). [18]This translation and interpretation come from Primasius (CCL 92:56). According to Gryson, the text of Primasius harmonizes Rev 4:8 with the wording of Rev 4:6 (CCL 121A:182). [19]The "intelligent creations" (*intellectualis creatura*) refers to the angels, who do not possess physical bodies. [20]Translating *Christi dispensationem*.

teries of the holy Scripture that were revealed through the incarnation of the Lord. Its harmonious unity contains, as it were, the Old Testament without and the New Testament within.

Sealed with seven seals. That is, it is concealed by virtue of the total fullness of the hidden mysteries, or it was written through the arrangement of the sevenfold Spirit.

[5:2] *And I heard a strong angel proclaiming with a loud voice, "Who is worthy to open the book?"* He is speaking of the proclamation of the Law. For many prophets and righteous persons desired to see what the apostles saw.[1] As Peter said, "And concerning this salvation the prophets diligently inquired and searched."[2] And this is the book that in Isaiah is closed both to the learned and to the unlearned. Nevertheless, already there the opening of the book is foretold: "In that day the deaf will hear the words of the book."[3] And of this book also Ezekiel spoke: "And I looked," it says, "and, behold, a hand was stretched out to me, and a scroll was in it, and he spread it before me, and it had writing within and without."[4] And he added that which John concealed, namely, what was written in the book, saying: "And there were written on it words of lamentation and mourning and woe."[5] For the whole narrative of the Old and New Testament forewarns that there must be repentance of sins, a search for the kingdom of heaven and an escape from the laments of hell.

[5:3] *And no one was able in heaven or on the earth or under the earth to open the book.* Neither an angel nor anyone of the righteous who are already freed from the bond of the flesh was able to reveal or to search out the myster-ies of the divine law.

Nor to look into the book. That is, to contemplate the splendor of the grace of the New Testament. Similarly, the sons of Israel had not been able to look on the face of the giver of the law of the Old Testament,[6] which contains the New.

[5:4] *And I wept much.* Seeing the common misery of the human race, he grieved.

[5:5] *And one of the elders said to me, "Do not weep; behold, the lion from the tribe of Judah has conquered."* He was prohibited to weep, since the mystery that had been hidden for a long time had already in the passion of Christ been fulfilled, when, as he handed over his spirit, "the veil of the temple was rent asunder."[7] And to him it is said, "Judah is a lion's whelp; toward the prey, my son, you have gone up," and following.[8] And he continues to describe how and when the lion from the tribe of Judah will conquer.

[5:6] *And I saw in the midst of the throne and the four living creatures and among the elders, a lamb standing, as though it had been slain.* The same Lord who is a Lamb by virtue of his innocent death was made also a lion in the strength of his victory over death. Tyconius says that the Lamb is the church, which in Christ has received all power.[9]

And the Lamb had seven horns and seven eyes. The sevenfold Spirit in Christ is compared with horns because of the eminence of its gifts[10] and with eyes because of the illumination of grace.

[5:7] *And he came and took the book from the right hand of him who was seated on the throne.* The Son of man is said to have taken the book

---

Revelation 5   [1]See Mt 13:17.   [2]1 Pet 1:10.   [3]Is 29:18; see also Is 29:11-12.   [4]Ezek 2:9-10.   [5]Ezek 2:10.   [6]Ex 34:29-35; 2 Cor 3:7-16. [7]Mt 27:50-51; Mk 15:17-18.   [8]Gen 49:9. The text of Bede reads *ad praedam, fili mi, ascendisti.*   [9]The influence of Tyconius can be seen in the comments of Caesarius (*Exposition of the Apocalypse*, Homily 4 [PL 35:2424]) and of Primasius (CCL 92:85).   [10]Translating *propter eminentiam munerum.* Other manuscripts read *propter eminentiam potestatis,* ("because of the eminence of its power").

from the right hand of God. By this is meant that he received the economy of the incarnation prepared both by the Father and by himself, because he is God. And both dwell with the Holy Spirit on the throne. For Christ, who is a Lamb according to his humanity, is at the right hand of the Father according to his divinity.

[5:8] *And when he opened the book, the four living creatures and the twenty-four elders fell down before the Lamb, each holding a harp and golden bowls.* When the Lord in his passion demonstrated that the proclamation of both Testaments was fulfilled in himself, the church renders thanksgiving and gives herself up to sufferings in order that, as the apostle says, she might fill up that "which is lacking of the sufferings of Christ in her flesh."[11] For the harps represent bodies made ready to die, since the strings are stretched tight on wood.[12] And by the bowls are designated hearts wide open by the breadth of charity.

[5:9] *And they sang a new song, saying, "Worthy are you to take the book and to open its seals."* They celebrate the sacraments of the New Testament that have been fulfilled in Christ, while they accompany his dispensation by songs of praise, confessing that it belongs to Christ alone.

[5:9-10] *"And you have redeemed us for God by your blood from every tribe and tongue and people and nation."* Here it is declared more fully that the animals and the elders are the church, which has been redeemed by the blood of Christ and gathered from the nations. And he shows them in heaven by saying "and they will reign over the earth."

[5:11] *And I saw and heard the voice of many angels around the throne and of the animals and of the elders.* Countless thousands of people coming together to the church praise the Lord to whom was given all power in heaven and on earth. For if the righteous are called children of God, why not also the angels? But the heavenly host is able to sing this song by joining us in giving thanks for our redemption. The holy Pope Gregory expounded it in this way, saying, "For the voice of the angels is in praise of the Creator and is itself the admiration of an intimate contemplation."[13]

[5:14] *And the four living creatures said, "Amen," and the elders fell down and worshiped.* When the people in the church give forth their songs of praise to the Lord, the teachers confirm the same, and, for the sake of example, add their own praise of the Lord.

REVELATION 6

[6:1] *And I saw that the Lamb opened one of the seals.* With good reason he has reversed the usual order, since the seals are first broken and then the scroll is opened. For by his suffering and his rising again the Lord taught that he was the end of the Law. And when he ascended into heaven and sent the Holy Spirit, he established the church with the gift of a more hidden mystery. Therefore, at that time he opened the book, but now he breaks its seals.

And so, in the first seal he beholds the glory of the ancient church; in the following three seals he sees the threefold war against it; in the fifth seal he sees the glory of those who triumph in this war; in the sixth seal he sees that which is going to occur at the time of the antichrist; and then there is a short recapitulation of that which had come earlier; and in the seventh seal he sees the beginning of the eternal repose.

[6:2] *And I heard one of the four living crea-*

---

[11]Col 1:24. [12]The harp or lyre was a common image of martyrdom, since the strings stretched out and tied to the wood imaged the arms of Christ stretched out and fixed to the wood of the cross. [13]See Gregory the Great *Moralia* 2.7 (CCL 143:65).

tures, saying, "Come and see!" We too are admonished by the loud voices of the gospel to behold the glory of the church.

And, behold, a white horse, and he who sat on it had a bow, and a crown was given to him, and he went out conquering and to conquer. The Lord presides over the church, which is made whiter than snow by grace and bears the weapons of spiritual doctrine against the ungodly. As a conqueror he receives the crown in those who belong to him. Concerning this it is said, "He received gifts in people."[1] And although in them he was reigning in heaven, he was persecuted by Saul.[2]

[6:3] *I heard the second living creature saying, "Come and see."* He is prudently told to observe the opposing horsemen, so that just as he takes joy in the prosperities of the church, he might also from foreknowledge take caution concerning her adversities.

[6:4] *And out came another horse, a red one.* A red horse comes out against the victorious and conquering church, that is, an evil people bloody from their rider, the devil. Although we read in Zechariah that the horse of the Lord is red,[3] in that passage he is red from his own blood, while here he is red from the blood of others.

And to him who sat on it was given to take peace from the earth. That is, he is to take the earth's peace. For the church has received an eternal peace, which Christ has bequeathed to her.

And there was given to him a great sword. This sword is to be used either against those who are betrayers[4] of the faith or against those whom he makes martyrs. Concerning this sword, it is said to blessed Job: "He who made him has caused his sword to draw near."[5] The

sword is drawn near either that he may not tempt the saints to the extent that the impious desire or that he might return the vengeance of his fury to himself.

[6:5-6] *And, behold, a black horse, and he who sat on it had a balance in his hand, and I heard what seemed to be a voice in the midst of the four living creatures.* This black horse is the troop of false brothers who have the balance of right confession but harm their friends through works of darkness. For when it is said in the midst of the living creatures, "Do not harm," it is clear that there is someone who is doing harm. And concerning this running horse, the apostle says, "Outside there were wars, inside there are fears."[6]

A quart of wheat for a denarius and three quarters of barley for a denarius; but do not harm wine and oil. Beware, he says, lest by an evil example you offend your brother for whom Christ died and who bears the signs of the sacred blood and chrism.[7] For whether one has perfect merit or very little, all who have been instructed in the church in the faith of the holy Trinity have been redeemed by the same perfect price of the blood of the Lord. Nor without reason is the perfection of faith or works expressed by the measure of two quarts and not just one, since both at bottom consist of a twofold charity.[8]

[6:8] *And, behold, a pale horse, and the name of him who sat on it was Death, and Hades followed him.* This image is of the heretics who clothe themselves as though they are catholics but are worthy to have death abide within them and who draw the army of the lost after themselves. For the devil and his ministers are, by metonymy,[9] called death and hell, since

---

Revelation 6   [1]Ps 68:18 (67:19 LXX).   [2]See Acts 8:1-3; 9:1-5. Heaven refers to the faithful believers of the church.   [3]See Zech 1:8.
[4]Translating *praevaricatores*, used especially of advocates who are guilty of collusion with the opposite party.   [5]Job 40:19.   [6]2 Cor 7:5.
[7]The signs of the sacred blood and chrism refer to the signs of the cross, applied with holy oil, during the rite of baptism.   [8]This seems to refer to the commandment to love God and the neighbor.   [9]Metonymy is the literary device by which the name of one thing is exchanged for a related term or concept. For example, Wall Street may be used to refer to the business activity of corporate America.

they are for many the cause of death and of hell. The passage may simply be interpreted to mean that eternal punishments there [in hell] follow those who are here spiritually dead.

And there was given to him power over the four parts of the earth. Behold the insanity of Arius, which arose in Alexandria and extended itself even to the Gallic ocean, that pursues the pious not only by a dearth of the word of God but also, as though by beasts, with the physical sword.[10] Another edition has translated "fourth part," because the three evil horses, trusting in their rider, the devil, attack the fourth, that is, the cavalry of the church.[11]

[6:9] *I saw under the altar the souls of those who had been slain for the word of God.* He who said that the church was afflicted in many ways in the present age also speaks of the glory of the souls after the punishment of their bodies. "I saw them," he says, "under the altar," that is, in the secret place of eternal praise. For the altar that is of gold and is placed within and is near the altar of the Lord's body does not present, as does the altar without, flesh and blood to the Lord, but only the incense of praise. And those who now present their bodies as a living sacrifice,[12] then, when the chains of the body have been broken, sacrifice to him the offering of praise.[13] However, it may also be by transposition that he did not see under the altar but those slain under the altar, that is, under the testimony to the name of Christ, as it is said of the Maccabees, "They fell under the covenant of God."[14]

And they cried out with a great voice, saying. The great cry of the souls is their great desire to do that which they know the Lord wills. For it is not right to believe that they desire anything against the will of God, when that which they desire is dependent on his will.

[6:10] *"How long, O Lord, holy and true, until you judge and avenge our blood from those who live on the earth?"* They do not pray for these things out of hatred of their enemies for whom they intercede in this world. Rather, they pray out of love of equity. For in concord with the judge in whose presence they are placed, they pray for the day of judgment when the kingdom of sin is destroyed and the resurrection of their dead bodies comes. For even at the present time, when commanded to pray for our enemies, we nevertheless pray to the Lord, "May your kingdom come!"[15]

[6:11] *And there was given to each of them a white robe.* The souls of the saints, which rejoice in their own blessed immortality, have only a single robe. However, according to Isaiah, when their bodies arise, "they will possess a double portion in their own land."[16]

And it was told to them that they should rest a little while longer until their fellow servants and their brethren should be complete. Their desire for the resurrection is not denied, but it is delayed for the sake of the increase of the brethren who were yet to be gathered in. For even the joy of souls itself may be represented by white robes, when through the revelation of the Lord they learn that the impious will be condemned at the end and that to the end of the age many will be joined to their number by way of martyrdom. And so, filled with an inward love and content with this consolation, they have preferred to delay their own joy until that time for the sake of completing the number of the brothers.

[6:12] *And when he opened the sixth seal, I looked and there was a great earthquake.* With the opening of the sixth seal, the last persecution is announced. And just as it was when

---

[10]Bede has in mind the various Germanic kingdoms that at first accepted Arian Christianity and only later were converted to the faith of Nicea. The Gallic ocean, as the Romans called it, is now the Bay of Biscay, that body of water that lies between the northern shores of Spain and the western shores of France. [11]This other edition that probably comes from Tyconius is represented by Primasius (CCL 92:97). [12]See Rom 12:1. [13]See Ps 116:17 (115:8 LXX). [14]2 Macc 7:36. [15]Mt 6:10; Lk 11:2. [16]Is 61:7.

the Lord was crucified on the sixth day of the week, the world was shaken with darkness and trembling.[17]

And the sun became black. When the servants of the antichrist are allowed to attack the servants of Christ, it is as though the power of Christ is concealed or his teaching is for a time obscured or hidden by a protective covering.

And the full moon became like blood. The church will shed her blood for Christ more than is usual. It says full moon, because the final earthquake will be in all the earth, while beforehand, as the Scripture says, there will be earthquakes in many places.[18]

[6:13] *And the stars fell on the earth as the fig tree sheds its fruit when shaken by a strong wind.* Those who shine as heavenly figures in the church, but only in appearance, will be proven to have been of the earth when the wind of the final persecution blows. And their works are rightly compared with unripened figs, that is, to that which is immature and useless, like the falling fruit of a fig tree.

[6:14] *And the heaven vanished, like a scroll that is rolled up.* As a scroll when rolled up contains mysteries on the inside but has nothing visible on the outside, so also at that time the church, known only to her own, will go into concealment, prudently avoiding persecution so that hidden away it may not be noticed by those without.

And every mountain and island was moved from its place. He speaks of the members of the church who differ in regards to the nature of their offices or powers, and he foretells that no one will be untouched by this turbulence. However, the movement will have differing effects. Among those who are good it will give prior warning for flight, while among the evil it will give opportunity for falling through conformity.

[6:15] *And the kings of the earth and the leaders and the tribunes.* We understand the kings to be powerful persons, for he wills that they be understood from every station and condition. Moreover, who will be kings at that time, except the persecutor alone?

[6:16] *And they hid themselves in the caves and among the rocks of the mountains, and they called to the mountains and to the rocks, "Fall on us."* Since all the weak at that time will seek to be strengthened by the examples of the highest in the church, to be fortified by their counsel, to be protected by their exhortations and to be sheltered by their prayers, it is as though they entreated the mountains themselves to fall on them out of compassionate affection. For "the high mountains are a refuge for the deer, and the rocks for the badger."[19]

"And hide us from the face of him who is seated on the throne and from the wrath of the Lamb." That is, when he comes, that he should not find us worthy of condemnation but steadfast in faith, our sins being covered by the intercession of the saints and the mercy of God.

[6:17] *"And who will be able to stand?"* Certainly that one will be able to stand who has now taken care to be vigilant, to be steadfast in faith and to live manfully. Because if one refers this earthquake literally to the day of judgment itself, it is not surprising if at that time the kings and princes of the earth out of fear seek the refuge of the holy mountains, just as we read has already occurred in the story of the rich man clothed in purple and the poor Lazarus.[20]

REVELATION 7

[7:1] *After this I saw four angels standing on the four corners of the earth.* The four angels signify the four principal kingdoms, namely,

---

[17]Mt 27:45. [18]Mt 24:7. [19]Ps 104:18 (103:18 lxx). [20]Lk 16:19-31.

those of the Assyrians, of the Persians, of the Greeks and of the Romans. For just as in the previous seals, after the threefold struggles of the church,[1] he saw the joys of the triumphant souls, so now as well he will demonstrate by examples the victory over the preceding kingdoms of the world that have already succumbed to the law of Christ and of the church, which follows the kingdom of the antichrist. For matters of great importance must of necessity be confirmed by greater demonstrations.

And they held the four winds of the earth that no wind might blow on the earth or on the sea or against any tree. Suffocating in some way all things by their might, these angels did not allow anyone to breathe freely of his own right. By "the earth" is indicated the various provinces, in "the sea" the various islands and among "the trees" the various qualities and conditions of people. Another interpretation: These four angels are to be understood as those four winds of which Daniel speaks in his prophecy: "Behold, the four winds of heaven stirred up the great sea, and the four beasts came up from the sea."[2]

[7:2] *And I saw another angel ascending from the rising of the sun, having the seal of the living God.* This is the Lord born in the flesh, who is the "angel of great counsel,"[3] that is, the messenger of the Father's will, "who has visited us as the dayspring from on high,"[4] carrying the standard of the cross by which he seals the foreheads of his own.

And he cried out with a great voice to the four angels. The great voice of the Lord is that exalted proclamation, "Repent, for the kingdom of heaven has drawn near."[5]

[7:3] *"Do not harm the earth and the sea or the trees."* From the time of the Lord's passion, not only has the dominion of the enemy who opposed him been destroyed but also that of the earthly kingdom, as we see both with our eyes and read on that statue that the stone from the mountain broke into pieces.[6]

"Until we have sealed the servants of our God on their foreheads." For this purpose was the rule of the nations destroyed, that the face of the saints might in freedom be marked by the sign of faith that the nations had resisted. For even the figure of the cross indicates that the kingdom of the Lord is everywhere extended, as the ancient distich[7] shows:

> Behold, the four-squared world, in distinct parts,
> that you might show the sign of faith to encompass all things.[8]

Nor in vain was the four-lettered name of the Lord written on the forehead of the high priest,[9] since this is the sign on the foreheads of the faithful, about which the psalm "for the wine vats" sings: "O Lord, our Lord, how majestic is your name in all the earth," and so on, until he says, "that you may destroy the enemy and the defender."[10]

[7:4] *And I heard the number of the sealed, a hundred and forty-four thousand sealed, out of every tribe of the sons of Israel.* By this finite number is signified the innumerable multitude of the whole church, which is begotten from the patriarchs either by way of the offspring of flesh or by the imitation of faith. For it says, "If you are of Christ, you are the seed of Abraham."[11] And it pertains to the increase of perfection that this twelve is

---

Revelation 7 [1]The text of Bede reads *post triformes ecclesiae conflictus.* Another manuscript reading is *post multiformes ecclesiae conflictus* ("after the various struggles of the church"). [2]Dan 7:2-3. This other interpretation comes from Primasius (CCL 92:106). [3]Is 9:6 (LXX). [4]Lk 1:78. [5]Mt 4:17; cf. Mk 1:15. [6]See Dan 2:34. [7]A distich is a couplet meant to stand alone. [8]The source of this ancient distich is unknown. Gryson doubts that the distich is quoted from a written source. He surmises that it was on some form of iconography of the cross, something like a monument of the cross or a mosaic (CCL 121A:165-66). [9]See Ex 28:36-38. [10]Ps 8:1-2 (8:2-3 LXX). [11]Gal 3:29.

multiplied by twelve and is completed by the sum of a thousand, which is the cube of the number ten, signifying the immoveable life of the church. And for this reason the church is rather frequently symbolized by the number twelve, since throughout the four-squared world it subsists by faith in the holy Trinity, for three fours make ten and two. And, finally, twelve apostles were elected that they might preach the same faith to the world, signifying by way of the number the mystery of their work.

[7:5] *From the tribe of Judah, twelve thousand sealed*, and the following. It is fitting that he begins with Judah, for from that tribe our Lord came. However, he omits the tribe of Dan, from which it is said the antichrist will come. As it is written: "Let Dan be a serpent in the way, a viper by the path, that bites the horse's heels so that his rider falls."[12] For he does not intend to give the order of earthly generations but to expound the virtues of the church by way of the interpretation of the names, for by its present confession and worship the church hastens to the right hand of eternal life—for this is the meaning of the name Judah, which is placed first, and of Benjamin, which is placed last. Therefore, Judah is placed first, who being interpreted means "confession" or "praise." For before the beginning of confession, no one attains the heights of good works, and unless we should renounce evil works through confession, we do not live by those works that are just.[13]

The second name is that of Reuben, which being interpreted means "seeing the son." By *sons* works are indicated, as the psalmist says when speaking of the various blessings of the blessed person: "Your sons will be as olive shoots," and further, "that you may see the sons of your sons."[14] For it is not that he who fears the Lord cannot be blessed unless he produces sons and grandsons, since a greater reward awaits the faithful virgins. But by *sons* is meant works and by *sons of sons* is meant the fruit of works, that is, the eternal reward. For this reason, Reuben comes after Judah, since after the beginning of divine confession there follows the perfection of work.

And since "through many tribulations it is necessary that we enter into the kingdom of God,"[15] after Reuben there follows the tribe of Gad, which interpreted means "temptation" or "girt about." For after the beginning of good works, it is necessary that a person be tested by greater temptations and be prepared for more serious battles, so that the strength of his faith might be demonstrated. As Solomon says, "Son, if you come forward for the service of God, stand in his righteousness and prepare your soul for temptation."[16] And the psalmist says the same thing: "You did gird me with strength for the battle."[17]

[7:6] And since "we bless those who have endured suffering,"[18] after Gad is rightfully placed the tribe of Asher, which means "blessed." For blessed is the one who endures trial, for "when he has stood the test, he will receive the crown of life."[19]

Because secure by a sure promise of this blessedness, they are not placed in distress, but "rejoicing in hope and patient in tribulation,"[20] they sing with the psalmist, "In tribulation you have given me room,"[21] and again, "I have run in the way of your commandments, while you enlarged my heart."[22] And exulting with the mother of blessed Samuel, they say, "My mouth is made wide over my enemies, for I re-

---

[12]Gen 49:17. See Hippolytus *On the Antichrist* 14 (ANF 5:207). [13]The Latin is *non informamur rectis*. The verb *informare* means "to give shape" to something, "to mold, to form." By extension it comes to mean "to educate, inform," as it were, giving shape to the mind through understanding. My translation wishes to suggest that in living by good works one gives shape to that which is just and good. [14]Ps 128:3, 6 (127:3, 6 lxx). [15]Acts 14:22. [16]Sir 2:1. [17]Ps 18:39 (17:40 lxx). [18]See Jas 5:11. [19]Jas 1:12. [20]Rom 12:12. [21]Ps 4:1 (4:2 lxx). [22]Ps 119:32 (118:32 lxx).

joice in your salvation."[23] And for this reason, Napthali comes next, for it means "breadth."[24]

And Manasseh, meaning "forgetting" or "necessity," follows him. For by the mystery of this name we are exhorted that, taught by the troubles of present temptations, we ought to forget that which is behind and, as the apostle says, strive for that which is ahead.[25] And in this way we might make no provision for the flesh in its desires[26] but be constrained by the sole necessity of the human condition, concerning which the psalmist, sighing for better things, prays, "Bring me out of my distresses."[27]

[7:7] Simeon is placed next and means "he has heard sorrow" or "the name of dwelling," so that by the character of this name he might more clearly teach what is here to be acquired and what is more advantageously to be awaited. For the joy of the celestial habitation is given to those whose mind is here made sorrowful by a fruitful repentance. And of these it was said, "Your sorrow will be turned into joy."[28]

Next listed is Levi, which interpreted means "addition," by which we understand either those who with temporal things purchase eternal things, as Solomon says, "The ransom of a man's life is his own wealth,"[29] or those who by following the counsel of God receive in this world a hundredfold with tribulations, but in the future age they receive eternal life.[30] Concerning these it has been written: "He who adds knowledge adds woe."[31] For this reason the bitterness of tribulations was added even to holy Job so that, having been found worthy, he might receive a greater reward.[32]

And so not without reason does Issachar follow him in a proper order. Issachar is interpreted to mean "there is a reward," for, as the apostle says, "the sufferings of the present age

are not worthy to be compared with the future glory which will be revealed to us."[33] For, indeed, we fight with greater effect when a sure reward is awaited.

[7:8] However, God works and perfects these things in the "habitation of strength," which is the meaning of Zebulun, since "strength is made perfect in weakness."[34] And God works in this manner so that the body, which is regarded as weak by its enemies and through which they strive to wreak destruction on the soul, might be found, with God's assistance and by the happy addition that will come to it,[35] to be invincible.

And this is indicated by the name Joseph, which means the "gifts of grace to be added." By this we must understand either the increase of the spiritual gift from the double return of the talents,[36] or you should think of those offerings that are rendered to God the Redeemer by the devotion of the faithful.

And that you might understand that all these, who by sequence and the interpretation of names are placed here in a meaningful way, are those who will in the future judgment be at the right hand of Christ, the eternal king, Benjamin, as we said before, is mentioned in last place. For Benjamin means "son of the right hand" because he is at the end of the series. For when the last enemy, namely, death, is destroyed, the felicity of the eternal inheritance will be given to the elect, either each one of the faithful rightfully being named "son of the right hand," or the whole congregation of the church, concerning which we sing, "A queen stood at your right hand dressed in various golden robes."[37]

Therefore, from each tribe twelve thousand are sealed. For in whatever virtues any one of the faithful may have advanced, it remains

---

[23]1 Sam 2:1. [24]See Philo *On Dreams* 2.36. [25]See Phil 3:13. [26]See Rom 13:14. [27]Ps 25:17 (24:17 LXX). [28]Jn 16:20. [29]Prov 13:8. [30]See Mk 10:30. [31]See Eccles 1:18. [32]See Job 42:10-17. [33]Rom 8:18. [34]2 Cor 12:9. [35]Bede probably has in mind the incorruptibility and immortality that will be given to the body at the resurrection of the dead. [36]See Mt 25:20-22. [37]Ps 45:9 (44:10 LXX).

always necessary that they are made strong in the faith of the ancient fathers and are influenced by their examples.[38] For it is most certain that because of the total of the apostles or of the patriarchs the number twelve often designates our teachers as a whole or the entire church. For whether as in Judah they are praiseworthy in confession or as in Reuben they are noble in the fruit of their works or as in Gad they are strong by the exercise of temptations; whether as in Asher they are happy by their victory in struggles or as in Naphtali they are enlarged by their great works of mercy or as in Manasseh they are forgetful of past things; whether as in Simeon they are as if sorrowful in a vale of tears yet are always rejoicing because of their dwelling place even as they yearn for the heavenly Jerusalem or as in Levi they rejoice together in the promises of both the present and future life, made strong in the temporal blessings that are added to the eternal good, or as in Issachar they are firm in the contemplation of their future reward; whether as in Zebulon they offer their lives for the sake of Christ or as in Joseph they both strive to increase their holiness[39] and offer something more beyond the commandments of God, whether in virginity or in the full use of their capacities, or as in Benjamin by unwearied prayers they await the right hand of eternal bliss—it is proper that each person in his own profession is sealed by the rule[40] of the foregoing fathers, as is indicated by the number twelve, and that through the merits of individual persons the fullness of the most perfect beauty of the church, indicated by the number of one hundred forty-four thousand, is gathered together.[41]

[7:9] *After this I saw a great multitude that no one could number.* When this recapitulation, which was inserted for sake of example, is completed, he returns to the previous sequence and foretells the glory of those who will conquer the iniquity of the final persecution.

And so he continues: *From every nation and tribe and people and tongue.* This can be interpreted to mean that when the tribes of Israel to whom the gospel was first preached have been named, John then wishes to recall the salvation of the nations.

Clothed in white robes and palm branches in their hands. By the robes he refers to baptism. By the palms he refers to the triumph of the cross and that they will have conquered the world in Christ. It is possible that the robes might also indicate the brightness that is given through the Holy Spirit.

[7:10] *And they cried out with a great voice, saying, "Salvation belongs to our God who sits on the throne, and to the Lamb."* With a great voice, that is, with deep devotion and an unceasing praise, they profess that the Father and the Son reign on the throne, that is, in the church, with the Holy Spirit no less co-reigning with them. For just as it is said, "to him who sits on the throne, and to the Lamb," so it is said in the Gospel, "That they might know you, the true and only God, and Jesus Christ whom you have sent"[42]—we should add "that they might know Jesus Christ, the one and true God."[43]

[7:11] *And all the angels stood around the throne and around the elders and the living creatures.* In all the angels he indicates the persons of the great multitude that worships

---

[38]Translating *informentur exemplis*, literally "they are given shape or form by the examples." [39]Translating *spiritualis substantiae*, literally to increase their "spiritual substance or wealth." [40]Translating *regula*, which refers to the habit or manner of one's daily life. [41]The thought of Bede seems to be that 144,000 symbolizes the church in the perfection of its virtue, each faithful contributing to it by following the virtuous examples of the twelve patriarchs. [42]Jn 17:3. [43]The wording of Jn 17:3 could admit the interpretation that the Father is the true and only God but that Jesus Christ, the one sent, is not. Bede wants to uphold the equal deity of the Son with the Father and so supplies the phrase used of the Father and applies it also to the Son (*subauditur*).

the Lord. "All who are around him," it says, "offer gifts."[44]

And they fell on their faces before the throne and worshiped him. In this passage he does not say that the multitude or the living creatures or the elders worshiped, but he mentions the angels only. For these are the multitude; these are the living creatures and the elders. Although it might be possible to understand this of the angelic spirits themselves, concerning whom it is said that they rejoice at the salvation of the nations: "Give praise, O nations, with his people, and let all the angels of God worship him."[45]

[7:12] *"Blessing and glory and wisdom and thanksgiving and honor and power and might be to our God."* The church offers a sevenfold praise of virtues to the Lord, which the church confesses to have received from him in each member.

[7:13] *And one of the elders said to me: "These who are clothed in white robes, who are they, and from where have they come?"* He asked the question for this reason, that he might teach.

[7:14] *"These are they who have come out of the great tribulation."* "Through many tribulations it is necessary that we enter into the kingdom of God."[46] However, who would not know that the future persecution of the antichrist will be greater than any other?

"And they have washed their robes in the blood of the Lamb." He is not speaking only of the martyrs, for they are washed in their own blood. However, the blood of Jesus, the Son of God, cleanses the entire church from every sin.[47]

[7:15] *"Therefore they are before the throne of God."* Those who here stood as faithful confes-

sors of his name in the midst of adversities are there considered worthy to stand in the service of God.

"And they serve him day and night in his temple." Speaking according to our custom, he indicates eternity.

"And he who sits on the throne will dwell over them." The throne of God is the saints over whom and among whom God dwells forever.

[7:16] *"And they shall neither hunger nor thirst any more."* This is what the Lord promised: "I am the bread of life; he who comes to me shall not hunger, and he who believes in me shall never thirst. For blessed are they who hunger and thirst for righteousness, for they shall be satisfied."[48]

"Nor shall the sun strike them, nor any heat." "We have gone through fire and water," it says, "and you have brought us into a place of rest."[49]

[7:17] *"For the Lamb, who is in the midst of the throne, shall rule them."* He says that the Lamb is in the midst of the throne. Earlier he had said that the Lamb received a scroll from him who sat on the throne. And so he teaches us that the one church is the throne for the Father and the Son, in which through faith the one God, that is, the whole Trinity dwells.

"And he will guide them to springs of the waters of life." That is, he will guide them to the community of the saints, who are the springs of heavenly doctrine. It is possible that he is indicating also the very vision of God, "in whom are hid all the treasures of wisdom and knowledge."[50] Concerning this also David said, "As a deer longs for springs of water, so my soul longs for you, O God."[51]

"And God will wipe away every tear from their eyes." When the fullness of the immortal joys has been obtained, every sorrow will be utterly consigned to oblivion. For "blessed

---

[44]Ps 76:11 (75:12 lxx). [45]See Deut 32:43. [46]Acts 14:21. [47]See 1 Jn 1:7. [48]A combined quotation of Jn 6:35 and Mt 5:6. [49]Ps 66:12 (65:12 lxx). [50]Col 2:3. [51]Ps 42:1 (41:2 lxx).

are those who mourn, for they shall be comforted."[52] However, it is possible that the vision of this great multitude dressed in white is to be understood of the present time, when we have been saved in hope and hoping for that which we do not see, we await it with patience.

REVELATION 8

[8:1] *And when the Lamb had opened the seventh seal, there was silence in heaven for about half an hour.* It is believed that after the destruction of the antichrist there will be a short rest in the church. Daniel prophesied of this: "Blessed is he who waits and comes to the thousand three hundred and thirty-five days."[1] The blessed Jerome commented on this passage of Daniel in this way: "Blessed, he says, is he who when the antichrist is killed waits for the forty-five days beyond the thousand two hundred and ninety days, that is, three and a half years. For during them the Lord and Savior will come in his majesty. It is a matter of divine knowledge why there is silence for forty-five days after the death of the antichrist, unless we make the conjecture that the delay of the kingdom of the saints is a test of patience."[2] We should note that the greatest afflictions of the church are envisaged in the sixth period, while a rest is seen in the seventh. For the Lord was crucified on the sixth day, and he rested on the seventh, awaiting the time of the resurrection.[3]

Until now the author has written of the opening of the sealed scroll and of the seven seals. Now he recapitulates from the beginning and will speak of the same things in a different way.

Here Begins the Second Book

[8:2] *And I saw seven angels standing before God, and seven trumpets were given to them.* The church, which is often indicated by the number seven, is given over to the office of preaching. The first trumpet of this preaching indicates the common destruction of the impious by fire and hail. The second trumpet indicates the expulsion of the devil from the church that he might burn more hotly in the sea of this world. The third trumpet shows the heretics apostatizing from the church and corrupting the rivers of the holy Scriptures. The fourth trumpet reveals the defection of false brethren by the darkening of the stars. The fifth trumpet reveals the great infestation of the heretics who are the forerunners of the time of the antichrist. The sixth trumpet shows the appearance of the antichrist and the war that his followers will wage against the church. Then, after a recapitulation from the coming of the Lord has been inserted, the sixth trumpet shows the destruction of that same enemy. The seventh trumpet reveals the day of judgment in which the Lord will reward his followers and banish those who have corrupted the earth.

[8:3] *And another angel came.* He did not say, "afterward he came," but having claimed that the angels had received the trumpets, he takes up the explanation how they had received them. For although the church was preaching before the coming of the Lord, that did not occur everywhere until it had been confirmed by his Spirit.

And stood before the altar with a golden censer. He stood before the altar, that is, he appeared in the sight of the church. He was himself made the censer, from which God received the smell of sweet savor and became more favorable toward the world. Another version reads "on the altar,"[4] because for us he

[52]Mt 5:5. **Revelation 8** [1]Dan 12:12. [2]Jerome *Commentary on Daniel* 4.12.12 (CCL 75A:943-44). [3]The passion, burial and resurrection of Christ, therefore, are a new creation, typified by the first creation. However, the first creation did not usher in an eighth day, as did the work of Christ: sixth day (death), seventh day (burial) and eternal eighth day (resurrection). [4]This other version comes from Tyconius and Primasius (CCL 92:135). For this other version Bede has *super aram*. According to Gryson, *aram* is typical of Tyconius; Primasius reads *super altarium* (CCL 121A:180).

offered to the Father on the altar of the cross his own golden censer, namely, his own sinless body conceived by the Holy Spirit.

And there was given to him much incense to mingle with the prayers of all the saints on the altar that is before the throne. He offered incense from the prayers of the saints. For the church entrusted to him her prayers, saying, "Let my prayer be brought before you as incense."[5] The same angel is said to have received the prayers of the saints and to have offered them, for through him the prayers of all come to the Lord in an agreeable manner.

[8:4] *And the smoke of the incense rose from the prayers of the saints from the hand of the angel before God.* When Christ offered himself to the Lord as an agreeable and acceptable sacrifice,[6] the sorrow of the hearts of the saints was made acceptable. And arising from the fire within, this sorrow elicits tears, as is usual from smoke.

[8:5] *And the angel received the censer and filled it with fire from the altar.* Rightly does he mention the censer as full with fire. "For God does not give the Spirit in measure,"[7] and we know that this was most especially fulfilled concerning the humanity of Christ, in whom "all the fullness of the Godhead dwells bodily."[8]

And he threw it on the earth. The Lord spoke in a similar way in the Gospel: "I have come to send fire on the earth."[9]

And there were peals of thunder and voices and flashes of lightning and earthquakes. He moved the earth by the thunder of heavenly threats and by the voice of exhortation and by the lightning of miracles. Although some refused to follow, some did follow. Those who followed said, "He is good," while those who

did not said, "He leads the people astray."[10]

[8:6] *And the seven angels who had the seven trumpets prepared themselves to blow them.* Made zealous by the sevenfold Spirit, the church prepared herself to preach with faithfulness and to cast down the pomp of the world by the heavenly trumpets, even as happened to the walls of Jericho.[11] For even walking around the walls of Jericho for seven days suggests the entire time of the church.

[8:7] *And the first angel blew his trumpet.* The foretelling of the plagues is rightly compared with a trumpet, which is the signal for battle. For the Scripture says, "Lift up your voice as a trumpet; declare to my people their transgressions."[12] And elsewhere it says, "Set the trumpet to your lips, as an eagle over the house of the Lord,"[13] that is, preach with a great voice that Nebuchadnezzar will come to destroy the temple.

And there was hail and fire mixed with blood, and it fell on the earth. That the punishment of Gehenna is the reward for works that spill blood is indicated by the voice of the preachers who say, "He will pass from the waters of the snow to very great heat."[14] It is possible that by the word *blood* the spiritual death of the soul is intended. Tyconius interprets this verse like this: "There followed the wrath of God, which possesses within itself the death of many."[15]

And a third part of the earth was burned up, and a third part of the trees was burned up. The life of those who are good exists in teachers and hearers. For it says, "Blessed is he who reads and they who hear the words of the prophecy."[16] To be sure, the third part of evil persons have neither teachers nor hearers. Therefore, the good earth that brings forth

---

[5]Ps 141:2 (140:2 LXX). [6]See Eph 5:2. [7]Jn 3:34. [8]Col 2:9. [9]Lk 12:49. [10]Jn 7:12. [11]See Josh 6:1-21. [12]Is 58:1. [13]Hos 8:1. [14]Job 24:19.
[15]See Tyconius *Turin Fragment* §150 (TS 2 7:90): "By the fire and blood he signifies the wrath of God which devours the multitude of the impious." [16]Rev 1:3.

fruit in patience[17] receives benediction from God, while the bad earth produces thorns and thistles whose end is to be thrown into the fire.[18] So also the Father who is the husband-man prunes the fruit-bearing tree but cuts down the barren tree and brings it as fuel to the fire.[19]

And all green grass was burned up. "All flesh is grass."[20] Now it is fattened by the softness of extravagance. But when the sun of judgment is hot, it loses the flower of its beauty. As the Lord says, "Today it is in the field, tomorrow it is thrown into the oven."[21] Tyconius comments on the third part in this way. He says that a third part is internal enemies, another third part is that which is outside the church, and the church is a third part that will struggle against this twofold evil.[22]

[8:8] *And as a great mountain, burning with fire, was throw into the sea, and a third of the sea was made blood.* As the Christian religion increased, the devil, puffed up with pride and burning with the fire of his own anger, was cast into the sea of the world, as the Lord said: "If you should say to this mountain, 'Be taken up and cast yourself into the sea,' it will be done."[23] It is not that the devil was not present before, but thrown out of the church, he began to rage even more against his own followers, inflicting on them spiritual death by the arrogance of fleshly wisdom. For to be wise according to the flesh is death.[24] For flesh and blood did not teach the apostles, but the Father who is in heaven.[25] For they guided the ship of faith on that sea that submitted itself to the feet of the Lord for walking.[26]

[8:9] *And a third part of those who have souls in the sea died.*[27] He said "those who have souls" in order to show the living as spiritually dead. As the apostle said of that self-indulgent widow, "although living, she is dead."[28]

And a third part of the ships were destroyed. Another version[29] renders "And they destroyed a third part of the ships" to indicate that the third part that is dead killed another third part, that which followed after it, by a poisonous tradition and by the discipline of a useless teaching.

[8:10] *And a great star fell from heaven, blazing like a torch, and it fell on a third of the rivers and on the fountains of water, and the name of the star was Wormwood.* The heretics, whom the apostle Jude calls "stars of seduction,"[30] fall from the height of the church and by the flame of their own iniquity endeavor to pollute the fountains of the divine Scriptures, fearing not to falsify their meaning and often even their words. And so they are worthy of the name Wormwood. For even a small admixture of this is able to make bitter a great sweetness.

[8:11] *And many people died of the water.* As the apostle says, "Many follow their dissipation, and through them the way of truth is reviled."[31] However, as Moses teaches, for the people of God all water may be drunk.[32]

[8:12] *And a third of the sun was struck and a third of the moon and a third of the stars, so that a third part of them was obscured.* The glory of the church, which shines like a star, is often obscured through false brethren who, whether in times of prosperity or in the adversities of the world, cause her to shine less brightly by their defection.

---

[17]See Lk 8:15. [18]See Heb 6:7-8. [19]Mt 7:19. [20]Is 40:6. [21]Lk 12:28. [22]See Tyconius *Turin Fragment* §§152-56 (TS 2 7:91-93). [23]Mt 21:21. [24]See Rom 8:6. [25]See Mt 16:17. [26]Mt 14:22-27; Mk 6:45-51; Jn 6:16-21. The sea is an image of a people. There is the sea of the world, but also here the sea of that people who submits to the Lord. [27]Bede writes *quae habebant animas in mari.* I translate literally, since Bede's comment rests clearly on the Latin phraseology. [28]1 Tim 5:6. [29]This other version comes from Tyconius (Gryson, CCL 121A:180). [30]See Jude 13. [31]2 Pet 2:2. [32]See Lev 11:36.

That a third of the day would not shine, and likewise at night. Another version[33] renders in this way: "That a third part of the day might appear, and similarly at night." That is, the heavenly bodies were struck for this reason, that a third of the day and a third of the night might appear, namely, that which belongs to Christ and that which belongs to the devil. I would add that they were struck in order that given up to their own desires, they might be revealed in their own time as their sins become more abundant and insolent.

[8:13] *And I saw and heard the voice of an eagle flying through the middle of the heaven, "Woe, woe, woe, to those who dwell on the earth."* The voice of this eagle flies each day through the mouth of the eminent teachers in the church when they announce the evil of the heretics and the rage of the antichrist and the day of judgment that with all severity will come to those who love the earth. It says, "In the last days there will come perilous times, and there will be people who are lovers of self."[34] And later in the same letter: "People of corrupt mind and counterfeit faith,"[35] and elsewhere: "Then that evil one will be revealed, who opposes and exalts himself over everything that is called 'god' or is the object of worship."[36] And again: "The day of the Lord will come as a thief in the night; when people say, 'Peace and security,' then sudden destruction will come on them."[37]

From the other voices of the three angels. This does not mean that the trumpets of the angels bring the plagues to the world. Rather, they foretell those plagues that are coming or will come in their own time.

REVELATION 9

[9:1-2] *And I saw a star fall from heaven to earth, and he was given the key to the shaft of the bottomless pit, and he opened the shaft of the bottomless pit.* He indicates by what tinder the flame of the heretics, concerning which he had spoken briefly, will burn. Indeed, the ancient enemy, whom the Lord saw "like lightning falling from heaven,"[1] opened the hearts of his followers with blasphemous teaching and taught them to rise up high, like smoke, by speaking iniquity against the Most High.

And from the shaft rose smoke like the smoke of a great furnace, and the sun and the air were darkened with the smoke from the shaft. Heretical insanity rages as an announcement of a great furnace, that is, of the last persecution. It labors not only to darken the light of the more feeble, who like air in some manner touches the ends of the earth and heaven, but also to darken the light of the more exalted. Yet it is not strong enough to extinguish the light. For "if it is possible, even the elect will be led into error."[2]

[9:3] *And from the smoke came forth locusts on the earth.* Just as the saints are the body of Christ and members of one another, so also the members of the flesh of the dragon cling to one another and are born one from the other. And the smoke of heretical blindness produces the arrogance of the impious that offends with the mouth. And although these are shaken by the wind of haughtiness, they nonetheless do not escape earthly things. For the smoke as well from which they come, although it seeks to ascend, always lacks the capacity to do so.

And power was given to them like the power of the scorpions of the earth. The heretics are compared with hostile powers that outwardly appear harmless but keep poison in their tails.

[9:4] *And they were commanded not to harm the*

[33]Apparently from Tyconius (see *Turin Fragment* §170 [TS 2 7:96]). See Gryson, CCL 92:180.   [34]2 Tim 3:1-2.   [35]2 Tim 3:8.   [36]2 Thess 2:3-4.   [37]1 Thess 5:2-3.   **Revelation 9**   [1]Lk 10:18.   [2]Mt 24:24.

grass of the earth or any green thing. He shows that the locusts are human persons, for they are sent not to the grass but to people. For in this passage we interpret grass literally.

But only those persons who do not have the seal of God on their foreheads. Those are said to have the seal of God on their foreheads by whom it is possessed as it was necessary. The number of these persons was reckoned above as unchangeable and fixed by that angel who brought the seal of the living God from the east. For here he wished to use that form of speaking by which it is said, "No one says that Jesus is Lord, except by the Holy Spirit,"[3] that is, perfectly and truly.

[9:5] *And they were allowed to afflict them for five months, but not to kill them.* Although supported by the secular power,[4] the heretics are for a time allowed to attack those who are good, yet, as the Lord said, they are not able to kill the soul.[5] By the five months he indicates the time of this age on account of the five senses that we use in this life. Another translation has "six months," which agrees with this interpretation on account of the six periods of the age.[6]

And their suffering was as the torture of a scorpion when it stings a person. As a scorpion dispenses its poison from its tail, so the impiety of evil persons injures from their hind parts, when by threats and allurements it causes temporal things, which are behind, to be preferred to that which lies before, that is, to eternal blessings. Contrary to the parable in the Gospel,[7] this "generation of vipers" gives this scorpion over to its own offspring.

[9:6] *And in those days people will seek death but will not find it.* They prefer that their life of misery be ended by a quick death. As the blessed Cyprian complained had happened

during the persecution under Decius, "It was not permitted to those who desired to die to be killed."[8]

[9:7] *In appearance the locusts were like horses arrayed for battle.* That is, they are like the last persecutors. For in the last war that will be described by the following angel, he says that horses fight. Or simply put: As horses are led into battle, not by their own reason but by the urging of their riders, so wicked teachers, moved by a demonical spirit, fight against the church.

On their heads were what looked like crowns of gold. The twenty-four elders, who are the church, have golden crowns. However, these have crowns similar to gold, since they fashion for themselves false triumphs out of an empty victory.

[9:8-9] *And their faces were like human faces, and they had hair like the hair of women, and their teeth were like lions' teeth, and they had breastplates like iron breastplates.* By the human face he represents the pretence of reason. In the hair like that of women is represented their changing and effeminate habits. In the teeth like those of a lion, that both mangle and carry a natural stench, he represents a ferocity of mind and the infamy of evil teaching. And in the iron breastplates he represents hearts made stubborn against the truth. For these are persons who "holding the form of piety but denying the power of it, come in the clothing of sheep, but inwardly they are ravenous wolves."[9]

And the noise of their wings was like the noise of many chariots with horses rushing into battle. We should be more alarmed than attempt to explain that so great a power accrues to this army. At first the smoke arises; then it brings forth locusts that are first compared with

---

[3]1 Cor 12:3. [4]Perhaps Bede has in mind the Arian kings of certain Gothic nations. [5]See Mt 10:28. [6]The text of Primasius reads "six months" (CCL 92:147). [7]See Lk 11:12. [8]Cyprian *Epistle* 56.2 (FC 51:156). The Latin of Bede's quotation does not exactly correspond to that of Cyprian. According to Gryson (CCL 121A:164-65), Bede's quotation corresponds to the approximate form that appears in the second chapter of Jerome *Life of Paul* (FC 15:226; PL 23:19). [9]A combination of 2 Tim 3:5 and Mt 7:15.

scorpions and then with horses and with lions. Their power would suffice, even if they did not come fully armed. But now they are said to be winged and similar to chariots of war.

[9:10] *And they have tails like those of scorpions.* As the scorpion moves silently but strikes with its tail, so the lying deceits of evil persons seem outwardly harmless and innocent, but since the scorpion destroys in secret, it is as though it carries death in a hidden way.

Their power harms people for six months. Again he is speaking of this life where falsehood is able to be strong, either to seize the useless or to afflict the spiritual for a time.

[9:11] *They have as king over them the angel of the bottomless pit.* Although God is supremely good, by a hidden yet just judgment he permits an angel, suitable for such persons, to rule over them.

[9:12] *One woe has passed; behold, two woes are still to come.* Since he had foretold that three woes were to come, he now mentions that one woe has already come in the deceit of heresy. However, he says that two woes remain, which will come against the perverse during the time of the antichrist and at the day of judgment.

[9:13] *And the sixth angel blew his trumpet, and I heard a voice from the horns of the golden altar, that is before the eyes of God, saying to the sixth angel.* The sixth angel indicates the preachers of the final struggle, who, as the gospel warns, uncover the lies of the antichrist. Certainly the horns of the golden altar are the Gospels, which are pre-eminent in the church.[10]

[9:14] *"Release the four angels who are bound at the great river Euphrates."* He indicates to what extent the ancient enemy along with his allies is going to persecute the church at the end of the world. He has been shut up in the hearts of the impious since the suffering of the Lord and by divine power is restrained lest he should harm the church as much as he wants. The Euphrates is a river in Babylon and symbolizes the power of the kingdom of the world and the waves of persecutors. The enemy is the great mountain that he had said beforehand would be sent, burning with fire, into the sea.[11]

[9:15] *And the four angels were released.* After the manner of prophecy that shows us what will come to pass, in the spirit he sees these things as having happened. Therefore, he spoke of four angels, since the persecution will rage in the four parts of the world. These are the same angels whom the seer previously saw standing at the four corners of the earth and restrained from harming the earth and the sea so that the servants of God might be sealed.[12]

Who had been held ready for the hour and the day and the month and the year, to kill a third of humankind. The wicked spirits desire the death of humankind at every hour and moment of time. These will be permitted to rage more freely so that the church might be made strong, but at the proper time they themselves will be destroyed. And what do you think such spirits will do when they are released, when they work such devastation even now when they are bound?

[9:16] *And the number of the troops of cavalry was twenty thousands times ten thousand.* This number signifies the deceitful duplicity of that perverse army. This may more easily be understood from another translation, which renders "twice ten thousand times ten thousand."[13] The parable in the Gospel opposes this num-

---

[10]Referring to the four Gospels that correspond to the four horns (corners) of the altar. [11]See Rev 8:8. [12]See Rev 7:1-3. [13]The text of Bede reads *vicies milies dena milia.* The other translation reads *bis muriades muriadum.* This other translation is explicitly attributed to Tyconius by Primasius (CCL 92:155). Primasius's own text reads "The number of that cavalry was eighty thousand" (CCL 92:154). See the discussion of Gryson (CCL 121A:181).

ber to the king who has ten thousand.[14] It is as though the duplicity of the wicked opposes the simple faith of Christ, since thousands of thousands serve him and ten thousand times a hundred thousand stand before him.[15]

[9:17] *And this is how I saw the horses in the vision. Those who sat on them wore breastplates the color of fire and of hyacinth and of sulphur, and the heads of the horses were as the heads of lions.* The wicked spirits are clothed with the punishments of those whose hearts they govern. For we read that those who worship the beast will be tormented by fire and sulphur and that the smoke of their torments will ascend forever and ever.[16] Note that in the plague of locusts he did not say that he saw horsemen but only horses.[17] Here the severity of the persecutions clearly reveals the presence of an opposing power. Moreover, in this passage the horses have the heads of lions, while in that passage the locusts had human faces with the teeth only being those of beasts. For heretics often make a show of humanity, but those who administer the last persecution will demand that as punishment that they offered merely by signs and words.

And from their mouths came forth fire and smoke and sulphur. He shows that he had used the word hyacinth for smoke.[18] However, these things will not openly come forth from their mouths. Rather, by their noxious preaching they bring forth punishment for themselves and for their hearers. "I will bring forth fire from the midst of you," it says, "and it will consume you."[19]

[9:19] *For the power of the horses is in their mouths and in their tails.* That is, their power is in their speech and in their work.[20] For "the prophet who teaches lies is the tail."[21] He hides a part that is in some manner unseen and unclean by the verbosity of flattering talk, saying to the impious, "You are good."

For their tails are like serpents, having heads, and by them they wound. The false teachers of the ancient serpent, who deceived humankind, like those who are upheld by the protection of princes, harm more than if they had convinced by word alone. "He sits," it says, "in ambush with the rich."[22]

[9:20] *The rest of humankind, who were not killed by these plagues, did not repent of the works of their hands,* and so forth. Since he had described the false Christians and the heretics, now that he might fully describe the whole body of the devil, he mentions also the error of the pagans. For it in no way profited them not to be killed by these plagues, since it is clear that they continue in their pagan wickedness. Nor in that persecution will the pagans be coerced to consent to that mentioned above, but they will die in their unbelief.

[9:21] *Nor did they repent of their murders or of their sorceries.* To their impious religion they add also their wicked behavior. Having described the ferocity of the antichrist in order to show his ruin, as is his habit the seer now recapitulates from the beginning of Christ's birth and the glory of the church.

REVELATION 10

[10:1] *And I saw another mighty angel coming down from heaven, wrapped in a cloud.* The Lord, who is "the angel of great counsel,"[1] descends from heaven clothed in the cloud of his flesh. As Isaiah said, "Behold, the Lord

---

[14]See Lk 14:31. [15]See Dan 7:10. For the opposition to Christ Bede writes *decies milies centena milia adsistunt.* [16]See Rev 14:9-11. [17]See Rev 9:7-9. [18]The previous comment had spoken of fire, hyacinth and sulphur. Here it speaks of fire, smoke and sulphur. Bede concludes that in the previous passage hyacinth referred to smoke. [19]Ezek 28:18. [20]By "work" I have translated the Latin *officium*. An "office" is an obligatory service or a duty laid on one because of one's public responsibility. [21]Is 9:15. [22]Ps 10:8 (9:29 LXX). **Revelation 10** [1]Is 9:6.

shall ascend on a swift cloud and shall come to Egypt."[2]

And a rainbow over his head. That is, the promise of propitiation remains around those who are good.

And his face was like the sun and his feet like pillars of fire. Since the face of the Lord shines brightly, that is, knowledge of him has become manifested through the glory of the resurrection, his feet, enlightened by the fire of the Holy Spirit and made strong like a pillar, will preach the gospel on the mountains and announce peace.[3] For James and Cephas and John were regarded as pillars of the church.[4]

[10:2] *And he had an open book in his hand.* This is that book previously mentioned.[5] Although it had been closed for a long time by a covering, it was at last unfastened by the grace of the Lord so that, as the prophet says, even "the deaf might hear the words of the book."[6] And rightly is "his face like the sun," for he now bears an open book.

And he set his right foot on the sea and his left foot on the land. The proclamation of the Christian faith is extended by land and by sea. But allegorically it means that the stronger members are put in greater dangers, while the others are placed in circumstances suitable to them. For God does not allow us to be tempted beyond what we are able.[7]

[10:3] *And when he called out, the seven thunders sounded their voices.* When the Lord preaches mightily, the church, filled with a sevenfold grace, also lifts her voices to preach. For "the lion will roar, who will not fear? The Lord God has spoken; who will not prophesy?"[8] Indeed, the seven thunders of which he is speaking are the same as the seven trumpets.

[10:4] *And when the seven thunders had sounded, I was about to write.* For he had heard above, "Write what you see in the book."[9]

"Seal up what the seven thunders have said and do not write it down." The mysteries of the Christian faith are not shown indiscriminately to all, lest they be regarded as of little worth. Nor are they closed to those who have been tested, lest they be altogether hidden. For the sake of these he heard later on, "Do not seal the words of this prophecy."[10] And both of these thoughts are brought together into one verse by Daniel, to whom an angel says, "Seal the book and shut up the word until the appointed time."[11]

[10:5-6] *And the angel whom I saw standing on the sea and on the land lifted up his hand to heaven and swore by him who lives forever and ever.* The angel swears by him who lives forever, while Christ comes in the name of the Father and confirms the unchangeable truth: "Heaven and earth will pass away, but my words will not pass away."[12]

Who created heaven and what is in it, and the earth and what is in it. He who stands on the sea and the land extends his hand to heaven and rightly swears by him who is the creator of the heaven, of the land and of the sea.

For there will be no more time. To be sure, as the psalmist says, "the time of the wicked will be forever,"[13] but the changing variety of the times of this world will cease at the last trumpet. For the trumpet will sound, and the dead will rise incorruptible, and their inheritance will be forever.[14]

[10:7] *And the mystery of God will be consummated, just as he proclaimed it through his servants, the prophets.* The mystery that is

---

[2]Is 19:1. [3]See Is 52:7; Rom 10:15. [4]See Gal 2:9. [5]See Rev 5:1-5. [6]Is 29:18. [7]See 1 Cor 10:13. The sea is figure for the instability of the world, while the land is figure for that which is less tempestuous. It may be also that the right foot represents the spiritually strong, while the left foot those who are less mature. [8]Amos 3:8. [9]Rev 1:11, 19. [10]Rev 22:10. [11]Dan 12:4. [12]Mt 24:35. [13]Ps 81:15 (80:16 LXX). [14]See 1 Cor 15:52.

now being proclaimed will then be brought to its fulfillment,[15] when the wicked will go into eternal punishment and the righteous to eternal life.

[10:8] *And the voice that I heard from heaven spoke to me again and said, "Go, take the open scroll from the hand of the angel."* When the Lord reveals the mysteries of the future time and says, "The kingdom of heaven has drawn near,"[16] the church also is admonished to receive the same book of preaching. These words may also be suitable to John himself, who after his exile is to return to preaching.

[10:9] *And I went to the angel and told him to give me the book.* Let him approach the Lord who wishes to receive the sacraments of teaching.

And he said to me, "Take the book and eat it." That is, graft it into your most inward parts and "write it on the tablet of your heart."[17]

"It will make your stomach bitter, but in your mouth it will be as sweet as honey." When you will have received it, you will be delighted by the sweetness of the divine eloquence, but you will experience a bitterness when you begin to preach and to live according to your understanding. Or undoubtedly this can be understood in view of Ezekiel. For when he said that he had eaten a book, he added, "And I went away bitter in the indignation of my spirit."[18]

[10:11] *And he said to me, "It is necessary that you prophesy again to the peoples and to the nations."* He expresses what the book that is eaten and what the sweetness mixed with bitterness signifies. That is to say, that when he is released from exile he was to preach the gospel to the nations. This would be a sweet task as regards love, but it would be a bitter work

on account of the persecutions that he would endure.

REVELATION 11

[11:1] *And I was given a measuring rod like a staff.* In the rod he received the ministry of writing the Gospel. This ministry is not unnecessary because of an empty splendor, but it is like the scepter of equity[1] and the scepter of the kingdom of God, for it will describe the eternal kingdom of Christ.

"Rise and measure the temple of God and the altar." He said, "Rise," not because John was sitting when he heard these words, but because by this word the heart of each person is aroused to measure the words and deeds of the gospel. For there each will discover to what extent he has progressed and to what extent he is in agreement with the divine rule.

"And those who worship in it." Not everyone who is seen therein is worshiping, as it says, "Whoever will have confessed me."[2] And therefore he commands that a part not be measured, saying:

[11:2] *"But the court outside the temple, leave that out and do not measure it, for it is given to the nations."* Those who are joined to the church in name only and approach neither the altar nor the holy of holies are cast out from the rule of the gospel and are associated with the nations. "For all the glory of her who is daughter of a king is from within."[3]

"And they will trample the holy city for forty-two months." Not only are they expelled from the church, but also they attack the church herself as allies of the nations for three and a half years. Not that they will trample on her only at that time, that is, at the time of the antichrist. Rather, the entire body of the wicked, among whom even now the mystery of iniquity

---

[15]See Mt 25:46. [16]Mt 4:17; 10:7; Mk 1:15. [17]Prov 7:3. [18]Ezek 3:1-3, 14. **Revelation 11** [1]See Ps 45:6 (44:7 LXX). [2]Lk 12:8. [3]Ps 45:13 (44:14 LXX).

is working,[4] will attach itself to him as though to its own head.

[11:3] *"And I will grant my two witnesses power to prophesy for one thousand two hundred and sixty days."* Lest the ferocity of evil persons terrify the hearer, he declares that also the church, united from two peoples, will be made glorious by the grace of virtues. And it is said that always attentive to its head, namely, Christ teaching in the flesh, the church will prophesy for three and a half years. For the months of three and a half years, that is, thirty times forty-two, makes for one thousand two hundred and sixty days.[5] Daniel writes that the days of the same period in which the abomination of desolation will be set up will be one thousand two hundred and ninety.[6]

"Clothed in sackcloth." This means that they are established in confession, as the prophet says: "But I clothed myself in sackcloth when they were an annoyance to me."[7]

[11:4] *These are the two olive trees and the two lampstands that stand before the Lord of the earth.* Made radiant by the light of the two Testaments, the church always stands near the commandments of the Lord. For the prophet Zechariah also saw a lampstand of seven lamps and these two olive trees, namely, the Testaments, pouring oil into the lampstand. This is the church with her oil that never runs out and that makes her to burn brightly as the light of the world.

[11:5] *And if anyone would harm them, fire will pour from their mouth and will consume their foes.* Should anyone harm the church, he is condemned to a judgment similar to his own attack and is consumed by fire. "For all who take the sword will perish by the sword."[8]

Therefore, also the Chaldean fire that was poured out on the children of God destroyed the ministers of impiety themselves.[9] Or the passage may mean that whoever is to be changed into something better is spiritually consumed in a good fire by the prayers of the mouth of the church. "You will heap coals of fire," it says, "on his head."[10]

[11:6] *They have power to shut the sky, that no rain may fall during the days of their prophecy.* In Christ all power in heaven and on earth is given to the church, for the keys of binding and loosing have been granted to her.[11] However, the heaven is also closed in a spiritual way so that it rains no rain, that is, that no blessing from the church descends on the dry land. As the Lord said to his vineyard, "I will command the clouds that they rain no rain on it."[12]

And they have power over the waters to turn them into blood. Not only do they cause the rain to cease, but also they make useless those waters that have come down by turning the waters into blood. For the good aroma of Christ that comes from the church is to some an aroma of death to death but for others an aroma of life to life.[13]

[11:7] *And when they have finished their testimony, the beast that ascends from the bottomless pit will war against them.* He clearly shows that all this will happen before the final persecution, for he says, "when they have finished their testimony." At least their witness will continue until the revelation of the beast that will emerge from the hearts of the wicked. It is not that they will not strive at that time valiantly to resist the enemy with the same testimony. However, it is believed that at that time the church will be made destitute of the gift of miracles, while the adversary will be openly

---

[4]See 2 Thess 2:7. [5]There are forty-two months in three and a half years. Bede reckons each month as having thirty days. [6]See Dan 12:11. [7]See Ps 35:13 (34:13 LXX). [8]Mt 26:52. [9]See Dan 3:22, 48 (LXX). [10]Rom 12:20. [11]Mt 28:18; 16:19; see Jn 20:22-23. [12]Is 5:6. [13]See 2 Cor 2:15-16.

active with deceptive signs. As the Lord says, "Want will go before his face."[14]

And he will conquer them and kill them. He will conquer in those who will have succumbed, and he will kill in those who by a praiseworthy suffering for the name of Christ will be slain.[15] Or should he conquer and kill in a spiritual manner, we understand this to refer to that portion of witnesses of which the Gospel speaks, saying, "They will deliver you up to tribulation and put you to death."[16] And the Evangelist Luke indicates that this was spoken of a part, saying, "Some of you they will put to death."[17]

[11:8] *And they will throw their bodies onto the streets of the great city.* "If they have persecuted me," it says, "they will also persecute you."[18] Therefore, it is not surprising if the city of the wicked, which did not fear to crucify the Lord, should also hold his servants in derision, even if they are dead. The history of the church relates that such things have often occurred.

Which is spiritually called Sodom and Egypt. *Sodom* and *Egypt* mean "silent" and "dark," for this city possesses neither the light of faith nor the sound of confession. For "man believes with his heart and so is justified, and he confesses with his lips and so is saved."[19] As a sign of spiritual punishment, these regions were oppressed with these plagues, that is, Sodom by a ravaging fire and Egypt by water turned into blood.[20]

[11:9] *And persons from the peoples, tribes, tongues and nations will see their bodies.* He did not say "the peoples and the tribes will see" but many "from the peoples" will openly ridicule the saints, for there will be others who believe.[21]

And they refused to allow their bodies to be placed in tombs. He speaks of their intention and of their hostile activity. Of course, they will not be able to accomplish their intention, lest the church be lost to memory. As it says, "You neither enter yourselves, nor do you allow others to enter,"[22] although some may enter, although the opponents fight against it. However, regarding the bodies of the living and the dead, they will clearly try to prohibit the living from gathering together for the celebration of services to their memory and to prohibit the dead from being recalled to memory, and to prohibit their bodies from being buried for their memory as witnesses of God.[23]

[11:10] *And those who dwell on the earth will rejoice over them.* As often as the just are afflicted, the unjust rejoice and celebrate with feasting, as it is said: "While the wicked person is exalted, the poor one is consumed."[24]

Because these two prophets had been a torment to them. In addition to the plagues that beset the human race on account of the witness of God, even the sight of the just is an agony to the unjust. As they themselves say, "The very sight of him is a burden to us."[25]

[11:11] *But after three and a half days a spirit of life from God entered them, and they stood up on their feet.* Until now the angel has narrated of the future and has reported what he hears will come to pass as though it has already happened, namely, that when the kingdom of the antichrist has been destroyed, the saints will rise to glory.

And great fear fell on those who saw them. He speaks of all the living, for even the just who are still alive will experience great fear at the resurrection of those who sleep.

---

[14]See Job 41:13. [15]The beast conquers in those who apostatize from the faith. He kills in those who suffer martyrdom from the persecution he inspires. [16]Mt 24:9. [17]Lk 21:16. [18]Jn 15:20. [19]Rom 10:10. [20]See Gen 18:16–19:28; Ex 7:14-24. [21]This interpretation comes from Tyconius *Turin Fragment* §390 (TS 2 7:161). [22]Mt 23:13. [23]This interpretation comes from Tyconius (see *Turin Fragment* §§384-87 [TS 2 7:158-59]); Caesarius of Arles *Exposition on the Apocalypse* 11.9, Homily 8. [24]Ps 9:23 (LXX). The LXX speaks of the wicked person exalting himself. [25]Wis 2:15.

[11:12] *And they went up into heaven on a cloud.* The apostle also spoke of this, saying, "We will be caught up in the clouds to meet the Lord in the air."[26]

And their foes will see them. Here he distinguishes the unjust from those whom he said feared in common with all.

[11:13] *And at that hour there was a great earthquake, and a tenth of the city fell, and seven thousand people were killed by the earthquake.* When the terror of judgment falls on them, the whole city of the devil, built as it is on sand, will collapse along with its builders. For both the number ten and the number seven are perfect. If that is not the case here, then the whole must be understood from the part.[27]

And the rest were terrified. "Who of men will boast that he has a pure heart, when the powers of heaven are shaken?"[28]

And they gave glory to the God of heaven. Those have built on the rock, who, when others are collapsing at the earthquake, out of their own stability praise God with a right confession. "The righteous person will rejoice when he sees the punishment of the wicked."[29]

Some interpret the two prophets to be Enoch and Elijah.[30] They will preach for three and a half years and strengthen the hearts of the faithful against the perfidy of the antichrist that is soon to come. And when they are killed, his ferocity will rage for the same length of time. When at last the saints, who through the protection of their hiding places were thought to be dead, resume the struggle, his rage will be overcome. For the sake of the fellowship of the one body, these prophets are said to rise, and when those who were thought to be dead are seen alive, the persecution is greatly intensified and

many of those who were thought worthy by the number seven or ten will fall away. For Daniel says, "And he will make a covenant with many for one week, and for half of the week he will cause sacrifice to cease, and in the temple there will be an abomination of desolation."[31] And in subsequent passages he says, "And the abomination of desolation will be in place for one thousand two hundred and ninety days."[32] This number is quite near to the course of three years and six months. Finally, Elijah once destroyed his enemies by fire, and hiding out for three and a half years he withheld rain. At last, when the false prophets had been put to death, he turned Israel to the Lord through the sacrifice that had been consumed.[33]

The recapitulation goes this far.

[11:14] *The second woe has passed, the third woe is soon to come.* This second woe is not part of the recapitulation. It rather concerns the battle of the horses that the trumpet of the sixth angel set in motion. For the eagle had predicted three woes that would come from the sound of the three trumpets. But he did not speak it then, lest it be thought that the third woe that concerns the seventh angel and the end would follow on immediately.

[11:15] *Then the seventh angel blew his trumpet, and there were loud voices in heaven, saying, "The kingdom of this world has become the kingdom of the Lord God and of his Christ."* The six previous trumpets, corresponding to the periods of the present age, proclaimed the course of the various struggles of the church. This seventh trumpet is the messenger of the eternal sabbath and of the victory and dominion of the true King.

---

[26]1 Thess 4:17. [27]Whichever of the two interpretive strategies is employed, the meaning is the same: the whole city of the devil is destroyed. [28]See Prov 20:9. [29]Ps 58:10 (57:11 LXX). [30]That Enoch and Elijah would be forerunners of Christ was a common opinion from the second century onward. See Tertullian *On the Soul* 50 (ANF 3:227-28); Hippolytus *On the Antichrist* 43 (ANF 5:213); perhaps also Irenaeus *Against Heresies* 5.5.1 (ANF 1:530-31). From the Greek tradition Oecumenius shared this opinion (*Commentary on the Apocalypse* 11.3-6 [TEG 8:163-64]). [31]Dan 9:27. [32]Dan 12:11. [33]2 Kings 1:9-12 (4 Kings 1:9-12 LXX); 1 Kings 17:1-3; 18:1; 18:36-40 (4 Kings 17:1-3; 18:1; 18:36-40 LXX).

[11:16-17] *And the twenty-four elders worshiped God, saying, "We give thanks to you, Lord God Almighty."* "Behold," it says, "at the voice of the seventh angel the third woe will come." And when he has sounded his trumpet, he speaks only of the church praising God and giving him thanks. And from this we understand that there is no recompense of the good without also the woe of the wicked.

[11:18] *"You who are and who was, you who have taken your great power and begun to reign; and the nations raged, but your wrath came."* To be sure, from eternity you have reigned, although the wicked are in rebellion, but now their anger is suppressed and ceases to exist. For "the Lord has assumed his reign, let the people be angry."[34]

"And the time for the dead to be judged and for the rewarding of your servants," and the following. This corresponds to the order we have in the Gospel narrative. First, all the nations are to be gathered before the judge; then those on the right will be placed in many mansions in the kingdom of the Father, while those on the left will be tossed outside the limits of the kingdom and cast into the flames of their condemnation.[35]

"And for the destroying of those who corrupted the earth." This is the final woe. Up to this point he has spoken of the seven angels who blow the trumpets. Now he recapitulates from the birth of the Lord and will speak of the same things in a different and more extensive manner.

[11:19] *Then the temple of God in heaven was opened, and the ark of the covenant was seen in his temple.* Formerly the temple of the Lord on the earth contained the ark of the covenant hidden behind the mystical veil. However, since the veil of the ancient temple and the wall of partition have been torn asunder by the sword of the blood of the Lord,[36] now in the church, that is, the temple of the living God and whose citizenship is in heaven,[37] the ark of his incarnation is laid open to all the world. For just as the manna from heaven was in a pure gold container,[38] so is his divinity in his holy body.

And there were flashes of lightning, voices, an earthquake and heavy hail. All of these phenomena represent the excellences of the brightness and of the preaching and of the struggles of the church. He said that such things took place also in his description of the preaching of the seven angels from the coming of the Lord when he stood on the altar,[39] but more generally from the beginning to the end. Finally, he described in each case how they took place. And so now, that the temple of God in heaven stands open and that struggles are to follow, he says . . .

REVELATION 12

[12:1] *And a great sign appeared in heaven.* The sign that now appears in the church is that God is born of man.[1]

A woman clothed with the sun and the moon under her feet. Clothed with the light of Christ, the church treads on temporal glory. "Righteousness will flourish in his days," it says, "and peace abound, until the moon is taken away or is destroyed."[2] These words of the psalm mean that there will be an increase in the abundance

---

[34]Ps 99:1 (98:1 LXX). The LXX has the aorist (ἐβασίλευσεν), which is reflected in Bede's perfect tense (*regnavit*). I have translated as an incipient aorist. The thought of Bede is that although God is eternally king over all, yet he has allowed the impious to have their way for a time. Now that God asserts his rule over them, they react with rage. [35]Mt 25:31-46. [36]See Mt 27:51; Eph 2:14-16. [37]See 2 Cor 6:16; Phil 3:20. [38]Heb 9:4. [39]See Rev 8:3, 5. **Revelation 12** [1]Translating *Deum ex homine fieri*. Here as elsewhere heaven is interpreted to be the church, the place of God's dwelling and presence. Bede will consistently interpret the experiences of the woman in the following passages to refer to experiences of the church. [2]Ps 72:7 (71:7 LXX). Bede adds the words *vel interficiatur* to the Psalm quotation. In this way he interprets "taken away" (*extollatur*) in terms of the quotation that follows (1 Cor 15:26). The waxing and waning of the moon made it an apt symbol for the changeableness of temporal existence. In this context the moon is figure for the "mutability of mortality."

of peace, until God will consume all mutability of our mortality, when "death the final enemy will be destroyed."[3]

Another possible interpretation is this. The church in part will enjoy Christ, the Sun, in heaven and in part sojourn in the body apart from the Lord.[4] From this perspective it is possible to understand what was said: "His left hand was under my head, and his right hand will embrace me."[5]

And on her head was a crown of twelve stars. The head of the church is decorated with the twelve apostles. By this image you may understand either Christ or the beginning of the nascent church, which is designated by the name of her head. "You placed on his head a crown of precious stone."[6]

[12:2] *She was with child, and she cried out in her pangs of birth.* The church spiritually gives birth to those with whom she suffers birth pangs, and she also never ceases to be in birth pangs with those who have already been born.[7] As she herself says, "My little children, with whom I am again in travail until Christ be formed in you."[8]

And she was in anguish for delivery. As the Lord says in the Gospel, "When a woman is in travail, she has sorrow, because her hour has come; however, when she is delivered of the child, she no longer remembers the anguish on account of the joy."[9] And speaking with his disciples, he adds this: "So you have sorrow now, but I will see you again and your hearts will rejoice."[10]

[12:3] *Behold, a great red dragon with seven heads and ten horns.* Made bloody by his

ferocity, the devil is armed against the church by the power of an earthly kingdom. For by the seven heads is meant all kings who are his allies and by the ten horns is meant every kingdom.

[12:4] *And his tail swept down a third part of the stars of heaven and cast them to the earth.* He speaks of the power and malice of the enemy whom the church conquers with the help of the Lord. For he cast down, as though by his tail, an innumerable host of angels and of people by means of deceit. For a tail is that member hidden from view and unclean, and by its own cover it conceals unclean parts that they might not be seen.

As is his habit, Tyconius interprets the third part of the stars that fell to be false brethren, the second third to be the church and the last third to be the enemy that is outside the church.[11]

And the dragon stood before the woman, that he might devour her child when she brought it forth. The devil lies in wait for the church attempting to extinguish the faith in Christ that is in the hearts of the believers. In this way he desires to kill the person to whom the church gives birth by teaching, as though he were killing the Lord. An image of such deceit was the person of Herod, for although he was an enemy within, he feigned the desire to worship the Lord. But in fact he wished to kill him.

[12:5] *And she brought forth a male child.* Although the dragon opposes her, the church always gives birth to Christ.[12] However, he spoke of a male child because of him who was the conqueror of the devil who had conquered

---

[3]1 Cor 15:26. [4]See Phil 1:21-26. In this interpretation the church triumphant enjoys Christ (sun) in heaven, while the church militant continues to live in the conditions of change and corruption (moon). [5]Song 8:3. [6]Ps 21:3 (20:4 LXX). [7]The church spiritually gives birth through baptism. Until that time the church is in birth pangs (evangelism, catechesis). Moreover, the church continues to nurture those born of baptism until such time as they are perfectly born in the resurrection of the flesh and fully conformed to Christ. [8]Gal 4:19. Although Paul writes these words to the Galatians, Bede thinks of them as spoken by the church (*ipsa dicit*). [9]Jn 16:21. [10]Jn 16:22. [11]According to the *Turin Fragments* (§§ 459-60), Tyconius interpreted the "third part of the stars" to be "the Jews and their leaders who rejected Christ" (TS 2 7:183). [12]This is a reference to the sacrament of baptism through which children of God are given birth by the church, the mother of the faithful.

the woman. For what son is not a male child?

Who is to rule all the nations with a rod of iron. He rules those who are good with an inflexible justice, and those who are evil he breaks into pieces. In fact, this was promised to the church in what was written above: "I will give him power over the nations, and he shall rule them with a rod of iron."[13] For the church also gives rise each day to the church that in Christ rules the world.

But her son was caught up to God and to his throne. To be sure, impiety is incapable of comprehending Christ, who is spiritually born in the mind of the hearer. For he reigns with the Father in heaven who has also "raised us up and made us sit with him in the heavenly places in Christ."[14]

[12:6] *And the woman fled into the wilderness.* Living in the hope of things eternal, the church rejoices in her walk in the present wilderness. For she has received power to walk on serpents and scorpions[15] and on every power of the red dragon, just as the people of Israel, who, fed in the desert with the celestial bread, conquered the fiery serpents by looking on the brass serpent.[16]

Where she has a place prepared by God. "Be to me," it says, "a God of protection and as a place of refuge, that you might make me safe."[17]

That there they might nourish her for one thousand two hundred and sixty days. By this number of days that make three and a half years, the entire time of Christianity is encompassed. For Christ, whose body is the church, preached a similar amount of time in the flesh.

[12:7] *Now a great war occurred in heaven;*

Michael and his angels fought against the dragon. Heaven signifies the church. In it, it says, Michael with his angels fights against the devil. For according to the will of God he contends for the church in her sojourn by prayer and the giving of succor. Also Daniel said that Michael would come to the aid of the church in the last and most serious test.[18] And for this reason they believe that the antichrist will be destroyed by him. And there are said to be his angels just as there are also our angels. As the Lord said, "Their angels always behold the face of my Father,"[19] namely, the angels of those with whom they are fellow citizens.[20]

And the dragon fought, and his angels. The angels of Satan are not the only ones who are like him in nature and will. This is true also of those persons who have become entangled in their snares.

[12:8] *But they were defeated* [that is, in view of all time], *and there was no longer any place for them in heaven.* That is, there was no longer any place for them among the saints who through his ejection have become heaven and who in their faith no longer receive him who has been cast out.

[12:9] *And that great dragon was thrown down to the earth.* Thrown out from those who are spiritual, the ancient foe is more narrowly confined in those who are earthly.[21] This is what it means that he was thrown down from heaven and sent to the earth. To him it was said, "Dust you will eat all your days."[22] And on the earth he will be trampled by the feet of the saints, as it is written: "You will tread on the asp and the basilisk."[23]

---

[13]Rev 2:26-27. [14]Eph 2:6. [15]See Lk 10:19; also Mk 16:18. [16]See Num 21:4-9; Jn 3:14-15. [17]Ps 31:4 (30:3 LXX). [18]See Dan 10:13; 12:1. [19]Mt 18:10. [20]Since the church is signified by *heaven*, the angels are fellow citizens (*cives*) with the members of the church. [21]Translating the reading *in terrenis includitur*, which is that of the Migne text (PL 93:167). Gryson's text reads *terrenos includit*, suggesting that the enemy confines the earthly more narrowly. However, the context favors the Migne text: the enemy is thrown out of the spiritual and is therefore confined to the earthly only. [22]Gen 3:14. [23]See Ps 91:13 (90:13 LXX).

[12:10] *"Now the salvation and the power and the kingdom of our God and the authority of his Christ have come."* He clearly shows in what heaven these things occur. For we know that in the church salvation has been accomplished by the victory of Christ. About this he says, "All authority is given me in heaven and on earth."[24] He does not speak of that authority that he eternally possessed. He speaks rather of that authority that he has in the church from the time he willed, namely, when he began to exercise authority in the members of his body as their head.

"For the accuser of our brethren has been thrown down." The angels express their joy at the salvation of their brethren, that is, of those who in the future will become their fellow citizens but who are now sojourners.

"Who accused them day and night before our God." He accused those whom he advised to make ill use of times of prosperity and whom he advised lack of patience in times of adversity.

[12:11] *"And they loved not their lives even to death."* Rightly do those disdain their lives for the sake of Christ who through the blood of Christ have conquered such a foe.

[12:12] *"Rejoice, then, O heavens, and you who dwell in them."* The inhabitants of heaven are here understood to be both angels and holy persons. And it is fitting for them both to be joyful in the Lord, for humankind is now joined to the angels and the angels administer to the human nature in Christ.[25]

"Woe to you, O earth and sea, for the devil has come down to you in great wrath." Just as he taught that the redeemed could expect joy, so he teaches that lamentation awaits those who are perishing. For a great woe threatens those whom this most wicked and wrathful foe possesses.

[12:13] *And when the dragon saw that he had*

been thrown down to the earth, he pursued the woman.* The devil attacks the church with an inextricable cunning, and the more he is cast out the more he persecutes her.

[12:14] *But the woman was given the two wings of the great eagle that she might fly into the wilderness.* Supported by the two Testaments, the church avoids the poisonous tumults of the world and by the affection of the mind each day seeks the solitude of a quick and gentle spirit. And so in joy the church sings, "Behold, I have gone far away in flight and remain in solitude."[26] Nor is it contradictory that in the psalm the church asked for the wings of a dove[27] while here it received the wings of an eagle. For just as the church, whose youth will be renewed as the eagle's, is represented in the former because of the gift of the Holy Spirit, so in the latter she is symbolized because of the lofty flight and sublime sight by which she sees God with a pure heart.

Where she is to be nourished for a time, and times, and half a time. He is speaking of the whole time of the church, which is comprehended in the number of days mentioned previously. For a "time" signifies one year, "times" signifies two years and "half a time" signifies six months.

[12:15] *The serpent poured water like a river out of his mouth after the woman, to sweep her away with the flood.* Water is symbolic of the violent force of the persecutors, and so it is said, "Perhaps as water they would have swallowed us up."[28] The church, therefore, is not only lifted up by the word of God but also is propelled forward by the force of persecutions as she hastens to fly away from the world.

[12:16] *But the earth opened its mouth and swallowed the river.* This earth is the holy flesh of the Lord, for by the flesh that he

[24]Mt 28:18. [25]See Mt 4:11; Mk 1:13. [26]Ps 55:7 (54:8 LXX). [27]See Ps 55:6 (54:7 LXX). [28]See Ps 124:4 (123:4 LXX).

assumed he swallowed up death,[29] although for a time it had the upper hand over him. And so he taught that we also will swallow up death. We can also understand the church in this image. For by the admonitions and prayers of her mouth, the treacheries of the enemy are avoided.

[12:17] *Then the dragon was angry with the woman, and he went off to make war on the rest of her offspring.* The dragon saw that he could no longer continue the persecutions since they were stopped by the mouth of the holy earth [i.e., the flesh of Christ], and so he armed himself all the more with the mystery of wickedness, so that he might be able to continue his plotting.

Who keep the commandments of God and bear the testimony of Jesus. To keep the commandments of God by faith in Jesus Christ is to fight against the devil and to provoke him to war. But thanks be to God who has brought to naught all that the evil dragon has begun! For, behold, although he tried to kill the Lord incarnate, he was frustrated in this by the Lord's resurrection. And afterward, he worked to take from the apostles the confidence of their teaching, and this was as though he had given himself the task of taking the woman, that is, the whole church, from human affairs. But since he has failed to accomplish this, he fights against the faithful in every age. Therefore there follows . . .

And he stood on the sand of the sea. This means that he stood on the multitude of the people, "which the wind drives away from the face of the earth."[30] For when he wishes to excite plots and wars, he stands on that multitude that is in the habit of adopting his plans.

REVELATION 13

[13:1] *And I saw a beast rising out of the sea.* Depending on the meaning of the context, a beast may have different significances.[1] Here it signifies the body of the devil that rises from the multitude of the impious. For, indeed, we must understand this sea to be that which above was called the abyss.[2] For this reason the dragon is called "the king of all that is in the waters"[3] whose heads, according to David, were broken in the sea.[4]

Having seven heads and ten horns, with ten diadems on its horns. He shows that the seven diadems and the ten horns are the same thing. Before he had said that the dragon wore seven diadems on his seven heads.[5] But now he says that the beast has ten diadems on his seven heads. For, indeed, the numbers seven and ten are the same, for "he will receive sevenfold in that age,"[6] while another Evangelist has "a hundredfold."[7]

And a blasphemous name on his head. For they call their kings "gods," whether it is those who are dead and, as it were, have been translated to heaven to be among the gods or those on the earth whom they call augusti, which is, as they think, a name of divinity.[8] However, in another passage it says that the same beast was "completely full of blasphemous names."[9]

[13:2] *And the beast that I saw was like a leopard, and its feet were like a bear's, and its mouth was like a lion's mouth.* He is likened to a leopard because of the variety of nations, to a bear because of his malice and madness, to a lion because of the power of his body and the haughtiness of his tongue.[10] In the book of Daniel we read that the kingdom of the

---

[29]Translating *qua suscepta deglutiens mortem*. Other manuscripts read *quae susceptam deglutiens mortem*: "which flesh swallowed up death that it had assumed" (PL 93:168). In the latter text it is death that is assumed, not the flesh. [30]See Ps 1:4 (LXX). **Revelation 13** [1]The following comes from Tyconius. Bede probably was following Primasius (CCL 92:193). [2]See Rev 11:7. [3]Job 41:25. [4]Ps 74:13 (73:13 LXX). [5]See Rev 12:3. [6]Lk 18:30 [7]Mt 19:29. [8]The Latin *augustus* means worthy of awe and fear because consecrated to deity. Hence, aweful, elevated. [9]See Rev 17:3. [10]These interpretations derived from Tyconius. See Caesarius of Arles *Exposition on the Apocalypse* 13.2, Homily 10 (PL 35:2435).

Chaldeans was compared with a lion, that of the Persians with a bear and that of the Macedonians with a leopard.[11]

And to it the dragon gave its power. The apostle says this about the body of the devil: "Whose coming is by the activity of Satan with all power, signs and pretended wonders for those who are perishing."[12]

[13:3] *And one of its heads seemed wounded to death, but his mortal wound was healed.* In imitation of our true Head the antichrist dares to exhibit himself to the heads of the earthly kingdom as though he were dead and had risen again and to have himself accepted as Christ, who really did accomplish this. The falsehood of this fiction is said to have been anticipated in Simon Magus.[13]

And the whole earth followed the beast with wonder. He speaks of the part in terms of the whole. He says that the beast is adored, since earthly people will marvel at this false head that imitates as the person of the head who truly was dead but now is living.

[13:4] *And they worshiped the dragon because he had given power to the beast.* They claim that they worship God, who gave power to Christ.

And they worshiped the beast, saying, "Who is like the beast?" They say, "Who is like Christ?" or "Who can overcome him?"

[13:5] *And it was given a mouth uttering haughty words and blasphemy.* "Who is exalted," it says, "above everything that is regarded as god or is worshiped."[14]

[13:6] *And he was allowed to exercise power for forty-two months, and it opened its mouth to utter blasphemies against God.* In the previous three and a half years he does not blaspheme with an open mouth, but his blasphemy occurs in the mystery of iniquity that will be revealed when the separation is effected and the man of sin is made known.[15] Then he will say, "I am the Christ," while now he says, "Here is the Christ and there is the Christ."[16] "To God" means "against God."[17]

To blaspheme his name and his dwelling. Usurping for himself the dignity of the divine name, this impious one will even presume to call the church his own.

[13:7] *And he was allowed to make war on the saints and to conquer them.* From the whole he speaks of that part that can be conquered when, if this is possible, even the elect will be shaken by the violence of the times.[18] This occurs so that those Jews might be condemned who did not believe the truth but accepted the lie.

[13:8] *And all who dwell on the earth worshiped it.* He said "all" but means those who inhabit the earth. For "those who turn away," it says, "will be written in the earth."[19]

Whose names are not written in the book of life of the Lamb. It is right that those who serve the author of death are not written in the book of life and that those who were deceived by the false death of the beast should have no fellowship with the Lamb who bore the sins of the world.

Of the Lamb, it says, who was slain from the beginning of the world.[20] As Peter says, "Of the

---

[11]Dan 7:4-6. [12]2 Thess 2:9-10. [13]See *Acts of Peter* 23-31. According to the *Acts of Peter*, Simon does many acts of sorcery, including raising some from the dead. At every point, however, Saint Peter outdoes him. As a final and glorious demonstration that he is the Power of God, Simon flies over Rome, only by the prayer of Peter to fall to earth and break his leg in three places. [14]2 Thess 2:4. [15]See 2 Thess 2:3, 7. [16]See Mt 24:5, 23. [17]Bede's text of Rev 13:5 has *in blasphemias ad deum*. He explains that *ad deum* here means *adversus deum*. [18]See Mt 24:24. [19]Jer 17:13. [20]By repeating the phrase "of the Lamb" Bede connects the two verses. The Latin, as does the Greek, favors the reading that Bede gives and connects the temporal phase with the Lamb: the Lamb slain from the beginning of the world (*ab origine mundi*). The Greek reads "foundation of the world" (ἀπὸ καταβολῆς κόσμου). The RSV agrees with Bede's second possibility and connects the phrase with the names written: "whose name has not been written before the foundation of the world in the book of life."

Lamb, without blemish, who was foreknown before the foundation of the world but was made manifest at the end of the times."[21] Another version reads that the Lamb was "sealed" from the beginning of the world.[22] It could also be understood by way of transposition, that the names of the saints have been written from the beginning in the book of life.

[13:9] *If anyone has an ear, let him hear.* Whenever the Scriptures introduce this saying, it seeks for an attentive hearer because of the obscurity of the subject matter. Lest the temporary kingdom of the devil be regarded as great, he anticipates human thinking on the matter and says,

[13:10] *"Whoever shall lead into captivity, into captivity he goes."* That is, the devil together with the beast, who seems at the present time to capture the nations in his nets, will suddenly be captured together with his followers.

"Whoever slays with the sword, with the sword must he be slain." Whoever now persecutes the church with physical or even spiritual death, him "will the Lord Jesus slay with the breath of his mouth and destroy by the brilliance of his coming."[23]

This is the endurance and faith of the saints. He promised that the murderer is to be killed, but since "no one is crowned unless he has legitimately contended,"[24] it says that now courage and a strong heart are needed.

Having at first described the beast in general by way of his hypocrisy and then by way of its open mouth, he describes the same blasphemer who similarly works his hypocrisy in those who lead his cause. Finally he describes him as revealed himself.

[13:11] *And I saw another beast rising out of the earth.* He calls it "another" because of its function, but otherwise he is the same. What was the sea is here the earth.[25] Daniel testifies to this, for when he saw four great beasts arising from the sea, he was told, "These four great beasts are four kings who shall arise out of the earth."[26]

It had two horns like a lamb, and it spoke like a dragon. He displays the horns of a lamb, and by these he secretly inserts the poison of the dragon. For through a sham show of holiness he puts forth the lie that the singular wisdom and life that the Lord truly possessed exists rather in himself. And concerning this beast the Lord said, "Beware of false prophets who come to you in sheep's clothing but inwardly are ravenous wolves."[27]

[13:12] *It exercises all the authority of the first beast.* The miserable disciples follow their master in all things.

And he made the earth and its inhabitants worship the first beast. He shows the power of seduction and causes both the body and the soul that inhabits it to be subjected to himself.

Whose mortal wound was healed. That is, he creates the illusion that by rising up he has overcome death. For the Scripture did not say that he was "slain," but it speaks of him "as though slain." As it was also said of the Jews, "They themselves did not enter the praetorium, so that they might not be defiled."[28] The Evangelist did not mean that those already wholly polluted would become polluted were they to enter the praetorium. Nor were the Jews, already complicit in so many crimes, really fearful of being contaminated. Rather, the Evangelist recounted what they were feigning to be the case, as though he was asserting it.

---

[21]1 Pet 1:19-20. [22]This other version most likely comes from Tyconius (see Gryson, CCL 121A:181). [23]2 Thess 2:8. [24]2 Tim 2:5. [25]See Rev 13:1. [26]Dan 7:17. [27]Mt 7:15. [28]Jn 18:28. Outward appearances do not always correspond to reality. By their rejection of Christ, the Jews were defiled and unclean although they did not enter the Roman fortress. Similarly, the outward show of the beast merely hides the fakery by which he confronts the world.

[13:13] *And it worked great signs, even making fire come down from heaven to earth.* He performs the miracle of fire as though it were the greatest of all. For since the Lord Christ gave the gift of miracles to his disciples through the Holy Spirit who had come in fire,[29] with a cunning ruse he deceives even his own disciples as though through a similar charism.

[13:14] *And by the signs that it is allowed to work, it deceives those who dwell on earth.* "For his coming," as it is said, "will be by the activity of Satan with all power and false signs and wonders."[30] It may be that these are called false signs and wonders because he will deceive the senses of people through phantasms and so seems to do what in fact he does not do. Or it may be that these signs, even though they will be astonishing wonders, will lead those to falsehood who, unaware of the power of the devil, will think that such things could not be accomplished apart from divine power. For it was not by a fake fire or storm that the devil destroyed the whole family of the saintly Job together with all of his flock, but by a real fire and a real whirlwind.[31] Whether, then, these are called false signs for this reason or that, without doubt this will prove to be the greatest temptation, that when the pious martyr submits his body to sufferings, before his eyes the torturer will appear to be doing miracles.

Bidding those who dwell on earth to make an image of the beast that was wounded by the sword and lived. That is, they should make an image of the beast by becoming like him. Another version reads, "as though he has a wound by the sword and yet lived."[32] This would mean that by that falsehood they would say that they have died and been raised with the Christ. By this claim he would make himself to be both

God and mediator between himself and his followers. For he does not have another one, as does our Lord Christ, between whom and his followers he might be mediator.[33]

[13:15] *And it was allowed to give breath to the image of the beast.* This means that by skillfully making himself an image of the beast, he pretended to give the "Spirit of truth" to the very people who will be filled with this falsehood.

So that the image of the beast should even speak. Not only will he delude the miserable multitude by the counterfeit spirit through fire, he will also make them suitable for the teaching of others.

And he will cause those who would not worship the image of the beast to be slain. He will do this so that they not become that image that they seduce but that they become that image to which they make the people similar.[34] Therefore, the people who live as the image of the beast adores the image of the beast, that is, as a people that adores whatever the devil conjures up.

[13:16] *And he will cause all, both the small and the great and the rich and the poor.* This does not refer to all without exception as if it included also the Gentiles. It refers to those who belong to this mystery of iniquity.

To have the mark on the right hand or on the forehead. The mark is the mystery of iniquity that under the name of Christ the hypocrites receive in deed and confession.[35]

[13:17] *So that no one can buy or sell.* By this mention of selling and buying he teaches that, just as the church for good delivered the creed for the benefit of our salvation, so they for evil confine themselves to such a definition, so that they allow no freedom for buying or sell-

---

[29]See Acts 2:1-4.　[30]2 Thess 2:9.　[31]See Job 1:16, 19.　[32]This reading probably comes from Tyconius (Gryson, CCL 121A:181).　[33]By deceit the antichrist assumes the place of both God and mediator. By contrast, Christ can be and is a true mediator, for he stands between the Father and humankind.　[34]The idea of Bede is that the beast works so that Christians do not become the true image of Christ but rather in their words and deeds the image of the beast. See Caesarius of Arles *Exposition on the Apocalypse* 13.15, Homily 11.　[35]The hand refers to work or behavior, the forehead to thought or doctrine.

ing, just as merchants who sail in one ship are bound to a uniform signal.

Unless he has the mark of the name of the beast or the number of its name. This refers to any person who participates in his fraudulent enterprise. For the mark, that is, the stamp, the name of the beast and the number of its name is one thing.

[13:18] *For it is a human number.* He says this lest we should think, as do some, that the beast is either the devil or a demon. He is rather one from the human race in whom the fullness of Satan will inhabit bodily. For he is "the man of sin" and the "son of perdition."[36]

And its number is six hundred and sixty-six. Among the Greeks this number is said to be found in the name Teitan, that is, "giant." They reckon in this way: T = 300, E = 5, I = 10, T =300, A = 1, N = 50. Moreover, they think that the antichrist will usurp this name for himself as though it surpassed all others in power and that he will boastfully proclaim himself to be that one of whom it is written, "As a giant he rejoiced to run his course; his going forth is from highest heaven."[37] However, Primasius advances another name that can also give this number. He suggests "ANTE-ΜΟΣ," which means "opposed to honor" and is reckoned in this way: A = 1, N = 50, T = 300, E = 5, M = 40, O = 70, Σ = 200. He suggests also the word "APNOUME," which means "I deny" and is reckoned as follows: A = 1, R = 100, N = 50, O = 70, U = 400, M = 40, E = 5.[38] Through these titles both the character of the person and the fierceness of the antichrist are indicated. However, why one so desirous of praise should desire to be designated by such a mark requires a detailed explanation.

Another interpretation: Who is unaware that the number six, the number of days in which the world was created, is symbolic of a completed work? Or, that this number whether in simple form or multiplied by ten or by a hundred signifies the fruit of the same perfection to be thirtyfold, sixtyfold or a hundredfold? "Now the weight of gold that came to Solomon in one year was 666 talents."[39] Therefore, this seducer tyrant will attempt to exact for himself that tax that is rightfully due and paid to the true king.

REVELATION 14

[14:1] *And I looked, and behold, the Lamb stood on Mount Zion.* That is, by the example of his power and the safety of his protection the Lord Christ guarded his church, which was toiling under the burden of her struggles. For although the body that had been confounded by the power of the devil and marked by his brand was shown,[1] lest you fear that the body of the Lamb had been overcome by the furor of the beast, he showed also the church rejoicing with her usual brightness and number. Note as well that the beast stands on the sand of the sea,[2] while the Lamb stands on Mount Zion.

And with him a hundred and forty-four thousand. This finite number should be regarded as representing an infinite number and by the meaning of a hidden mystery suitable for that virginal throng that loves God with all its heart, all its soul and all its mind,[3] and by the integrity of the body, which consists of four qualities, is consecrated to him. For three times three makes nine, and four times four makes sixteen, and sixteen times nine completes the number of 144,000,[4] so that there should be no doubt concerning the remaining members of the church when such a perfect

---

[36]2 Thess 2:3. [37]Ps 19:5-6 (18:6-7 LXX). [38]See Primasius (CCL 92:203-5). Perhaps Primasius interprets ΑΝΤΕΜΟΣ to be equivalent to ΑΝΤΙ + ΤΙΜΟΣ ("contrary to honor") in order to refer to Antemos, emperor of the west from 467 to 472, who was much hated in Italy. [39]1 Kings 10:14 (3 Kings 10:14 LXX). **Revelation 14** [1]That is, in Rev 13:11-17. [2]See Rev 12:18. [3]See Mt 22:37. [4]The three refers to the heart, soul and mind.

multitude is seen by those who placed in the midst of a more difficult life are rightly seen with the Lamb on Mount Zion.

Having his name and the name of his Father written on their foreheads. This is by way of analogy with the mark on the forehead of the body of the beast,[5] for it says that God and Christ were written on the foreheads of the church.

[14:2] *And I heard a voice from heaven like the sound of many waters.* The loud voice of the saints is the great devotion of love which, it says, he heard from heaven. When he said that those who uttered the voice stood on Mount Zion, it was to indicate that by *Mount Zion* he referred to nothing other than to the church, which, encouraged toward overcoming the distresses of her afflictions by the sublime joy of the contemplation of her king, celebrates his struggles at the same time by praise and by imitation. This is truly to sing to the Lamb who is standing on Mount Zion.

And the voice that I heard was like harpists playing on their harps. Although all the saints are harpists of God who crucify their flesh with its vices and lusts and praise him with psalter and harp,[6] how much more are they who, by the privilege of an angelic purity, render themselves totally a sacrifice to the Lord and in a particular way deny themselves and, taking up their cross, "follow the Lamb wherever he goes."[7]

[14:3] *And they sang as if a new song before the throne.* The old song was this: "Blessed is he who has his seed in Zion and his household in Jerusalem."[8] However, the new song is this: "Rejoice, O barren one, who did not bear,"[9] and again, "To the eunuchs in my house and within

my walls, says the Lord, I shall give a place and a name better than sons and daughters."[10]

And no one could say that song except the hundred and forty-four thousand who had been redeemed from the earth. To sing the song to the Lamb is especially to rejoice with him for eternity before all the faithful, especially concerning the incorruptibility of the flesh. Nevertheless, the other elect are able to hear the song, although they cannot sing it, because through love they have been made glad in their high status, although they do not rise to their rewards.[11]

[14:4] *For they are virgins; it is these who follow the Lamb wherever he will go.* The blessed Augustine has beautifully expounded these words in his exhortation to the virgins: "Press on, saints of God, youths and maidens, men and women, celibates and virgins; press on and persevere to the end. Praise the Lord more sweetly, whom you think on more richly. Hope in him more happily, whom you serve more readily; love him more ardently, whom you please more attentively. With loins girded and lamps burning, wait for the Lord, when he comes from the marriage.[12] You will bring to the marriage of the Lamb a new song that you shall sing on your harps, such as no one shall be able to utter but you. For in the Apocalypse this is how you were seen by a certain one beloved above others by the Lamb, who was in the habit of lying on his breast.[13] He saw you, twelve times twelve thousand of holy harpists, of undefiled virginity in body, of inviolate truth in heart. Follow the Lamb because the flesh of the Lamb is also virginal; follow him by the virginity of heart and of flesh wherever he shall go. For what is it to follow, unless to imitate? For 'Christ suffered for us, leaving

---

[5]See Rev 13:16. [6]See Gal 5:24; Ps 150:3 (149:3 LXX). Bede is using the image of the harp as symbol of crucifixion, here as a symbol of crucifying the flesh by refusing its desires. [7]See Mt 16:24. In this context Bede is speaking of the virgins and monks. [8]Is 31:9 (LXX). [9]Is 54:1. [10]Is 56:5. [11]Bede seems to be distinguishing between the elect who presently enjoy the delights of heaven and the elect who yet remain in their earthly sojourn. [12]See Lk 12:35-36. [13]See Jn 13:23-25.

us an example that we should follow in his footsteps.'"[14]

These have been redeemed from all as first fruits for God and the Lamb. From that holy and unblemished flock of the church they are chosen by the Holy Spirit as sacrifices more holy and more pure because of the merits of their will. The apostle, having no command of the Lord concerning them, implores them to present their bodies as a living sacrifice, holy and pleasing to God.[15]

[14:5] *And in their mouth no lie was found.* Virgins are not joined to the divine following because of chastity only, unless they also lead a life unblemished by any infection of sin. Tyconius does not interpret this vision to refer especially to virgins but generally to the whole church, which the apostle betroths "to one husband, to present a pure virgin to Christ,"[16] and he concludes in this way: "He did not say 'no lie was in their mouth,' but 'no lie is found.'" As the apostle says, "And such were you, but you have been washed,"[17] and "the iniquity of the unjust will not harm him on the day he will have turned from his iniquity,"[18] and he will be able to be a virgin, and deceit will not be found in his mouth. For those who are chaste and pure he calls virgins.

[14:6] *And I saw another angel flying in midheaven, with an eternal gospel.* Since he had described the anticipated and diverse battles that the church sojourning in the world wages against the dragon, it remains now to assign to either army the appropriate prize, showing what penalty will follow those who are evil and what reward will follow those who are good. For this reason, the preacher who runs about within the church carries the gospel of the eternal kingdom.

To proclaim the gospel to those who sit on the earth. It is appropriate that those who are lifted up by celestial flight should also, through preaching, lift their earthly minds from the place of their present sluggishness.

And on every nation and tribe and tongue. "This gospel," it says, "will be preached throughout the whole world, and then the end will come."[19]

[14:7] *"Fear the Lord and give him honor, for the hour of his judgment has come."* The more you look to your salvation, it says, the quicker the retribution, which forever is unchangeable, awaits you who fear the Lord, who made the world, rather than the temporal tyranny of the beast.

[14:8] *"Fallen, fallen, is Babylon the great."* It says that the ruinous city of the devil has already fallen. It says this either according the custom of the Scripture, which often presents something as past that it knows will inevitably be accomplished, or it means that the haughty have been cast down by the Lord at that very time when they were puffed up by the devil, as the psalm says: "You did cast them down, while they were being lifted up."[20]

"She who made all nations drink the wine of the wrath of her fornication." The city of the impious, which is gathered together from all nations, makes the nations, that is, its members drunk from the wine of error. However, the city of the Lord, which cultivates the vineyard of Sorek,[21] does not desire to be inebriated by that wine in which there is excess, lest it be deprived of the promised payment of life.

---

[14]1 Pet 2:21. See Augustine *On Holy Virginity* 27 (FC 27:173). Primasius also quotes Augustine in his commentary on Rev 14:2-4 (CCL 92:211-14). It is possible that Bede knew of the Augustine material by way of Primasius. In his *Homily on the Gospels* 1.13, Bede presents a long application of Rev 14:4 to Benedict Biscop, founder of the monasteries of Wearmouth and Jarrow and teacher of Bede (CS 110:130-31). [15]See Rom 12:1. [16]See 2 Cor 11:2. [17]1 Cor 6:11. [18]Ezek 33:12. [19]Mt 24:14. [20]Ps 72:18 (LXX). Bede is following Primasius, who seems to be following Tyconius (CCL 92:215-16). [21]See Is 5:2. The Hebrew word *soreq* probably refers to the grapes native to the valley of Sorek, west of Jerusalem.

[14:9] *"If anyone worships the beast and its image."* That is, if anyone worships the devil and the head that was as though slain.[22]

"And receives a mark on his forehead or on his hand." When he says "on the forehead or on the hand," he indicates that some are marked by the devil with a heinous confession and some simply by their work.

[14:10] *"And he shall drink from the wine of God's wrath, which is unmixed in the cup of his wrath."* When he says "and he shall drink," he shows that there is also another who will drink, lest he exclude him who, although he is not visibly mixed with the nations, nevertheless worships the same beast under the name of Christ. Rightly, however, are those who extend the cup of the wrath of fornication brought low by the cup of the Lord's wrath, not, as according to Jeremiah,[23] that they might vomit out the malice of their hearts that are to be cleansed, but that being condemned and in a senseless stupor they might perish by an eternal death.

"And he will be tormented with fire and sulphur in the sight of the holy angels." The saints who reign with the Lord are always able to observe the punishment of the wicked, so that they might give the greater thanks to their Redeemer and sing forever of the mercies of the Lord. For the torments of the wicked that are seen do not distress those who are in agreement with the just Judge, just as the rest of Lazarus that was seen was able to give no refreshment to the rich man who was buried in the flames.[24]

[14:11] *"And they who worship the beast and its image have no rest, day or night."* They say that a lion will spare a man who is lying on the ground. But this beast is more ferocious than a lion, for the more he is adored, the more he inflicts sufferings.

"And if anyone receives the mark of its name." Saint Augustine interprets the beast to be the impious city. That is, his image is his simulation, namely, those who are Christians by a deceitful image, for he interprets the mark as the brand of guilt, which they adore and to which they are subjected and consent.[25]

[14:12] *Here is the endurance of the saints.* Although the beast will be ferocious, nonetheless this momentary suffering, which will be rewarded with eternal bliss, will not distress the saints. For the saints will see their persecutors, who were arrogant for a short time, suffering eternal penalties along with the beast.

[14:13] *And I heard a voice from heaven saying, "Write!"* The harmony of those who preach is beautiful. For, see, now the one announces that the kingdom of the Lord is come; the other announces the fall of the city of the devil. One indicates the flames of the wicked, while another announces the rest of the blessed. This last one projects his voice from heaven and instructs the seer that for an eternal memory it is worthy to be committed to writing. For the righteous rejoice that their names are written in heaven, while the impious are blotted out of the book of the living.

"Blessed are the dead who die in the Lord." Thank you, Jesus, that you make blessed in heaven those who on earth die in you. How much more, then, those who place their happy souls both in you and in your faith?

"From this time forward," says the Spirit, *"that they may rest from their labors, for their deeds follow them."* Just as he had said that the impious never have any rest,[26] so he teaches that the faithful, assisted by their previous works, will rest "from henceforth," that is, from the time of death. For "when he shall have given sleep to his beloved, this is the inheritance of the Lord."[27] However, "the slug-

---

[22]See Rev 13:3. [23]See Jer 25:27. [24]See Lk 16:23-24. [25]Augustine *City of God* 20.9 (FC 24:278). [26]See Rev 14:11. [27]Ps 127:2-3 (126:2-3 LXX).

gard would not plow in the cold; therefore he will beg at the time of harvest, but nothing will be given him."[28]

[14:14] *And I looked, and, behold, a white cloud, and seated on the cloud one like a son of man.* Until now we have heard the voices of heralds. However, now the person of the judge himself is revealed, who, when he comes for judgment, covers the glory of his divinity with a cloud of flesh so that the wicked might behold him whom they pierced.[29]

With a golden crown on his head. What kind of crown this is was described above concerning the adornment of the woman: "And on her head a crown of twelve stars."[30] But perhaps it may signify the victory of the king.

And a sharp sickle in his hand. The sharp sickle refers to the judicial sentence of separation, and this judgment can in no way be avoided. We are most certainly within it, no matter where we might try to flee, for whatever is felled by the sickle falls within.

[14:15] *And another angel came out from the temple, calling with a loud voice to him who sat on the cloud.* The angels, who in the Gospel are the reapers of the earth[31] and who are all "sent to minister for the sake of those who are to obtain the inheritance of salvation,"[32] consider every merit of the church and daily report them to the Lord.

"Put in your sickle and reap, for the hour to reap has come, for the harvest of the earth is ripe." Behold, they say, as iniquity increases, the love of many grows cold,[33] and because the heat of evil people presses on it, the harvest of the world has virtually ceased to be green. Therefore, lest any grain already mature fall down, the days will be shortened for the sake of the elect,[34] and the chaff and

tares will be cast into the flames, but the heavenly fruit will be stored in the granaries of blessedness.[35]

[14:17] *And another angel came out of the temple that is in heaven, and he too had a sharp sickle.* If Christ was seen on the white cloud as a reaper, who is this vintager, unless the same person is aptly repeated because of the twofold fruit of the church? For he who sowed good seed in his field is also he who planted a vineyard in a fertile place.[36] However, both plantings have come to ruin because of the neglect of the caretakers.[37]

[14:18] *Then another angel came out from the altar who has power over fire, and he called with a loud voice.* As Jerome says, "The duty of the angels is twofold. Some assign rewards to the righteous; others preside over the various torments."[38] As it is said, "Who makes the winds to be his messengers and the flaming fire his ministers."[39]

The two angels who announce that the harvest is dry and that the vineyard is ripe can be understood to represent the prayers of the church, which with a loud voice, that is, with a fervent desire, daily prays that the kingdom of the Lord come, saying, "Put in your sharp sickle and gather the clusters of the vine of the earth." As it was with the harvest, so also the vintage is partly of the earth and partly of heaven. But the maturation of both indicates the end of the age.

"For its grapes are ripe." This means that their sins have reached their completion, although the perfection of those who are good can also be called ripeness. As the holy Pope Gregory said, "Although the end of the world is dependent on its own course, nevertheless, finding some who are more perverse, he makes

[28]Prov 20:4. [29]See Zech 12:10; Jn 19:37. [30]See Rev 12:1, where Bede interpreted the crown to be either the twelve apostles or Christ. [31]See Mt 13:39. [32]See Heb 1:14. [33]See Mt 24:12. [34]See Mt 24:22. [35]See Mt 13:30. [36]See Mt 13:24; Is 5:1. [37]By *caretakers* Bede refers to the priests and bishops. [38]See Jerome *Commentary on Daniel* 7:10 (CCL 75A:846). [39]Ps 104:4 (103:4 LXX).

known to them that they are justly oppressed by its destruction."[40]

[14:19] *And the angel swung his sickle on the earth and gathered the vintage of the earth.* He who has the sickle for the harvest is also he who has the sickle for the vintage. For there is one judgment, and it shall occur at one time. But in the harvest and in the vintage he shows the beginning and the end of the same suffering.

[14:20] *And threw it into the great wine vat—or the wine press—of the wrath of God, and the wine vat was trodden outside the city.* Should this harvest and vintage pertain only to the evil, the wine press signifies punishment. However, should they also pertain to the good, then the treading of the wine press and the threshing of the floor grinds down that which is useless and tests that which is useful. For it is as the apostle said, precious metals are tested by fire, but wood, hay and stubble are consumed by fire.[41] And both are accomplished outside the heavenly Jerusalem. The wine vat of wrath is so called by a manner of speaking, as it is said, "On the evil day the Lord delivered him."[42]

And blood flowed from the wine vat to the bridles of the horses. Vengeance comes out, even to the rulers of the peoples. For in the final struggle vengeance for the shedding of the blood of the saints will go to the devil and his angels, as it is written: "You have sinned in blood, and blood will pursue you."[43] We discussed the horses above.

For one thousand six hundred stadia. That is, through all of the four corners of the world. For four is multiplied by four, as in four square-shaped faces and in wheels; for four times four hundred is one thousand six hundred.

Tyconius interprets the harvester and the vintager to be the church, which shines after the fires of persecution and holds the power of binding and loosing. He says that the angels from the temple and from the altar announce the kingdom of the Lord, not with an audible voice but by the suggestion of the Holy Spirit who works in Christ's body and teaches that now is the time for the evil to be accursed. And the Spirit has power over the fire, that is, that which comes out of the mouth of the witnesses and consumes their enemies.

The text speaks thus far of the struggle of the church and of the final end of both contests.

Here Begins the Third Book

REVELATION 15

[15:1] *And I saw another portent in heaven great and wonderful.* The order of the narrative is once more restored. Since he is about to narrate the same plagues of the final persecution, he wishes the hearer to become attentive, and so he says a "portent great and wonderful."

Seven angels, that is, the church full of the sevenfold grace, *with seven plagues, which are the last, for with them the wrath of God is ended.* He calls the seven plagues the "last," because the wrath of God always strikes a rebellious people with seven plagues, that is, he strikes them utterly and completely, as it is often stated in Leviticus: "I will strike you with seven plagues."[1] And these future persecutions are the last, since the church will have come out from the midst of them.

[15:2] *And I saw what appeared to be a sea of glass mingled with fire.* That is, he saw the translucent font of baptism consecrated by the fire of the Holy Spirit. Or, he saw a sea made red by martyrdom, since that color is typical of fire.

---

[40]Gregory the Great *Homilies on the Gospels* 35.2 (CS 123:303; CCL 141:323). [41]See 1 Cor 3:12-15. [42]Ps 41:1 (40:2 LXX). [43]Ezek 35:6. **Revelation 15** [1]For example, Lev 26:24, 28.

And those who had conquered the beast and its image, standing on the sea of glass. Those who conquer the deceits of the beast are seen in consequence of this to stand on the fire of baptism, desirous, as the apostle says, "to contend for the faith once delivered to the saints."[2]

[15:3] *With harps of God, and they sing the song of Moses, the servant of God, and the song of the Lamb.* That is, they bear hearts that have spoken praise to God and that are melodious with the truth of both Testaments. Or, this is the flesh extended on the cross of the passion[3] where not only the sound of a voice but also the benefit of a good work is signified.

"*Great and wonderful are your deeds, O Lord God Almighty! Just and true are your ways, O king of the ages!*" and the rest. This song is located in both Testaments where the Lord is sung as true and merciful and to be adored as judge by all ages.

[15:5] He repeats what he had said before, saying, *After this I looked, and behold, the temple of the tent of witness in heaven was opened.* The vision corresponds to the hymn. For in order that the Lord might be adored by all nations, the temple of the mysteries of God, once enclosed in the walls of one city, now begins to be opened spiritually to the whole world.

[15:6] *And out of the temple came the seven angels with the seven plagues.* This is what Mark spoke about: "And they went forth and preached everywhere."[4]

Robed in a pure white stone.[5] The apostle says, "For as many of you as were baptized into Christ have put on Christ."[6] For Christ is the elect chief Cornerstone.[7] Or, if one should understand the singular stone to represent a plural, the stone signifies the various beauties of the virtues.

Another translation renders "white linen." This would indicate the mortification of the flesh that our teachers endure. It says, "I pommel my body and subdue it to servitude, lest after preaching to others, I myself should be disqualified."[8]

And their breasts girded with golden girdles. Whoever desires to preach mighty things, let him not only mortify the body but also bind his breast with the gold of wisdom. Or, to bind the breast with golden girdles is to bind every movement of our changeable thoughts by the chains of love alone.

[15:7] *And one of the four living creatures gave the seven angels seven bowls full of the wrath of the living God.* These are the bowls that are carried with their odors by the living creatures and the elders, who are the church and who also are the seven angels. Indeed, when they are poured out by the saints before the coming of the kingdom of God, these bowls are said to contain both the sweetness of supplications as well as the wrath of punishments. For at that time the judgments of God, no longer hidden as in an abyss but opened as in bowls, are said to carry salvation to the righteous but damnation to the impious. As the apostle says, "For we are the good odor of Christ to God among those who are being saved and among those who are perishing."[9]

[15:8] *And the temple was filled with smoke from his majesty and from his power.* When she is about to preach to the nations, the church is first set aglow with the fire of love and emits the smoke of a pious confession, "giving thanks to God for his inexpressible gift."[10]

---

[2]Jude 3. [3]Again the harp is an image of the cross on which the flesh is extended as are the strings. [4]Mk 16:20. [5]The text of Bede reads "stone" (*lapide*) corresponding to the variant Greek reading λίθον (A C 2053 2062). Most manuscripts read λίνον ("linen"), which is the reading of most translations (except RSV). For discussion see Gryson (CCL 121A:182-83). [6]Gal 3:27. [7]See Is 28:16; 1 Pet 2:6. [8]1 Cor 9:27. [9]2 Cor 2:15. [10]2 Cor 9:15.

And no one could enter the temple until the seven plagues of the seven angels were ended. No one may be incorporated among the members of the church except that one who hears the mysteries of the faith and is taught by our teachers that Jesus is "ordained by God to be the judge of the living and the dead."[11] However, if one interprets the smoke to be the hidden mysteries of the judgments of God, these remain impenetrable and closed to mortal beings until the plagues of the present age are ended and the Lord then shall come, who both illumines what has been hidden in the darkness and makes manifest to what extent the coming of the antichrist will be useful either for the testing of the faith of the church or for the blinding of the Jews, who have not received the love of the truth that they might be saved.

REVELATION 16

[16:1] *"Go and pour out on the earth the seven bowls of the wrath of God."* Authority was given to the church to inflict judgment on those who are to be damned and in mercy to give absolution to those who had converted. And to be sure, all angels were commanded to pour out judgment on the earth. But likewise earthly people are given various names for the variety of their sins. In this way the number seven reckons not only the fullness of preaching and of vengeance but also the fullness of sin.[1]

[16:2] *And the first angel went out and poured out his bowl on the earth.* Those who preach pour out the bowls of the wrath of God in a twofold manner. By a spiritual judgment they inflict the punishments given out by the impious on those very same impious, as Peter said to Simon, "May your money perish with you."[2] Or those who preach by their preaching

reveal the impious to the holy church, as Peter said, "From of old their condemnation has not been idle, and their destruction has not been asleep."[3]

And we may understand this passage also in a third way. When the preaching of the truth is heard, every sinner is corrupted by the more severe wound of unbelief. About this the Lord said, "If I had not come and spoken to them, they would not have sin."[4]

And a foul and evil sore came on people who bore the mark of the beast. Those who have forsaken the Lord and worship the devil will spiritually perish from the most grievous sore of that very impiety.

[16:3] *And the second angel poured his bowl on the sea, and it became as the blood of a dead person, and every living thing died that was in the sea.* Those who not only are marked by the sign of the beast but also attack the steadfast servants of Christ by the waves of bitter persecution will be punished by a spiritual revenge, which here he calls blood. And those who boasted that they are alive will be proved to have served the author of death.

[16:4] *And the third angel poured out his bowl on the rivers and on the fountains of water, and they became blood.* Those who feign to offer that which is sweet so that they might pour out their poison on the unaware will be smitten by the deserved revenge of an unceasing plague.

[16:5] *And I heard the angel of the waters say, "Just are you, who is and was, the Holy One, for you have judged these things."* By the angel of the waters he refers to all the messengers of the peoples who by an inner affection raise up in unison a cry of praise to God, for he will avenge the blood of his servants by giving their murderers death to drink.

---

[11]Acts 10:42. **Revelation 16** [1]"Sin" translates the Latin *noxa*, which can mean a harm, offense or punishment. The context seems to require the meaning of offense or sin. [2]Acts 8:20. [3]2 Pet 2:3. [4]Jn 15:22.

[16:7] *And I heard another angel say from the altar,*[5] *"Yes, Lord God Almighty, true and just are your judgments!"* That which the angels are that also is the altar that gives thanks to God, namely, the inner affection of the saints, whether of the angels or of those human beings who lead the people by teaching.

[16:8] *And the fourth angel poured out his bowl on the sun, and it was allowed to scorch people with heat and fire.* The persecutors of the church, who like the burning sun attempt to dry up the seed of the word of God, will be burned in the future fire by the flames of Gehenna. Or, if one interprets the sun to be the splendor of the wise, it is not given to the angel to pour out on the sun, but it is given to the sun itself to punish people with heat and fire. For while wise people, conquered by torments, are affected by the error of having done evil, the weak, persuaded by their example, are inflamed by temporal desires. However, the heat may also be understood to be that by which the body of the devil is incurably tormented by the steadfastness of the saints and is incited to blasphemy. The prophet has spoken concerning this fire, "Zeal overcomes a people without understanding, and now fire consumes the adversaries."[6] It says "and now" because the fire of the last judgment is reserved.

[16:9] *And people were scorched by the fierce heat.* In the present time, so far as it is permitted, the devil glorifies his followers, although the Holy Spirit has designated such glorification and joy to be nothing but plagues and sorrows. For we also read above that the army of the devil has killed people with fire, smoke and sulphur. Not that he killed them openly, but rather that with these plagues he binds to himself those who were in agreement with him.

[16:10] *The fifth angel poured his bowl on the throne of the beast, and its kingdom was placed in darkness.* The throne of the beast, or his kingdom, as it were, his judicial authority is darkened by plagues of this kind, that is, by the false joy of earthly happiness. It became dark by being destitute of light, as the psalmist says: "You did cast them down even while they were being lifted up."[7] He did not say, "after they had been lifted up" you cast them down.[8]

And they gnawed their tongues in anguish. Just as a righteous person will eat the fruit of his labors, so also an ungodly person, given punishments worthy of his blasphemy, is sated, as it were, with his own tongue. Therefore, those who blaspheme are simply harming themselves, thinking that the wrath of God by which they are impaled is in fact gladness.

[16:11] *And they blasphemed the God of heaven for their pain and sores.* He does not refer to their hardness of heart but to the righteous indignation of God, who gave to them such a plague that in it they would not remember. For when afflicted by a bodily punishment, who does not feel the hand of God, as did Antiochus?[9] It says "they cursed," not that they did this openly, but in that they reveled in their sins.

[16:12] *The sixth angel poured his bowl on the great river Euphrates, and its water was dried up to prepare the way for the kings from the east.* While the abundance of the people of Babylon perishes, in which nothing living and nothing green shall remain that is not fit for the fire—for this is what it said above, "The harvest of the earth is ripe"[10]—the saintly

---

[5]The text of Bede reads *alterum ab altari dicentem*. This reading occurs also in a very few Greek manuscripts (046 2329) and in the Latin a (61). Most manuscripts have the altar itself speaking, which also is the sense of Bede's comments. [6]See Is 26:11. [7]Ps 72:18 (LXX). [8]The idea of Bede is not that the haughty are cast down but that the exaltation of a false happiness is itself a divine judgment, for it serves to further entrap the sinner in his sin. [9]See 2 Macc 9:5-12. [10]See Rev 14:15.

kings hasten toward the sun of righteousness. There is another interpretation. Just as "while the impious person is exalted, the poor person is consumed,"[11] so also "when the scoffer is stricken, the wise person becomes more prudent."[12]

However, as is his habit, the author passes over the seventh angel and briefly recapitulates from the beginning.

[16:13] *And I saw from the mouth of the dragon and from the mouth of the beast and from the mouth of the false prophet three foul spirits like frogs.* The spirit of the devil and of the antichrist and of those who are placed over his body, which is said to be threefold for the number of the parts of a body, is likened to frogs. For frogs are creatures horrible in their places, in their appearance and in their disgusting croaking. Although they seem to dwell in the waters, they nevertheless roll around in the muck and filth. Hypocrites likewise promise the water of life to their followers but lie dead in the filth that those who believe have deposited in the water.[13] So also Pharaoh, who sought to destroy the people in the watery deep, was killed in that same place when he ventured to enter in after them.[14]

[16:14] *For they are the spirits of demons, performing signs.* Just as was the case concerning the magicians of Pharaoh, so we are also to believe that these spirits will do signs. Nor without cause did he recall these to mind when he mentioned the frogs, for he wished to foretell that the ministers of Satan would then do similar signs. For until the sign of the frogs, the magicians were permitted to prevail

through their words of magic.[15]

And they go abroad to the kings of the whole world, to assemble them for battle on the great day of God Almighty. Just as there are holy kings for whom the way of the east is laid open when the Euphrates is dried up, so also there are evil kings of the earth. These are not assembled from all the world into one place, but each people will fight against the saints in their own place. By "the great day of the Lord" he means the entire time from the Lord's passion to the end of time. It is also possible to understand this as the day of judgment, when the army of the devil, gathered together from the whole time of the present life, will confront the Lord, the king, to be destroyed.

[16:15] *"Lo, I am coming like a thief."* Another translation renders this more suitably: "On the great day of God Almighty, behold, he comes as a thief."[16]

"Blessed is he who is awake and keeps his garments that he may not go naked and they see his dishonor." "Blessed are those whose sins are covered,"[17] who before the eyes of the saints cover the dishonor of a reprehensible life at the judgment with the covering of a subsequent good work.[18] Also in the Gospel, the Lord commands his servants to be vigilant by the example of a thief for whom they must be on guard.[19]

[16:16] *And he will gather them at the place that is called in Hebrew Armageddon.* Elsewhere he mentions this place and says, "He gathered them for battle, and they surrounded the camp of the saints and the beloved city,"[20] that is, the church. On the other hand, the

---

[11]Ps 9:23 (lxx). [12]Prov 19:25. [13]Bede seems to refer to heretics or to schismatics who proffer an invalid baptism that does not wash away sin, although they claim that it does. Caesarius of Arles thinks of the false Christian who is baptized but does not live accordingly: "Hypocrites likewise do not spend their time in the waters, as they seem to, but in filthy acts that those who believe lay aside in the water" (*Exposition on the Apocalypse* 16.13-14, Homily 13 [PL 35:2439]). [14]Ex 14:26-29. The phrase "in the watery deep" translates *in baptismo,* which word allows Bede to continue with the image of baptism. [15]See Ex 8:1-11. [16]This other translation comes from Tyconius (see Gryson, CCL 121A:181). [17]Ps 32:1 (31:1 lxx). [18]These words are taken from Gregory the Great *Moralia* 2.81 (CCL 143:109). [19]See Mt 24:43. [20]Rev 20:8-9.

place of the ungodly can be understood to be the devil, who in the man of perdition, puffed up with an usurped deity, will be glad to resume his former plots, which were formerly forbidden by the Lord. For Armageddon is interpreted to mean "a general uprising in former things" or "a spherical mountain."[21]

[16:17] *The seventh angel poured his bowl into the air, and a great voice came out of the temple, from the throne, saying, "It is done!"* Just as we said before,[22] the blood of vengeance extends as far as the bridles of the horses, that is, to the unclean spirits, so also here, when the final revenge was poured over those same powers of the air, it is said, "It is done." That is, the end is come when, as the apostle says, "the last enemy, death, will be destroyed."[23]

Until now the final persecution has been described under the guise of plagues. However, Tyconius wants to interpret all these things in a different way.[24] The plague that cannot be healed and the great wrath, he says, is to receive the power of sinning, especially against the saints, and as yet not to be overcome by the greater wrath of God. What appears to be the blessedness of those who are evil is death, even as the torments and humiliation of the church is its glory. For at that time all of the impious people will remain uninjured by any plague of the body, as those who have received the full power to effect their savagery. Nor will there be any need then, at the completion of sins and the consummation of wrath, for any one of the wicked to be whipped and restrained from fury.

He recapitulates from that persecution and now describes the fall of the impious city.

[16:18] *And there were flashes of lightning, voices and peals of thunder, and there was a great earthquake such as had never been since there were human beings.* When at the end of time there will be such "a tribulation as has not been from the beginning,"[25] the greatest signs will similarly be evident. However, whether they come from the side of those who are good or from the side of those who are evil or come from both sides, as was the case with Moses and the magicians,[26] is in this passage not sufficiently made clear.

[16:19] *The great city was split into three parts.* The impious city wages a threefold war against the church of Christ. The nations and the Jews attack the church in open conflict, while the heretics attack it by way of secret defections, and the false brethren trouble it by evil examples.[27] This very thing was also symbolized above in the images of the three evil horses, namely, the red one, the black one and the white one.[28]

And the cities of the nations fell. That is, all the strength and confidence of the nations fell. "For the rejoicing of the ungodly is their utter ruin, and the joy of the iniquitous is their destruction."[29]

And God remembered great Babylon, to give to her the cup of the wine of the fury of his wrath. Babylon falls or drinks the wrath of God at that moment when she receives power against Jerusalem, especially against the last Jerusalem. For this reason it said that Babylon fell by an earthquake that she caused for the church. If, however, you refer this passage to the day of judgment, then the ungodly, who now "says

---

[21]See Jerome *Onomasticon, de apocalypsi Johannis* (CCL 72:159). Jerome gives four possibilities for Armageddon: *Armageddon consurrectio tecti sive consurrectio in priora. Sed melius mons a latrunculis vel mons globosus.* ("Armageddon means either an uprising of the roof or an uprising in former things. But a better meaning might be a mountain from robbers or a spherical mountain.") [22]See Rev 14:20. [23]1 Cor 15:26. [24]The Tyconian background of this interpretation can be observed in the remarks of Caesarius of Arles *Exposition on the Apocalypse* 16:17, Homily 13 (PL 35:2440). [25]See Mt 24:21. [26]See Ex 7:8-13. [27]This interpretation seems to arise from Tyconius, although exactly who comprise the three parts can vary. Primasius thinks of the nations, the heretics and Jews, and the false brethren (*Commentary on the Apocalypse* 16.19 [CCL 92:235]). Caesarius thinks of the nations, the heretics and false brethren, and the catholic church (*Exposition on the Apocalypse* 16.19, Homily 13 [PL 35:2440]). [28]See Rev 6:4, 5-6, 8. [29]See Job 20:5 (LXX).

in his heart, 'God has forgotten,'"[30] will come into the remembrance of God.

[16:20] *And every island fled away, and no mountains were to be found.* The church, which is compared with islands and mountains because of the excellence of her stability, wisely hides herself from the onslaughts of the persecutors.

[16:21] *And great hailstones, heavy as a hundredweight, dropped on people from heaven.* The hailstone of God's wrath is likened to a hundredweight, which by its heavy weight and the equity of its judgment is inflicted on all persons according to the diversity of their transgressions. The plagues of Egypt were all figures of these spiritual plagues.

And people cursed God for the plague of the hail. Some sins are the cause of sin, and some sins are the punishment of sin, and some sins are both. As Isaiah said, "You were angry, and we sinned."[31] In this passage, to curse God for the hail is recognized as both sin and the punishment for sin.[32]

REVELATION 17

[17:1] "*Come, I will show you the damnation of the great harlot, who is seated on the many waters.*" The multitude of the lost, who, abandoned by the Creator, have given themselves over to the corruption of demons are said to sit on the waves, that is, on the seditious discord of the nations. "The company of those who believed were of one heart and soul,"[1] whom the apostle betrothed "to one husband, to present her as a pure bride to Christ."[2]

[17:2] "*With whom the kings of the earth have committed fornication, and with the wine of her fornication the dwellers on earth have become drunk.*" The whole is greater than the parts. For the kings and the inhabitants of the earth each seek arrogantly after the things of the earth, and through the lust of vice they are corrupted by the allurements of the world and are made drunk by the madness of their minds.

[17:3] *And he carried me away in the spirit into a wilderness.* By *wilderness* he means the absence of God, whose presence is paradise.[3]

And I saw a woman sitting on a scarlet beast that was full of blasphemous names. Bloody with ungodliness and puffed up with blasphemies, the devil extols the corruption of the wicked with the haughtiness of presumption.

And it had seven heads and ten horns. That is, it possessed the kings and the kingdoms of the world whose glory he also showed to the Lord on the mountain.[4] For as we said above, the number seven and the number ten often are used to indicate universality.

[17:4] *The woman was arrayed in purple and scarlet.* By purple is indicated the deceitfulness of false rule, while scarlet indicates the bloody garb of impiety.

And she was bedecked with gold and precious stones and pearls. That is, she was clothed with every allurement of that which falsely claims to be true. And then he explains what is within this beauty, saying:

She holds in her hand a golden cup full of abominations. The golden cup full of abominations is hypocrisy. For outwardly hypocrites appear to others as just, but within they are filled with every impurity. For poison, hidden

---

[30]Ps 9:32 (lxx). [31]Is 64:5. [32]This interpretation comes from Tyconius, probably mediated to Bede through Primasius, who writes, "In this passage the blaspheming of God for the hail is recognized to be both sin and the punishment of sin by which the impious are so blinded that they do not come to their senses even when corrected, and so by these punishments they become even worse and more demented" (*Commentary on the Apocalypse* 16.21 [CCL 92:236]). **Revelation 17** [1]Acts 4:32. [2]2 Cor 11:2. [3]This comment is taken directly from Primasius (CCL 92:237). Similarly, Bede's comments on the description of the woman sitting on the scarlet beast come largely from Primasius. [4]See Mt 4:8-9; Lk 4:5-7.

within a golden cup, remains poison. So, although hidden beneath the dress of the whore, the beast remains who he is.

[17:5] *And on her forehead was written a name of mystery: "Babylon the great, mother of fornications and of earth's abominations."* To be sure, this corrupter is immediately shown in her very face to be the nurturer of vices. However, since she is recognized only by the wise mind, for she is dressed in such precious clothing, he indicates that this name is that of a mystery.

[17:6] *And I saw the woman, drunk with the blood of the saints and with the blood of the martyrs of Jesus.* The body of the adversary is one within and without.[5] For although it appears to be separated by means of place, yet it works in common by a unity of spirit. And so the ancestors of the wicked are in a sense said to have stoned Zacharias, although they themselves did not do it.[6]

[17:7-8] *And the angel said to me,* and so on until it continues, *"the beast that you saw was, and is not, and is to ascend from the bottomless pit and go to perdition."* That is, the devil ruled in the world at one time, but when the Lord was crucified, he was cast out. However, at the end of the world, when he has been released from the confinement of his prison, he will perish for eternity by the breath of the mouth of the Lord.

Tyconius interprets the beast to be the entire body of the devil, which is supplemented by the course of generations that pass away and succeed themselves.[7] And especially for this reason he shows the woman to be seated on the beast whom he had promised to show seated on the many waters, that is, on the peoples.

[17:9] *"The seven heads are seven hills on which the woman is seated. And there are seven kings."* It says that the heads of the beast are the kings of the world. Because of the swelling of their pride, they are compared with high mountains on which wanton ungodliness rests, so that they oppress by force and deceive by fraud.

[17:10] *"Five have fallen, one is, the other has not yet come."* Since the number seven indicates the full duration of earthly dominion whose final period, that of the kingdom of the antichrist, had not yet come, it accordingly indicates that five have passed away, the sixth now exists and the seventh is yet to come.

"And when he comes, he must remain only a little while." Since the Lord considers us, both the proud and the weak, it says that those days that he will inflict on us and that will be especially evil will be made short for mercy's sake.[8] This will be so that he might terrify their arrogance by the adversities of that time yet might revive their weakness because of its brevity.

[17:11] *"As for the beast that was and is not, it is an eighth, but it belongs to the seven, and it goes to perdition."* The antichrist, who is going to rule at the end of the age, belongs to the number of the kingdoms of the world on account of the unity of the body of the impious, whose head he is. However, on account of the singular power of his iniquity, he also retains his own proper place in the order.

[17:12] *"And the ten horns that you saw are ten kings who have not yet received royal power."* In persecuting the church, the kingdoms of the world have not yet fully demonstrated

[5]Bede's comments correspond to those of Caesarius of Arles, who explains that within there are false Christians while without there are heretics and pagans (*Exposition on the Apocalypse* 17.6, Homily 14 [PL 35:2442]). [6]See Mt 23:35. [7]Illustrated also by the comment of Caesarius of Arles: "An evil people is born out of an evil people . . . because wicked children copy and replace their wicked parents, and while some are dying, others succeed them" (*Exposition on the Apocalypse* 17.8, Homily 14 [PL 35:2442]). See also Primasius (CCL 92:242). [8]Mt 24:21-22.

their power. For although now they indeed rule over most, nevertheless the power of their insane boasting will be the more acute when they will deceive most through signs. Some[9] interpret this to mean that when the last persecution draws near, there will be ten kings who divide the world among themselves, according to the prophecy of Daniel, who said concerning the fourth beast, "It had ten horns, and behold, there came up among them another horn, a little one, before which three of the first horns were plucked up."[10] These interpreters further say that the antichrist would arise from Babylon and would overcome the kings of Egypt, Africa and Ethiopia, and that when these had been killed, seven other kings would submit their necks to the conqueror.[11] However, others say that the antichrist is placed as the number eleven as an indication of his collusion. For they think eleven is a departure from the number ten, which is perfect.[12]

"*But they are to receive power as kings for one hour after the beast.*" It says "as kings," for those who oppose the kingdom of Christ rule as though in a dream.

[17:13] "*These are of one intent and give over their power and authority to the beast.*" That is, with common consent they fight on behalf of the devil with all their might and energy. For this is what it means to receive a kingdom after the beast, to imitate the devil by opposing Christ.

[17:14] "*They will make war on the Lamb, and the Lamb will conquer them.*" Lest human weakness be terrified at the ferocity of the ancient foe, he describes the seven-headed beast, armed with the horns of an earthly kingdom, as vanquished by the triumphant Christ.

Indicating that Christ triumphs in his own followers, he adds:

"*And those with him are called elect and faithful.*" With good reason it placed "elect" first, for "many are called, but few are chosen."[13]

[17:16] "*And the ten horns that you saw, they will hate the harlot.*" When they see that at the end they are going to be damned by the conquering Lamb, then they will begin with the greatest hatred to detest the glory of the world, which at the present time they hold fast with a wanton love. This passage may also be otherwise interpreted to mean either that "among the proud there are always quarrels"[14] or that "whoever loves iniquity hates his own soul."[15]

"*They will make her desolate and naked.*" For through the wrath of God they themselves make the world desolate, since they are given over to it and use it unrighteously.

"*And they will devour her flesh and burn her up with fire.*" Made destitute of her usual enjoyments, they will consume her with the fires of Gehenna.

[17:17] "*For God has put it into their hearts to carry out what is pleasing to him.*" God, who is the righteous and mighty judge and to whom justice is always pleasing, allows the ungodly to do such things as punishment for previous sin. For such deeds he rightly might have made an end to the whole world, just as the Gospels say he did at the time of Sodom and at the flood.[16]

"*That they might give their royal power to the beast, until the words of God shall be fulfilled.*" That is, they obey the devil until the Scriptures are fulfilled in which God said that during the fourth kingdom he would consummate the world, as we read in Daniel: "There

---

[9]See Primasius (CCL 92:238). [10]Dan 7:7-8. [11]See Jerome *Commentary on Daniel* 2.7.7-8 (CCL 75A:844). [12]Augustine often expresses this opinion. See, for example, *City of God* 15.20 (FC 14:464). [13]Mt 22:14. Bede is following Primasius (CCL 92:245), who followed Tyconius in these remarks. [14]See Prov 13:10. [15]Ps 11:5 (10:5 LXX). [16]Mt 10:15; 24:37-39.

shall be a fourth kingdom on earth that shall be more powerful than all these kingdoms, and it shall devour and overthrow and destroy the whole earth."[17]

[17:18] *"And the woman that you saw is the great city that has dominion over the kings of the earth."* Later, when the seer is commanded to behold the wife of the Lamb, he sees the holy city coming down from heaven, and he says concerning her, "The kings of the earth carried their glory into her."[18] For in the world there are two cities, one that arises from the abyss and the other that comes down from heaven. And so now he compares the same ungodliness, which he had described in the form of a harlot made naked and burned up, with the ruins of a deserted city.

REVELATION 18

[18:1] *After this I saw another angel coming down from heaven, having great authority; and the earth was made bright with his splendor.* This angel, who is strong and brightens the earth, may be regarded as both the Lord incarnate as well as the teachers of the church who, granted heavenly light, preach the fall of the world, saying, "The kingdom of heaven is at hand."[1]

[18:2] *"Fallen, fallen is Babylon the great! It has become a dwelling place of demons, a haunt of every foul spirit."* "O Jerusalem," it says, "do not fear the power of the earthly city, which collapses from that very thing by which it subjugated you through the hatred of its wicked citizens." Isaiah also describes Babylon as inhabited by impure monsters.[2] For there is no other city than that of the devil that receives every unclean spirit and in which

every impurity remains throughout the world.

[18:3] *"And the merchants of the earth have grown rich with the wealth of her wantonness."* Those are called rich in sins who by an unhappy barter have exchanged their own souls for temporal abundance. For an excess of luxury renders people poor rather than rich.

[18:4] *"Come out of her, my people, lest you take part in her sins."* Isaiah also speaks in the same way: "Go out from their midst and touch no unclean thing; purify yourselves, you who bear the vessels of the Lord."[3] Since the ruin of Babylon has been foretold, he introduces the division, which is the ruin of Babylon.[4] For when Lot departed from Sodom, they were totally destroyed.

[18:6] *"Render to her as she herself has rendered to you."* For plagues, both visible and invisible, come out of the church into the world.

"And repay her double for her deeds." Repay her double that she who took delight in temporal enjoyments might be afflicted with eternal torments.

[18:7-8] *"Since in her heart she says, 'A queen I sit, I am no widow, mourning I shall never see,' so shall her plagues come in a single day."* Because she took delight in the luxury of the present time, she made no effort to prevent the coming retribution. Therefore, in a short time she will be punished with both spiritual and bodily disaster. However, the citizens of the heavenly fatherland, who place Jerusalem before their own happiness, do not want to sing the Lord's song in a foreign land, that is, to receive in the present time that joy that belongs to the future age.[5]

---

[17]Dan 7:23. [18]See Rev 21:24. **Revelation 18** [1]Mt 4:17; 10:7. [2]Is 13:21-22. [3]Is 52:11. [4]The removal of the pious from the evil city is its ruination, prefigured in Lot leaving Sodom. See the comments of Caesarius of Arles on this passage (*Exposition on the Apocalypse* 18.4 [PL 35:2444]). [5]See Ps 137:4-6 (136:4-6 LXX).

[**18:9**] *And the kings of the earth, who committed fornication with her, will weep and wail over her.* This wailing of the kings, of the merchants and of the seamen of Babylon may be interpreted in a twofold sense. On the one hand, it may mean that on the day of judgment, when all the glory of the world is passing away, only penitence for their former life will remain for the impious, who will then say, "What has pride profited us? Or what has the vaunting of riches brought us?"[6] All these things will pass away as a cloud." On the other hand, it may mean that when in the present age an abundance of things ceases and the downfall of various nations is occurring, the opportunity for carnal pleasures, which was everywhere present for the sating of the desires of the wicked, will have been taken away.[7]

When they see the smoke of her burning. That is, when they see the evidence of her destruction, for smoke arises from fire. Indeed, what else is the rioting of the world and its crumbling than the smoke of Gehenna, which is close to hand?

[**18:10**] *They will stand far off, in fear of her torment.* They will stand afar off, not physically but in their souls. For each one will fear for himself when he sees what another suffers through maliciousness and power.

And say, "Alas! Alas! That great city, Babylon! That mighty city! For in one hour has your judgment come!" The Spirit speaks the name of the city. Indeed, they lament the world, which is overtaken by punishment in such a short time and all of whose industry has come to an end so violently.

[**18:11**] *And the merchants of the earth will weep and mourn over her, since no one buys their cargo anymore,* and the following. They

bemoan the loss of all the spectacles of the world and those things that are pleasant to the senses of the body and that are suitable for external use. For the various kinds of metals pertain to sight, the odors to smell, the unguents to the touch, the wine, wheat and oils to the taste. In the mention of the beasts of burden and of the slaves, they lament the loss of other aids to humanity, and this in a double sense, as I have said. For either they fail when this world passes away, or the miserable survivors of those who have left the joys of the world through death lament their ruin as though it were the ruin of their own city. There those who stand afar off out of fear of a similar punishment are mentioned,

[**18:15**] *Who gained wealth from her will stand far off.* Whenever the Spirit says that they were made rich from her, he indicates the abundance of their sins. Later, when there is the voice of the unjust saying, "Alas! alas! for the great city where all who had ships at sea grew rich,"[8] material wealth is understood. For they believe that they are made wealthy by the skill of their manufacture.

[**18:16**] *That was clothed in fine linen, in purple and scarlet.* Is it the city that is clothed in fine linen and purple and not rather the people who live in it? In any case, they lament for themselves, since they are despoiled of those riches mentioned above.

[**18:17-18**] *And all shipmasters and seafaring men stood far off, as they saw the smoke of her burning.* Could all those who sail the sea be able to be present and watch the burning of the city?[9] No. It means rather that all workers and laborers of this age fear for themselves when they behold the ruin of their own hope.[10]

---

[6]Wis 5:8-9. [7]This second interpretation comes from Primasius (CCL 92:255). [8]See Rev 18:19. [9]The question implies a negative answer. [10]Caesarius of Arles perhaps makes clearer the intention of Bede: "It says that all who loved the world and were the workers of iniquity fear for themselves" (*Exposition on the Apocalypse* 18.15-17, Homily 16 [PL 35:2445]).

Saying, "What city was like the great city?" That is, the world cannot be restored to its previous condition.

[18:19] *And they threw dust on their heads.* This means that they reproached the persons of their leaders by whom they were deceived and so perished. Or, perhaps it means that they were accusing the insanity of their own heart, which is the guiding principle of every person, with a repentance that is too late.

"For in one hour she was laid waste." Note that every one of those who mourn weeps not only for the loss of riches but also because of the unexpected and unforeseen ruin of this deceitful world.

[18:20] *"Rejoice over her, O heaven, O saints and apostles and prophets."* According to the Gospel, when the Lord was foretelling the destruction of the world, he added, "Now when you see these things taking place, look up and raise your heads,"[11] that is, make your hearts glad.

"For God has given judgment for you against her." This is that judgment that the souls of the saints sought for with a loud cry, "How long, O Lord, holy and true, before you will judge and avenge our blood?"[12]

[18:21] *Then a mighty angel took up a stone like a great millstone and threw it into the sea, saying, "By this violence shall Babylon, the great city, be cast down,"* or, as another version has it, *"with violence shall Babylon in this way be thrown down."*[13] The city of this age is compared with an unstable millstone because of the weight and the error of sins. For "the wicked walk in a circle."[14] Babylon is rightly swallowed up by the waves of retribution, for its citizens oppressed Jerusalem with the waves of infidelity when, sitting by the rivers of Babylon, they bemoaned their absence from the heavenly Zion. For the Lord says that those who cause one to fall are to be punished with a similar punishment.[15] To be sure, the church is also likened to a stone, but one that is stable and firm and withstands the assaults of the tempestuous waves.[16] The millstone may also be understood to represent the crushing of punishments, for even the blessed Ignatius is reported to have said as he was about to suffer, "I am the wheat of God; I am being ground by the teeth of beasts, so that I might be made pure bread."[17]

[18:22] *"And the sound of harpers and minstrels, of flute players and trumpeters shall be heard in her no more."* Of the five senses, the text had until now neglected to mention the sense of sound, which will be taken away from the world along with the other senses.[18] It is as though it said, "What is beautiful to the eye, and melodious to the ear, and smooth to the touch, and sweet to the smell and delicious to the taste, all of that will pass away from the world."

"And every craftsman of every craft shall be found in her no more," and the rest. Everything, it says, that contributes to human use and to the happiness of human life is taken from the wicked. And he adds the reason for this when he says,

[18:23] *"For your merchants were the great men of the earth."* That is, because in your lifetime you received good things.[19]

[18:24] *"And in her was spilled the blood of prophets and of saints, and of all who have been slain on earth."* Was it the same city that killed the apostles and that killed the prophets and all the saints? Of course not. It refers rather

---

[11]Lk 21:28. [12]Rev 6:10. [13]See Gryson, CCL 121A:181. [14]Ps 12:8 (11:9 LXX). [15]See Mt 18:6-7. [16]See Mt 7:24-25. [17]Ignatius of Antioch *To the Romans* 4:1. This is the only use of Ignatius. According to Gryson, Bede did not take this quotation directly but derived it from Jerome (*De Viris Illustribus* 16.9 [FC 100:33]). [18]See Bede's comments on Rev 18:11-14. [19]See Lk 16:25.

to that city that Cain established with the blood of his own brother and that he called by the name of his son, Enoch, indicating in this manner all of his posterity, for the seven generations of Cain are described.[20] On the foundation of this city is poured out "all the righteous blood from the blood of innocent Abel to the blood of Zechariah,"[21] that is, the blood of the people and of the priest.

REVELATION 19

[19:1] *After this I heard what seemed to be the mighty voice of many trumpets*[1] *in heaven, saying, "Hallelujah! Praise and glory and power belong to our God!"* The church speaks these things now only in part, but she will then speak them perfectly, when the separation will have been accomplished and its vindication is manifest.

[19:2] *"She who corrupted the earth with her fornication, and he has avenged the blood of his servants from her hand."* He mentions two deeds of the harlot, namely, that she has corrupted herself with evil deeds and has persecuted the good. It seems to me that in these two works all errors of evil people may be comprehended.

[19:3] *And once more they cried, "Hallelujah!"* In never-ending love the church praises the Lord for his judgments. For "hallelujah" means "praise the Lord." Accordingly, psalms that begin with the words "praise the Lord" begin with the word *hallelujah* among the Hebrews.[2]
"And her smoke goes up forever and ever." It says that the smoke "goes up," not that the smoke "will go up." For Babylon always leads into perdition, and she is in part already set

afire even as Jerusalem already is passing over into paradise, as the Lord made clear in the story of the beggar and the rich man.[3]

[19:4] *And the twenty-four elders fell down, and the four living creatures worshiped God.* The church worships her Lord not only with her lips but also with the affection of the highest devotion.
Saying, "Amen. Hallelujah!" The words *Amen* and *Hallelujah* can be interpreted, for they refer to faith or to the truth and praise of the Lord, as I have said. However, out of reverence for the holiness of the original language, the use and authority of these words is preserved. The church continues to sing Hallelujah on the days of the Lord and throughout the period of Quinquagesima[4] because of the hope of the resurrection, which in the praise of the Lord is still in the future.

[19:5] *And from the throne came a voice, saying, "Give praise to our God, all you his servants, who fear him, the small and the great."* When he commands that this be done and then mentions that it has been done, he is indicating the approved praise of his elect. It says "the small and the great," because to be small in natural abilities does not matter if one's heart and tongue are full of the praise of the Lord.

[19:6] *And I heard what seemed to be the sound of a great trumpet and the sound of many waters and as the sound of great thunder peals, saying, "Hallelujah! For the Lord our God the Almighty has begun to reign!"* The great voice of those singing indicates the great devotion of the heart. By the manifold repetition of praise the voice rejoices in the destruction of the wicked

---

[20]Gen 4:18-22. [21]Mt 23:35. **Revelation 19** [1]The Latin of Bede reads *multarum tubarum*. Some manuscripts read *multarum turbarum*, "many multitudes," that corresponds to the Greek ὄχλου πολλοῦ. [2]For example, Ps 106:1; 111:1; 112:1; 113:1; 117:1; 135:1; 146:1; 147:1; 148:1; 149:1; 150:1. [3]Lk 16:19-31, esp. Lk 16:22. [4]Quinquagesima is the final Sunday before the season of Lent. It means "fiftieth" and so indicates fifty days before Easter, inclusive of Easter Sunday itself. The days of the Lord refer to Sunday, which traditionally was also the day of resurrection.

and in the eternal glory of the Lord and of those who are his.

[19:7] *"Let us give him glory, for the marriage of the Lamb has come."* The marriage supper of the Lamb occurs when the church will be united with its Lord in the wedding chamber of the heavenly kingdom.

"And his bride has made herself ready." By always persisting in works of righteousness the church has shown herself worthy of the spiritual banquet and the eternal kingdom. One can also interpret this according to the parable of the Gospel that speaks of the virgins who, when the bridegroom was coming, rose up to prepare their lamps,[5] that is, among themselves to consider their deeds for which they hope to receive eternal blessedness.

[19:8] *"It was granted to her to be clothed with fine linen, bright and pure."* It was granted to the church to be clothed with her own deeds. But it is not so with the wicked who, according to Isaiah, "weave a spider's web and will not be covered by their works, for their works are without benefit."[6]

[19:9] *And he said to me, "Write this: Blessed are those who are invited to the marriage supper of the Lamb."* It says that they were invited to a supper, not to a mere lunch, for at the end of days the supper will certainly be a great feast. Therefore, when the time of the present life is ended, those who come to the refreshment of the heavenly contemplation are truly invited to the supper of the Lamb.

"These are true words of God." That is to say, those future events that I have foretold will without any doubt certainly happen.

[19:10] *"You must not do that! I am a fellow servant with you and your brethren."* He had said above, "I am the first and the last."[7] Therefore, it shows that the angel that has been sent is the figure of the Lord and of the church. For also at the end it says, "I am Jesus; I have sent my angel to testify these things to you among the churches."[8]

"Who hold the testimony of Jesus." After the Lord Jesus elevated the humanity he assumed above the heavens, the angel was afraid to be adored by man, without doubt worshiping him who is man and God above himself. For before the incarnation of the Lord we read that what was done by human beings was in no way prohibited to the angels.[9]

The testimony of Jesus is the Spirit of prophecy. Whatever the Spirit of prophecy said is the testimony of Jesus of whom both the Law and the prophets testified. Therefore, he says, "Do not worship me rather than God, since I came to give witness to his mighty works."

Up to this point the narrative has spoken of the destruction of Babylon. From now on what lies in the future relates to the glory of Jerusalem.

[19:11] *Then I saw heaven opened, and behold, a white horse! He who sat on it was called Faithful and True.* The Lord, who is "the way, the truth and the life,"[10] and to whom it is said through the prophet, "For you have done wonderful things, plans ancient and faithful, Amen,"[11] mounts the throne of his white body, that is, his pure body, in order to conquer the powers of the air.

And in righteousness he judges and makes war. He judges as the "King of the ages,"[12] and he makes war, for he struggles at all times by suffering in his members.

[19:12] *His eyes were as a flame of fire.* Sometimes it speaks of the commandments as the eyes of the Lord; sometimes it is speaking of the

---

[5]See Mt 25:1-13. [6]Is 59:5-6. [7]Rev 1:17. [8]Rev 22:16. [9]See Gen 19:1. The exaltation of Christ in his humanity exalts all of humanity above the angels. [10]Jn 14:6. [11]Is 25:1. [12]See Rev 15:3.

Spirit. Of the commandments, it says, "Your word, O Lord, is a lamp to my feet,"[13] and of the Spirit it says, "I came to cast fire on the earth."[14]

And on his head are many diadems. In him "in whom we shall perform great deeds,"[15] the multitude of the saints are said to have the beauty of crowns.[16]

And he has a name inscribed that no one knows except himself. It says "except himself" for the whole church exists in him. Perfect knowledge of the Word of God is manifested to those who are counted worthy to be the body of Christ and members of him. The Lord also spoke in the same manner: "No one has ascended into heaven but he who has descended from heaven, namely, the Son of man who is in heaven."[17]

[19:13] *He was clad in a robe dipped in blood.* The robe of Christ must be interpreted according to context. Apparently in this passage the robe refers to the passion, as his immaculate birth was indicated in the white horse and his innocent death is indicated in the bloodstained garment.[18]

And his name was called the Word of God. He who appeared in time as a man who was going to suffer was he who in the beginning was God with God.[19] He is called Word, because nothing in the substance of his nature is visible or corporeal or because through him the Father created all things. As it says above, perfect knowledge of his nature is known to himself and to the Father. "For the peace of God passes all understanding,"[20] that is, that peace by which God himself has made peace with himself surpasses the understanding of every creature, whether that of a human being or even that

of an angel. For "his wisdom is without end."[21] When it is says, "And to whom the Son chooses to reveal the Father,"[22] it means that one who knows the Son and the Father knows them after the manner of the creature.

[19:14] *And the armies that are in heaven followed him on white horses.* With pure white bodies the church imitates Christ. Because of the struggle of her battle, she has by right received the name of army.

They are arrayed in fine linen, white and pure. Above[23] he displayed the righteous deeds of the saints according to the words of the psalm, "Let your priests be clothed with righteousness."[24]

[19:15] *From his mouth issues a sharp sword.* Isaiah speaks in the same manner: "He made my mouth like a sharp sword."[25] The apostle speaks similarly: "And the sword of the Spirit, which is the word of God."[26]

And he himself will tread the wine press of the fury of the wrath of God the Almighty. He treads the wine press also now until at length he will tread it outside the city.[27]

[19:16] *On his robe and on his thigh he has written "King of kings and Lord of Lords."* This is the name that no one of the arrogant knows. However, it is inscribed on the church not with ink but with the Spirit of the living God, that is, on the tablets of the heart.[28] By the thigh is indicated the posterity of a seed. And so, lest his posterity become intermingled with foreign persons, Abraham put forward his thigh as a third witness between himself and his servant.[29] And the apostle too, as though raising

---

[13]Ps 119:105 (118:105 LXX). [14]Lk 12:49. [15]Ps 60:12 (59:14 LXX). [16]This comment comes from Tyconius by way of Primasius (CCL 92:264). [17]Jn 3:13. [18]Caesarius of Arles interpreted the bloody robe to be "the martyrs who are in the church" (PL 35:2447). [19]See Jn 1:1. [20]Phil 4:7. [21]Ps 147:5 (146:5 LXX). [22]Mt 11:27. [23]See Rev 19:8. [24]Ps 132:9 (131:9 LXX). [25]Is 49:2. [26]Eph 6:17. [27]The comments of Caesarius clarify Bede's meaning: "He treads [the wine press of God's wrath] even now, when he permits the evil to persecute the good and leaves them to their own desires. However, later he will seek repayment, when he sends those into Gehenna who have not repented" (*Exposition on the Apocalypse* 19.15, Homily 17 [PL 35:2447]). [28]See 2 Cor 3:3. [29]See Gen 24:2-3.

up seed for a dead brother, says, "For I begot you in Christ through the gospel."[30] This passage may also be interpreted in this manner. By remaining subject to Christ, the church will reign and shall be a lord of those who are lords. The same name is said to be on the robe, for by the mystery of the nativity and by the work of his passion his majesty and his kingdom is revealed to us.

In the following passages, the text expounds the significance of this king and his army, that is, the struggle of the final battle and the glory of the kingdom that follows upon it.

[19:17] *Then I saw an angel standing in the sun, and with a loud voice he called out.* The angel standing in the sun represents the preaching in the church, which shines the more brightly and thunders the more freely the more she is oppressed.

Saying to all the birds that fly in midheaven. He calls the saints who live a heavenly life birds, "for wherever the body is, there the eagles will be gathered together."[31] Considered as one body, he had referred to the saints as an eagle flying in midheaven.[32]

[19:18] *"Come, gather for the great supper of God, to eat the flesh of kings,"* and following. "Come," it says, "you who hunger and thirst after righteousness,"[33] to the supper of the kingdom that is to come, when the anger of the proud has been suppressed, and you will eat your fill by the light of the divine righteousness.

"And the flesh of horses and their riders." In my opinion these horsemen are the same as those who at the opening of the seals were described as having come against the white horse of the Lord.[34]

[19:19] *And I saw the beast and the kings of the* earth *with their armies gathered to make war,* and what follows. It explains how the supper of God is prepared, namely, when the devil assails the church but is defeated.

[19:20-21] *These two were thrown alive into the lake of fire that burns with sulphur, and the others were killed by the sword of him who sits on the horse.* This refers to the devil and the antichrist. They will be punished much more severely than other human persons or demons, for it is more terrible to be burned alive in flames of sulphur than to die straightway by the lethal stroke of the sword. Unless perhaps this passage refers to that opposition to God that has taken possession of them. For "whoever does not believe is condemned already."[35] And so one might interpret the passage to refer to the antichrist and the false prophet or to the heretics. For of those who are dying no one sins more grievously than do the heretics who deny Christ after they had come to know him.

And all the birds were gorged with their flesh. If at the present time "the righteous person will rejoice when he sees the punishment"[36] of the impious, how much more then when the judge himself is present and the righteous are made one spirit with him? However, the birds might be interpreted to be unclean spirits who are sated with their own destruction.

Tyconius expounds this supper in the following way: "At all times the church eats the flesh of her enemies. While she is consumed by them, she will however be filled at the resurrection when their carnal works are punished."[37]

REVELATION 20

[20:1] *Then I saw an angel coming down from heaven, holding in his hand the key of the bot-*

---

[30]1 Cor 4:15. [31]Mt 24:28. [32]See Rev 8:13. [33]See Mt 5:6. [34]See Rev 6:1, 2, 4, 6, 8. [35]Jn 3:18. [36]Ps 58:10 (57:11 LXX). [37]Quoted by Beatus of Liebana (see Gryson, CCL 121A:502).

tomless pit and a great chain. Summarizing again from the beginning, the author explains more fully what he had earlier said: "The beast that you saw was, and is not, and is to ascend from the bottomless pit and go to perdition."[1] Therefore, possessing the power of the Father, the Lord came down into the flesh, for he was going to wage war on the leader of the world, and when he had been bound, the Lord was going to free his captives.[2]

[20:2] *And he seized the dragon, that ancient serpent, who is the devil and Satan.* The devil is interpreted to mean "flowing downward," although in the Greek it means "accuser," while Satan means "adversary" or "deceiver." Therefore, he is called "dragon" because of the wicked harm he inflicts; he is called "serpent" because of the cunning of his deception; he is called "devil" because of the fall from his previous status; and he is called "Satan" because of the stubbornness of his opposition to the Lord.

And bound him for a thousand years. He restrained and hindered the devil's power to lead astray those who were going to be freed. If the devil had been allowed to use his full power and deception, in such a long period of time he might have ensnared even more of the weak in his fraud. When he mentions the thousand years, he is speaking in part and refers to the days remaining in the thousand years of the sixth day on which the Lord was born and suffered.

[20:3] *And threw him into the pit.* He threw him into the hearts of a persecuting people. It is not that the devil was not already there before. However, shutting him away from the faithful, the devil begins more completely to lay hold of the wicked who not only are estranged from God but also even hate the servants of God without cause.[3] And the Lord showed this in a visible manner when he cast the devil out of persons who were demon possessed and cast him into the pigs.[4]

And he shut it and sealed it over him, that he should deceive the nations no more. As though with a royal seal the angel forbids and hinders the devil, lest he further seduce the nations, namely, those whom he previously used to lead astray so that they would not be reconciled to God although they were destined to life.

After these things he must be loosed for a little while. As Saint Augustine says, "The devil will be loosed when there will be little time remaining, since we read that he and his forces will rage with full power for three and a half years. Moreover, those against whom he will make war are such persons as cannot be conquered by his attacks and plots. However, were he never set free, his malignant power would be less apparent, nor would the very faithful patience of the holy city be put to the test, and yet more, we would not so clearly see the good use that the almighty God makes of the great wickedness of the devil."[5]

[20:4] *Then I saw thrones, and seated on them were those to whom judgment was committed.* He indicates what transpires during these thousand years in which the devil is bound. For although the church will sit in Christ on twelve thrones in order to render judgment, she already sits and judges, for she was counted worthy to hear from her king, "Whatever you bind on earth shall also be bound in heaven."[6]

Also I saw the souls of those who had been beheaded for the testimony of Jesus and for the word of God. Already implied is what he is going to say after this, "They reigned with Christ a thousand years." To be sure, the

---

Revelation 20 [1]Rev 17:8. [2]See Mt 12:29. [3]See Ps 35:19 (34:19 LXX). Bede's comments follow closely those of Augustine (*City of God* 20.7 [FC 24:267-68]), perhaps by way of Primasius (CCL 92:273-74). [4]See Mt 8:28-34. [5]See Augustine *City of God* 20.8 (FC 24:271). [6]Mt 18:18; also Jn 20:23.

church reigns with Christ in the living and the dead. As the apostle says, "For to this end Christ died, that he might be Lord both of the living and of the dead."[7] However, he mentions especially the souls of the martyrs, because after death they reign in a special manner who struggled for the truth even to death.

What now follows, *and who had not worshiped the beast or its image, and they came to life and reigned with Christ a thousand years*. We must interpret this passage to refer to both the living and the dead, who, whether they are still living in this mortal flesh or have died, reign with Christ even now in a manner appropriate to this time. For the thousand years signifies the complete duration of this interval of time.[8]

[20:5] *The rest of the dead did not come to life until the thousand years were ended*. Whoever did not hear the voice of the Son of God and move to life from death during this time of the first resurrection, that is, of the resurrection of the soul, will most certainly at the second resurrection, which is that of the flesh, go with that very flesh into the second death, that is, into eternal torments.

This is, it says, *the first resurrection*. This is the resurrection by which we rise through baptism. As the apostle says, "If you have been raised with Christ, seek the things that are above."[9] For just as the first death consists in this life through sins, since "the soul that sins shall die,"[10] so also in this life the first resurrection consists in the forgiveness of sins.

[20:6] *Blessed and holy is he who shares in the first resurrection*. That is, blessed and holy is that person who will have preserved that which was born anew.

But they shall be saints of God and of Christ.

Another translation reads "they shall be priests of God and of Christ."[11] However, this is said not only of bishops and presbyters, who are properly called priests in the church. Rather, just as all are said to be of Christ on account of the mystical chrism, so also all are priests since we are members of the one Priest. Concerning the members of Christ the apostle Peter says, "a holy nation, a royal priesthood."[12]

And they shall reign with Christ a thousand years. Although he had already written this, the Spirit repeats that the church is going to reign a thousand years, that is, to the end of the world. And how could anyone doubt this? It is clear from the fact of its eternal rule that it will reign to the end of the world.

[20:7] *And when the thousand years are ended, Satan will be loosed from his prison*. When he speaks of the years having ended, he is speaking of a part from the whole. For the devil will be loosed so that there yet remains the three years and six months of the final struggle. However, except for this figurative speech it rightly speaks of the end of time. For that which remains is short and is not to be computed, since the seven hundred years or whatever it is that God shall wish are called by the apostle an "hour."[13]

And he will come out to deceive the nations that are at the four corners of the earth, that is, Gog and Magog, and he will gather them for battle. At that time he will deceive the nations in order to gather them together for this battle. Before this time and in whatever ways he could, he had deceived them through many and various evils. It says that he "will come out," for he will erupt out of the hiding places of those who are full of hate into open persecution. Therefore, Gog and Magog signify either

---

[7]Rom 14:9. [8]The interval of time between the death and resurrection of Jesus and the final judgment. [9]Col 3:1. [10]Ezek 18:4, 20. [11]The reading "priests of God and of Christ" is, in fact, the reading of all manuscripts except for a few codices of the Vulgate. Gryson comments that Bede's reading raises the question of what text of the Vulgate he was using (CCL 121A:183). [12]1 Pet 2:9. [13]See Rev 17:12.

the whole from a part, or according to the interpretation of the names, which mean "roof" and "out from the roof," these names indicate that the enemies are both hidden and open. For they are a roof because in them the enemy is closed up and concealed, and they will be out from the roof when they shall burst forth into open hatred.

[20:8] *And they marched up over the breadth of the earth, and they surrounded the camp of the saints and the beloved city.* This does not mean that they have come and will come to only one place, as though the beloved city, that is, the church, is united and located in any single location. Rather, by the breadth of the earth it indicates that at that time the church will be persecuted in all nations. Nor by the mention of the camps does he wish to assert that his army is going to desert.

[20:9] *But fire came down from heaven and consumed them.* This is not to be interpreted as the last punishment. It is rather the fire of envy that torments the hostile enemy because of the steadfastness of the saints. For heaven is something strong and secure. This is also the fire that comes out of the mouth of the witnesses of God and devours their enemies. For on the last day he will not pour fire on them; rather, he will send those who are gathered together before him and who have been judged into eternal fire.

[20:10] Concerning this he adds: *And the devil who had deceived them was thrown into the lake of fire and sulphur where both the beast and the false prophet were.* At the last judgment the devil will be thrown into the eternal fire, where all those whom he had sent before, that

is, the greatest part of the wicked city, also are. The beast is to be interpreted according to the context. At times it refers to the devil, at times to the antichrist and at times to the wicked city itself. Perhaps the fire that is said to come down from heaven can also indicate the sudden destruction of the wicked. For when the Lord comes, he will kill the antichrist with the breath of his mouth.[14]

How at the judgment of Christ the devil along with his followers will be sent into the fire he now explains more fully.

[20:11] *Then I saw a great white throne and him who sat on it; from his presence earth and sky fled away.* It says that he saw him who sits on the throne and from whose face the earth and the heaven fled away. For, to be sure, when the judgment has been effected, the heaven and earth cease to exist, since the new heaven and the new earth begin to exist. That is to say, there will be a change by way of a transformation of things and not in the sense that things are going to be utterly annihilated. "For the form of this world is passing away."[15] He did not say "and the substance" of the world will pass away. For we believe that this is going to be transformed into something better.[16]

[20:12] *And I saw the dead, great and small, standing before the throne.* For "when the Son of man shall sit on the throne of his majesty,"[17] then "all the nations shall be gathered before him."[18]

And books were opened; and another book was opened, which is the book of life. Another translation renders, "which is the book of the life of each person."[19] The open books refer to the two Testaments of God, for humankind will be judged according to both Testaments.

---

[14]2 Thess 2:8. [15]1 Cor 7:31. [16]See the discussion of Irenaeus *Against the Heresies* 4.3.1; 5.35.2 (ANF 1:465, 566). Against Gnostic pessimism concerning the capacity of the material order to receive the incorruption of the Spirit, Irenaeus insists that the substance of the creation does not pass away but is transformed into something infinitely superior, quoting 1 Cor 7:31 for support. [17]Mt 19:28. [18]Mt 25:32. [19]Bede is referring to the text of Tyconius and Augustine, which is also that of Primasius and Caesarius of Arles. See Gryson, CCL 121A:182.

The book of the life of each person refers to our recollection of our deeds. It does not mean that each person will learn of his or her deeds through a book that mentions what is unknown.[20]

And the dead were judged by what was written in the books, by what they had done. This means that they were judged from the two Testaments according to what they had done and what they had not done. It is possible also to understand these books to refer to the deeds of the righteous. For in comparison with these the wicked are damned, since in the opening of these books they read of that good that they did not choose to do.

[20:13] *And the sea gave up its dead who were in it, and Death and Hades gave up their dead.* Without doubt, this occurred before the dead were judged.

And so he recapitulates what he had interrupted and returns to the order by saying, *And all were judged by what they had done.* He indicates that the bodies and the souls are to be brought together, the bodies from the earth and the souls from their own locations. By *death* he indicates those good souls who endured only the separation of the flesh but would not suffer punishment, while by *Hades* he indicates the wicked souls. It is also possible to interpret this literally to mean that all bodies that the waves of the sea carried away or that the beasts had devoured would be resurrected.

Tyconius interpreted the passage this way: "Those nations that he shall find here still living are the dead of the sea; while 'death and Hades gave up their dead' refers to the nations that are dead and buried."[21]

[20:14] Although he had said, "And all were judged by what they had done," he briefly adds in what manner, *Death and Hades were thrown into the lake of fire.* It is speaking of the devil and his followers. In a previous passage Hades followed the devil, who was the rider of a pale horse.[22] It repeats move clearly what in anticipation it had already said. "And the devil who had deceived them was thrown into the lake of fire and sulphur."[23] What there he had added more obscurely of the beast and false prophet, he here explains more clearly.

[20:15] *And whoever is not found written in the book of life.* This passage is speaking of those who are not judged by God to be living. For this reason, it seems to me that those interpreters are correct who say that the open books above are the thoughts and deeds of each person that have been made known.[24] However, the book of life is the foreknowledge of God, which cannot fail concerning those to whom eternal life will be given. They are written in this book, that is, they have been foreknown by God.[25]

When the judgment in which he sees the damnation of the wicked has come to an end, he continues the narrative so that he might speak also of the blessed.

REVELATION 21

[21:1] *And I saw a new heaven and a new earth, for the first heaven and the first earth has passed away.* Whereas by way of anticipation he mentioned above that he saw one seated on the throne from whose face heaven and earth fled, that is, when the wicked were judged, he now returns to that order. Then the form of

---

[20]This last sentence somewhat freely translates *non quod librum habeat commemoratorium occultorum cognitor.* For the meaning, see Augustine, who thinks that the book symbolizes some action of God by which each person recalls his deeds and reviews them mentally (*City of God* 20.14 [FC 24:287-88]). [21]Here, as frequently elsewhere, the sea is a figure for the world and its troubles. Caesarius of Arles follows this interpretation of Tyconius (PL 35:2449). [22]See Rev 6:8, where the devil has the name of Death. [23]Rev 20:10. [24]Bede has Augustine especially in mind. [25]Bede is following the interpretation of Augustine: "[The book of life] is a figure of the predestination of those who are to receive eternal life" (*City of God* 20.15 [FC 24:290]).

this world will pass away in a blazing fire so that as heaven and earth are transformed into something better, the nature of the change of each may be fitting to the incorruption and immortality of the bodies of the saints.

And the sea was no more. From these words it is difficult to say whether the sea was dried up by the great heat or whether it also was changed into something better. For while we read that there will be a new heaven and a new earth, we do not read that there will also be a new sea—unless here the word *sea* signifies the turbulent life of this world that will then cease to exist. For it is the habit of the prophets to mix figures of speech with their words.

[21:2] *And I saw the holy city, the new Jerusalem, descending out of heaven from God.* This city is said to descend from heaven, since the grace by which God made it is heavenly.

Prepared as a bride adorned for her husband. There is another Jerusalem that is not adorned for her husband but for an adulterer.

[21:3] *"Behold, the dwelling of God is with humankind, and he shall dwell with them."* For the elect, God himself will be the reward of eternal bliss, which, since they are possessed by him, they will possess into all eternity.

[21:4] *"And God will wipe every tear from their eyes."* The glory of that city will be so great and so exalted from the goodness of God that no remnant of its former agedness will remain, namely, when the celestial incorruption will raise up all the bodies of the saints and the contemplation of the eternal King will feed their minds.

"And death shall be no more, neither shall there be mourning or crying or pain, for the former things have passed away." It was earlier said that death had been sent into the lake of fire. We can also now understand these statements in the same way, namely, that when the holy city has been glorified at the last judgment, mourning and crying and mortality will remain in Gehenna alone.

[21:5-6] *And he said to me, "Write, for these words are most trustworthy and true." And he said to me, "It is done!"* It is best not to expound these things only but to believe them. This is especially so, since he says "It is done" concerning what has already taken place, so that no one would be in doubt about the future.

"I am the Alpha and the Omega, the beginning and the end." Just as he testified at the beginning of the book that he was the Alpha and the Omega,[1] so this is repeated three times,[2] so that no one might believe that there is any other god before him or any other god after him, as Isaiah says.[3] Indeed, since he is speaking of the end of the world, the one who consummates the world should be understood to be the same one as he who was its creator.

"To the thirsty I will give from the fountain of the water of life without payment." From this fountain he now moistens the throats of believers in this life.[4] However, at that time he will draw abundantly from this fountain and give them to drink in the fatherland. In both instances, however, he gives by grace. For "the grace of God is eternal life in Christ Jesus our Lord."[5] And "from his fullness we have all received grace for grace."[6]

[21:8] *"But as for the cowardly, the unbelievers, the vile,"* and the following. He always mixes harsh sayings in with the easy and appealing words so that watchfulness is encouraged.

Revelation 21   [1]See Rev 1:8. [2]Here and at Rev 22:13. [3]Is 43:10. [4]Moisten translates the verb *irroro*, which suggests a gentle use of water, so to moisten or to bedew. In this manner Bede compares the relatively modest gift of grace in this life compared with the abundant use of the water of life in heaven. [5]Rom 6:23. [6]Jn 1:16.

Psalm 144 does the same when it mentions the grace of God's abundant mercies and suddenly mentions also his impending judgment: "The Lord watches over all who love him but will destroy all sinners."[7] He mentions the cowardly along with the unbelievers, since those who doubt the rewards of those who conquer will certainly be afraid to undergo trial.

"And for all liars there will be a place in the lake of fire." He shows that there are many classes of liars. However, the greatest and most detestable liar is the one who sins in religion. The author spoke of such persons above: "They say that they are Jews but they are not, for they are lying; they are the synagogue of Satan."[8]

[21:9] Then came one of the seven angels who had the bowls full of the seven last plagues. The preachers who had earlier poured out the seventh plague, that is, the universal plague on the impious, are those who now reveal the future joys of the church.

"Come, I will show you the bride, the wife of the Lamb." He calls the church bride and wife, for while remaining herself pure and immaculate, she is always giving birth to spiritual children for God.[9] Or, she is called bride and wife because although she is now betrothed to God, she will at that time be led to the never-ending wedding feast.

[21:10] And he carried me in the spirit to a great, high mountain, and he showed me the holy city Jerusalem. After the destruction of Babylon, the holy city, which is the bride of the Lamb, is seen located on a mountain. The stone that was cut out of the mountain without hands broke the image of the world's glory into small pieces, and it grew into a great mountain and filled the whole world.[10]

[21:11] Coming down out of heaven from God, having the glory of God. The church's beauty will then be seen more fully, when she will have merited fully to bear the heavenly image through the Spirit by whom her bridegroom is believed to have been conceived and born.

Her light was like that of a precious jewel. The precious stone is Christ, who said, "The glory that you have given to me, I have given to them."[11]

Like a jasper, as crystal. The city's light is likened to jasper because of the clarity of her virtues and to crystal because of the inner purity of her mind and her sincere faith.[12]

[21:12] It had a great, high wall. The wall represents the unconquerable strength of the church's faith, hope and love. The Lord himself can also be understood to be this great wall that protects the church on every side. Isaiah spoke of this: "A wall and a bulwark is set up in it."[13] Isaiah is speaking of the protection of the Lord and of the intercession of the saints who make a path to the city by addressing their teaching to the hearts of the faithful.

Having twelve gates. The twelve gates are the apostles who by their writing and their work first made the entrance into the church known to all the Gentiles.

And at the gates twelve angels. The twelve angels are the teachers who in the mystery of faith and word follow in the footsteps of the apostles.

And the names inscribed are of the twelve sons of Israel. The names of the twelve sons of Israel signify the remembrance of the ancient fathers that is implanted in the hearts of preachers. For this reason when the high priest entered the tabernacle, he was commanded to carry the remembrance of the fathers in his mind and understanding.[14]

[7]Ps 145:20 (144:20 LXX). [8]Rev 2:9; 3:9. [9]Bede is referring to the spiritual birth through baptism (see Jn 3:3, 5). [10]See Dan 2:34-35. [11]Jn 17:22. [12]See 1 Tim 1:5. [13]Is 26:1. [14]See Ex 28:12.

[21:13] *On the east three gates, on the north three gates, on the south three gates, on the west three gates.* In my opinion this skillful description of the gates intends to indicate the mystery of the number twelve. It can therefore suggest either the whole number of the apostles or the perfection of the church, for through it the faith in the holy Trinity is made known to the four corners of the earth.

[21:14] *And the wall of the city had twelve foundations, and on them the twelve names of the twelve apostles and of the Lamb.* What the gates are, that is also the foundation. What the city is, that also is the wall. The patriarchs can be designated by the word *foundation*, for in themselves, that is, by way of figure they entail the persons of the apostles. Through them [the patriarchs] this city was founded, although it is through the apostles, as though through gates more wide open, that the city is open to the nations that are going to believe. It should also be noted that when *foundation* is used in the plural, it means either the teachers of the church or its virtues. However, when *foundation* is used in the singular, it signifies the Lord, who is the foundation of foundations.

[21:15] *And he who talked with me had a measuring rod of gold.* "Reaching from one end of the earth to another mightily and ordering all things sweetly,"[15] Christ, who is the Wisdom of God,[16] measures the holy city. That is to say, Christ determines all things by way of number and measure and weight[17] and so distributes to each one of the faithful the gifts of the spiritual graces.[18]

One could also think of the teachers of the church, who though weak in their bodies are heavenly in their mind and with wisdom examine the merits of each person.

[21:16] *And the city lies foursquare.* The city is said to be laid out in a square, and each side is given an equal dimension, for nothing is allowed to be marked by inequality. According to the apostle, to be perfect is to have wisdom and to have peace,[19] that is, truly to exist in the strength of a square.[20]

And he measured the city, twelve thousand stadia. That he measured the city means that he looked on the church in her faith and works and made her to be perfect. For the perfection of the four cardinal virtues is lifted up by faith in the holy Trinity, and so by the number twelve the dignity of the church is indicated.[21]

Its length and breadth and height are equal. This signifies the stability of unconquered truth by which the church, supported by the length of faith, the breadth of love and the height of hope, is not allowed to be blown about by every wind of doctrine.[22] Were it to lack any one of these, the perfect stability of the church would not exist.

[21:17] *Its wall was measured, one hundred and forty-four cubits.* This number is the total of the number twelve squared, for twelve twelves equal one hundred and forty-four. This number, therefore, signifies the immovable perfection of the holy city.

The measure of men, or of a man, that is, of an angel. The church consists of persons gathered together and exalted by the promises of Christ, and so she hopes for equality with the angels. However, according to the literal sense, it indicates that the angel appeared to him in the form of a man.

[21:18] *The wall was built from jasper.* This is what the apostle Peter urged: "Like living stones be yourselves built into spiritual houses."[23]

---

[15]Wis 8:1. [16]See 1 Cor 1:24. [17]See Wis 11:20. [18]This first interpretation that Bede gives comes from Primasius (CCL 92:292). [19]See 1 Cor 1:10; Phil 2:2. [20]A square is stable and only with difficulty overturned. [21]The four cardinal virtues are temperance, prudence, justice and fortitude. The scheme seems to derive from Plato (*Republic* 427e) but appears in the intertestamental books of the Scriptures (Wis 8:7; also 4 Macc 1:18-19). [22]See Eph 4:14. [23]1 Pet 2:5. The text of Bede reads the plural (*domus spirituales*).

The city itself was pure gold, similar to clear glass. The church is signified by gold, for she is often described as decorated with golden lampstands and bowls because of the worship of wisdom. The glass refers to true faith, for what is seen on the outside also exists on the inside. Within the saints of the church there is nothing that is counterfeit and not open to sight.

This verse might also refer to that time when the thoughts in each are clearly declared to one another.

[21:19] *The foundations of the wall of the city were adorned by every precious stone.* By the names of the various stones it signifies either the kinds or the order or the diversity of virtues by which the whole of the heavenly Jerusalem is built up.[24] For it is difficult for every individual person to be filled of all the virtues. Therefore, when Isaiah described the ornamentation of this city, he said, "Behold, I will set your stones in order and lay your foundation in sapphires."[25] And as though giving an explanation, he adds, "All your children will be taught by the Lord."[26]

The first foundation was jasper.[27] There are many kinds of jasper. Some are green in color and have the appearance of being dipped in the color of living plants. Some have the appearance of the wetness of an emerald but of an uncultured type. These are said to have the power to chase away phantasms. Another has the appearance of snow and the foam of great waves, although with a reddish hue as though mixed with blood.

The jasper stone, then, symbolizes the unflagging vigor of faith. Such faith arises in the sacrament of the Lord's passion through the living water of baptism, and, with assisting aid, it grows into the blossoms of spiritual graces. For one who has this faith chases away all fear, as the blessed apostle Peter reminds us: "Your adversary, the devil, prowls around like a roaring lion seeking whom he might devour. Resist him, firm in faith."[28] Such a person is able to say with the bride, "My beloved is radiant and blushing red."[29] Therefore, with good reason is both the structure of the wall built up with this stone and, as Isaiah says,[30] the fortress of the city is also adorned by it.

The second stone is sapphire. Moses explains both the color and the significance of this stone when he describes the dwelling of God: "Under his feet was a work of sapphire stone, clear as the sky."[31] Ezekiel also says that the place where the throne of God is has the appearance of sapphire and that the glory of the Lord, who bears the image of the highest heaven, consists of that color.[32] Therefore, whoever is such a person is able to declare with the apostle, "Our abode is in heaven."[33] As if struck by the rays of the sun, sapphire glows in itself with burning brightness. So also the thoughts of the saints are always occupied with heavenly things, and so they are daily renewed by the rays of divine light. Therefore, they continually and ardently, in whatever way, search after eternal things and urge others as well toward those things for which they ought to seek. For what happened in the Red Sea is said to occur again when through the passion of the Lord and through the laver of holy baptism, the minds of mortals are raised high to taste beforehand heavenly things.

The third stone is chalcedony. Chalcedony

---

[24]Benedicta Ward writes of this section: "Fascinated by their appearance and the significance he discovered in these gems, he provided an extended commentary which is in fact a lapidary, in which the ancient tradition of significance in gems was turned into Christological commentary" (*The Venerable Bede* [Harrisburg, Penn.: Morehouse Publishing, 1990], 34). [25]Is 54:11. [26]Is 54:13. [27]The text of Bede has *fundamentum primum* concerning the first stone, jasper. Concerning the remaining stones the text has the masculine, *secundus, tertius* and so forth. The masculine form of the numbers suggests that the implied noun was *lapis* ("stone"). Some manuscripts have the neuter form throughout, *secundum, tertium,* hence the translation "the second foundation, the third foundation," and the like. [28]1 Pet 5:8-9. [29]Song 5:10. [30]See Is 54:12. [31]Ex 24:10. [32]See Ezek 1:26; 10:1. [33]Phil 3:20. The text of Bede reads *nostra autem conversatio in caelis est.*

shines like the pale fire of a lamp out of doors in the daylight. By this is shown those who, supported by heavenly desires, remain hidden by their humility to people as they practice in secret their fasting, almsgiving and prayers.[34] But when they are commanded to demonstrate their teaching or other acts of saintly service in public, they quickly do so in order that their inner glory might be shown forth. For that which remains after the sculptor has done his work draws dross to itself by the working of the sun's rays or by the handling of warm hands. This property of chalcedony rightly agrees with those who do not permit their own strength to be conquered by anything but rather by their own light and ardor draw to themselves the more fragile, joining them to their own strength. Concerning one of these it was said, "He was a burning and shining lamp."[35] Clearly he was burning with love, and he was shining in speech. For in order that their own virtues might never go dark, they are always refreshed by the oil of internal charity. The fact that this stone occurs among the Nasmoneans, which is a region of Ethiopia, indicates those who by an obscure reputation, as though under a dark skin, are held in low esteem although they possess the ardent fervor of love.

The fourth stone is emerald. The emerald[36] has the quality of very deep green to the point that it surpasses all green plants, branches and buds. It is colored all around with the green of reflective copper, and to the extent that its nature allows, it approaches the appearance of a pure and green oil. There are many different types of this stone. However, the more noble are the Scythian; the Bactrian have second place, and in third place are the Egyptian. This stone further signifies those souls who are always growing in faith and when tested more and more by the adversities of this world (indicated by the coldness of the Scythian climate) the more fully do they hold on to that unfading inheritance kept in heaven.[37] These souls advance to a contempt of this world through the chalice of the Lord's passion and by the fullness of the inner charity given to them by the Holy Spirit.

Also, the very beautiful ancestral homeland of these stones is fitting. It is a rich but uninhabitable land. The ground there abounds with gold and gems, but griffins hold all of them. These griffins are very ferocious birds or, rather, flying beasts, for they are four-legged and have the body of a lion while their heads are similar to birds. When these griffins fight the Arimaspi,[38] who carry the mark of one eye in the midst of their forehead, the griffins take these stones, and with amazing ferocity and fierce snatching, take the Arimaspi captive. The psalmist refers to this land filled with an abundance of virtues when he says, "Behold, I have fled afar off, and I remain in solitude."[39] That is, I have withdrawn my soul from the enticements of the world. He then strikes out at the hostile beasts when he prays, "Let the lying lips be dumb that speak iniquity against the righteous in pride and contempt."[40] He shows himself to have found desirable riches when he says with remarkable affection, "How abundant your goodness, O Lord, which you have laid up for those who fear you,"[41] and on to the end of the psalm. Against the desire of such birds to snatch away the seed of the divine word, some of the saints with a heavenly desire keep watch with undivided attention, as though admiring with one eye, in order that

---

[34]See Mt 6:3-4, 6, 18. [35]Jn 5:35. Jesus was speaking of John the Baptist. [36]Emerald is the usual translation of *smaragdus*, a transliteration of the Greek ἡ σμάραγος, that refers to any precious stone of a green color. [37]See 1 Pet 1:4. [38]The Arimaspi were a legendary people of north Scythia who were said to have one eye in the middle of their foreheads and to engage in frequent battles over the gold protected by the bird-like griffins. They are mentioned in a lost poem by Aristeas of Proconnesus (c. seventh century) quoted in Herodotus (4.13.1). The theme of these battles became a favorite motif on ancient Greek pottery. [39]Ps 55:7 (54:8 LXX). [40]Ps 31:18 (30:19 LXX). [41]Ps 31:19 (30:20 LXX).

they might discover and unearth the precious jewel of faith and other virtues. Where the need for strength is greater, there are fewer laborers and fewer of those who bear the terrible persecution by unclean spirits. As the dreadful earthly griffins fight for riches by violence, these few struggle tirelessly for spiritual riches, not to possess the riches for themselves but to offer them to others. And since such an exalted faith is made known throughout the whole world through the gospel, it is fitting that as there are four books of the gospel, the emerald is placed in the fourth place.

[21:20] *The fifth stone is sardonyx.* This stone has the luster of onyx yet shows the redness of carnelian, and therefore from both of them receives the name of sardonyx. There are many kinds of this stone. One has the likeness of red earth. Another has the appearance of two colors, as though it were blood shining through a human fingernail. Another consists of three colors, on the bottom is black, the middle is white and the top is red.

This stone represents those who are red in the passion of the body, white in the purity of the spirit, but in the humility of their mind examine themselves and say with the apostle, "Although our outer man is wasting away, our inner man is being renewed every day."[42] And again, "I am aware of nothing against myself, but in this I am not justified."[43] Similarly the psalmist says, "A person walks in the image of God," that is, by the virtue of the mind, "however, in vain will he be disquieted,"[44] that is, by the weakness of the flesh. Since this suffering exists in the weakness of the body—"for they who kill the body are not able to kill the soul"[45]—and humility comes from the weakness of the body, as it is said, "Wretched man that I am! Who will deliver me from this body of death?"[46] it is fitting that sardonyx is said to be the fifth foundation, since our bodies possess five senses.

The sixth stone is sardion. Sardion[47] has the color of pure blood and signifies the glory of the martyrs, of whom it is said, "Precious in the sight of the Lord is the death of his saints."[48] Rightly is it placed in the sixth position, for our Lord was both incarnated in the sixth age of the world and was crucified on the sixth day for the salvation of the whole world.

The seventh stone is chrysolite. Chrysolite shines as though it were sparkling gold. Its appearance represents those who shine with the knowledge of the heavenly and true wisdom and who by the words of exhortation to their neighbors or even by signs of power sparkle as though sparks of fire. Of such persons it is true, as Arator says, "Love bestows justice to our thoughts, but ardor gives passion to our words."[49] Since this occurs only by the gift of spiritual grace, it is most proper that chrysolite stands as the seventh foundation, for the grace of the Holy Spirit is often symbolized by the number seven,[50] of whom it was said above, "and from the seven spirits who are before his throne."[51]

Corresponding to this interpretation is the fact that a kind of this stone is found in the color of blue-green, for which reason the Hebrews call this stone Tharsis[52] because it has the color of the sea. The color green indeed corresponds to the reality of faith, which is said to be the beginning of wisdom, and water is a figure of the Holy Spirit, as the Lord

[42]2 Cor 4:16. [43]1 Cor 4:4. [44]Ps 39:6 (38:7 LXX). [45]Mt 10:28; Lk 12:4-5. [46]Rom 7:24. [47]Bede's Latin has *sardius*, and I have kept this in my translation. English translations usually render *sardius* "carnelian." Both sard and carnelian are varieties of the mineral chalcedony and are often used interchangeably. When distinguished, sard refers to the harder and darker variety. [48]Ps 116:15 (115:6 LXX). [49]Arator 1.147 (PL 68:108). Arator was a sixth-century Christian poet. He served in the Ostgothic court of Theodoric and later in the church at Rome under Pope Vigilius (537–555). His most important poem was *De Actibus Apostolorum*, a symbolic account of the book of Acts. The poem was much studied and quoted during the Middle Ages, existing in standard curricula at least until the twelfth century. [50]See Is 11:2-3. [51]See Rev 1:4. [52]Perhaps a reference to the region where the stone was thought to originate. Tharsis is the name given to the most western regions of the known world. However, perhaps it refers merely to Tharsus in Cilicia. See Jonah 1:3.

indicates, saying, "He who believes in me, as the Scripture says, 'Out of his heart shall flow rivers of living water.' Now this he said about the Spirit, which those who believed in him were to receive."[53]

The eighth stone is beryl. Just as water reflecting the brightness of the sun, beryl gives off a beautiful reddish color. However, it does not shine unless it has been shaped and polished into a six-sided form, for its brightness is accentuated by the reflection of the angles. This stone represents those persons who indeed are wise by their natural disposition but who reflect even more the light of divine grace. Solomon indicates that water might symbolize the depth of understanding when he says, "The words of a man's mouth are deep waters."[54] But neither human nor divine wisdom is perfect in its light unless the performance of works is joined to it. For often the completion of a work is represented by the number six, especially when in this number it is a finished work of this world. Without doubt it is clear why it is said that the hand of one holding this stone is burned, since one who is joined to a holy person is truly recreated by the fire of his good behavior.

The ninth stone is topaz. Since topaz is rarely found, it is very valuable. It comes in two colors, one of purest gold and the other glittering with an ethereal clarity. In color it has a pure rosy and reddish hue and is similar to chrysophrase in the brilliance of its color. When it reflects the splendor of the sun, it especially shines, surpassing the most costly brilliance of all other stones and in its appearance giving uniquely the greatest delight to the eyes. Should one polish this stone, however, it becomes dull; yet should one leave it alone, it shines by virtue of its own natural properties. Kings regard this stone as marvelous and consider nothing else among their riches as

its equivalent. This most beautiful quality of its nature is most fittingly compared with the contemplative life. For saintly kings, whose hearts are in the hand of God,[55] display this nature by the riches of good works and by the gems of all of the virtues. Especially guiding in it the contemplation and keen vision of their pure minds, they shall be more frequently struck by the splendor of the heavenly grace the more fervently they behold the sweetness of the heavenly life with their soul.

Therefore, saintly people possess a golden color by the fire of their inner love, while they have also a heavenly color from the contemplation of a supernal sweetness. Sometimes these persons become worthless through the turmoil of the present world, as though they were rubbed by a file. For at one and the same time a soul cannot easily be agitated by the difficulty of earthly toils and by cares and sorrows and, having taken delight in the joy of the heavenly life, also contemplate this with a tranquil mind. Rather, in its groaning such a soul protests, "My eye is troubled because of anger; I have grown old on account of my enemies."[56]

This stone is said to be found on an island of Thebaide, which is named Topazion, and from that it also receives its name. We can understand this in two ways. First, these regions, that is, of Egypt, are especially filled with crowds of monks, and whoever dwells near to the Son of righteousness is truly colored by the brightness of the heavenly light. And since the perfection of the active life is designated by the eighth place, this stone, which represents the delight of the contemplative life, is fittingly put in ninth place either because there are nine angelic orders mentioned in the holy Scriptures, whose life is imitated, or because the contemplative life is removed from the ten of perfect bliss, as I shall put it, by the single step of death.[57]

---

[53]Jn 7:38-39. [54]Prov 18:4. [55]See Prov 21:1. [56]Ps 6:7 (6:8 LXX). [57]The monastic life was frequently thought to be an imitation of the angelic life, for it was dedicated solely to the service of God. Yet, says Bede, this imitation is not yet perfect, as is that of the angels. But it will be when the saint dies and lives in the perfected life of heaven.

Longing for this highest joy, the prophet said, "Therefore, I have loved thy commandments more than gold and topaz."[58] That is to say, above the glory for every approved work and above every height of contemplative joy that is possible in this life, I have delighted in your commandments with the sweetest love. And the first and greatest of these commandments is that "you will love the Lord your God with the whole heart, the whole mind and with all your strength."[59] It is most certainly true that this cannot be perfected in its completeness except in the height of the celestial kingdom.

The tenth stone is chrysophrase. Chrysophrase has a mixed color of green and gold and even brings forth a certain purple gleam intermingled with spots of gold. It is found in India. This stone symbolizes those who by the brightness of perfect charity deserve the verdant garden of the eternal fatherland and reveal it even to others by the purple light of their own martyrdom. Since those who despise the present life and prefer the eternal glory follow the example of the Lord who appeared in the flesh, by the brightness of their merits they already display that glory as though in India, that is, near the rising of the sun. And because they expect to shine as the sun in the kingdom of the Father and desire then to reign with their king for whom they are now suffering, rightly are they listed in the tenth place. For through the denarius by which the workers in the Lord's vineyard were paid,[60] the image of the eternal king is to be perceived. There—and this would not have been possible in the ninth position—the Decalogue will be in every way fulfilled by a perfected love of God and of the neighbor.

The eleventh stone is hyacinth. Hyacinth is found in Ethiopia and has a dark blue color. At its best it is neither of loose texture nor dull by density, but rather it shines moderately and gives a pleasant, pure gleam. But this stone does not gleam the same all the time. Rather, it changes with the appearance of the sky, for when the sky is fair and clear, it is transparent and pleasing, but when the sky is cloudy, it becomes faint and pale to the eyes.

This stone suggests those souls that are always devoted to the purpose of heaven and who, to the extent possible for mortals, approach in some manner to the angelic life. These are admonished to preserve their hearts with every diligence, lest they grow callous by an excessive subtlety of their understanding and dare to seek after higher things and to examine that which is more powerful. "For the glory of God is to conceal a word,"[61] that is, one is to intellectually scrutinize God and the human Christ only with caution. They are also to preserve their hearts lest through an idle torpor they fall back again to the weak beginnings of faith and to the rudiments of the words of God. Those rather who travel the royal highway advance protected on the left and on the right by the weapons of righteousness,[62] and by apt observation of the times they change their style and form with the sky and say to their overseers, "If we are beside ourselves, it is for God; if we are in our right mind, it is for you."[63] As a hyacinth underneath a cloud, such a person says, "You are not restricted by us, but you are restricted in your own affection."[64] And again, "For I decided to know nothing among you except Jesus Christ and him crucified."[65] And as a hyacinth seen in the bright sun, he says, "We speak wisdom among the mature."[66]

The twelfth stone is amethyst. Amethyst is purple, a mixture of violet and the luster of a rose, and it gently gives off little sparks. But it has a certain glow that is not purple through and through, but rather it appears like the red of a wine. The beauty of purple suggests the

---

[58]See Ps 119:127 (118:127 LXX). [59]Deut 6:5. [60]See Mt 20:2. [61]Prov 25:2. [62]See Num 20:17; 2 Cor 6:7. [63]2 Cor 5:13. [64]2 Cor 6:12. [65]1 Cor 2:2. [66]1 Cor 2:6.

deportment of the heavenly kingdom, while the rosy violet indicates the humble modesty and the precious death of the saints. For to be sure, their minds are chiefly concerned with things on high, and although externally they must endure misery, they remember among these adversities the Lord's promise, "Fear not, little flock, for it is your Father's good pleasure to give you the kingdom."[67] These persons do not extend the fire of love only toward one another but also toward their very persecutors, imploring on bended knee, "Lord, do not hold this sin against them."[68] Moreover, along with the cup of suffering that they must drink, by a continuous recollection they drink even more of that wine that gladdens the heart and that the Lord promised that he would drink new with his disciples in the kingdom of the Father.[69]

Jasper, therefore, symbolizes the greenness of faith, and the sapphire suggests the height of celestial hope. Chalcedony indicates the fire of inner love, while the emerald is figure of the confession of a strong faith in the midst of adversity. Sardonyx symbolizes the virtue of humility in the saints, and sardion indicates the glorious blood of the martyrs. Chrysolite symbolizes spiritual preaching with signs, while beryl suggests the perfected work of those who preach. Topaz demonstrates their fervent contemplation, while chrysophrase indicates both the work and the reward of the blessed martyrs. Hyacinth symbolizes the seeking after heavenly things by those who teach as well as their humble service for the sake of human weakness,[70] and the amethyst designates the memory of the heavenly kingdom that is always in the mind of the humble.

Each of these precious stones was allotted to one of the foundations. For although all the stones by which the city of our God on his holy mountain is adorned and established are perfect and shine by the light of spiritual grace, nevertheless "to one is given through the Spirit the utterance of wisdom, to another the utterance of knowledge, to another gifts of healing, to another various kinds of tongues, to another faith by the same Spirit,"[71] and the like. "Its builder and maker is God,"[72] who is the Foundation of foundations and who for our sake was also found worthy to be high priest, so that by the sacrifice of his own blood he might both wash clean and dedicate the walls of this city, and that whatever the Father has he might possess as his own. For this reason these same stones with the names of the patriarchs inscribed on them were commanded to be placed on the breast of the high priest,[73] so that by this most wonderful mystery it might be shown that every spiritual grace that each saint received individually and in part has been wholly and perfectly fulfilled by the mediator of God and man, the man Jesus Christ.[74]

Perhaps it seems that I expounded these precious stones more extensively than was fitting for a commentary of short comments. However, it was necessary to expound on their characteristics and places of origin, then also to inquire with care after their significance and to add a comment on their order and place in the sequence. And so whatever pertains to the significance of the matter, I thought that I should say some few things about it in a brief and summary way. And I humbly beseech the reader[75] that if he thinks that I have proceeded on the right path, he give thanks to God. If, however, he should detect that the result is otherwise than I wished, may he, with me, pray forgiveness from the Lord for my error. But this suffices for these things; let us now consider what remains.

---

[67]Lk 12:32. [68]Acts 7:60. [69]Mt 26:29. [70]Bede distinguishes between an ascent (*sublevatio*) toward higher things (*ad alta*) and a descent (*descensio*) toward humankind (*ad humana*). I have translated *descensio* as service. [71]1 Cor 12:8-10. [72]See Heb 11:10. [73]See Ex 28:17-21. [74]See 1 Tim 2:5. [75]Bede writes *lectoremque supplex obsecro*. The word *supplex* refers to something bent underneath, often to the bent knee underneath a person. Hence, one could translate, "I beseech the reader as on bended knee."

[21:21] *And the twelve gates, each of a single pearl.* All the glory of the head is referred to the body. Just as "the true light that enlightens every person"[76] has granted the saints to be the light of the world, so also he himself, since he is the single pearl that the wise merchant purchased after selling all that he had,[77] in similar manner compares his disciples with the bright appearance of pearls.

And the street of the city was pure gold, transparent as glass. The streets are made of the same materials that adorn the city that was just described.[78] Although there are many lives, some more important and some less important,[79] gird in the church with the highest virtues, they shine with a purity of mind and with the light of their work.

[21:22] *And I saw no temple in it, for the Lord God Almighty is its temple, and the Lamb.* Although, he says, I have said that the city is constructed of stones, nevertheless I have not meant by this that the eternal rest of the saints will be in a material building. For God himself will be their sole abode and light and rest.

[21:23] *And the city has no need of sun or moon to shine in it.* The city has no need of sun or moon because the church is not governed by the light or by the elements of the world. On the contrary, she is led through the darkness of the world by Christ, the eternal Sun.[80]

For the glory of God will illumine it. In the fatherland we will enjoy that very Light that now guides us as we walk on the way. Taught by it, we now distinguish between that which is good and that which is evil. Then, when we have been made blessed by it, we will see only that which is good.

[21:24] *The nations will walk by its light.* This indicates that the Lamb himself, who is the way for those who are underway[81] toward the heavenly city, is he who then will be the life of the citizens of the heavenly city.

And the kings of the earth will bring their glory and honor into it. In this passage he is speaking of spiritual kings who add all the riches of their virtues to the praises of the church.

[21:25] *And its gates will not be closed by day, for there will be no night there.* The passage speaks of the future light of the Lamb that is perpetual. Indeed, in that city the Lamb will be the eternal light when the time of night has been removed. That the gates are not closed is an indication of the most complete security. For in that city it is no longer said, "Watch and pray that you may not enter into temptation,"[82] but rather, "Be still and see that I am God."[83]

[21:26] *And they will carry the glory and honor of the nations into it.* That is, the city will be assembled together from all peoples.

[21:27] *But nothing unclean shall enter into it.* It is describing the church of that time when evil persons have been completely removed from her midst and those who are good will alone reign with Christ. But even now no impure or deceptive person is in the church,[84] nor do they who hate the light see the light of the city of God. For the darkness has made blind their eyes.

---

[76]Jn 1:9. [77]Mt 13:45-46. [78]See Rev 21:18. [79]Bede is following Primasius (CCL 92:296-97). The streets symbolize the simple Christians who, as Primasius puts it, seem not to have been included in the description of the city and so placed in an inferior position. The Latin of Bede speaks of lives that are *latioris et inferioris*, "wider and smaller," language suitable to describe streets. [80]Perhaps Bede is contrasting faith in Christ to pagan superstitions based on natural phenomena. [81]Translating *peregrinantibus*. A *peregrinatio* is a journey in a foreign land, hence a sojourn. Following Augustine, Bede thinks of the life of the Christian in this world as a *peregrinatio* in a foreign land whose destiny is the spiritual city in the fatherland (*patria*). Bede's comments echo those of Primasius (CCL 92:298). [82]Mt 26:41. [83]Ps 46:10 (45:11 LXX). [84]The true church of the elect even now contains no impure or hypocritical person.

REVELATION 22

[22:1] *Then he showed me the river of the water of life, bright as crystal, flowing from the throne of God and of the Lamb.* The river of life that flows in the midst of the city no longer indicates the administration of baptism. Rather, the fruit of that sacrament will be revealed in the river. For now the church "sows in the Spirit so that then it might reap eternal life."[1]

[22:2] *On either side of the river there was the tree of life.* The tree of life is seen on either side of the source of life. One may interpret this to refer either to the glory of the sacred cross or to the Lord Christ. While even before baptism he was revealed in the Old Testament, also now when the mystery of baptism is made clear, he fills the saints with heavenly fruit. "For there is no other name under heaven given among people by which we must be saved."[2] The tree that John saw in golden Jerusalem is the same that Moses described in the lush of paradise.[3] Solomon said that the tree of life is for those who embrace it.[4] I think that the Jordan River was a figure of this river in the heavenly city. On the far side of it Moses exhorted the people who had been saved, and on the inside of it Joshua opened the land of promise.[5]

Bearing twelve fruits and yielding its fruit each month. In the twelve months he suggests the whole of time, namely, of the life of him, where it is said, "And your years shall not fail."[6] And again: "It will be from month to month and from sabbath to sabbath."[7] Where the face of the Lord is present, there is eternal health and the eternal food of life. One could also simply understand this to mean that the cross of Christ is made fruitful through the teaching of the twelve apostles.

And the leaves of the tree was for the healing of the nations. If the fruit is understood to be the reward of a blessed immortality, then the leaves are rightly interpreted to be the perpetual hymn, because by a happy lot it already falls to health for those who sing. For there in that city is the true health of the nations, there is the full redemption, there is the eternal happiness.[8]

[22:4] *And they will see his face.* The vision of God is preserved for us as a reward of faith. This is the highest good, as Philip understood when he said, "Lord, show us the Father, and we shall be satisfied."[9] For it was of great urgency to commend that the saints would have this vision and would dwell in this way, for they believe and live from faith.[10]

And his name shall be on their foreheads. The confession of the holy name is now preserved in the midst of enemies. Then it glorifies the conquerors in the fatherland.

[22:5] *And night shall be no more, and they will need no light of lamp or of the sun, for the Lord gives them light.* In the city above the weakness of our bodies will require neither the quiet of night nor the light of a fire. For then "God will be all in all,"[11] namely, he who is the true light[12] and the eternal rest of the saints. One might also interpret these words figuratively. The exhortation of the prophets and the preaching of the divine Law will not be necessary there, for these are now said to be lights in a dark place. But then, when all things have been fulfilled, the promise will be perfected in the vision and contemplation of God.

[22:6] *And he said to me, "These words are most trustworthy and true."* He is not expressing any lack of confidence in John. Rather, he is commending the vision as true for the whole

---

Revelation 22   [1]Gal 6:8. [2]Acts 4:12. [3]See Gen 2:9, 15-17. [4]See Prov 3:18. [5]For Joshua Bede writes *Jesus*, a correspondence of names that occurs also in the Greek ('Ιησοῦς: see, for example, Josh 1:12). [6]Ps 102:27 (101:28 LXX). [7]Is 66:23. [8]Bede's comments are taken directly from Primasius (CCL 92:301). [9]Jn 14:8. [10]See Rom 1:17. [11]1 Cor 15:28. [12]See Jn 1:9; 8:12.

church, for he knew that in the church there would be also in the future children in the faith.[13]

"And the Lord, the God of the spirits of the prophets, has sent his angel." Do not doubt, he says, the one who exhorts and warns you. For the God who often inspired the spirits of the prophets with a heavenly vision is he who sent me to you that I might reveal these coming events to you.

"To show his servants what must soon take place." As I have said, he taught that he foresaw what is generally useful and beneficial for all.

[22:7] *Blessed is he who keeps the words of the prophecy of this book, and I am John who heard and saw these things.* The words "I am the blessed one" are to be supplied. For this is how the blessed Dionysius, bishop of Alexandria, connected these versicals when he was refuting certain heresies that were springing up on the basis of this book and was attempting to purge the sense of this prophecy from any darkness of a fleshly understanding and to relate the prophecy to the eternal and heavenly promises.[14]

[22:8] *I fell down to worship at the feet of the angel who was showing these things to me.* Either he does again what he did once[15] and is restrained that he dare not repeat it, or overwhelmed by the great astonishment of the vision, he confesses that he again wished to worship the angel.

[22:9] *"I am your fellow servant and the brother of your prophets."* Note how frequently it mentions both the prophet John and the prophecy of this book. For there is a considerable harmony between this book and the prophets, not only in their meanings but also in their vocabulary. For what verse can you find that is not from Isaiah or Zechariah or another of the prophets?

[22:10] *"Do not seal up the words of the prophecy of this book, for the time is short."* Since the future judgment is approaching, it is necessary that the divine commandments, judgments and promises be made known. For by obedience to them those who are humble shall acquire their reward, while the proud and obstinate will incur condemnation by their neglect.

[22:11] *"Whoever does evil, let him do evil still, and whoever is filthy, let him be filthy still."* He shows that the judgments of God by which evil people are allowed to become even more evil are hidden yet just. That is, God permits evil persons to progress to the greatest iniquity so that he can receive his just judgment. Similar to this is the statement in the Gospel, "Either make the tree good and its fruit good, or make the tree bad and its fruit bad."[16]

[22:13] *"I am the Alpha and the Omega, the First and the Last."* By the Alpha he indicates the divinity of the Word and by the Omega he indicates the humanity that the Word assumed. He is in the beginning and without end. This is affirmed frequently by repetition in this book either to assert the deity and humanity of the one Christ or to suggest the one nature of the whole Trinity who says through the prophet, "Before me no god was formed, nor shall there be any after me."[17]

---

[13]Translating *in qua et parvulos futuros noverat*. Those who are children require teaching and encouragement. The Revelation was written not only for those who were alive at that time but also for all future Christians who would be equally benefitted by its visions. [14]See Eusebius *Ecclesiastical History* 7.25.6. Dionysius was bishop of Alexandria (248–c. 264). He was active both as theologian and exegete, arguing against Sabellianism and Paul of Samosata. Eusebius preserves long extracts from his work "On the Promises" in which Dionysius argues against the view that the John of the Revelation was the apostle who wrote the Gospel. In this work Dionysius rejects the millenarianism of some who base that doctrine on the Revelation. Bede refers to the passage in which Dionysius connects Rev 22:8 with Rev 22:7. In so doing Dionysius identifies the "blessed is he who keeps the words of the prophecy of this book" with John himself. Rev 22:8 begins κἀγὼ Ἰωάννης which may be translated "that is, I, John, am he." [15]See Rev 19:10. [16]Mt 12:33. [17]Is 43:10.

[22:14] *That their power may be in the tree of life.* In the image of the white robes he promises a worthy and suitable reward, namely, that of a pure and stainless life. Evidently he promises this so that one might obtain the vision of the Lord, who is eternal life. For "blessed are the pure in heart, for they shall see God."[18]

And that they may enter the city by the gates. Those who keep the commandments of the Lord who said, "I am the door; if any one enters by me, he will be saved, and will go in and out and find pasture"[19]—these are the pastures that are also promised here, that is, the tree of life—they without doubt enter into the church through the gates, that is, through the gates of righteousness that the psalmist says are opened to him. "However, he who climbs in by another way, that man is a thief and a robber."[20]

[22:15] Concerning these also this is added, *Outside are the dogs and the sorcerers and the unchaste,* and the following. Every kind of madness that characterizes the impious now tempts the church from without. But when the father of the household enters in and the saints enter in with him to the wedding banquet, he shall close the door, and then the wicked will stand outside and begin to pound on the door.[21]

[22:16] "*I am the root and the offspring of David.*" He is referring to the two natures of his person. For he who is the creator of David according to his divinity is he "who was descended from David according to the flesh."[22] In the Gospel the Lord put this question to the Jews: How it could be that the Christ could be the son of David, when David, inspired by the Spirit, calls him his Lord?[23]

"*The bright morning star.*" The morning star is he who after the night of his suffering appeared living and so revealed to the world the light of resurrection and life by both words and example. Of him Job speaks to the blessed One, "Have you ever brought forth the morning star at its own time?"[24]

[22:17] *The Spirit*[25] *and Bride say, "Come!"* The Head and body of the church exhort each member to faith.

And let him who hears say, "Come!" Whoever has received and possesses in their mind the interior light of faith and love calls also others to share in this.

And let him who desires take of the water of life without price. He speaks appropriately of free will when he says, "Whoever desires, let him take," when straightway grace is proclaimed in that which follows, "of the water of life without price." Indeed, since no merit comes before, even the willing to take of the water is a gift of God.

[22:18] *If any adds to these words, God will add to him the plagues written in this book.* He said this because of those who would falsify the Scriptures, not because of those who speak their opinions in a simple manner yet in no way wrongly change the prophecy.

[22:20] *He who testifies to these things says, "Surely, I am coming soon."* The same Christ who gave this testimony is he who proclaims to the church that he is coming. And in the manner of the Song of Songs the church devoutly responds to him,

Amen, Come, Lord Jesus Christ![26] The church declares these words every day when it prays, "Let your kingdom come!"[27] and in the words of the psalm, "I will sing and be wise in a blameless way when you will come to me."[28]

---

[18]Mt 5:8. [19]Jn 10:9. [20]Ps 118:19 (117:19 LXX). [21]See Lk 13:25. [22]Rom 1:3. [23]Mt 22:42-43. [24]See Job 38:32. [25]An alternate reading of Bede has *sponsus et sponsa,* "the Bridegroom and the bride." Given the commentary of Bede, this may be the preferred reading. [26]See Song 2:8, 10, 13; 4:8; 7:11. [27]Mt 6:10; Lk 11:2. [28]Ps 101:2 (100:2 LXX). Bede's text follows more closely that of the LXX. However, both in the Hebrew and in the LXX the final words of verse 2 are a question: "When will you come to me?" Bede interprets the psalm eschatologically. When the second coming of Christ occurs, the faith will praise God with a perfected wisdom and with a being that is wholly without sin.

[22:21] *The grace of our Lord Jesus Christ be with you all. Amen.* Let the Pelagians be confident in their own power and deprive themselves of the grace of the Lord. However, when the apostle Paul was seeking for help, he said, "Who will deliver me from this body of death?"[29] Mindful of his own condition, let John respond and say, "The grace of God through Jesus Christ, our Lord."[30] And lest the Donatists deceive themselves concerning the singular gift of God, let them hear that when John commends the grace of God, as if it were a final farewell, he adds, "and with you all. Amen."[31]

Since at last this large and rather perilous labor has been laid out before you, I humbly and fervently pray that should any by their reading or by their copying consider our little work worthy, they would remember to commend also the author of the work to the Lord. In this way I will have labored not for myself alone but also for them. And while I am rewarded by the vows and prayers of those who find delight in my effort, by their merits they might enable me to obtain the vision of fruit of the tree of life with whose odor and glory I have, to some extent, bedewed them. Amen.[32]

---

[29]Rom 7:24. [30]Rom 7:25. [31]The Pelagians believed that grace was primarily the gift of free will. Our holiness, therefore, lay in the correct use of the free will, not by virtue of the remedial, creative grace of God. The Donatists believed that they alone were the holy church. The universality of the church was thus called into question. [32]Bede is expressing the communal importance of his work. He expects that it will be read and copied. In this way he will have benefitted others, and they, having received such benefit, will commend Bede to God. The significance of text for the life of the church is thus expressed.

Scripture Index